HEAD FOR MEXICO

THE RENEGADE GUIDE

Don Adams

http://www.headformexico.com
e-mail: don@headformexico.com

First Edition

Edited by Teresa A. Kendrick

With
Karen Blue, Mark Farley, Bill Haslbauer, Judy King,
Bill O'Brien, Georgina and Ron Russell

Illustrations by William Gentes

Trafford Publishing Company

Dedication

This book is for my grandchildren, Asa and Madison,
and for my children Abigail and Matthew.

Head for Mexico
The Renegade Guide

FIRST EDITION
First Printing – March 2003

PUBLISHED AND PRINTED BY
Trafford on-demand publishing service
Suite 6E
2333 Government Street
Victoria, BC, Canada, V8T 4P4
250-383-6864
1-888-232-4444
http://www.trafford.com

Adams, Don, 1945-
    Head for Mexico : the ren-
egade guide / Don Adams ; Teresa
A. Kendrick, editor ; Karen Blue
... [et al.], contributors.
ISBN 1-55369-562-3
    1. Mexico—Guidebooks.   2.
Retirement, Places of—Mexico—
Guidebooks.   I. Kendrick, Teresa
A.   II. Title.
F1209.A32 2003   972.08'37
C2003-902578-0

All photographs used with permission of the owners, the original copyright holders. Illustrations used with permission from the artist's estate.

ISBN: 1-55369-562-3

Author: Don Adams
Editor: Teresa A. Kendrick
Contributing Writers: Karen Blue, Mark Farley, Bill Haslbauer, Judy King, Bill O'Brien, Ron & Georgina Russell
Illustrator: William Gentes
Photography: Teresa A. Kendrick
Production and Design: Mary Rickman-Taylor, email: *publisher@coalinga.net* and
            Marianne Carlson, email: *mariannecarlson@prodigy.net.mx*
Cover Composition and Design: Joseph Philipson, Principal, THE PHILIPSON AGENCY, Marketing Communications & Graphic Design,
            Boston/Ajijic. Email: jxxp@prodigy.net.mx.
Cover Photography: Teresa A. Kendrick, *http://www.chapalaguide.com*
Horse "El Venado" courtesy of Rejino Rojas, Ajijic, MX
Moccasins by Sparrowhawk, Yatahai Beads & Buckskin, Tacoma, WA., http://www.yatahai.com
Shirt and vest by Alejandro Julian Nunez, Guadalajara, San Miguel de Allende, Polanco, Puerto Vallarta, MX., and Austin, TX
Pirata the "One-Eyed Wonder Dog", the author's faithful canine companion

Please send comments and questions to: http://www.headformexico.com, e-mail: don@headformexico.com

This book was published independently by the author, who is responsible for all content. No particular individual, business, or sponsor was served during the research, compilation, and printing of this book except in the case of contributors to the book. The author and publisher have exercised diligent care to assure that all information presented is accurate as of the date of publication. The author and publisher do not accept, and hereby disclaim any liability to any party for any loss or damage caused by errors, omissions, or any potential disruption or problem due to application of information contained in this book, whether such incidences result from misuse, negligence, accident, or any other cause.

Acknowledgments

There are many people who encouraged me when I was discouraged, provided solutions when I thought I'd hit bottom, and celebrated with me when things occasionally went right. Thanks to Sara Henze for reading my (very) rough draft and urging me to keep going. And thanks to her beautiful daughters, Mayan who helped me capture the *coatimundi* and search our tiny village for the circus wagons, and Miriam of the sweet enigmatic smile, who helped keep me on an even keel as I pounded out the early versions of this book.

Special thanks and blessings go to Ellie Fiscella and the lovely but reclusive "Loretta" who volunteered to type my first draft hard copy onto disks after my computer crashed and wiped out a more polished version.

Los Picaros, my friends and support group: Lea Ward, Rick Devoy, Bill and Neva Haslbauer, Anne Lewis, Dru Pearson, Rick Steadman, Howard Botz, Gladys Grand and Tim Harlin (and Nana Jennie), Rich and Ellie Fiscella, and, of course, our combination Grande Dame/den mother, Judy King, who all have my undying gratitude and affection for their friendship and encouragement. Our newest Pics, Wayne and Wanda Vincent have been extremely supportive, and are also greatly appreciated.

I knew I was on the right track when Cynthia Franklin told me which parts of the book made her weep, and I thank her and Barbara Adams for their kind comments and constructive help as they read through the first draft. Thanks also to my daughter Abby Tolbert. I not only love her, I respect her opinion. When she offered her supportive analysis I felt as if I already had a best-seller. And thanks to my wonderful son Matt, my personal inspiration, for his confidence and pride in my work.

Heartfelt thanks go to H.Prospero Avegno who is gone from us now, and to my friend Professor Tom Hoffman for their encouragement and guidance as I was earning my degree at Midwestern State University in Wichita Falls, Texas, and learning to write.

Mary Rickman-Taylor has been the answer to a prayer. Her exceptional design talents made this book actually look like a book.

Isabel Fuente and Lara Gallardo generously offered their collection of William Gentes prints that allowed the book to take on an entire other dimension. Without their cooperation I could not have assembled this large body of Bill's work. Thank you, Isabel and Lara. Thanks also to Luisa Julián of The Studio Art Gallery, Linda Samuels, Bob and Smokee Wilson, David Merryman, Laurel

Kelley, Dr. Gil Silverman, and Marguerite and Carl Marxsen who also loaned prints.

Heartfelt thanks to the children of William Gentes who allowed me to honor their father's talent and memory by giving permission to reproduce his work in this book. Thank you very much, Bill and Gaye.

Thanks to David McLaughlin, Publisher and Editor of *http://www.mexconnect.com* for providing me another forum in which to publish my work.

Special thanks to the contributors, Karen Blue, Mark Farley, Bill Haslbauer, Teresa A. Kendrick, Judy King, Bill O'Brien, and Ron and Georgina Russell who displayed their confidence in this endeavor by their participation. I appreciate them all.

Deep appreciation to Nick Paulini and Deidre Kennedy for the generous and timely loan of their equipment at Cafe Internet Ajijic, CIA, Ajijic, Jalisco.

Isabel Fuente has my undying gratitude for checking and correcting my efforts at using the Spanish language.

Special Acknowledgement

This book would have not been published without the exceptional efforts of Teresa A. Kendrick. Her specific knowledge, good judgment, honesty, patience and good humor, her supportive attitude, and gentle guidance all kept me focused and semi-sane throughout a very difficult process. All of her contributions as well as her friendship are highly valued.

Essential Acknowledgement

Most authors stand on the shoulders of, or in some measure rely on the good work of those who have gone before them. In the case of this book, I owe a huge debt of gratitude to the many website owners and the webmasters who have added to our collective knowledge of life in Mexico. The information offered to the public through their sites made a good deal of my research easier.

Colophon

This book was designed and typeset in Arial MT 11/13 for the body text, in Little Ancients, a graphic font, for the artful band at the beginning of each chapter, and in Posada Irregular for the chapter numbers and titles. Posada Irregular is named for and inspired by the turn of the 20th century Mexican artist José Guadalupe Posada, whose clever protest art graced posters and newspapers of revolutionary Mexico.

FOREWORD

Getting Used to Things

TERESA A. KENDRICK, EDITOR

Traveling to Mexico is like having a fling, a stunning romance, a love affair so intense that everything seems washed in a radiant and benevolent mist. Senses are heightened, feelings revive, and travelers find themselves newly innocent and unfettered by the constraints of their own societies. We find ourselves so profoundly moved that, depending upon our temperament, we live on oxygen alone or gorge ourselves at an endless table of sensual feasts. Our deepest longings find a voice to express the stirrings of our hearts, the range of our feelings, and the sleeping voices of our souls. Magic is rediscovered.

Moving to Mexico, however, is not unlike getting married. Perhaps we'll marry Mexico for romance, for adventure, or to elevate our spiritual or economic status, but once the honeymoon is over we begin to notice that the language and customs of our beloved are strikingly dissimilar to our own. The informal intimacies of our native interactions clash with the formality of Mexican decorum. When once all we saw were bougainvillea-covered walls and cobblestone streets, we now see different attitudes toward ecology, animals, consumerism, democracy, and in much of the country, huge differences in technology, education and prosperity. For all the genuine beauty Mexico offers, there are considerable differences between the societies of "northern" North America and Mexico. And so the real work of compromise begins, as it does in all marriages, and it must be noted for the record that divorce is an honorable option.

The eight years I've spent in small Mexican villages have shown me more about our cultural differences than I ever expected. My natural "can do" attitude, fueled by an economic dominance I vaguely understood, emboldened me so that I overestimated the value of gleaned information from the value of authentic experience. Armed with a guidebook or two, I thought I could know about Mexico by reading about it, not knowing that the reality of another country is something else indeed. Because my relocation occurred in small villages, I wasn't pitted socially or economically against those who would have been my peers. Like many newlyweds, I found myself developing a storehouse of peculiar notions and frustrations "about Mexico" that edged their way into the early days of my wedlock. I needed to get used to things.

For starters, Mexico is only just now inching toward the kinds of democratic principles northern North Americans expect. It continues to be tied to a tradition of military coercion and political and economic feudalism. Widespread fiscal accountability is not yet a reality and payoffs and bribery at every level are common. Unconsciously, visitors from the North expect a classless society, mistaking the life of the people in the villages, with their gentle attitudes toward children, commitment to family, and boundless hospitality, to be a microcosm of the country. It isn't necessarily so. As class rank rises, so does the angst of the privileged teenager, the ennui of the bored housewife, and the compulsions of the trapped executive. Many newcomers, hailing from the great middle classes of the U.S. and Canada, carry conflicted ideas about domestic help. Mistaken cultural cues lead to unwanted overtures, and unrealistic expectations surprise us all.

Because of the geographical isolation of Canada and the U.S., we are not really challenged to embrace another culture, except for those of us who live near Quebec and in the states that share their borders with Mexico. Even then, we know we can rely on the comfort of our native tongue when conversation proceeds beyond simple greetings and transactions. Once the wordless language of infatuation fades, we find that we cannot communicate our simplest needs, not to mention our complex feelings and ideas, to our beloved. As a rule we are woefully unprepared to deal with the realities of mastering another language.

In Mexico, especially in the rural areas, animals are often regarded more as tools than soulful companions to be watched over and cared for like children. The roadside carnage of free-ranging cats, dogs, horses, burros and cows mowed down by cars and trucks can be shocking. The ubiquity of trash; plastic bags, garbage, debris, and refuse of all kinds takes visitors back a generation or two when our own streets and lanes looked more like Tobacco Road than the sterile showplaces that are the norm today. Only after national crusades in the U.S., for example, were younger generations educated about littering, a campaign just being talked about in Mexico. Still on the edges of an organic society where food and the other necessities of life are wrapped or managed in naturally decomposing materials, people have yet to make the mental leap of the plastic bag and the disposable diaper. While Mexico still energetically retains its holistic traditions of herbal remedies and homeopathy, it remains naïve about the long-range effects of dangerous chemicals. Gardeners routinely dust with Diazinon and many natural healing clinics over spray pesticides for insect control. Animals are poached, exotic birds are illegally captured, and pollution by industry and automobiles goes virtually unchecked. Mexico is just now learning the hard lessons of environmental responsibility the developed nations of the world have been forced to embrace.

Other things, especially in the small villages of Mexico need some getting used to. For one thing, houses are different. Concrete, brick, block and rebar rule; building codes don't exist in most areas, and a kind of technological backwardness exists side by side with a building tradition that can be wildly luxurious.

There are differences in the way people dress, too. Apart from the indigenous people, there are rules for dressing in mainstream Mexico. Modesty is still observed according to local standards, and European, not North American, styles are emulated. Our middle class slouchwear, regardless of how much we paid for it is not *de rigeur*.

Mexican village society is not a consumer society. Once newcomers have purchased their fill of the country's mind-staggering array of *artesania*, they'll find that recreational shopping is out. Necessities are still purchased in the market, accompanied by the subtle social interaction of bargaining. Hard-nosed attitudes about getting the best deal, paranoia about being cheated, and obsessive preoccupation with getting minute amounts of change have created more cultural ill-will than perhaps anything else. This is not to say that there aren't those nationals *and* foreigners out there who are not worthy to be "the object of our affections", there are. A balanced, patient, and instinctual savvy is called for when approaching matters of money.

As if the challenges of our union with Mexico are not enough, there is the matter of our "in laws"—our relationships within the foreign community. The Lake Chapala and Ajijic area is said to embrace one of the larger extrinsic communities in the world. By virtue of our common language, we are expected to juggle the expectations, proprieties, and sometimes ill-conceived advice of this diverse group along with those of our newly adopted culture.

Carolyn Myss, co-author of *The Creation of Health* observes that "one of the false goals of (northern North American) life is that we can somehow maneuver our lives in such a way as to avoid difficulties (and)...this is impossible". We have been steeped in the idea that our institutions, though we say we loathe them, should shelter us and keep us from experiencing hardships. People expect fewer things from the government here—the population is large, resources are limited and what cannot be shared is often done without. There is a significant degree of fatalism in the Mexican psyche that accepts problems. It is abundantly reflected in the Day of the Dead ceremonies, the blend of indigenous beliefs that embraces, teases, endures and respects death. Death and other difficulties, though profoundly experienced, are not denied in Mexico, whereas in our cultures we want guarantees that the unthinkable won't happen. Statistics reveal that 94 percent of all the lawsuits in the world originate in the U.S. When things go wrong in Mexico, recourse, if any, is accomplished outside the institutions.

Those who enter into their nuptials with Mexico armed only with childish dreams can expect frustrations and possibly irreparable disappointments. Those who bring mature, accepting, and flexible talents to the task will assimilate well and flourish. Once we move past the romantic vision, the sentimental outlook, our conceit as experts, and our insistences that Mexico be "our way," we can move on to really living within the reality of the country. It is from there that we can choose to love it.

TERESA A. KENDRICK, AUTHOR
MEXICO'S LAKE CHAPALA AND AJIJIC: THE INSIDERS GUIDE TO THE NORTHSHORE FOR INTERNATIONAL TRAVELERS
HTTP://WWW.CHAPALAGUIDE.COM

CONTENTS

CHAPTER 13: COMMUNICATIONS 197

CHAPTER 14: BUYING A WHOLE NEW ENCHILADA 205

CHAPTER 15: HOW MUCH IS THAT PERRITO IN THE WINDOW ? 211

CHAPTER 16: IS THAT A STETHOSCOPE IN MY POCKET, OR AM I JUST GLAD TO SEE YOU? 219

Chapter 1

Living in Mexico: Basic Training

"This is what I thought I'd be living in" she whined as we sat admiring the sturdy and spacious white adobe casa. Wide and solid, it had a deep porch of arched columns and dark red floor tiles complemented by the earthy ochre roof tiles. Beautifully worked wrought iron bars protected the windows. A wide, hand-carved wooden door ensured privacy and security for the home. A tall free-standing fountain bubbled and gurgled in an immaculately maintained garden. Vines grew up the lofty walls surrounding the grounds and provided a casual counterpoint to the formal lines of palms, ferns, flowers, shrubs and trees and a maze of walkways. Hummingbirds flitted busily from one red flower to another as a huge tabby snoozed on the brightly colored cushions of an equipal sofa.

I'd sensed this sentiment many times but this was the first time anyone had articulated it so openly and honestly. Many of the people I know here believed that as they crossed the border they were entering some sort of tropical Shangrai-la where all the rules of

NOSTALGIA, WILLIAM GENTES, 1992

reality would be suspended in order to let them live out their fantasies of Mexico, whatever they might be. We broke out of this pity party fairly quickly as I feared the owners might come out to see why we'd shimmied up that tree and were sitting there on that limb and looking over the top of their wall; a weeping gringa *and her totally befuddled accomplice in peeping tomism.*

This book was written for those of you who are now living in the U.S. or Canada and who will soon retire on a relatively small fixed income and are considering a retirement home in Mexico. I want to help you avoid some of the more common misconceptions about such a move, while providing access to the solid information you need to make an informed decision about such an undertaking.

In order to make your decision you will first need to determine if you have enough income to qualify for an FM-3, the *no inmigrante visitante* permit. If you meet the legal financial requirements of the FM-3 it will allow you to bring your Canadian or U.S. plated car into the country and to move your household goods into Mexico, if you choose to bring them, and to legally reside in the country. Let's go ahead and do a quick pre-qualification to determine if you're financially eligible to enjoy life South of the Border (SoB) or if you'll need to stay North of the Border (NoB).

Legal Financial Requirements

Whatever you do, please, do not waste your money on books that say you can live in Mexico in luxury for $800 or $1000 US a month! You might be able to do it but at present the Mexican government says to live here with FM-3 status you must prove a minimum monthly income of 250 pesos times 40.35 per month. This figure is based on the minimum wage in Mexico City at the time you apply for your FM-3. As of this writing, that comes to 10,087.50 pesos for one person. Each additional person of the same household will require an additional 2,521.88 pesos. Some consulates are requiring the initial amount as well as 50% of that amount for each additional family member. The *Migración* representative in Manzanillo gave these figures to me on June 12, 2001. The quantity required to qualify for the FM-3 varies from time to time. It also varies from consulate to consulate. Whatever the amount is when you get ready to move, it's a non-negotiable figure set by the authorities to ensure that you can support yourself while living in Mexico. The exchange rate at the time I received this information was about 9 and a fraction to 1, which means that in dollars you'd need an income of a little more than $I,000 US for one person and a corresponding 25% or 50% more for each additional member of your household.

Here comes the disclaimer: some Mexican Consulates in the U.S. and Canada have differing ideas of what constitutes an acceptable monthly income and which percentage rate you're going to be required to pay. I've provided a complete list of these folks so you can check for yourselves. On the Internet go to *http://www.move-to-mexico.com* or to *http://www.enespanol.com/home.html.* At these sites you'll find a list of all the Mexican Consulates located in the U.S. and Canada. Find the contact information for the one that serves your area and direct your questions to them. The Consulates are the final arbiters. If you don't like what you hear, you may want to contact the consulate in the area of Mexico you think you'd be most happy—just to see if they have a story you like better.

Register with your Consulate

While I'm on the subject, I strongly urge all of you, Canadian as well as U.S. citizens, to register with your local Consulates as soon as you relocate to Mexico. Canadians can register online at *http://www.voyage.gc.ca/consular_home-e.htm.* Go to the Registration for Canadians Abroad (ROCA) link and follow the instructions.

Do You Receive a Monthly Pension or Benefits Check?

If your income arrives in the form of monthly benefit payments of any type or from pensions from Canada or the U.S. and it meets or exceeds the minimum requirements set by Mexico City, then keep reading.

If it's from a U.S. or Canadian government institution or program, Social Security in any of its forms, Canada Pension Plan, Department of Veterans Affairs in any of its forms, Department of Defense in any of its forms, Old Age Security, Quebec Pension Plan, or any other program that will still pay you benefits if you leave the country, you're in great shape. If I'm not too far off the mark I believe that most of these entities require that you have a bank account into which these benefits can be deposited electronically. If this is the case we're doing fine so far. The question comes up quite often so let me tell you that yes, you can receive Social Security disability and legally live in Mexico. Some of my friends are doing it.

However, I must inform you about something EXTREMELY IMPORTANT. If you are drawing any type of SS benefits and plan to live anywhere other than the U.S. you may be asked to submit paperwork and follow specific procedures to safeguard your monthly payments. PERSONALLY CONTACT THE SS ADMINISTRATION, THE CANADIAN OAP, OR ANY PLAN THAT PAYS YOU ANY TYPE OF BENEFITS to explain your plans and to get current and correct information regarding your particular situation. It may all depend entirely upon how you plan to receive your monthly check

but I am not going to presume to advise you in this matter when the risks of passing on misinformation are so great. Go directly to the experts at the appropriate office nearest you.

If you've come SoB without doing this then I suggest you contact the closest American Consulate as soon as you arrive. Ask for the Federal Benefits Unit and explain that you need information about the Residence Status Form. This item must be filled out each year by recipients who are living abroad and receiving SS payments. **DO NOT accept the information I'm providing as anything other than a referral.** For up-to-date and official SS information consider subscribing to the e-newsletter they offer. It's free and requires only your e-mail address for the quick sign-up. Go to *http://www.ssa.gov/enews*.

Canadians seem to face even more daunting obstacles than those of us from the U.S. Here are some sources that should answer most of your questions about taxes and retirement incomes.

First, go to *http://www.voyage.gc.ca* and look for the list of Consular Affairs Publications. There are several books listed there that will be of great help.

The Canadian Snowbird Guide by Douglas Gray is a highly acclaimed book that gives you an almost overwhelming amount of information about the complexities of Canadian law, taxes, pensions, health care, mail, money, investments, voting, and the uses of the Internet, just to name a few of the subjects he covers. You can ask a local bookstore to order it. If by chance they don't stock this bestseller, look at the publisher's website at *http://www.mcgrawhill.ca*, or try *http://www.amazon.com*.

Also go to *http://www.expatax.com* which is the website of the Canadian Relocation and Expatriate Taxation Resource Centre. Go to the Expatriate Resource Centre link to see the information that will be of greatest interest to you.

If you'll have a tax obligation or two the following section will list websites for various government and commercial organizations that will be able to help you if you have questions or problems. But first…

Let me give you a tip about web addresses. When you type in the complete addresses below, some might respond with a message informing you that the page cannot be opened. Re-enter the address but this time stop typing when you reach the first single backslash. For example, if *http://www.ssa.gov/foreign* refuses to open, re-type *http://www.ssa.gov* to get to the main page of the site and then search for the page(s) you really need. If you absolutely can't get anyone to help you with information and you're experiencing continuing difficulties, you can always e-mail me at *don@headformexico.com* if you get really frustrated. I'll be able to either help you, or further frustrate you. Some of my exes report that both situations look and feel about the same.

We're From the Government and We're Here to Help

http://www.ssa.gov/international is a Social Security Administration website. On the left side of the homepage is a sidebar titled Benefits Information. You'll want to scroll down to the Benefits Payments heading and right below it click on Payments Outside the U.S.

http://www.ssa.gov/enews is where you can subscribe to the Social Security newsletter.

http://www.irs.treas.gov is the website of our good buddies of the Internal Revenue Service. There is apparently no way to escape them. Check it out.

http://www.aarp.org is an American Association of Retired Persons website. Scroll down to Retirement Abroad and choose the appropriate option.

http://www.ustreas.gov is a Treasury page. Click on the Sitemap link and then go to International.

http://www.va.gov is the Veterans Affairs website which is very easy to navigate. You won't have any problems here.

And We're Their Canadian Accomplices

http://www.www.ccra-adrc.gc.ca is a Revenue Canada website. Go to the Tax heading and then down to the International and non-resident link and click for more information.

http://www.expatax.com is the website of the Canadian Relocation and Expatriate Taxation Resource Centre that is a commercial site, but it gives you plenty of info, and a lot of things to consider before you make a move.

http://www.hrdc-drhc.gc.ca/isp/common/home.shtml is the website of the Old Age Security and Canada Pension Plan. This is a good site and I suggest you spend some time here.

http://www.fifty-plus.net is the website of the Canadian Association of Retired Persons and has some valuable information for those moving from Canada.

Immigration Status

Some "old hands" will suggest that you come down on a Tourist Visa (FM-T) and return to the border every six months to renew it instead of getting FM-3 status. My personal advice is to avoid this option. The Mexican government is roaring into the 21st century and one of the tools assisting them is the computer. The law says that you may have only one six-month Tourist Visa per year, but in the past immigration officials had no way to track you. Things are rapidly changing and this option may soon disappear.

Get A Passport

If you don't have one, get a passport. Call your local Post Office for the location of the nearest office where you can pick up an application and instructions. U.S. citizens and Canadians don't actually need a passport to enter Mexico but you'll be surprised how much easier dealing with banks and bureaucracies will be with one. If you're a U.S. citizen visit *http://www.travel.state.gov/ passport_services.html* to download a passport application form. Be sure to read all the instructions carefully and pay special attention to the following two items. First, when you print the form, two pages will come out, and you'll need both of them. Second, read the size requirement regarding the photograph and make sure your printer has given you a full sized form. My HP Deskjet 540 printed out a copy that was slightly too small. I suppose you could use a copier to properly size it if you needed to. Canadians will go to *http://www.dfait-maeci.gc.ca/passport/menu_e.asp.*

To get your tourist visa you'll also need a picture ID, like a state or international driver's license or ID card. If you absolutely refuse to get a passport, you can use your notarized birth certificate or a notarized statement of citizenship. Canadians can use the Canadian Citizenship Certificate.

How Did You Get Into That Mess and More Importantly, How Do You Get Out Of It?

In spite of all our efforts to achieve perfection, occasionally a zit does erupt. Here's a list of folks who may be able to help depending on how badly you blew it. Keep in mind that everything is subject to change at a moment's notice or on a whim. Don't panic, there's always some kind of option hanging around out there somewhere and a lot of your questions can be answered by visiting one or more of these websites.

The very nature of the WWW dictates that it be in a constant state of flux. Computers help us make more mistakes at a higher rate of speed than any other creation in history, with the possible exceptions of friendly blondes, loaded handguns, and *tequila*. Nonetheless, here's a whole grist of websites and e-dresses you can use to your advantage. If you discover that some are not working, just go to your search engine and type in your request.

Instituto Nacional de Migración (Immigration)

Phone: 55-387-2400 or 55-626-7200 or 55-529-9500

Toll free: 01-800-707-0000 (Spanish required)

Policia Federal Preventiva

Toll free: 01-800-440-3690 (Have a Spanish speaker by your side)

Here come some specific addresses, but for information that's updated on a daily basis you might want to look at *http://www.embpage.org*. This site offers a comprehensive listing of worldwide embassies, travel tips and advisories, immigration and visa resources, and general information on various countries. The site has a message board where you can post your questions or read information posted by others. It's definitely worth your time to take a look.

U.S. Embassy

    Paseo de la Reforma 305

    Colonia Cuahutemoc, 06500

    Mexico, D. F.

    Phone: 209-9100 exts. 3505 and 3529

    011-52-55-209-9100 from the U.S.

    01-55-209-9100 within Mexico

    FAX: 55207-0091

    E-mail: *ccs@usembassy.net.mx*

    http://www.usembassy-mexico.gov

Canadian Embassy

    Schiller 529

    Colonia Polanco, 11560

    Mexico, D. F.

    Phone: 011-55-724-7900

    FAX: 011-52-55-724-7980

    http://www.canada.org.mx

U.S. and Canadian Consulates—52 is the Country Code for Mexico—(000) is each individual Area Code. I've written these numbers in a form that will be familiar. The Mexican form (52-000-0-00-00) or any number of variations can be confusing. From the U.S. or Canada dial 011 first. Within Mexico if you're calling long distance dial 01 first. Under the new system, initiated in September of 2001, Mexico City, Guadalajara, and Monterrey have two digit area codes, although the prefixes now seem to contain four digits instead of the previous three. All other cities and towns use three digits.

U.S. Consulates
  Avenida Lopez Mateos 924-N
  Cuidad Juarez, Chihuahua
  Phone 52-861-611-3000
Progreso 175
Guadalajara, Jalisco
Phone 52-33-3825-2998 or 2700

Avenida Monterrey 141 Pte.
Hermosillo, Sonora
Phone 52-658-217-2375

Avenida Primera 2002
Matamoros, Tamaulipas
Phone 52-871-925-5011

Paseo Montejo 453
Merida, Yucatan
Phone 52-999-925-5011

Calle Allende 3330, Colonia Jardin
Nuevo Laredo, Tamaulipas
Phone 52-867-714-0512

Tapachula 96
Tijuana, Baja California
Phone 52-666-681-7400

In addition to the Consulates, there are Resident Consular Agents in several cities. They can be of assistance in the event of an emergency. The cities where they are stationed, as well as phone numbers are listed below.

Acapulco	52-744-484-0300 or 469-0556
Cabo San Lucas	52-624-143-3566
Cancun	52-998-883-0272
Cozumel	52-987-872-4574
Ixtapa/Zihuatanejo	52-755-553-1108 or 557-1106
Mazatlan	52-669-913-4444 ext. 285 or 916-5889
Oaxaca	52-951-514-3054 or 516-2853
Puerto Vallarta	52-322-222-0069
San Luis Potosi	52-444-812-1528 or 811-7802
San Miguel de Allende	52-415-152-2357 or 152-0068

Canadian Consulates

Hotel Fiesta Americana Local 3

Aurelio Aceves 225, Sector Juarez

44100 Guadalajara, Jalisco

Phone: 33-3615-6215

FAX: 33- 3615-8665

e-mail: *guadalajara@canada.org.mx*

Edificio Kalos

Piso C-1, Local 108-A

Zaragoza 1300 Sur y Constitucion

06400 Monterrey, Nuevo Leon

Phone: 81-344-2753

FAX: 81-344-3048

e-mail: *monterrey@canada.org.mx*

There are a number of Honorary Consuls who may be able to provide assistance in the event of an emergency. The cities in which they are posted, as well as telephone numbers and e-dresses are listed here.

Acapulco   52-744-484-1305   FAX 7-484-1306

Acapulco@canada.org.mx

Cancun   52-998-883-3360   FAX 9-883-3232

Cancun@canada.org.mx

Mazatlan   52-669-913-7320   FAX 6-914-6655

Tijuana@canada.org.mx

The Consular Agents and Honorary Consuls seem to change phone numbers and locations more often than Imelda Marcos changes shoes, so good luck.

The U.S. State Department website is *http://www.state.gov* and the Canadian site is *http://www.canada.org.mx* so you can check there for updated information regarding Consular Agents and Honorary Consuls, their phone numbers and possibly their shoes. If you have trouble getting to these sites, try *http://www.usembassy-mexico.gov/emenu.html*. Canadians can go to *http://www.costalegre.ca/Passport_Visas.htm*.

Centers for Disease Control and Prevention (CDC) can be reached at the International Traveler's Hotline at 1-877-394-8747. There is also an automated faxback service at 1-888-232-3299. Their website is *http://www.cdc.gov*.

Health Canada Online is located at *http://www.hc-sc.gc.ca*.

Mexico Government Tourist Organization 1-800-463-9426

Mexican Ministry of Tourism 24 hour hotline 01-55-250-0123

Toll free from Mexico, call 01-800-9-0392 or 800-482-9832

Toll free from the U.S., call 1-800-482-9832

Green Angels (Ministry of Tourism hotline again) 01-800-903-9200 or 01-55-250-8221 x 130 or 250-8555 x 297.

Policia Federal Preventiva (Federal Highway Patrol) 01-55-481-4345

Toll free: 01-800-440-3690

Embassy of Mexico

1911 Pennsylvania Avenue NW, Washington, D.C. 20006

Phone: 202-736-1000

The U.S. Customs website is at *http://www.customs.ustreas.gov.*

The Canadian Food Inspection Agency is at *http://www.inspection.gc.ca.*

Canada Customs and Revenue Agency is at *http://www.ccra-adrc.gc.ca.*

For consumer complaints you can notify PROFECO (Procuraduria Federal del Consumidor), the Mexican consumer protection agency in Mexico, D.F. The menu bar gives you links to the English language pages so you won't have a problem there.

Phone: 52-55-5211-6414 or 5568-8722 or 5761-4371.

Toll free: 01-800-903-1300

http://www.profeco.gob.mx

If your problem is caused by a Mexican bank, stockbroker, insurance company, retirement fund, investment house, or any other provider of financial services, you'll need to contact CONDUSEF (Comision Nacional para la Proteccion y Defensa de los Usarios de Servicios Financieros).

You can file your complaint by going to their website and downloading the form provided. To access the English and French language versions you'll need to look on the menu bar at the left and click on the bar that says "Attention to foreigners". Fill out the form and send it, along with copies of pertinent documents to the address given, fax it in to the number given, or e-mail them. The website is *http://www.condusef.gob.mx*

Mexico Secretary of Health 52-55-5553-7145

At *http://www.tomzap.com/legal.html#consumer* Jonathan Rapoport has compiled a list of legal resources offered by both government and private organizational entities. These are all specifically aimed at helping us *gringos* who encounter difficulties SoB. Thank you, Jonathan.

The Apostille

When you apply for your FM-3 someone may ask for your apostilled papers. I personally was not required to submit these because I used a Mexico-based immigration service. The Mexican Consulate in your area will detail their specific requirements, including what documents may need to be apostilled. Find your nearest Consulate at one of these sites:

http://www.move-to-mexico.com

http://www.enespanol.com/atlanta/mexconsulate/list.htm

http://www.embamexcan.com/english/indexenglish.html

http://www.mexonline.com/consulate.htm

http://www.canada.org.mx

An apostille is simply a statement by an approved authority that validates or proves the authenticity of a Notary Public's seal and signature. In other words, you might look at it as a "super notary" or an "international notary".

This action is required for the acceptance of documents exchanged between countries which are party to and abide by the Hague Convention Abolishing the Requirement of Legalisation for Foreign Public Documents. Many countries and commonwealths are party to the Convention, including the U.S. and Mexico. At present, Canada is not. In Canada you'll need to have your papers "legalized" by an official representative of the Mexican government. Contact your nearest Mexican Consulate for instructions.

For a longer and more detailed explanation you can go to:

http://www.sre.gob.mx/seattle/ing_ser_legaliza.htm, the website of the Mexican Consulate in Seattle.

The Secretaries of State of each U.S. state and the District of Columbia are the entities authorized to issue the apostille. You will find a complete list of addresses and fees at: *http://travel.state.gov/hague_foreign_docs.html#states.* Fees range from $3.00 up to $10.00 US.

What should you have apostilled? This is one of those "Who knows?" situations. I had nothing apostilled, but friends who applied for IMSS Medical Coverage were required to submit apostilled birth certificates and marriage licenses. It's a relatively inexpensive process and shouldn't take too long so I'd get those two documents apostilled before you come down.

I've tried to avoid listing commercial sites but here's one that's both interesting and potentially useful. If you find yourself in a position where you need a lot more information than you're able to gather on your own, you may need the services of a professional investigator. Try this site: *http://www.mexicoinvestigations.com.* The e-dress is *mchenry@unisono.net.mx.*

Their mailing address is Mexico Investigations, PMB 98B, 521 Logan Avenue, Laredo, Texas 70840. The physical address is Prolongacion de Aldama #21, Centro, San Miguel de Allende 37700, Guanajuato, Mexico.

There you go, folks. This should put you well into information overload. Some of the sites I listed here will give you pre-planning information, some will be of use after you're in Mexico, and some may be useful in both places, but I clustered them here for easier use. Relax and take your time working your way through this book. Mexico will wait until you're ready. Plus, we haven't even scratched the reference surface yet so you'll need to pace yourself.

If this seems like a lot for a single person or even a couple to attempt, here's how one group of folks provided mutual support for one another in their quests to make Mexico their new home.

Moving to Mexico-How We Did It

BILL HASLBAUER, RESIDENT
AJIJIC, JALISCO, MEXICO

Neva and I began looking for a place to retire in early 1996. She was 57 and I was 62. We took an exploratory trip to Ecuador, but were not impressed. Oh sure, the cost of living was impressive, but the country and it's environs just didn't fit us. Two years later, we received our first copy of International Living magazine, and that first issue had an article on the wonders of Ajijic.

That November, with nothing else pressing us, we decided to visit for ten days or so over our Thanksgiving time frame. Neva fell in love im-mediately.

While I was taken with the area, I continued to ask "What's wrong with this place?" since there HAS to be something wrong with every location. It was Fiesta time, so there was much excitement and revelry. We had a blast! With emotions running high, we decided that we'd better come back at a different time of year to see if we were still impressed.

The following May we visited for the weekend of Mothers Day. The weather was a treat from the Texas heat, and we were again impressed with the hospitality and attitude of the people. If twice is good, three times is better, so we returned in August to enjoy the rainy season and the new Mexican friends we had made as well as the gringo *friends.*

It was on this trip that we met a young lady named Karen. She too, was quite taken with the place, and began talking about moving here and starting an e-mail letter about moving to Mexico for newcomers. Thus was born Mexico Mama and her newsletter. It was to become the springboard from which all of our activities would occur.

By this time we were beginning to think pretty seriously about Ajijic as a new home, but there was much to do before such a move could be made. Also, more research was needed. Most of us have many, many questions when considering such a move and how to get answers to them. Karen's idea seemed very appropriate in this context, so we encouraged her. We, in turn, set about disposing of almost all of our worldly goods and properties in preparation for the move.

She went back to her home in Davis, California, sold everything, and moved to Mexico to start her newsletter. We visited with her in January of 2000 and continued that encouragement. It was a beautiful time in Ajijic, what with the total eclipse of the moon occurring then, and the glorious days and nights. At this point we were pretty sure that this was where we wanted to be.

Along with the newsletter, Mexico Mama also started an open forum. At first, it was open to anyone who clicked on her web site, and later, to subscribers of the newsletter only. Through this medium, we met and came to enjoy a number of like-minded people who seemed to have the same thoughts about Mexico as we did. One of the participants was Judy King who had been a resident and realtor here for about ten years at that time. In May, on yet another visit, we were privileged to meet Judy and learn still more about this unique village. She was the first acquaintance we made, in person, of the group that was yet to come.

Since we were in almost daily contact with the forum, many of the names and styles became very familiar to us. We looked forward with anticipation to see what posts came up every day. There was Don from Texas, who was the big kidder and always had something humorous to say. Dru from North Carolina was a schoolteacher who was ready to move on. Lea in Maine still had a couple of years to teach and wasn't sure where she was going to retire. Anne in New Jersey had made up her mind, and was busily trying to sell her house. Ellie, who became the cheerleader of the group, was still working and with her husband, Rich, was ready to get out of the Pennsylvania winters.

Up in Virginia was Rick D. who was our expert with the computer, and could keep us out of serious trouble most of the time. Rick S. in Colorado was always the "searcher", visiting and checking out everything. Gladys in New Jersey had her house there decorated in a Mexican style and was kept busy with an invalid mother. Then there is Howie up in Seattle, a pharmacist who is also a gardener who can't wait to get here and grow orchids.

Then there was Neva and me from Texas. Along the way there were Gary, Mary Jo, and some others, but as time went on, this little group became sort of "Pen Pals". Since one thing leads to another, we decided that we needed a name for ourselves. Judy suggested Los Picaros for The Rebels, and it stuck. We each supported the other and brought different things to the party. A more disparate group you've never seen. We come from all over the continental U.S., and almost any background you can imagine. I suppose Neva and I are the oldest of the group, and gratified that we could be included with all of these youngsters.

Needless to say, we became a support group that continues to this day. We are a FAMILY! I never believed in support groups, but this most certainly is one. Judy is our matriarch as she has been here to see many changes in the area. The rest of us, all of whom have at least visited the area, have been trickling on down since Dru arrived in June 2000.

Don and Anne were the next to head this way. They met up in Greenville, Texas and caravanned down. We were fortunate to have them stop by our place in Quinlan, Texas for a short break in the drive. That, of course, encouraged us to get high behind and work harder to make the trip. We finally got everything sold, thrown away, or given away, and made one more visit in October of

2000 to find a place to live. We then moved in November after deciding to rent. Ellie and Rich arrived in May of 2001, Gladys, her husband Tim, and invalid mother Jennie, got here in August right behind them.

Lea has decided not to come down after all. She will come for a visit from time to time, but is moving to North Carolina instead. She's still part of the family though. Rick D., Rick S., and Howie are still locked to duties in the U.S., but we're hoping they can make it soon. We will gain a new Picaro, when Rick S. marries his lovely Linda.

Since we became the Picaros, we have had other folks participate in the conversations, but never really become part of the group. Most have dropped out, but Wayne and Wanda from Oklahoma have stuck around and probably will make the move down this year. As the time passed, we also sent pictures of ourselves to the group, so that when we were finally able to meet, we weren't complete strangers. But then we never were.

Neva and I have been here for over a year now, still enjoy being retired, and look on each day as a new adventure. Our Spanish is horrid, but we're doing better. Luckily, both the Mexicans and the area are VERY forgiving. We are enjoying the visits of friends, both old and new. A big thrill was the Christmas visit of our grown, and very supportive, children. Now they know why we enjoy it here so much. We have also had the privilege of meeting each others families and children, and when anyone new arrives, it's an opportunity for a really big "family reunion"!

We know that Mexico isn't for everyone, but life is great as far as we're concerned. Perhaps you could come and visit. You may want to enjoy this lovely village with us.

One Year Later

So what has happened to this group of e-mail friends who became family?

Those of us who are now here stay in close contact with those who aren't and each other by e-mail. While we go in different directions, we still remain family and get together periodically as a group. Naturally, we see each other individually as well.

Dru, the first one down, rented a place in Mirasol where she still lives. She likes to travel, and has been investigating this part of Mexico. She has also gotten involved with the Lake Chapala Society and is co-editor of their Newsletter.

LOS PICAROS IN MÉXICO, JUNE 2002 FRONT LEFT TO RIGHT: NEVA HASLBAUER, BILL HASLBAUER, TIM HARLIN, SECOND ROW: RICH FISCELLA, ANNE LEWIS, GLADYS GRAND, THIRD ROW: ELLIE FISCELLA, JUDY KING, TOP: DON ADAMS

Anne immediately got involved with a number of projects in addition to buying a house. She has organized the Jewish community, works with handicapped children and is active in the Lakeside Little Theater group.

Don, of course, has been writing. He has also been moving around. First he lived in San Antonio Tlayacapan, then San Nicolas de Ibarra, La Manzanilla, and San Juan Cosala. He continues to travel throughout Jalisco, Nayarit, and Colima states researching his articles and future book projects.

Judy has more jobs than any of us can keep up with. Her monthly newsletter shows us that she still has a lot to tell the rest of us.

Neva and I are now in our second rental. We've been in this lovely house for a little over a year, and will be here for another year and a half at least. We love our surroundings and enjoy being retired.

Ellie and Rich moved to a new rental and are thinking about buying or building in the near future. They are enjoying retirement with the help of their adopted street dog, Molly.

Gladys and Tim rented for a short time, then bought a home in San Antonio Tlayacapan that is more comfortable for her mother. Travis made the trip from New Jersey with them and they have adopted two more dogs that regularly eat the new furniture and rugs. They've been busy shopping in the craft town of Tlaquepaque to find treasures for their home.

While all of us have gone our separate ways, we still visit with a reasonable degree of regularity. We all have made new friends and I think we fall into a lot of the habits that we had stateside. As for those who haven't made it yet, they continue to dream and work on getting here. It appears that we will all be here within the next three years except for Lea who has chosen not to come.

Life is definitely different and we are all adjusting. Some have had an easier time than others. Those of us who lived a somewhat rural lifestyle seem to have an advantage over those from metropolitan areas. There are many similarities between these villages and small, rural Texas towns. Many of the problems we experience here are the same ones we encountered back home – like brownouts, problematic dial up internet connections, loose animals on the highway, and limited shopping.

Some of the joys, however, are the beautiful sunny days, the birds and flowers, waiting for a herd of cattle to cross a street, watching a one-horse plow cultivating a field, and a slow pace of life that offers the opportunity to stop and smell the roses.

BILL HASLBAUER, RESIDENT
AJIJIC, JALISCO, MEXICO

From Canada to Mexico

Ron and Georgina Russell, Residents Ajijic, Jalisco, Mexico

As a working couple, Georgina and I always tried to live within our means, pay off our debts, pay down the mortgage when possible, and help our children plan their careers. Yearly holidays were important but retirement plans were never in the forefront of our thinking.

In July 1991, I took over as a Department Director at the University of Waterloo where both Georgina and I worked. The former Director had retired and unfortunately, just a few months later, was widowed. He came in to my office one day, sat down and said, "Life is just not fair". They had been planning his retirement for many years. They'd helped their girls begin their lives and were set to enjoy their retirement. Now he was alone.

That incident prompted us to look at our future. For the next couple of years Georgina and I began to search for a way to change our lives, but we weren't sure what that change should be. We worked long hours and our jobs supplied us with daily doses of stress. We saw that the time we had for each other was diminishing. The children were winding up their school years, planning their moves away from home, and beginning their careers.

Ron Russell

I'd always thought that my husband and I would retire to our lakefront cottage on the Bruce Peninsula in midwestern Ontario. We both enjoyed our summer holidays there and had talked about someday building a permanent home. But it really was a very distant point in time for me, some 10 or 15 years in the future. I had not really entertained any other retirement ideas. But after some thought we began to have questions. How would we feel in the dead of winter? How much isolation would we be in for? Would we fit into the social structure of a small rural community? What would we do with ourselves?

In the fall of 1996 Ron came home from work one day and asked if I would like to attend a seminar about retiring in Mexico. Retiring in Mexico? Why would I want to do that? I have to confess that the whole idea of living in Mexico was unattractive to me. The only images I had about Mexico came from newspaper headlines, expose TV shows and stock Hollywood cliches. Saddled with misgivings, I managed to accompany Ron to the seminar. Even though the seminar gave us another avenue to consider, I didn't come away from it convinced that Mexico was where I wanted to be. Looking back, however, that evening was to become a turning point in our lives.

Shortly after attending the seminar, Ron was offered an early retirement package by the University. After many long discussions and restless nights, he accepted the package the University offered. While I continued to work, Ron had time on his hands to investigate other retirement possibilities. Even though I still believed that the 'cottage' was where we ought to be, we began to look around. We visited Vancouver Island and were enchanted until we discovered how much rain they received each year. My arthritis quickly ruled that option out. We looked at Spain, Nova Scotia, California, Arizona, and Costa Rica. Did we really know what we wanted? Well, I still thought it was the 'cottage.' Ron wasn't convinced. He kept researching Mexico and in particular, the Lake Chapala area. In April of 1998 he asked me to join him for an exxploratory visit. Reluctantly I agreed.

As we flew into Guadalajara I wrestled with one negative notion after another. I believed that we wouldn't be safe. I believed that

people in Mexico lived in abject poverty. I had no interest in timeshares or all-inclusive vacations, so why would I want to live here? What would I do with myself "down here", away from all my family and friends?

I began my education about the "real" Mexico the day we arrived. It was a far different reality than the banditos, timeshares and super coastal resorts I'd imagined. Our guides began to break down the myths that I had created in my mind. They talked to us about safety and crime, the cost of living, the weather, and the language. We listened to people who worked in the medical professions, investment banking, immigration, and real estate. We talked to lawyers and economists. Our guides showed us the beauty of the Lakeside community. They offered me an opportunity to make that change in my life that I'd been looking for.

We bought a place in Ajijic that April of '98 with the goal of living there for six months of the year, starting in March 2000. When we returned to Kitchener, we sold our lovely old Victorian home and moved to a tiny 1,000 square-foot condo that we assumed would be our northern home for the next five to eight years. There was still a BUT in my mind, and even though I came away knowing that we'd bought a wonderful 'retirement' home, I was not ready to give up my job or move away from my family and friends. I could not visualize living in Mexico on a permanent, or even semi-permanent basis, for some time to come.

We spent our first extended visit, five weeks, in our new Mexican home the next December. Lakeside Christmas celebrations were a delight. One evening in the small village of San Antonio Tlayacapan we joined the Christmas posadas. The parish priest, accompanied by a small children's choir, walked the dark streets re-enacting Mary and Joseph's quest for lodging in Bethlehem. Mimed Biblical scenes were re-enacted in front of the homes. A mass was held at the end followed by festivities with piñatas for the children. It was memorable. During this first visit we shopped in the local tianguis where we found fresh vegetables and fruits and a myriad of produce that we couldn't begin to identify. We saw local live theatre and attended Sunday morning church services. Our children joined us for Christmas break and, without a vehicle, we explored everywhere we could on foot, stopping to soothe our tired feet in the hot-spring mineral baths in the nearby village of San Juan Cosala. Internet cafes kept us in contact with our cynical families up north and local buses took us to Guadalajara and the tiny villages farther down the Lake. The four of us realized that the real magic of Mexico was her delightful people--their warmth, hospitality and ability to celebrate life touch us enormously.

Suddenly, when it was time to leave, I didn't want to return to Ontario or to my job. I had been working extremely long hours and was so wrapped up in what I was doing that I wasn't aware of the effect it was having on our lives. In the five weeks I'd spent in Mexico with my family I'd found the time to reflect on my life and to examine my priorities. By the time I returned to Ontario I'd made a decision. I gave the University notice and left six months later.

But one worry continued to haunt me. Could we afford it? We were convinced that the cost of living would be lower in Mexico but would our lifestyle suffer? Friends and relatives gossiped about our crazy plans.

After careful research and discussion with our accountant we found a way to reduce our tax burden by establishing ourselves as non-residents of Canada. An advantage for Canadians living in a foreign country lies deep within Canadian Income Tax Law. By breaking all major and many minor ties to Canada, taxes can be greatly reduced. Intermittent Canadian pension payments may be taxed as low as 15% for Canadians who reside in Mexico.

We are still Canadian Citizens and carry Canadian passports, but since we do not live in Canada and have carefully cut the major ties, we are deemed non-resident Canadians for tax purposes. At a future date it is possible for us to return and re-establish residency, however CCRA, the Canadian tax authority, has the right at any time to question our non-residency status.

With this information in mind, we packed our van to the roofline and began our new lives. It was September, 1999.

Those early impressions of Mexico were confirmed once we made the country our home. One evening we looked over to find five pair of brown eyes staring at us from across a table. The five- and six-year old girls who were studying us with their watchful eyes wore crisply-ironed colourful dresses with woollen sweaters draped loosely over their shoulders. They charmed us with their stares, smiles and shy laughter and someone suggested that these kids had probably never seen a gringo before--much less a whole table of them.

Friends had invited us to accompany them to a small village just over the mountain for a band competition. The entire village, from the very young to very old, had turned out. Elderly couples watched from darkened doorways as teens courted and young families held hands and

danced together. Our Ontario Spanish lessons quickly failed us but smiles and handshakes made it plain that they were honoured to have us join their festivities. The salsa band overwhelmed our conversations so we gave up, joined in the dancing and couldn't have imagined a more enjoyable evening anywhere.

Our misgivings and reservations behind us at last, we look forward to the best years of our lives in our wonderful, adopted country.

GEORGINA RUSSELL

Okay, buckaroos, there's how some did it but if you want just a bit more here are some websites set up by folks who made the decision to move to Mexico. They've been kind enough to share the process and the results with us, and I, for one, thank them for their generosity and for allowing me to include them here. You'll see mention of them in other places too, but for now here they are. Enjoy!

Chris Bublin may not know what a great service she's performed by setting up the website at *http://www.newbeginningsmexico.com* but I can assure you she will answer many of your questions if you spend a bit of time here. She and Harry have posted a "diary" of their move to Mexico. Very informative!

http://www.Rollybrook.com is the site of a single man who moved to northern Mexico. I had the pleasure of meeting Rolly and we regularly communicate via e-mail. He's a lovely man with a kind soul and a desire to help others.

DonandCarmen Sellers have a beautiful site at *http://www.swiftsite.com/SayulaRetirement.* You'll discover a lot about life SoB as you explore their retirement story, and they've included many beautiful photos.

At http://www.donporter.net you'll find an excellent narrative about a couple's three month visit to the city of Colima. Don shares his experiences about finding housing and about learning to live in a different culture.

You should already be off to a good start, but there's a lot more to learn, so after you've looked at some of the sites found in this chapter, let's move on to more good stuff.

Chapter 2

Money Honey

For some reason many folks appear to develop a real concern about being in Mexico and leaving their money in another country. I fail to see the problem since I'm perfectly capable of mishandling currency in any country.

Are you getting the idea that this might be a pretty short section? Turning to me for financial advice is like asking Ted Bundy for dating tips.

Are U.S. and Canadian Dollars Accepted Here?

There are lots of places in Mexico that will be happy to accept your *gringo* dollars. Some won't. In one of the more popular retirement areas I tried to pay for a purchase at the hardware store with a twenty dollar bill that someone had given me but the cashier wouldn't accept it. That was a rare occurrence, but it *does* happen occasionally. I always assume that the person who declines the money isn't able, for whatever reason, to figure the exchange rate correctly. It won't be anything directed against you personally, or the Stars and Stripes. Or the Maple Leaf. Maybe the Star and Sickle, though.

Canadian dollars are not as easily spent down here. It's just a fact of economic life, nothing personal.

Anyway, what are we gonna do about that strange looking cash? Let's exchange it for *pesos*! How and where? Easy, just look around. See those banks? If they're open they'll change it for you. Most of the ATMs in border towns will allow you to withdraw money from your Canadian or U.S. account and will dispense either *pesos* or dollars US, your choice. Except for border towns and some airports though, you'll usually only be able to get *pesos* out of the machine.

Casas de Cambio

Another alternative is one of the many independent businesses called *casas de cambio.* These are money exchanges that will be open even when the banks are not. They're perfectly safe to use and they'll usually give you an adding machine tape showing how they figured the rate of exchange. If the exchange rate is 9.3 to 1 and you're changing $100 US, your slip will read 9.3 X 100 = 930. You'll then receive 930 *pesos* for your hundred dollars. At an exchange rate of 10 to 1 your slip will read 10 X 100 = 1,000. This time you'll get 1,000 *pesos.*

Here's where you can find dollar to *peso* conversion information on the Internet: *http://www.bloomberg.com/markets/currency.html,* and *http://www.xe.net.* Again, if you have trouble accessing these sites, or any others I give you later on, just stop typing after "com" and you'll be able to get to a homepage where you can find directions to the info you need.

What Mexican Money Looks Like

How will you know if you got the correct amount of money? Count it. If you'd like to familiarize yourself with the currency before you come go to *http://www.chapalaguide.com* and click on the money link where you'll see color pictures of Mexican coins and bills. At *http://www.maztravel.com/maz/money.html* you'll find black and white reproductions of the bills. The photos at both sources are of bills that will be slightly different by the time you get down here. The government has recently issued newer versions which have the denomination printed on them in smaller numerals but you'll still be able to recognize them. This is being done to combat counterfeiting. The *maztravel* site also provides you with an explanation of the identity of each of the people represented on the bills. Good little history lesson.

Now let me explain "large" and "small" in regard to the size of these bills. The difference will be considerably more subtle than someone saying that an elephant is large and a mouse is small. Small bills are about 2 X 5 inches and large bills will be about 2 X 6 inches long. Same width, different lengths.

Now on to colors. The 20 *peso* bill is small and blue. The 50 *peso* bill is small and magenta. The 100 *peso* bill is large and red on goldish tan. The 200 *peso* bill is large and green. You'll also frequently get 500 *peso* bills from ATMs if you're not lucky. They're large and maroon.

Here's one to screw up your day. Beginning September 30, 2002, the Bank of Mexico began replacing the 20 *peso* notes with new plastic ones. They estimate that it will take a year to make the transition and they may convert the others in the future.

Next, coins. These come in the following denominations: 10 *centavos*, 20 centavos, 50 centavos, 1 peso, 2 pesos, 5 pesos, 10 pesos, 20 pesos, and 50 pesos. They range in size from smaller than a dime up to about the size of a half dollar. Look at each one to determine its value. To simplify matters, and for the sake of discussion, let's consider the peso to be worth a U.S. dime. At the exchange rate of 10 to 1 this will be accurate. Unless something drastic happens in the economy of either the U.S. or Mexico this will serve as a good rule of thumb for figuring conversion rates in your head.

If anyone hands you a coin differing from the pictures drop it like a hot horse-shoe. It's old currency. Tons of those coins were sold to U.S. scrap metal dealers. South of Mismaloya is an abandoned crafts store. Inside the store, easily available to all, is a small shrine to the Virgen. There's a large basket full of coins given in thanks and tribute. The owner of the store was murdered seven or eight years ago. The unattended basket is still full. Of worthless coins.

And speaking of worthless coins never give U.S. or Canadian coins to kids or panhandlers. They can't spend them or convert them at the bank.

As we pulled into the village, prepared to explore the old silver mine and the ancient church and have one of the best pastries in all of Nayarit State, they approached the car. Three children. Two girls about seven years and a boy of about five, all with outstretched hands. I braced for yet another begging epi-sode but I saw that they were offering coins to me. U.S. coins. Canadian coins. Useless to them, and frustrating. I took the coins and replaced them with pesos at a generous exchange rate.

Then it was time for bidness. They were selling tiny carvings of the church and other buildings of the village. We bought an entire little town.

But back to the coins you're unfamiliar with.

Ready for this? The centavos are fractions of a peso. Of a dime. 10 centavos = 1 penny. 20 centavos = 2 cents. 50 centavos = a nickel. 1 peso = a dime. 2 pesos = 20 cents. 5 pesos = 50 cents. 10 pesos = $1.00. 20 pesos = $2.00. 50 pesos = $5.00. 100 pesos = $10.00. 200 pesos = $20.00. 500 pesos = $50.00. These conversions, once again, are figured at the 10 pesos to one U.S. dollar exchange rate.

At first folks express some difficulty in dealing with Mexican currency. It's fairly simple though and it works exactly the same way on both sides of the border. If you've made a purchase and been told the price is three hundred and twenty-seven pesos all you need to do is hand over a combination of coins and bills totaling three hundred and twenty-seven.

Like this. One 200 peso bill, one 100 peso bill, one 20 peso coin, one 5 peso coin, and one 2 peso coin.

Or one 100 *peso* bill, four 50 *peso* bills, two 10 *peso* coins, two 2 *peso* coins, and three 1 *peso* coins.

Or let's buy something small, something that costs *veintiocho y diez,* 28.10. You've just set down on the counter four cans of tuna and a Coke. In the U.S. you're gonna pay about $4.50 or so at the 7 Eleven or Stop 'n Shop. Here, a bit over half. You can figure you're looking at somewhere over $2.00 and less than $3.00.

You could take the safe route and hand over a fifty *peso* note and wait for change. Or you could hand over a 20 *peso* note and a 10 *peso* coin and wait for change. Here's a tip for you. If you hand over money to pay for your selections and the clerk makes no move to offer change, that's usually a fair indicator that you haven't passed enough currency across the formica. You could simply hold out a handful of coins and bills or spread them out on the counter and let the clerk pick and choose until the correct amount has been reached. I still do this when I'm tired, or when a case of stupidity overtakes me.

Or you *could* hand over a 20 *peso* coin or bill, a 5 *peso* coin, a 2 *peso* coin, a 1 *peso* coin, and a 10 *centavo* coin, wait for the smile and nod, gather your goodies and stroll out into the sunshine feeling as though you're finally begin-ning to understand what's happening. You're bound to get that little smile as a reward and hear "*Que la vaya bien*", the Mexican "You have a good day". Not literally, but in spirit. I love to hear it. Some folks interpret it as " May you travel well" or something similar. I just think it sounds cool regardless of how it's interpreted. A while back I read someone's complaint that "in the old days" he heard it all the time, but now nobody uttered it. Nonsense!

But if this is your first time out of the chute, you could simply hand a pen and paper to the clerk and say *Por favor, escribalo.* Or you could Marcel Marceau it.

Or you could just look at the cash register or the hand-held calculator, or the scrap of paper that was used to figure the total, and using it as a guide, count out the correct amount.

Will I Be Cheated?
I know this is a bit unusual but I need to digress for a moment. I know you want to ask "But if I just throw down a bunch of money, won't I get cheated?" In my experience, no. Or yes. Well, sometimes. Maybe.

One time several years ago I *did* inadvertently pay a cab driver 800 *pesos* for a ride from the train station to a hotel on the other side of Tepic. The temporary love of my life spent months and months reassuring me that I erred for a pur-pose. The driver was very helpful and very impressed by the fact that we were both teachers. He was dressed very neatly and didn't really seem to be a full-time cabbie. It was the middle of the night and I'd been roused from a sound sleep to disembark in a town I'd never heard of, after a long, hot and stinky train ride about six hours behind schedule. I still wasn't all that comfortable with the currency that had just made the transition from old *pesos* to new *pesos*. Old *pesos* had lots of zeros on them.

When I asked for the fare and heard an answer that might well have been offered up in one of the more obscure Ugandan dialects, I began peeling bills from the stash in my front pocket. Each time I laid a 200 *peso* note in his hand, the driver looked directly into my eyes. After four, he turned away, then asked a question that I answered with a wave of dismissal, and a smile.

Later my traveling companion almost convinced me that the *Virgen* took a hand in that night's proceedings. Her theory was that the cabbie was a moonlighting teacher who was trying to earn enough to pay for a life-saving or sight-saving operation for one of his children and that the money I gave him was exactly the amount he needed to pay for the job. I like that idea. And I *do* believe that everything happens for a reason. Do I feel cheated? No. Dumb is another matter altogether.

My neighbor, who is evidently fluent in every language but Tagalog went to buy some water pipe. One place quoted a price twice as high as what the first store was asking. Cheaters? Nah. You better shop around.

However, lots of folks look for an excuse to piss and moan about being cheated by nearly anyone, but especially those "dishonest Mexican shopkeepers." It's been my experience that the vast majority of the folks I deal with are scrupulously honest. Again, everyone has their own personal take on things. Consider where you're living now. Why do all the cash registers tell the operator exactly how much change to return to you, and even then, how often are mistakes made?

Keep Most of Your Money in Your Home Country Bank

All or most of your money should probably stay in the U.S. in an FDIC protected account or in a CDIC protected Canadian account. In a minute we'll discuss moving some, but not yet. We earlier talked about the fluctuation of the *peso* in relation to the value of the dollar. Although at present the *peso* is as strong as a yak fart, it can change overnight. And in the past has. Folks have lost lots of money playing the odds on daily *peso* exchange values. I don't do it. If you want to play that game, I'm sure someone down here will be glad to "advise" you. It ain't gonna be me.

Keep your money in a U.S. or Canadian bank that provides online banking services. That's one of the reasons you need to learn to use a computer if you don't know how. If your bank doesn't provide this service, my suggestion is to change banks. There are several reasons for this:

One, the mail service is slow and undependable. Even the private companies can be slow and undependable. However, I recently sent off a packet to the National Cotton Council in Washington, D.C. which arrived in only six days, so you really never know. I use the Mexican Postal Service rather than one of the expensive private systems, although I recently began using an inexpensive locally owned service that takes my stuff to the border for mailing through the USPS.

Two, you can pay bills through your bank account using automatic payments options. Talk to your banker to see what s/he can do for you. Ongoing stuff like credit cards, child support, the eternal payment to the hospital for your latest hernia transplant, or anything else you're responsible for should be easy to arrange.

Three, you have almost instant communication with the bank if you have a problem or need to make changes. It'll cost a few bucks a month but it'll be a bargain. My advice here is to establish some sort of personal relationship with your banker before you move to Mexico. Candlelit dinners and soft murmurs of undying love won't be necessary, but you *do* need your banker to know and care who you are if you call or e-mail him or her with a problem.

No, you won't need to buy a computer. Mexico is full of *cibercafes*--places where you can rent time on a computer for $2 to $4 US an hour. You can use one of the free e-mail services like Hotmail, or in my case Yahoo!. Go ahead and sign up before you leave home. Even if you don't have a computer I'm sure you can go to the public library or a friend's house to do this. Simple, quick, and free. Ask a ten year-old for help. Seriously. They love teaching stuff to dinosaurs, they're good at it, and they all seem to know their business.

Four, you need a debit card issued by your bank. You can use it to make cash withdrawals from an ATM machine at Mexican banks, some stores, kiosks, or at bigger airports. Regardless of where your card was issued, these machines will dispense *pesos.* You're in Mexico. In Paris you get francs. Or I did anyway.

You can make withdrawals every twenty-four hours for as long as your money holds out. In my case, not long. Your bank will have a set daily limit and a set number of daily transactions. For example, my bank in Texas allows me to withdraw up to $400 US per day, and gives me three transactions in which to do it. Sometimes I need all three transactions and here's why.

Some Mexican banks will have a lower daily withdrawal amount than your home bank will. If you encounter this situation draw out what you can at one bank and then go to another for the rest of it. Sometimes you can do multiple withdrawals at the same machine. Or stack your withdrawals by using your

Mexican bank debit card. Hell, just try everything you can think of--something will eventually work.

ATMs are available in most towns. Nearly all the banks will have one. Or two. More in cities, none in small villages. If the ATM is down at one bank then try another. If you hear someone say the "computers are down" it might mean that all the ATMs in the area aren't working. You could get lucky by driving to another town to try their machines or you could wait out your local delay. Sometimes it turns out that a particular machine has already dispensed all of the cash that was loaded into it earlier that day or yesterday.

Here's a short list of what could happen during your ATM withdrawal adventures:

1.   the ATM actually dispenses the amount requested

2.   the ATM dispenses a *portion* of the amount requested

3.   the ATM whirs and burps and dispenses a receipt for the requested amount, but *no* cash

4.   the ATM screen reports that you have exceeded your daily withdrawal limit

5.   the ATM screen posts a report to the effect that the machine is unable to provide the requested service

6.   the ATM eats your card.

In the event of number 2 or 3, notify your U.S., Canadian, or Mexican bank immediately. The bank that issues your debit card is the one that must be notified to have the lost amount credited to your account. This happened to me on the first day of the month, a Friday afternoon, and by the time I finally figured out that I needed to contact my Texas bank, rather than trying to rectify the mistake through the Mexican bank connected to the ATM I'd used, the problem was solved. The money was back in my account by the sixth, so it actually took two working days to remedy the situation.

In the event of numbers 4 or 5, re-insert your card and PIN and request a smaller amount of money. I drove my banker to distraction with phone calls and e-mails after early ATM transactions left me wondering why I couldn't withdraw my daily limit. The head bookkeeper and one of the officers finally figured out that I was miscalculating the exchange rate of dollars to *pesos*. I hadn't allowed for the daily fluctuation. I requested a smaller amount and money came pouring out. Sometimes when number 5 shows up on the screen it means the machine has been tapped out and there's no more cash to be had. Be careful on week-ends and holidays, because they empty out quickly in popular locations.

In the event of number six you'll need to make your decision based on the circumstances. One evening in Manzanillo I had to go to a small grocery store and buy two steak knives to use like chopsticks to retrieve a card that was hung up in an ATM slot. I've seen folks camped in front of remote location ATMs waiting for someone to come from the bank in response to their call for help. If you encounter this problem in the middle of the night just check in with the bank first thing in the morning. Past this, I'm as much in the dark as you.

What Does 24 Hours Mean to Your Bank?

Before you come you need to know your bank's definition of "twenty-four hours". At my bank one particular twenty-four hour period begins at three p.m. every Friday and runs until three p.m. on the following Monday. I found this out the hard way. Luckily, I really *do* like water and stale *tortillas*.

Keep in mind that each time you use that card the banks charge for the privilege and convenience. Sometimes both your NoB bank *and* the Mexican bank take a bite. Make sure you understand how much and allow for this in your budget.

Pay Your Bills Online

Five, you can pay bills online through many banks. If yours is progressive and service oriented enough to offer online banking, they'll probably offer this service too. I have one fixed payment deducted from my account each month and have had no problems.

Get a Deck of Cards

Six, it's a good idea to leave an extra debit card with a trustworthy friend or family member in your home country so that if you need to get cash to someone there you can have your trusted friend withdraw the money and send it on. I'd *really* try to get three cards if you go this route. One to leave, one to carry, and one to hide to use for a replacement when you lose the other one. I live with my doors open and my former junior dog, Panchito, filched my wallet from the bedside table one night and scattered cash, cards, and important classified nuclear secrets all over the place. I found my wallet and two cards, one of them my debit card, out by my truck. It's always good to have a backup.

You *must* get this taken care of before you leave home because your bank probably won't take an application for replacement or additional debit cards unless you're there in person. However, there are no absolutes.

If you lose your debit card nobody else can use it unless they know your Personal Identification Number (PIN) which is the four digit code you selected when you applied for the card. If you accidentally leave it in a machine somewhere, and if you later remember where, and if you'll go back, you may find that someone turned it in as a good deed, because it's worthless without the PIN. Yes I've walked away from the ATM sans card, as have some of my friends.

Just a few days ago a gentleman walked into the store where I was selecting some new cassettes and I heard the clerk say to him, "*gringo*". I looked around because I knew I was the only *gringo* in the place. He saw me and came over to hand me a card. I looked and saw it wasn't mine but he explained that it was my *amiga's.* Sure enough, I'd seen a friend at the bank earlier and she'd left her card. Yes, he received a *very* nice tip.

I'm sure you already know that you can also use your credit cards to access money through an ATM. Sometimes. A few years ago in Paris a friend and I were unable to get money from one particular machine with any of our credit cards. As a last effort I inserted my debit card from a little three-branch home-town bank in Galveston and money popped right out.

If you're not comfortable or familiar with using an ATM card start practicing now. Practice at different locations and get used to using a variety of machines. It's much easier to learn before you move.

Western Union
If you find that you've mismanaged yourself into a financial bind and can convince someone North of the Border to send you cash, there are a few options. Western Union, of course. It's fast but expensive. Look around your area to see who provides the same service besides your bank.

Emergency Bail Outs
But this is better. If your trusted friend lives close by, the easiest and least expensive method is to have them deposit money into your U.S. or Canadian bank account so you can withdraw it using your ATM card. They could also do a bank-to-bank funds transfer if they can't manage to get to your bank to make a deposit. That's a process by which they transfer money from their bank account to yours. It may take from several hours to a day or so to get the transfer credited and posted. In the meantime you *could* re-heat those *tortillas.*

If you really don't want to wait that long, here's a new option if your saviour is located in one of the areas serviced by this program. Tell them to go to a participating Post Office (call 1-888-368-4669 to find out which ones are participating) and ask for an application for the DineroSeguro program. They'll fill out the form, give it and the money to the Postal Clerk, listen while that person gives them the daily exchange rate and the amount of the service fee, issues a Confirmation Number and receipt, and fires the cash off to one of the nearly 2,300 Bancomer locations in Mexico.

All they have to do now is call you and give you the Confirmation Number, the exact *peso* amount they sent, and just to be safe, the exact name under which they completed the transaction.

Now, fifteen minutes later you can walk into a local Bancomer facility and show your valid photo ID, give them the Confirmation Number, collect your money, and heave a deep sigh of relief.

Your friend can send a maximum of $2,000 a day this way. If more than $1,000 is being sent in any single transaction they must show a valid photo ID. It may be a bit pricey, but it's definitely a useful option.

Se Habla ATM?

One last thing in this segment. The ATMs are usually much more bilingual than we are and you'll see your instructions in English as well as Spanish. Some don't display English until after you've inserted your card, but these will usually be in towns where you'll perish anyway if you can't figure out that the machines function exactly the same all over the world. If you have a Mexican bank account and insert the debit card from that bank, count on seeing Spanish on the screen.

Stick That Monthly Check Where?

Since you need to be able to prove monthly income for your FM-3 application and renewal you *could* have your check deposited into a Mexican bank. This is, in my opinion, a monumentally bad move because of possible devaluation of the *peso* in the middle of the night so that when you drop by the bank the next morning the gray-faced and quaking cashier tells you that the message on the ATM screen is exactly right and you really are officially a pauper. I'll contradict *this* piece of advice in just a minute.

Or you could have your check deposited into an independent financial institution such as Multivalores or Lloyd. Still risky since it's a *peso* account, but since the Bank of Mexico has prohibited banks from opening new dollar accounts, that's how it goes. For more information you can go *http://www.lloyd.com.mx* or e-mail them at *lloyd@lloyd.com.mx*. I've read books by less experienced writers who say that Lloyd is the choice of most of the gringos here. This is *not* true, since we use a variety of services, depending on our individual situations. They advertise that 70% of all money market funds in the areas where they have branches are handled by them, so maybe that's what they mean. I have an account with them and consider them to be solid, professional, safe, and extremely helpful.

Multivalores is an investment institution and is not set up for day-to-day banking services. For more information about the services they offer you can check their website at *http://multiva.com.mx* or e-mail them at *ajiprom@multiva.com.mx.*

You might want to explore the feasibility of an account with California Commerce Bank. They're affiliated with Banamex and allow you relatively easy access to your money through a special arrangement called the *"Programa Amistad",* or Friendship Program. There are several other benefits to this offer.

For details you can call them at 1-800-222-1234. Keep reading because this next part is important. This number connects you to a recording. A very nice recording. A recording that won't give you one single damn piece of information you want or need. Ain't it murder? Here's the secret to making contact with a real person. As soon as the recording starts, press "O" and you'll get an operator. Tell her, or him, that you need information about the *Programa Amistad* for Mexico and they'll take your mailing info and you'll have it *muy pronto.* Took four days to get mine delivered to Texas. Do I use this system? No, just my local bank in Galveston.

The website is *http://www.ccbusa.com.* Snail mail address is PO Box 30886, Los Angeles, CA 90030-0886. Check 'em out. If you do decide to use this system you'll find a dedicated phone in many Banamex locations that you can use to make free calls to the California bank once you're SoB.

Contradiction time. Earlier I advised against putting your money into a Mexican bank account. If you get an FM-3, which I suggest you do, you're going to need to prove that you have a regular monthly income of at least the minimum required by the government. Your bank statements from your U.S. or Canadian account will suffice for the initial FM-3 but after that you'll need to prove that the minimum monthly requirement is actually coming into, and theoretically at least, being spent in Mexico. The simplest way to do this, and what the regulations actually state you *must* do, is to deposit that amount into a Mexican financial institution *each* month. I can guarantee you that when you go to renew your FM-3 that the *Migración* officials will ask to see the original copies of at least the last three months of statements from your Mexican bank.

There are several versions of this requirement and the best I can do is tell you what the folks in the business of assisting us say the law says, and then what I've observed. The law evidently states that you must show the proper amount of income for each of the twelve months preceding the renewal of your FM-3. I went to *Migración* in Manzanillo with my neighbor when she renewed her FM-3 for the first time. The gentleman she dealt with told her he needed to see the bank statements for only the *three* months prior to the application, from both her Mexican bank and her European bank.

Another friend just renewed her FM-3 in Chapala. They just asked for three months of her Lloyd statements. A lot of things changed with the inauguration of the new administration so these examples are based on the most current information available to me. Let me also tell you that the nice folks at Lloyd filled out all of her paperwork, issued the receipt for the renewal tax of 913 *pesos*, and had her aces up, shipshape, watertight, and ready to rumble with absolutely no effort on her part. It's one of the benefits of having a Lloyd account.

When I renewed my FM-3 in Chapala, they asked for the originals of my Mexican bank statements for the preceding three months, but accepted downloaded copies from my U.S. bank account.

Keep Some NoB and Some SoB

Here's what I did, and what I do. Open a Mexican bank account or a Lloyd account. In some cases, unless you live in a fair sized town, your choices are limited to whichever bank serves your area. In my case Banamex was my only choice in Melaque, so I just stuck with them when I moved to an area that offered me a choice. Most larger towns will offer a choice.

Then you have two options, at least. First, have your bank use whichever method is fastest and cheapest to deposit into your Mexican bank the minimum amount required to keep you legal. Or you can adopt the more time consuming method that I use:

Use your ATM card to withdraw the amount of money you need to deposit and then go in and actually deposit it. By the way, Banamex makes banking very easy. When I make a deposit all I have to do is hand the money and my Banamex debit card to the teller. She swipes it through an electronic reader, types in the amount, prints my receipt, stamps and initials it, hands it back, smiles, and sends me on my way.

Yes, it *does* require several days and several visits to the bank. Keep in mind that you probably don't have a job, so why get uptight about time? Relax and enjoy the outings. Turn off the AC and roll down the windows on the way to town so Rocky can stick his head out the window and pant and slobber in the breeze. The dog might want to do this also.

The Mexican bank will give you an ATM debit card when you open the account, so once you've satisfied the government requirements you can start pulling money out by the fistful. Assuming your fists are no larger than Jiminy Cricket's.

How to Open a Mexican Bank Account

Show up with chocolate. Brownies. Bars. Anything brimming with that Aztec ambrosia. Share. Freely. With everybody. Smile. Someone will eventually offer to help. At that point anything can happen. It all depends on what they require because every bank will not require the same items. Here's a list of things you might take with you to make the application process easier.

1. Chocolate in almost any form.

2. A letter from your municipal authorities or police department stating your address, as well as the fact that you actually live there. This is called a *Constancia de Domicilio*. Once you get it, make several copies because you'll use it a lot and each entity with which you deal will want a copy. You don't have to pay attention to this piece of advice but I'll bet you'll regret not doing so.

3. A copy of your Tourist Visa or of every page of your FM-3. Some banks will let you open an account with only a Tourist Visa, but I wouldn't count on it.

4. A copy of every page of your passport.

5. A copy of a utility or phone bill showing your address, along with a copy of your lease. The bill doesn't necessarily have to be in your name but it shouldn't be more than a month old. This will be required only if you didn't get the *Constancia de Domicilio* like I suggested.

6. A passport sized photo or two.

7. At least one thousand *pesos.*

8. A Mexican mailing address. Go rent a post office box prior to applying for a bank account. You'll need items #2 and #4, as well as about 80 *pesos.* If you don't have a passport, you're on your own at this point. Try pouting. Or tears. Or throw a fit. Or offer up some of that chocolate. Probably none of these will actually induce the clerk to sign you up for a box, but it'll be a nice diversion for him and the rest of the customers. In Chapala they asked for none of these. In Melaque they wanted it all.

9. Lots of time and patience.

Are you actually going to need all these items? Maybe. Maybe not. How many trips do you want to make just to open a bank account? Trust me, err on the side of too much, rather than not enough. Fan everything out on the desk and let 'em pick and choose. The letter from a local authority that verifies your address, the *Constancia de Domicilio*, will be very valuable to you as you do your regular day to day business transactions. It's much more acceptable in most places than a utility receipt, which most folks use. Just a suggestion, but a really good one.

Banamex requires only your ID (passport or FM-3), proof of residence address (letter from the municipal authorities or telephone bill), address where you want statements sent, and your initial deposit money. As they promise, *es muy facil.* If you read Spanish. Take someone to the bank with you. Someone fluent in Spanish. The paperwork you'll be expected to fill out will be in Spanish.

Again, some banks will not allow you to open an account if all you have is an FM-T. Some will. You gotta shop around. If one bank refuses, try somewhere else. *All* are going to require an initial deposit of at least a thousand *pesos.* One hundred dollars US. And they're gonna fit you for a debit card, too. And have someone show you how to use it. Be polite and watch the demonstration. Smile, nod, say *gracias.*

What if You Don't Receive a Monthly Check?
If you are planning to live here on the proceeds from investments or trust funds or the like, you will need to get documentation showing your monthly disbursement.

For instance, your broker could work up a chart for you; or your CPA could set up a monthly schedule of payments or write some sort of plan for you; or your banker could do something similar. Talk with these folks, explain the situation to 'em, and see what they suggest.

If You're on the Lam
For some odd reason I feel compelled to offer up a strange bit of information right now. If you have a police record of some kind you'll be able to enter the country on a Tourist Visa. They will not question you at the border regarding any past indiscretions, and even if you lie they won't be running a criminal background check on you.

However, if you're applying for an FM-3 and you have some sort of conviction that might show up, you may have a problem. One of the requirements for an FM-3 is that you be able to produce a Certificate of Moral Solvency or a document of any name that certifies that you have no criminal convictions or pending charges. You'll need to get this from your local police department. In Canada you get a Certificate of No Police Record from the RCMP. Sometimes they ask for it, sometimes not. I had one but nobody seemed to want to see it. Other friends, who on sight and in comparison to me would appear to be morally straight and ethically pure, have had to show their documentation. When you're dealing with a foreign bureaucracy, anything can happen. Hell, when you're dealing with a *domestic* bureaucracy, anything can happen.

Paying With Canadian or U.S. Checks

Nobody will take your U.S. or Canadian check. OK, a few desperate *gringo* realtors will, if you're absolutely determined to deal with them, and maybe the occasional down-and-out local businessman. At some point you may come into contact with someone who claims that they handle *all* of their business in Mexico with U.S. or Canadian checks. Deal with that situation exactly as you would if suddenly confronted by a rabid wolf or a fully armed and war-painted Zulu warrior. Keep your guard up, maintain eye contact, speak softly in a non-threatening manner, and get out of the vicinity as quickly as possible. Avoid sudden moves.

It can take anywhere from fourteen business days to seven or eight centuries for your foreign check to clear a Mexican bank, and it's subject to any number of service charges on any or each of those days. Most folks are not gonna want the hassle. So few that *nobody* is only a minor exaggeration. The doctors in Guadalajara who repaired my nose and eyes accepted a check written on my Galveston, Texas bank, but this is a rare occurrence and needs to be approved in advance.

Paying With Mexican Checks

If you really have a bad jones for check writing, then write them on your Mexican account. Almost all daily transactions are done using cash, and in the smaller outlying areas I'll guarantee that the local *tienda* queen is absolutely *not* gonna accept a check in payment for her goods.

Using Credit Cards

And the same goes for credit cards. Many places in the larger cities, tourist areas, popular retirement gulags and the like accept most major credit cards. Except maybe Discover. And American Express. Just like in the U.S. or Canada, if you plan to rent a car you'll need one and they come in handy for making airline and hotel reservations. Some folks keep one card active for emergency situations, like having to get back to the U.S. or Canada immediately, but many do quite well without one. If you decide to do without, my advice is to leave an amount in a bank account sufficient to get you home if needed.

If your financial needs and questions are too extensive and complicated to have been dealt with within the parameters of these few pages, congratulations! And could I borrow a couple grand until book sales pick up a bit?

Chapter 3

Am I Right for Mexico?

By now maybe you've found that you can legally and financially live SoB, but what about culturally? Let's do a quick self-evaluation. Be honest because these questions are important and they're a pretty good indicator of your ability to make a successful transition to Mexican life. If you can truthfully answer "yes" to most of the following questions you should do fine. If you answer "no" to half or more and still insist on coming down, that could mean you probably believe that Evel Knievel never really took as many chances as he should have.

A Quick Quiz

- Do you have a good sense of humor? If not you're going to be really sorry that you stole this book.

- Are you flexible? Mentally, emotionally, and physically?

- Are you self-sufficient?

- Are you in relatively good health?

- Are you ambulatory without mechanical aids or the help of Bruno and Garth?

- Are you interested in your quality of life?

- Are you interested in and willing to learn a new language—or at least a few words?

- Are you interested in and willing to learn a new culture?

- Are you able to entertain yourself? Can you be happy without TV and a daily newspaper? They're both available here if you need and want them.

- Are you now able, or are you willing to learn to use the Internet? *This one is important.*

- If you're married, does your spouse support and embrace the idea of living in Mexico?

- Will you be able to contend with a variety of flying, crawling, and slithering creatures—including the occasional blind date or whiny neighbor?

- Are you somewhat adventurous and resourceful?

- Can you survive without frequent visits with Cousin Lutie, Deacon Bob, and the other assorted slugs and hangers-on you regretfully call family and friends?

- Do you have a talent or skill that you can share with the local community such as teaching English, art, belly dancing, computer programs or high-stakes poker?

- Do you have a clearly defined reason for wanting to move to Mexico—other than to avoid those few minor problems down at the D.A.´s office?

- Are you willing to do the work involved in checking out retirement locations?

- Do you have the ability and desire to talk to people and to learn from their experiences?

- Are you as mentally and emotionally stable as most people you know?

The last question may be the least important and a "no" answer shouldn't discourage you one bit in your planning. A friend assures me that most of us who are down here are not crazy. We just have "lots of personality".

Perhaps you should stop for a few days of serious reflection before you take a wild-ass leap into the unknown. The information you'll get here, along with your own personal research, may give you an idea of what to expect, but you'll never know exactly how it's all going to affect you until you're in the middle of it. Vacations are always exciting. Everything is exotic and new and things are quaint and fascinating. The real world is held at bay. It's during periods like this that many folks make major mistakes around organizing their lives and managing their finances. Ask yourself what you want and what you need. Is it just a cheaper way to get through the month? Or is it to have all the amenities of "back home" but with a better climate? Or something else?

If you really plan to move to Mexico, for whatever reason, I suggest that you come down and spend a few months trying her on for size. You may find that what's amusing and interesting in small doses is intolerable on a daily basis. If for some reason you absolutely can't visit before moving down, at least gather as much information from as many sources as you possibly can. Nothing substitutes for your own personal inspection and observation.

Maybe you *are* ready to embrace a new life, in a new place, with new people. Maybe you *are* ready to become a part of a new culture, a different way of life, and can do so without attempting to impose your own will and desires on the existing social structure. Some people who come here are able, some aren't. A lot of us wish that those in the latter group would stay where they are.

We No Longer Dance on the Plaza

We no longer dance on the plaza. *We used to gather each Saturday, young, old, all of us. Music was played, dances were stepped, and everyone joined in. The old ones sat and talked of the far past, of the events of the day, of those on the dance floor, and of the ones at home tonight. And they allowed themselves to be pulled onto the* plaza *themselves, to dance with the younger ones.*

LOS DANZONES, WILLIAM GENTES, NO DATE

We no longer dance on the plaza. *The parents no longer come to watch their children learn the lessons of community. They now run unattended, irresponsible, without* la musica. *The young ones socialize, the old ones socialize but the breach is there; the void with no bridge. Each group socializes separately.*

We no longer dance on the plaza. *The plaza is a beautiful place. Behind us,* el templo, *the church, and behind her,* las montañas, *the mountains. Before us is* la bahía, *the bay. Wild and beautiful, it is a source of work for many, and a source of comfort for all. The new kiosko must be the most beautiful of any village in Mexico. The* plaza's *walks are wide and clean. The plants are tall and lush.*

We no longer dance on the plaza. *They came, these* gringos *from the cities high in the mountains. They bought that house, the one just across the street from the* plaza, *on the beach. And when their friends came and saw it, they were envious of the beauty. And then* they *bought a house, just across the street from the* plaza, *on the beach. And others came. And then others.*

We no longer dance on the plaza. *Complaints were filed. How can we rest with this noise at all hours of the night? And can't something be done about all these people wandering about? Something must be done! And it was.*

We no longer dance on the plaza.

See how we can upset the balance with our imported ideas and values? I've never understood why some folks want to change everything down here to be exactly like it was "back home".

Why I Love Mexico

I've finally figured out the answer to The Question. You know the one. There are a number of variations, but it always boils down to the same thing.

You know, The Question...

Why do you live in Mexico? Why do you love that place? How can you be happy there? What's the attraction? The phrases are different, but The Question is the same. Why? And now I've finally figured out the simple one word answer.

Magic!

Magic—not the astounding stage-crafted illusions of Houdini or Henning, but the real magic of Merlin and Moses. Not tricks, magic! The kind of magic that appears unexpectedly to even the most prepared and watchful.

Magic—that power that shows us the mundane as miraculous and majestic.

CERCA DE ISLA ALARCRÁ, WILLIAM GENTES, 1980

The Indian baby, lying quietly in a shaded hammock, offering up a diminutive shy smile as her bare-footed mother kneels at her back-strap loom to produce yet another beautiful weaving. Magic!

That gorgeous small flower growing unattended and unaccompanied high up on the face of a solid rock cliff. Magic!

Last night's full moon, hovering low in the western sky just above Mezcala Island, allowing the clouds to diffuse her soft yellow glow to illuminate the craggy rock cliffs and sandy beaches with an unsurpassable light show; a reward for the farmers, fishermen and their families who sat resting in her light after another long day of subsistence labor. Magic!

I've seen it many times and shared it on occasion but I've only recently learned to seek it out and fully appreciate it. Magic!

We had stopped at the Nueva Posada *for a late cup of coffee and slice of cheesecake. Our evening of exploring the town had been pleasant. Our hours-earlier dinner too close to perfect to be labeled as anything else, our conversation mutually interesting and engaging. The dimly lighted ambiance of the small dining room next to the patio, the muted piano music, and the small dishes of ambrosia all gently worked to provide what we thought would be the perfect end to a perfect evening. Our personal enchantress though, had one more gift to bestow upon us before her work was done that night.*

As we prepared to leave we both detoured to los baños, *common stops after refreshments. As males usually do, I completed my acts and ablutions first and wandered out to sit on the old wooden bench at the side of the hotel lobby nearest the bar. George, one of the hotel's giant felines had laid claim to the lion's share of the seat so I picked him up and draped him across my lap. There he seemed to be perfectly content to lie and purr while I stroked his silky fur and his ample supply of cat fat.*

George and I were both lost in the moment until the louder-than-we-were-prepared-for entrance of Rojelio disturbed our individual reveries. One of the local *vaqueros, Rojelio was small, quick, and wiry. He moved with a slight swagger born of his confidence to do his job well. And he was mildly intoxicated.*

He stopped at the reception desk and propped his elbows up on the high polished terrain of the counter, crossed one booted and spurred foot over the other, and leaned slightly forward to settle himself into a comfortable flirting position. The lovely young desk clerk was out of my line of vision for the moment but it was obvious from Rojelio's body language that she had no time to spare in appreciation of his advances. After a valiant attempt he broke off his efforts and straightened, turning toward me, George, and the barroom behind us.

I watched quietly as he strode purposefully toward us in search of something. This was not a place where you would expect to find a vaquero in work clothes. The beautiful and elaborate charro *dress with sash and sombrero, maybe, but not work clothes—the same kind of gear you'd find on a ranch hand in Texas or Montana. Worn, scuffed boots, faded jeans just exactly too long bunched over his instep and spurs, a heavy leather belt, a chambray work shirt, a red bandanna knotted loosely around his neck, and a very good straw hat, neatly creased and worn with just a hint of a tilt to the right. His black beard was closely trimmed and served as the perfect foil to the wild black hair curling and twisting in every direction from under his hat.*

She appeared in the lobby just in time for him to pass between us, spurs singing, boot heels tapping; each element playing counterpoint to his soft muttering. With a glance at Rojelio and then quickly back to me, her eyes asked a dozen questions, all of which I answered with raised eyebrows, a tilt of the head, and a short shrug. We tarried for a moment, fussing over George before we stepped from the lobby onto the narrow sidewalk.

The night had turned stormy as we sat inside enjoying the pleasures of the Posada. *Lightning fired the sky above the mountains at the head of the street with brilliant, short-lived bursts of pink-and gold-tinged white light. The wind roared over the cobblestone street carrying and driving not just dust, but full grains of sand and dirt. Only an instant behind us, Rojelio bounded out the door and across the windy street to the pole where his horse was tied. With a quick snap of the wrist to release the restraining knot, a slight tug to move the animal away from the pole, and one astonishingly acrobatic leap onto the horse's back, the two creatures melded.*

The wind drove against the vaquero's *back as his booted feet found the stirrups. A sharp jerk wheeled the horse to face the wind and the uphill path to their next destination. Rojelio held the reins high and loose as he tore his hat from his head in a spontaneous salute to life, freedom and to doing what pleases you. It was a challenge to the wind, a salute to the glory of Nature, an unvarnished display of impulse.*

In the same motion, as fluid and sure as the most practiced of dancers he spurred the mount into a gallop and his partner, twitching with expectation and excitement, sensing the spirit of the rider, and running for the pure pleasure of racing through such a wonderful storm, leapt forward. Mane and tail flew, steel shod hooves sprayed sparks in every direction as they slammed onto the stones. A flash of lightning highlighted the flared nostrils and the wide-eyed exuberance of both man and horse, and in that split second before they dashed past, they shared a spontaneous and unrehearsed display of the absolute essence of life.

There's a lot to life, but those two, in a small Mexican village, on a stormy summer night wrote volumes on the subject in only a few short heartbeats; volumes I'm sorry that I can share only so poorly with you. That night we saw the true spirit of life. We saw grace, poetry, appreciation, freedom, and most importantly we saw...magic!

CHAPTER 4

THE DAY TO DAY NITTY GRITTY

Even as we appreciate the magic, we must still keep at least one foot in the real world. You're probably wondering how many of the services you're used to will be available here. Most of 'em; although they may be in a somewhat different form. Beware of succumbing to *gringo* amnesia. That's where you remember things up North a bit differently than they actually occurred.

If you have the misfortune to sit in on *gringo* gripe sessions you might actually come to believe most, if not all, of the following things about "back home"…

- Electric service was never interrupted.
- Water distribution was never restricted, rationed or interrupted.
- The sewer never clogged or backed up.
- You were never, ever short-changed by a clerk.
- Every time you walked into any store, they had in stock exactly what you wanted.
- Service technicians politely responded to your calls and showed up exactly at the time they promised.
- The telephone never went dead.
- There was never a speck of trash in the streets.
- There were no stray animals anywhere in your town.
- The streets were quiet and safe to walk at night.

❧ Nocturnal wild creatures never entered the city limits.

❧ The trash guys were so quiet you never heard them coming and going, and they never put a dent in your can, or scattered refuse on the street.

❧ Your neighbors were all saints--comely, intelligent, well-mannered, cultured, witty, interesting and very concerned about your personal happiness--and willing to do anything for you at a moment's notice.

❧ The weather was always delightful, regardless of the season.

❧ Prices were incredibly low.

❧ You were never bothered by mice, insects, spiders, mosquitoes, houseflies, snakes or scorpions.

❧ No one ever ran over an animal and left the carcass lying on the road or street.

❧ There were never any mistakes in your billing from the utilities.

❧ Your mail was never lost or mis-delivered.

❧ Everyone sought your advice and counsel on all matters of importance and you were always selected to head up every charitable project for the township.

❧ There was no pollution.

❧ Your town had the fastest Internet connection in the universe.

❧ All the politicians were honest and efficient, concerned only with your needs and wishes.

❧ Taxes were neither high enough nor plentiful enough for the degree and diversity of services rendered.

❧ You moved from Eden to Hades.

Don't worry, I'm sure there will be lots of folks standing by to help you load up for the trip back North.

This place ain't for everybody.

If you are interested in the services that *are* available in most places, here's a short list:

❧ Electricity, at about the same cost per unit as North of the Border. It works the same way too: 110 volts, 60 cycles, whatever that means. Actually it means that if you plug your stuff in, it'll function the way it was designed to. As a warning, I must tell you that not all the receptacles are grounded, so if your gear has three-pronged plugs you might need to use adapters in some places. You can buy them here and can have one of the locals install grounded plugs for a very reasonable fee. If you intend to use your computer, this is an essential.

❧ Public water supplies, most of which are not potable. There are in-home filtering and purification systems available at a reasonable cost; most of us drink bottled water.

❧ Gasoline at higher than North of the Border prices: Texas 1.30/gal, Nawlins 1.40/gal, Mexico about 2.40/gal at present.

❧ Major automobile dealerships: Ford, Chevrolet, Dodge, Jeep, Chrysler, Nissan and Volkswagen, although some parts will not be available.

❧ Good health and dental care, a reasonably-priced national health care system, and doctors who still make house calls.

❧ Pharmacies with extensive stocks of medications and health and safety related products, although they may not stock the newer drugs that you need.

❧. Sewage systems and treatment plants, although many are taxed to their limits due to age, expanding population, new businesses, the expansion of industrial facilities, and in some areas to new home construction, much of it *gringo.*

❧ Law enforcement agencies who, contrary to popular fiction, are probably no more corrupt than say the L. A. or Detroit boys in blue.

❧ Natural gas suppliers who deliver to your door, or let you pick up.

❧ Residential trash pick-up services, some six days a week.

❧ Skilled craftspeople and technicians in all fields.

❧ Excellent roads and highways in many areas.

❧ Wonderfully fresh produce, although commercial growers spray with chemical insecticides.

❧ Modern shopping malls, strip centers and other retail establishments in many of the larger towns, and all the cities.

❧ An astonishing diversity of cuisines.

❧ Laundries, dry cleaners, self-service laundromats.

❧ Travel agencies. (You can even fly to Cuba.)

❧ Furniture stores, modern as well as rustic and traditional.

☞ Fire departments and emergency medical service personnel and vehicles in many places.

☞ Electronics stores.

☞ Hotels in all price ranges, from about $10 US on up to outrageous luxury.

☞ Rehabilitation clinics and nursing home facilities, as well as AA and NA groups in many parts of Mexico.

☞ Technical schools and universities, as well as medical and dental schools.

☞ Cable and satellite television services which provide U.S. and Canadian stations, as well as worldwide access.

☞ Excellent transportation services: locally, nationally, and internationally.

☞ Telephone and internet services. There are almost 200 ISPs in Mexico so you have a lot of choices here, although damn near everyone complains about service, or the lack thereof.

Paying the Piper

Okay, once you're here and you've used the electricity, the water, the cable TV and the telephone the time comes to pay up. Don't plan on mailing any of these payments. Remember, the mail service is pretty unpredictable. How you pay your bills is determined by where you live so you're going to have to ask some of the locals about this. In La Manzanilla I paid my bills in Melaque, either at the bank or the telegraph office, depending on which line was shorter at the time. In some areas a *kiosko* or trailer will be set up at certain times of the month to receive payments, and in other places one or more of the local businesses will accept your payments. In Puerto Vallarta and many other cities you can pay at Elektra, one of the department store chains. In some areas there are automatic payment machines, somewhat like ATMs where you can use a debit or credit card to pay both electric and telephone bills.

Phone

If a TELMEX office is close by you can go there to pay your telephone bill, or if not, find out where the locals pay. In many places you can pay at one of the banks. I had internet service provided by Prodigy through TELMEX and paid 999 *pesos* once a year with my telephone bill. If you use a different ISP, Internet Service Provider, one of the more than 200 in Mexico, they'll provide billing and payment information. I was once in a long distance dial-up area for Prodigy so I used a private local ISP and paid at their office in Jocotepec. An interesting note about TELMEX service in San Juan Cosalá and most other small towns is that no bills are sent to customers. You just go to the main office in Ajijic, or wherever your local service area office is, and give them your phone number and they'll tell you how much you owe for the month. Simple. Or as I mentioned earlier, if an automated teller is available, use it.

GAAAAHHSSS...EL GAAAAHHSSS...

Some day not too long after you've settled in you're going to hear the peace-rending call, *GAAAAHHSSS!!* Repeated moans of *EL GAAAHHSSS!!* have driven more than one teetering psyche to the Dark Side, followed by a long recuperative period at the *Linda Vista* Laughing Academy. For some odd reason, I find this wail really spooky. Thankfully, the Mexican National Gas Call is not universal throughout the country. Wherever you live you'll notice a system of bells, whistles, horns, music, and recordings to alert you to the approach of service men ranging from the knife and scissor sharpener, to the trash man, the water man, the pastry man, and everyone else who might pass by. You'll learn your local signals pretty quickly.

If your gas tank is stationary you'll normally place a call to the gas company to order a delivery. The driver will park in the street, run a long hose to your tank and proceed to pump it full. If you have gas cylinders that need to be filled the driver will exchange your tank, issue your receipt, and that's it. I usually tip the guy 10 *pesos* or so for his trouble, although it's not expected or required.

Here's a suggestion that may save you a lot of aggravation. In areas where bills are mailed out, have them sent to your APDO, or post office box. If you have them delivered to your home, you may or may not get it. I've seen bills laid on fences, propped on wall ledges, tossed onto walkways and generally left to the mercy of the elements and the neighborhood animals. They're your bills, and it's your choice, but they're much safer in that P.O. box. In some areas the bills are all given to one person who is authorized to collect payments and you just go to the store or kiosk where they are and pay up. Again, you need to ask your neighbors what to do. In many places you can pay any and all of your bills at the local banks, but it's likely they'll charge a small fee for the service.

Or, if you're renting, your landlord may just pay the bills and present the receipts to you for reimbursement. This is the easiest way, and the one I prefer when I have a choice

Airing your Dirty Laundry

Here's an area where you'll use a lot of water. Some folks down here have washers and dryers at home. I prefer to take my laundry to *Doña* Cata, or any local lady who needs the work, and pay her to wash, fold and press mine.

One day when I stopped by, *Doña* Cata's grandkids were frolicking about in the huge cement trough she uses as one of her washing machines. They were having fun, the clothes were being agitated, and *Doña* Cata was getting a short break. In many cities you'll find full service laundromats, dry cleaners and self-service laundries. You'll have basically the same options you have NoB, but sometimes the prices will be staggering. In the Lake Chapala area I paid nearly as much for one load as I paid for three at the beach in La Manzanilla. You'd better shop around. Or ask your maid to handle this one more detail for you.

Tricks with *Agua*

I strongly suspect that you'll be drinking a lot more water here than you do now. This is a fairly simple matter but one that can get expensive if you're not careful. Many of us buy our drinking and cooking water in five gallon (19 liter) bottles, or *garrafons.* They're heavy, and they're bulky, and they have to be manipulated onto or into a dispenser. There are several types available. Rubbermaid, as well as a number of Mexican companies, makes a plastic unit that sits on your countertop. Locally, you'll find lightweight metal stands into which you place the bottle so that it swivels down each time you need to pour water. If getting the bottle into or onto the dispenser is a problem for you the guys on the delivery trucks will be happy to help or you could ask a neighbor to assist. Some places have purified water to your tap. Ask.

Many people use purified water to cook with because they are uncomfortable using tap water, even when it will be boiled. Again, personal preference. Some folks tell you to boil the water for as long as twenty or thirty minutes to kill the germs. Try it sometime and see how much is left in that pot or pan after that length of time. All you really need to do is get the water to a good rolling boil and that will be enough to kill whatever might try to kill you. Trust me, I do it this way every damn day. Emeril, Martha Stewart, the CDC, Health Canada, and OMHs may have different stories to tell you, but I know that my method is effective. Or at least it hasn´t killed me yet. The Red Cross says three minutes.

Back to drinking. In most places there will be at least one company that will deliver water to every street in town every day. The truck will slowly cruise the neighborhoods and when you flag him down the driver or his helper will carry the bottles into your house and put them where they need to be. You don't actually need to be home in order to have water delivered. Follow these instructions and you'll be in good shape. Make a sign that reads "*agua*" and rig a string or wire to it so that you can hang it on your gate, door or fence, or wherever it can be easily seen by the truck driver. If you live where there is more than one supplier and you have a favorite, just include the name of the company you choose to buy from. Next you need to tape the correct amount of change on the bottle you'll set beneath the sign. I usually add a tip amounting to a couple of *pesos.* The cost of water is currently controlled by the government and 12 *pesos* will buy you a 5 gallon *garrafon*. NoB, that money taped to the jug wouldn't last as long as a snowball in a hot skillet, but down here it's very rare that anyone takes it. You must put that jug out because the deposit on it is around 50 *pesos*. Here's where the "expensive" part comes in. The smaller bottles that you buy at the *tiendas* usually cost from 3 to 6 pesos each. You'll be way ahead of the game if you buy a funnel so you can fill those small bottles at home, rather than spending the money to buy new ones during your travels and rambles.

Just like with water, you can signal for a gas delivery with a sign reading "gas" if you have the portable cylinders at your house. You'll need to be home when he comes by though. The sign will get him to stop at your house.

Can you drink the tap water? Yes, if you have installed and properly maintained a whole house water filtration system. There are several types available and most seem to be relatively inexpensive, initially. There will be ongoing costs involved with these systems of course. Be sure to ask about maintenance, service, and the cost of replacement filters, lights and chemicals for the system you plan to use. I see gardeners and construction workers drinking from hoses quite frequently but I advise you to avoid doing this.

Soaking vs. Stomach Cramps
And…

You *did* know you were supposed to soak those fruits and veggies before you eat them raw? Or peel them. Nothing will disturb a peaceful night of slumber like gut churning, stomach clenching, intestinal distress caused by eating unpurified produce. How do you avoid it? Piece of *pastel*. Just soak everything in clean water laced with purification drops. They're sold as "*microbicida*" under a number of brand names, or as the most commonly heard brand name "*Microdyn*". It's usually found near the produce section of most stores in tiny 15 or 30 ml squeeze bottles. It also comes in larger bottles and it's worth grabbing one or two when you find them. Brands vary as to how much you use but the label will tell you how many drops to place in a liter of water. Soak the *frutas y verduras* for at least 10 minutes, toss the water, shake the excess from the produce and get down to bidness.

Incidentally, never waste water. Here or in Seattle or Sand Springs or anywhere else. Pour that water over your plants. And take Navy showers. Or shower together, assuming you're not just in a platonic relationship with someone. If so, wash the dog or cat or the dishes while you're in there.

It's not necessary to purify foods you'll cook because the heat will take care of that for you. I heard of a woman who soaked her beans in *Microdyn* and cooked them in the same water. Big mistake. The taste must have been nasty, nasty, and a bean is a *terrible* thing to waste.

You can rinse your toothbrush under the tap after you brush. You'll still need to use purified or bottled water for the actual brushing and mouth rinsing but the tap's okay for clean-up. I do it every day and so far I've suffered no ill effects. The eye tic and the speech impediment were in place long before I got to Mexico.

Other Liquids

In addition to water, there will be a big selection of canned, bottled, and card-board packaged fruit and vegetable juices available in a variety of sizes. You'll also find a good range of domestic and U.S.-brand soft drinks. For my fellow Texans, I *have* on rare occasions seen a case or two of Dr. Pepper in a small store, but don't count on ever being able to find it here. Treats I suggest you try are bottled mineral waters mixed with fruit flavors, as well as the regular unflavored mineral water. Plastic containers of pasteurized milk are also in the stores, as are small boxes of milk that don't require refrigeration until after they're opened. A lot of folks don't have refrigerators and this milk is a boon to them. It tastes just fine and I use it on my *Zucaritas,* Mexican Frosted Flakes all the time.

Aguas Frescas

Here´s a quick word about *aguas frescas*, the fruit flavored waters sold by many restaurants and street vendors. Unless you can confirm that they´re made from purified water, stay away from them. In restaurants you´ll be fine, the water will be good, but sometimes the street product can be contaminated. I mentioned fruit flavors, but my personal favorite is *jamaica*, made with dried hibiscus blossoms. You might find an alfalfa-pineapple version in some places.

Designer Java and Other Addictions

If you're addicted to $12 US cups of designer coffee froths and slushes you may be in for a rather distressing adjustment period. You ain't gonna find that stuff in most of the places we're talkin' about, although Starbucks plans to move in to Mexico sometime in 2002. There are entrepreneurs who are import-ing some pretty fancy brew toys under their own names, so you can hit pretty close for a whole lot less. If this is a big deal to you you'll soon hook up with others of similar addiction and be led to what you consider a proper cuppa. If you´re really fanatical about coffee, fresh beans grown in Mexico and other countries are available for your do-it-yourself efforts. The thought of putting out that much time and effort for coffee makes me a bit light-headed.

Usually, when you order coffee you'll be presented with a big jar of Nescafé Clasico instant coffee, a container of sugar, a spoon, and a small dish of cream, all of which will be ceremoniously laid out before you. Delivered shortly there-after will be a cup of piping hot water. Sometimes it's tepid and you'll need to send it back. If the water is near-boiling when it reaches the table, you'll need to wait for it to cool a bit before you add coffee or sugar. If you don't, you'll be treated to a bubbling overflow that would impress most of the world's volca-nologists. It's always quite a sight. And quite messy. And if the coffee lava runs off the table and onto your lap you won't get a multi-million dollar court settle-ment like the plantiff and her lawyers received in the infamous McDonald´s case. One of the great joys of life in Mexico is the almost total lack of plaintiff´s attorneys and their whining clients. It's based on the wonderful Mexican as-sumption that if you're going to go out in public you should be intelligent enough to handle life's simpler chores without assistance or guidance.

The Day to Day
So what can an average day look like? Hard to say, but you and the Mrs. might get up, have a cup of coffee and head your separate ways. She to some of her club meetings or volunteer activities, and you to the coffee shop or the Legion Post or some of the community service work that interests you.

If you're in a retirement mecca you're bound to find volunteer efforts you'd like to join or you might decide to develop new talents or disinter interests that might have fallen by the wayside during your working years. There are reading circles and study groups, library support groups, volunteers who teach En-glish, the chess club, or the computer club. Some places have a music appre-ciation society or a little theater group. In a few places you may find a writer's group, or a garden club, or a travel group. You might find cooking classes, or a sewing circle. You can sign up to attend or teach adult education seminars, or volunteer to help out at the orphanage or one of the local schools. Some people enjoy helping out at the local animal shelter. You may enjoy participat-ing in the ham radio club, or the Navy League, the Daughters of the American Revolution, Sons of the Confederacy, Lions, American Legion, Alcoholics Anony-mous, Narcotics Anonymous, along with other like-minded individuals.

Or you may decide to sit in the house all day watching TV. Hell, you're retired, go on and do what'cha wanna.

I strongly encourage you to get involved in some of these activities though. They'll keep you busy and integrate you into the community. Plus they'll give you and the spouse a little break from each other. I've had exes tell me that this is necessary. Actually I think they said it was *very* necessary.

And after a morning of jollyfrockin' from group to group you may want to meet other expats for lunch somewhere for a dose of good company and conversa-tion, and then set off for a little shopping or sightseeing.

After returning home from your travels and taking a few minutes to garden or read, it's time to fix dinner—unless of course you're going out to one of the more reasonably-priced local restaurants.

Conchita cleaned the place while you were gone. You'll probably need to spend 30 to 45 minutes rearranging everything she moved. Some Mexican maids have their own ideas about furniture placement. Your opinion may not count and will not be sought. It can be a battle of wills. How often you have to shuffle furniture depends entirely upon how many days a week you've employed her to clean. It's quite possible to wear out your furniture from the bottom. Very likely actually, depending upon the strength of your maid and how much physical stamina you possess.

And Enrique stopped by to flood the yard while you were out. He pulled the "weeds" from the planting beds that you and the spouse spent all of yesterday afternoon setting out as soon as you got them home from the nursery. In Chapter 12 I discuss supervising gardeners.

Oh and there's a tapping at the gate. Two well-dressed, scrubbed-to-a high-sheen, little silver-haired *gringas* are standing there. Let's see what they want. Oh cripes! Gee, I'm sorry I can't invite you in but my cat's hemorrhaging in the kitchen and I really should try to save her. Oh, the latest <u>Watchtower</u>! Thanks ever so much. Ta!

Or…

You get up early and meet Wallace and Sylvia (Wally and Syl) over at the *Barranca* Breakfast Bar for a hearty meal before you set out on a tour of the mountain villages.

There's a family in a nearby village who sculpt religious figures from clay taken from a local riverbank. Over in the next village are the rug and *serape* weavers. And we'll have lunch at the little place overlooking the waterfall. And then we'll swing by that 300-year-old church in the old mining town. And isn't the country-side beautiful? We really need to plan some overnight trips to see…

Finally, you're back home for a light snack of the *tamales* Conchita left for you, along with a fruit salad.

All's well. Enrique cut the grass today *before* he watered, and he trimmed the roses and mulched the planting beds. Maybe he's getting a grip on things after all. Conchita even fixed a pitcher of *agua jamaica* and left it in the fridge to chill. And cleaned the cat box. And most of the furniture is fairly close to where you want it.

Life is definitely good! Then again, your day might go like this:

Trash Talkin'

Today is trash day so you need to get up early and hang your trash bag on the gate so the dogs don't tear into it. Then the gas man is coming to fill the tank. Need to make sure you have the money to pay him, and have enough left over for a nice tip. After that you'll have time to walk to the *plaza* for a quick shopping tour of the fruits and vegetables and then back home for a *siesta* before your dance class in the evening at the Murphy's house. The potluck afterward will be a good time to show off that dish you learned how to prepare at last week's Mexican cooking class. And maybe there'll be a spare minute to send a quick e-mail to the kids back in Duluth. Oh, and you need to call Chely and get an appointment for a cut and tint and maybe a manicure and pedicure too, since they're all so inexpensive.

Life is *still* definitely good!

Be the First on Your Block to do the *Molcajete*

Guys, here's one you can pull off and look extremely cool while doing it. At some point you'll break down and buy a *molcajete*. That's the little round gray bowl made of lava rock. The little rock that comes with it is called *la piedra del molcajete*. They're the Mexican cook's mortar and pestle. Most folks use them for decoration but you're gonna move up a step and actually use it for it's intended purpose.

First you need to season your *molcajete*. Here's how. Set it on the patio floor or somewhere else that's really sturdy. Take your *piedra* in one hand and with the other drop a half-cup or so of rice into the *molcajete*. Now start grindin' the rice. Go 'til it's good and gray. Throw it out. Go get a cold Modelo. Call your bride over to show her what to do. She'll need to repeat this process ten or twelve times or until the rice stays white after the grindin's done. You need to go next door to make sure that whatever your neighbor Juanito is doing is being done correctly. It should be safe to come back home in a couple of hours.

When you get back you'll need to take a handful of salt and a big clove of garlic and toss 'em into the *molcajete* and work them in for a few minutes. There are about 5 or 6 million ways to do this particular task. Many folks substitute corn (*maiz*) for the rice. Take a shortcut and you may end up with gritty *salsa*. And don't scrub that thing when you think it needs cleaning. A bit of water and a rag will get it as clean as it needs to be.

Now you're ready to fix a feast. Invite the neighbors. Invite whoever has the say over whether you get initiated into the *Grupo Misticos de Gringo Charros* or whichever other bunch you're tryin' to hook up with, and anyone else that looks like they'd enjoy havin' to put up with you for a couple of hours in exchange for a decent meal and free drinks. Ready to go?

Here's your menu. First, we'll set out two pre-dinner nibblies for those who can't shoot the breeze without a mouthful of food. We'll be heavy into *avocados* tonight and we'll start with a good *guacamole*, and a simple little *pico de gallo* from the recipe my friend Married Bill uses. For dippers we'll just buy whichever ready-made *tortilla* chips you like. No need in slavin' over a pot of bubblin´ hog fat just to fry a few *tortilla* bits.

MERIENDA, WILLIAM GENTES, 1996

Next, the main meal will be grilled steak with dollops of the *salsa* you'll prepare in your *molcajete*, a cold black bean side dish, *nopalito* salad, grilled onions, and *tortillas*. Then we'll finish off with an *avocado* dessert.

It's time for you to get to work. Your bride should have gotten down the bean pot, the ceramic *olla,* last night and put a couple of liters of water in it. Then she should have sorted and de-rocked a *kilo* or so of black beans. Sure they're more associated with Cuba, but they'll be great. Rinse 'em and throw 'em in the pot. Now that they're sufficiently soaked they need to be set on the fire. Boil 'em in the same water they soaked in. She needs to do this on a gas burner outside the house in steamier climates because they're gonna be cookin' for at least an hour and you don't need the heat and discomfort. Have her get the fire goin'. When the water gets to a good rollin' boil, she needs to cut the heat and let 'em simmer for about an hour or so. If the water level drops too far, your bride can add HOT water to the pot. Hot only, because cold water might toughen the beans and we don't wanna risk it.

Now, after an hour, or whenever the beans start softenin' up, it's time to get 'em off the heat. After they cool a bit you'll need to suggest that Sweetbuns drain the beans and put them in the fridge to chill. Set out the bean juice for the dog. It won't upset his system a bit, 'cause if he's like Pirata, he passes gas all day anyway.

While she's waitin' for the beans to cook you may as well have your bride get the dessert ready. This one is super simple. *Dulce de Aguacate*. An avocado sweet.

Get some nice big ripe *avocados*. Next you'll need a liter or so of freshly squeezed orange juice. Or squozen, if you prefer. How much you need depends on how many *avocados* you're planning to use. Here's the really hard part. Sugar. You'll need to play it by taste bud on this one.

Dig out the meat of the *avocados* and drop it in the blender. Add some orange juice and two or three spoons of sugar. Experiment a bit 'til you hit it just right. It's different every time. You'll want to end up with something light green, sweet, with the consistency of a good custard. When you've attained that degree of perfection it's time to have your helper spoon the mix into some really neat individual serving vessels. Jelly jars or your shaving mug collection just will not do.

Stick everything into the fridge to chill. When she gets ready to serve, just twist a lime slice and arrange it against the mint leaf you've artfully placed near the rim.

Now you should already have a whole mess of porterhouses layin' out for at least an hour before you're ready to toss 'em on the grill. They need to be at room temperature before you lay 'em up there to cook. It's also preferable to have them as free of cat nibbles and paw prints as possible, so cover 'em up. This has never happened at my house, but I've heard stories…

You'll also need to ask your lovely bride to cut the roots off two or three small onions per person for however many you managed to coerce into comin' tonight. Make sure she cleans away the dry outer layers, and trims the blades to about an inch or so from the bulb. Lay 'em aside 'til later.

One last little piece of prep work and you're good to go. The light of your life needs to get the iron skillet out and heat up 6 or 7 *chiles serrano* , five or six *Roma* tomatoes, and eight or ten *tomatillos*, until they soften and wilt enough for easy peeling. Let her peel 'em all. Keep 'em separated, at room temperature, in small individual dishes.

Clean a couple of cloves of garlic and set 'em aside, along with a small coarsely chopped onion. And a handful of chopped fresh *cilantro* leaves needs to go into a dish now. Lay the garlic on top of the *cilantro* if you want to, but everything else needs to be held separately. These are the ingredients for your steak *salsa.*

Make sure your bride gets a plate, a bean bowl, and a small salad bowl ready for each guest. And a tray or cart for the *molcajete* and all the *salsa* ingredients. Later on I'll tell you what to do with all this, but now all you need to know is that the ingredients should be at room temperature when you're ready to use them.

Let's go ahead and prepare the salad since we want it refrigerated. Take the sliced *nopalitos* that you bought this morning at the *tianguis* and boil them until they barely begin to soften and wilt, about thirty minutes or so. Drain them and toss them into a bowl and mix in chopped tomato, long strings of onion, and some chopped fresh *cilantro* leaves. Put it all in the fridge to chill and blend. You'll serve it cold, in individual bowls, with half a *limón* placed on top so your guests can flavor it as they wish. Drop a lime half on top of each serving of beans, too.

Here's the recipe, but don't make this *guacamole* until just before the guests arrive since it has a tendency to turn brown if it sits for a while. Refrigeration doesn't retard the oxidization, and besides, it shouldn't be served cold anyway. For years I've heard the tired old story about saving the seeds when you make *guacamole* so you can drop them back into the completed mixture to retard oxidation. Seemingly honest individuals have sworn to me that this actually works, but I've never seen a noticeable difference.

Anyway, back to the bidness at hand. Sweetcheeks should slice several *avocados* (adjust the proportions in all these recipes to accommodate your guest list) in half lengthways. Pop the seed out and then scoop out the meat, leaving the skin intact. Set the skin aside because it'll be used in just a minute. In the bowl you've dropped the meat into, add just a bit of minced tomato, minced *cilantro* leaves, finely chopped scallion greens, just a touch of minced or crushed garlic, a bit of salt, and begin to blend the ingredients with a fork, making sure you leave it just a bit lumpy. As you're mixing, drizzle on a bit of lime juice, just enough to add a mild flavor. You don't want too much of any of these ingredients, because you want the flavor of the avocado to prevail.

Now it's time to stuff the skins with this mixture. Garnish each boat with a tiny wedge of the smallest *Roma* tomato you can find, along with a small sprig of parsley. Arrange them all on a tray lined with shredded lettuce, and a goodly number of lime halves (some folks like to squeeze a bit more juice on) and you've created a tasty work of art. You're definitely in bidness now. On to the *pico de gallo*!

I do a mean variation of this mix, but Married Bill has a recipe that I really like, so with his kind permission, here it comes. After all ingredients are combined, you should have a relatively equal show of the colors of the Mexican flag—red, white, and green. Before you start, keep this in mind: you're going to be working with *jalapeños.* You'll want to remove all the seeds as well as the pith. After you do, be careful not to rub your eyes or other tender areas for about a month. As an alternative you might wear rubber gloves or get your sweet lovin' partner to do the prep work. If you do, don't let *her* touch any of your tender parts for about a month. And use green *jalapeños*. They also come in yellow and red.

Here we go. This is going to be scooped up with some of those *tortilla* chips, so chop all the ingredients into small bits, but don't mince them. They need a little bulk in order to hold their flavor, as well as the right texture. Again, adjust the volume to fit the crowd, but use the following as a guide: one large tomato, one large onion, two or three *jalapeños* sans seeds and pith, two small *arbol* chilies *(chiles de arbol)* with seeds and pith, enough *cilantro* to balance the color, and just enough lime juice squeezed over the mix to moisten it all. Mix it all together in a bowl and set it aside until you're ready to offer it up. If you have an extra, very large *molcajete* it will make a cool serving dish.

Oops! One more tiny detail. Tonight your *margarita* recipe cannot have as a part of the instructions, "take a can of frozen limeade concentrate" or "add Jose Cuervo Margarita Mix". Better make sure the little lady squeezes up a pitcher or two of lime juice and gets it in the fridge. And have Herradura brand *tequila,* or another premium brand made with 100% blue *agave* on hand. It doesn't matter if your guests *are* all *gringos*, don't serve that Cuervo to people you're trying to impress.

Now everyone I know, or know *of,* claims to possess the secret formula for the perfect *margarita*. I don't have a dog in that particular fight since I believe the correct way to drink *tequila* is straight up and lonesome. That lime juice is better suited for pies, *limonada*, wound disinfectant, and squeezing over any cooked fish and *all* street food.

Here's one of many "true original" formulas, this one supposedly invented by the writer and silver pounder William Spratling back in the late '20´s at Berta's *Cantina* in Taxco. The story, told by Spratling, is that after a long horseback ride he and John Dos Passos stopped by Berta's for a refreshing drink. Spratling had Berta prepare a *limonada* for his friend and instructed her to add a generous shot of *tequila* to the juice. As simple things often do, the drink, originally named a "Berta", became popular among the upper crust of Mexico City and was re-named the "*margarita*" (daisy) to divert attention from its plebian country birth. Evidently, at that time John Dos Passos had not yet become John Dos Passos. So I guess that anything other than an "original" recipe should actually be identified as the personal creation of whoever modifies the drink— making it Leon's *margarita* or Wolfgang's *margarita* and so forth.

There are other versions of how the drink came to be so here's another one for you. Some claim the drink came into existence in Palm Springs back in the forties where a bunch of hard drinkin' Hollywood types spent their upright hours sluggin' down straight tequila. An anonymous bartender, obviously a Nervous Nellie, felt, or perhaps saw, that the brew was a bit much for the fragile damsels. That sweet soul then took it upon himself to cut the power a bit by adding lime juice and salt.

If you believe that one I've got a prize breeding steer I'd like to give you an opportunity to invest in. If you're not from the country, get a farmer or rancher to 'splain this to you. And if you want more *margarita* stories you can go to *http://www.mexicanwave.com/food/drink/margarita.asp*. A good source of information about *tequila* is *Tequila – The Book* by Ann and Larry Walker. It's put out by Chronicle Books in San Francisco and you can get your local bookseller to order it for you. You'll find plenty of good recipes in there, too.

Okay, for the present we're all set. I'll give you cooking instructions for the steaks when the time comes but right now you need to have Love Blossom sprinkle them with Worcestershire Sauce, sea salt, and freshly ground pepper. Coarse. Trust me on this one. You've just eliminated the need for flavored wood chips and any other yuppie or pseudo-range-cowboy-cook pretensions and added tons of flavor to a damn fine piece of meat.

You'll probably need to lie down and rest for a bit before the guests arrive, because you still have plenty to do later on. But first you need to instruct Sugar Babe on what to do with the beans. She'll need to get some Roma tomatoes and a red onion and chop them into small chunks. Then finely chop a handful or so of *cilantro* leaves. It's a pain to pull them off the stems but what else does she have to do? Just get her to deliver up all the prepared ingredients so you can mix them together in a large serving dish. Now cover it and return the dish to the fridge until time to serve. Go lie down.

Your better half could help out by makin' sure the grill is clean and that a prep table is set up close by. You're also going to need a very large platter for the steaks. Also, she'll need to check to make sure there's plenty of beer iced down in that washtub she set up over there in the shade. It's the least she can do to ease your burden. This is a team effort, after all.

Following your nap and shower it's time to meet and greet. Time now for the bride to just mingle and take it easy, but first she needs to make sure all the fixin's are around the grill and that the *margaritas* are whipped up nice and fresh. Remind her to put the *tortillas* that she bought this morning on to heat.

It's time for you, big fella, to put your shoulder back to the wheel. You need to go ahead and get the steaks on the grill. Rub each one down with a generous coating of vegetable oil. Sprinkle on a little more salt, grind on a little more pepper and cook everydamn one of 'em medium rare. *No mas!* Toss those onions up around the edges of the grill and dab on just a bit of oil mixed with the juice that seeped from the steaks while they were resting. They'll roast up just fine. Leave Honeybuns at the grill with instructions to cook the steaks about 5 minutes on each side and turn them 2 or 3 times to cook them all the way through. Some purists in Texas say a steak should only be turned once. If you decide to grill these that way, blame them for the mess you make.

Wash your hands and head inside to mix and mingle for a few minutes and then get everyone seated. After suckin' down Mama's *margaritas* or a whole passel of those cold *cervezas,* most of your guests should be half in the bag by now, so you could probably get by with serving Alpo patties—but don't risk it, there might be a ringer in that mob of sots. Place a bowl of beans and a bowl of salad by each plate that has a big springy bed of shredded greens in the middle of it. Put a warmer of *tortillas* in the middle of the table and make sure a big platter is sittin' beside the grill.

It's *Showtime!*

Your assistant should have delivered all the *salsa* ingredients and implements to the dining table. You're on, Big Guy!

Position that *molcajete* where you can comfortably work with it and begin the magic. Explain that your great-great-great-great-grandmother was an Aztec noble, a member of a tiny band that escaped Cortes' destruction of the One World and lived undiscovered and undisturbed until your great-great-great-great-grandfather stumbled across them as he searched for the Treasure of the Sierra Madres. Perhaps some of your dinner guests have heard of the movie of his exploits. You'll need to explain that Hollywood took a few liberties with the script.

Anyway you can explain that this is her secret royal *salsa* recipe to spoon onto the steaks cut from cattle rustled from the nearby *ranchos.*

Go to it. Toss the *serranos,* the onion and the garlic into the *molcajete* and use the *tejolote* to crush and blend them. A small wooden spoon will help with the mixin' and blendin'. Now, with a flourish, begin to add the other ingredients one at a time. Tomatoes, grind lightly. *Tomatillos,* grind lightly. *Cilantro,* grind it good.

The bride should be deliverin' up the steak-filled platter about now. She should have let them rest for about ten minutes or so to make your slicin' chore a bit easier. Slice each steak into thin strips. Not all of this meat will be eaten to-night, so when the plates are taken away, be sure to mark each one. You'll feel better if you can decide which will be safe for you to re-heat for dinners the rest of the week, and which should be fed to Bowser. Now you'll make the rounds, artfully arranging several strips of medium-rare beef on the bed of greens on each plate, and placing two or three of the roasted onions on each plate. As soon as all are served, pick up the *molcajete* and carry it around so that each person can scoop a big dollop of salsa onto their steak. No Heinz, no A-1, *nada* except your great-great-great-great-grandmother's recipe.

And no *pan blanco*, either. Hot *tortillas*. And at this point you're going to offer up a different drink, something lighter and tangier. This recipe is from the magazine, 100% Tequila, that you can access at *http://www.100tequila.com* (no % in the web address). Even though the focus is on tequila, it's very eclectic and artistic with articles to interest most everyone.

So here we go. Serve this drink in a pilsner glass or a tall Collins glass. Okay, use water tumblers if you need to, or jelly jars. Again modify the recipe to fit the crowd. Set this one up beforehand and keep it in pitchers in the fridge. For each drink you need to pour a large glass of cold mineral water, minus three shot glassfuls, into the blender. Add a shot of freshly-squeezed lime juice and two shots of a good *tequila*. Toss in half a handful of parsley, slap on the lid and hit the power switch. Blend, strain, and pour.

Most of the conversation now will be centered around your culinary prowess, and after the dessert, you're a shoo-in for President of the Dog Pound.

Now it's time for the wife to pitch in and do her part. You've had a busy day, buckaroo, and it's only fair that she clean up this mess after all you've been through. Get some rest, for heaven's sake. You're only human!

For other great recipes go to *http://www.mexconnect.com*. Or buy any book by Diana Kennedy or Rick Bayliss. If you think French cooking is wonderful just wait until you get a plateful of real Mexican food. You ain't gonna find *those* dishes at Taco Bell. And if for some odd reason you're not a carnivore, you might want to check out *The Best 125 Meatless Mexican Dishes* by Susann Geiskopf-Hadler and Mindy Toomay. Despite the lack of meat many of these recipes are quite delicious.

Now that you know how some folks, and maybe someday you yourselves, spend their days, let's look at what kind of housing will be available to you.

CHAPTER 5

HOUSING

Can you afford to come to Mexico and pay, in cash, from $75,000 up to $1,500,000 US or beyond for a retirement home? Me neither. Critics will now scream that real estate loans are available in Mexico. They are. In certain areas and at certain rates, and under certain conditions. I offer some alleged sources of financing but you'll find that many are restricted to a few geographical regions. Or you may be able to work out a way to buy directly from a Mexican National who will finance the deal for you. And to be honest you *can* buy some nice little efficiency condos in some areas for $20,000 up to $25,000 US. Occasionally a small house will be available in the same price range or maybe even less, if you're not too particular and you own a very large selection of tools with which you are extremely proficient and creative. *And* if you understand Mexican construction methods. But more than likely your first home in Mexico will be a rental.

Like my friend in the first chapter, a surprisingly large number of people seem to believe that Mexico is full of abandoned *haciendas* just waiting for them to move into and redecorate so they can turn them into showplaces to be admired by their less fortunate friends up North. Not gonna happen, especially in our income range. Let's put the situation in perspective. You folks in the Southwest, how many abandoned ranches are available for rent at any price? And you guys in the Northeast, how many old money mansions or summer homes are available for rent at any price? See what I mean?

Also tied to the belief that you'll be living in a luxurious old *hacienda* for pennies is the idea that beautiful and personable smiling servants in colorful traditional dress will be quietly hovering about to keep your home spotless and to fulfill your slightest whim. Never asking, they appear just at the right moment to refill your glass with cold *limonada* as you lounge about on the breeze-cooled terrace. Or to rush forward with another *cerveza*, or to blot the drool from crazy Uncle Cyrus' chin as they wait to prepare and serve another indescribably delicious meal. Uh, not gonna happen, especially in our income range. Here's a more realistic scenario.

¡¡¿LEÑA?!!, WILLIAM GENTES, 1980

Timeshare Sharks

Let's say you've just breezed into one of the more heavily promoted retirement or tourist towns and checked into a hotel or B&B or some other accommodation. After you've cleaned up and set out to see the sights you pass by the front desk and see a stack or two or three or four or more of business cards advertising local real estate people. In some areas (Mazatlan pops into my mind, along with Puerto Vallarta) you may be approached, repeatedly and aggressively or smoothly and subtly, by a very friendly *gringo*. Ask questions, enjoy the conversation, maybe even buy him a drink, but unless you're interested in "investing" in a timeshare, don't show up for the appointment tomorrow morning for the "free" breakfast and the "short presentation". You may be tempted to accept the offer to rent a Jeep for only $10 a day, or to take a "free" moonlight dinner cruise on the local excursion boat. How can they afford to offer those kinds of deals? One signature on a dotted line, plus an accompanying deposit, buys a *lot* of cruises and Jeep rides. There are easier and more practical ways to retire to Mexico. Timeshares just don't cut it for full-time retirees.

Realtors

Hang in there folks cause this is the only really brutal section of the book but you need to know some things about the real estate business in Mexico. I mustn't forget to mention that the vast majority of real estate agents in retirement areas are good ol' North of the Border types. Ain't it nice to do business with someone you can understand? Somebody that looks like you? Somebody you can *trust?* Some *can* be trusted...and once I met a hooker with a heart of gold.

In Mexico the real estate licensing requirements are nearly non-existent. Some areas have voluntary licensing and regulatory organizations but at present this is strictly a *caveat emptor* situation. The Mexican Association of Real Estate Professionals (AMPI) is supporting a program proposed by the Mexican government that will require real estate agents and brokers to pass a realtor certification examination in Spanish. If that requirement ever actually gets put into play you can expect to see fewer agents out hustling business. I can see both sides of the issue, but since I don't have a dog in that fight, I´ll just stay quiet.

It's easy to be seduced into a false sense of security when many of the real estate signs you see advertise familiar U.S. or Canadian-based companies. But if something happens and you need to register a complaint about one of their Mexican franchises, the voice at the other end of the line is more than likely going to say they can't help you—they have no authority over them. Be careful.

Real Estate Leasing Agents

Real estate folks everywhere have several ways to earn money—sales, rentals, listings, referrals, etc.—but you're most interested in the rental aspect right now. You have a card in hand, a note scribbled by someone you met at dinner last night (Yes, they *can* tell you just hit town), or maybe you just liked the look of a certain sign and schlepped into an office of your own volition. At this point you've still got that that goofy "Jeez, ain't it all just great?" grin plastered all over your face. If you're lucky it'll always be there but right now when you're looking for a place to live, it's best to reign in the romance a little. Do you want to pay $600 to $3,000 US or so for a two or three bedroom rental? Me neither, but every day our fellow dreamers do exactly that, egged on by real estate developers, organized tour groups, contractors, and real estate salespeople. This isn't meant as a criticism of any of these folks, but for those of us on a fixed budget an overpriced rental could be deadly. Without our feet on the ground, a starry-eyed rookie will be what salespeople in all types of businesses call "dead meat".

A lot of realtors don't like the low-priced rental or sales deals so you'll need to find one willing to work with you. Seems low-ticket deals provide a smaller commission for the agent in return for lots more work. Huh? The feeling among some agents is that there are more questions, complications, trepidations, imprecations, molestations, and general ill will and headaches caused by clients looking for the low-priced rentals than those looking for the pricey ones. The same goes for sales.

Once you do land an agent, he or she will make you believe that they're going to make your transition to Mexico smooth and carefree. They're also going to cost you money, tell you horror stories about non-realtor sponsored or approved rentals, and then they're going to staple on a little disclaimer for the day you wise up and realize you've paid more than you needed to. I can hear the wails and screams and shrieks of indignation now but watch how this works.

"In what price range are you looking?" Regardless of what figure you fidget with and finally gasp out, be prepared to receive that *look* from the agent who now grudgingly drags out "The Book". If your figure was ridiculous but promising—that is, capable of being bumped into a higher range—he or she may hand you the book so you can see for yourself that your figure falls short of what would be necessary for reasonable housing. If your offer was well within the limits of an acceptable monthly commission the agent may point out that some properties are only a few dollars more each month but far nicer than those in the price range you've mentioned. Like this one for instance, right next door to the president of the local art association. Or this one, right down the street from a famous writer, or this one, right across the street from the president of the dog pound.

The next thing you know, you're tied into a long-term lease at a much higher monthly rate than you'd planned. And did I mention actual move-in costs? Three months rent up front. First, last, and deposit. Oh, the gas tank is probably empty or nearly so, so plan on $40 to $60 US to fill that. And there might be a water assessment due that you'll have to pay. (This varies according to the area and in some places you'll just pay a regular monthly fee.) And finally—it usually won't be mentioned—you'll pay for all repairs under $50 US.

If you've been following the subtext you now might have the nerve to say, "Oh hell, we can't afford these prices. Maybe we'd better try to find a Mexican landlord who'll rent directly." This is where you get to sit back and see how desperate and entertaining your agent can be. If you're lucky you might get to hear stories that would frighten Stephen King or others that would have tickled Mark Twain. Here are some actual statements:

- ☞ "This is the *only* house for rent in town and it's only $700 US. You'd better jump on it." There were actually dozens of rentals available at the time, in a wide range of prices, just not in *that* realtor's "Book".
- ☞ "You don't want to rent from a Mexican landlord. We know how to protect you."
- ☞ "You'll have to pay for all your own repairs."
- ☞ "It's nearly impossible to find a rental on your own, especially if you don't speak the language."
- ☞ "If you do any work on the place you'll lose your investment."
- ☞ "If you improve the place they'll raise the rent."

Well polish up the scoop Agnes, and let's clear out some of this horse manure. There are plenty of good ways to get a sense of the market and to locate rentals. Just keep reading. But first, take this into consideration. If you're looking at the possibility of moving to an area well known to *gringos*, start your search in the off-season, usually the summer months. Why? Many of the folks who rent down here are snowbirds, part-time residents who move South in the wintertime to escape the cold weather up North. If you come while they're gone prices are usually lower and you'll have more options. And after 9-11 the number of visitors from NoB dropped dramatically and so did sales prices--at least temporarily.

You'll soon discover that contradictions are an integral part of the Mexican experience. Here's one. You'll find enterprising entrepreneurs have set up housing locator services. For a one-time payment, they'll find housing for you. In contrast, the real estate folks add a fee each month. An excellent company in Mazatlan is at *http://www.mazatlan.homestead.com*. The Santanas are good people and I recommend them. Marlene can help you.

How to Find Rental Deals on Your Own

First, find a place you can rent for one month or on a month-to-month basis. If you came down in the off-season you should be able to get a good rate at a B&B or a small hotel. If you take a few days to look around you might find an ad posted by the snowbird owner of a rental property. Lots of them want to rent their places out for short periods, around three months, when they're out of the country. Now, use this short–term rental as your headquarters to conduct a serious search for the long-term rental that really works for you.

Start checking any place that allows flyers to be posted on bulletin boards. The first place to look is the local grocery store where most *gringos* shop. There will probably be more than one. Just ask someone, the lady at the next table, the guy eating ice cream in the plaza, the desk clerk at your hotel. There are *gringos* or English-speaking Nationals almost everywhere, even in the smallest towns. Talk to EVERYBODY.

Now check out the bulletin board at the post office—both the Mexican Post Office and any of the private companies. I've even seen rental notices posted in restaurants. Internet cafes are good places to check. They can be found in many reasonably-sized villages and *all* of the cities. And again, talk to EVERYBODY.

Larger cities will have English language newspapers that publish current rental listings in every issue. You'll find some of these in Appendix 1.

And then do like the encyclopedia salesmen and Mormon missionaries do. Go door to door. Seriously. Many really good rentals will never be advertised except for a small sign on a building or door. I've seen everything from a nicely lettered, commercially printed sign announcing "*Se Renta*", to a phone number scribbled beneath a scrawled "*Se Renta*" on an old 3X5 political campaign sign pasted to a door. Now keep in mind that the place for rent may not necessarily be the one where the sign is posted. Stop and check it out if anyone's home, or call later.

Yes, I know your Spanish is not that good and chances are the person who answers that phone probably won't be proficient in English either. Ask for help. Ask the desk clerk at your hotel, or the waiter at that little place you like so well, or that nice gentleman or lady you met near the plaza. You *have* been talking to EVERYBODY haven't you? And you *will* remember to tip him or offer to buy her a drink, or whatever is appropriate, won't you? It may not be accepted at first, but do it anyway.

After spending some time talking to EVERYBODY and trudging the streets looking for those *Se Renta* signs take a little advice: *slow down*.

Here's why. Right now you're probably running on a full tank of emotional energy and are feeling exhilarated by the new experiences you're having. Or maybe you're feeling desperate that the right place won't turn up or worried about how quickly your money is disappearing. Or perhaps you're facing for the first time those doubts that Mexico isn't really for you. Exhilarated or worried, you could be under a lot of stress.

If you're finding it hard to relax, take a moment to find out why. Maybe you don't like the area that you've been searching. If this crops up, choose another one. The character of a place changes from neighborhood to neighborhood and that's one reason you didn't take the first overpriced, long-term rental the leasing agent showed you. If you don't like *any* of the places you've seen, then take a deep breath and pull out the list of towns you considered when you planned this trip and look at the other prospects.

At this point you haven't made a major mistake from which you can't recover. If it turns out that you just flat out don't like anything about Mexico, then you're free to enjoy the rest of your "vacation".

Even if you *are* enjoying looking and think you've found *The Place,* you still need to relax. Try this. Eat breakfast in one of the little places where a lot of the locals eat. By locals I mean both Mexicans *and gringos.* Choose a few *fondas* and eat many of your meals in them.

The establishments frequented by locals rely on repeat business. Folks are not going to keep showing up everyday at places likely to poison them. I'm not inferring that the more touristy places are gonna kill you but they probably serve a customer once or twice at most. The second reason to eat where the locals do is that it's nearly always going to be less expensive. It probably won't be as fancy either. Look around until you find one or two that appeal to you.

Have you been wondering where your money's been going so quickly? A big part of it disappears in those touristy restaurants. You may as well get in the habit of living as close to the local economy as you can. Later, after you've moved into your new home you'll save by eating in but now you're on a mission: get out and talk to EVERYBODY, gather as much information as possible and get as many leads as you can. You don't need to spend a fortune doing it.

Even if you're not a breakfast person you still need to make an effort to get out there. Order juice and coffee. It'll give you a chance to talk to everybody in the place. Often, after they've seen you around a bit and have had a chance to size you up, some people can become very helpful. They'll remember that *Doña* Maria has that small vacant house or that Esteban knows a place or— well, you get the picture.

After an hour or two of hunting, stop somewhere for a cool drink and sit down. You'll want to drink *plenty* of water and you can buy bottles of it in nearly every store you see, even the *farmacias.* Take a short rest, and when you do, really try to relax and gear down. This portion of your day is where the "relax" advice really needs to be heeded. You're busy, both physically and mentally, and you're preoccupied with your primary task. You may not realize just how much effort and energy you're expending. Remember your goal is to be diligent, consistent, and persistent, not masochistic.

Afterwards if you need to use the bathroom here's a hint or two on that subject. Some towns have public bathrooms (*baños* or *sanitários*) on or near the *plaza.*

A lot of bus stations have them. You'll pay to use them, usually a *peso* or two. Private establishments may charge too. I've seen restaurants charge non-patrons as much as five *pesos*. If you encounter that situation just spend eight or ten *pesos* for a cold drink and pee for free. You need the fluid intake anyway. Always carry tissues or a small amount of toilet paper with you. You'll thank me for this piece of information.

Since you're taking a break and drinking and eating at the *fondas* and *taco* stands, watch the person who's preparing your food to see if they're also the one who takes your money. It's fine if they do both chores as long as they slip a clean plastic bag over their hands when they handle the cash. The best situation is one where there's a separate cashier.

I know, you're worried about *turista*, Moctezuma's Revenge, the border quick-step. In most cases it's caused by a change in diet, a variation of your normal routine, and stress. Mexican meals are somewhat different than your stomach is used to receiving and there may be some bacteria strains that your system isn't geared to handle. I always seem to have a problem as soon as I head North and again when I head South. And then again you could get sick because of substandard hygiene or improper food handling and storage. Another culprit could be dirty, germ-covered hands—yours or someone else's. That's why I told you to watch the guy preparing your food. Several people have told me that men are more likely to develop stomach problems than their spouses. Why? If they're the ones handling the money they're at risk. Wash your hands often and if you're in a situation where you can't, use baby wipes. I *know* they're designed for behinds, but they'll work just as well on your paws.

You've probably figured out by now that I'm *not* a doctor. I don't even play one on TV, so I can't dispense medical advice but I can recommend a couple of things to reduce the time you spend on the toilet. For several weeks before you come, as well as during your stay and for a few days *after* you return home, take *acidophilus bifidus* capsules. You can buy them at a drugstore or health food store. Or you can accomplish the same thing by eating or drinking yogurt with active culture. Yogurt is widely available here. Both Yoplait and Danone (that's the Mexican spelling) are widely available in enough flavors to satisfy you. The capsules and the yogurt will increase the variety of bacteria in your digestive system and help your system adapt. A lot of the locals drink a fermented dairy product called *Yakult*. It comes in a little plastic bottle about three inches tall and is made from milk, a little sugar, and active acidophilus. You'll also eventually come upon a local who makes yogurt at home and sells it quite reasonably.

If, in spite of your best efforts, you do develop a problem, plain old Pepto-Bismol is just about the most effective medication out there. Slug down a big snort right after the first hint of a problem. Hint might be too subtle. You need to empty your bowels if you're having stomach distress, so don't start too soon with the Pepto. I suspect that after *tequila,* it might be the number-one selling beverage in Mexico because you can buy it everywhere. If you don't get to the Pepto-Bismol after the first twinge and end up spending some time on the throne, buy a bottle or two of Pedialite or Electrolit. These drinkable liquids offset the effects of dehydration by restoring your electrolyte balance. You'll feel better eventually. They're available in just about every pharmacy on a shelf near the Pepto-Bismol.

I felt a bit apprehensive about giving health advice so I checked the website for the Center for Disease Control in Atlanta and discovered those guys recommend the same things *and* they gave specific dosage information. "Take two ounces of liquid Pepto-Bismol four times a day, or two tablets four times a day to control the flow." There are warnings, though. "Don't use Pepto-Bismol or a bismuth compound if you're allergic to aspirin, have renal insufficiency or gout, or if you're taking anticoagulants, probenecid, or methotrexate." They say that Pepto-Bismol has a prophylactic benefit but it shouldn't be used regularly for more than three weeks at a time.

As long as we're discussing physical comfort I have one quick question—two actually. You *are* wearing sensible, comfortable shoes aren't you? And they *were* broken in before you came down here, weren't they? Good. There are few things worse than hobbling around on tired blistered feet. Wear rubber-soled shoes.

After a morning of walking around checking bulletin boards, talking to everyone, and having a little lunch, you may want to follow the lead of many, if not most, of the locals and head in for a *siesta* between 2:00 and 4:00. A lot of the businesses will be closed, you'll be tired, and it'll be good for your soul. Go back to your place, lie down for a while and take a dip in a pool if there's one available. You'll feel better and you won't be losing any house hunting time. There'll be more this evening.

On the Town
Wasn't that *siesta* nice? You're rested up, relaxed, in a good mood and ready for more exploring. When my daughter Abby was a youngster she called it "adventuring". At the ranch she'd take her brother Matthew by the hand, and away they'd go down the wooded trails.

As evening comes, follow the lead of the locals and drift on over to the *plaza*. In the larger towns and cities you'll have quite a few to choose from. There are plenty of reasons for this: entertainment, relaxation, recharging your batteries, or just letting yourself be lulled into the rhythm of local life. There's a lot of street life in most Mexican towns and you're depriving yourself of a big reward for moving here if you fail to take advantage of it.

In San Luis Potosí, there was always something happening on one of the *plazas*. One night as I walked around the city I found an orchestra from the university playing show tunes and classics from the bandstand in the *plaza* of the oldest church, a choir performing on the steps of one of the museums, clowns and mimes performing in a couple of locations, a book fair, bicycle trick riding, a huge tent crowning a Christmas bazaar, several groups of strolling *mariachis*, an art exhibit, and stalls of craftspeople selling their wares.

The last time I was in Puerto Vallarta a Cuban band was presenting a free concert on the *malecón,* the boardwalk. My grandson, Asa, and I found front row seats even though the area was packed. We settled in for a couple of hours of great music. He had a *flan* (custard) purchased from a roving vendor and I had a soft drink. Cost? Maybe a buck.

In Guadalajara you can sit in *Mariachi Plaza* and enjoy a refreshment or two and listen to the music for hours. Besides entertainment, there's *always* something going on—religious, historical, political or social. If you avoid the *plazas* in the evenings you're going to miss out on a lot of the soul and spirit of Mexico. If you make evenings in the *plazas* a habit early on, you'll find out that some exceptional benefits will come your way.

Remember that nice young waiter from the restaurant where you've been eating breakfast? Here he comes, walking around the *plaza* with his family. Greet him, "*Buenas tardes*", and smile at his lovely young wife and their gorgeous children. Fuss over the children and try to express how precious they are. The parents *will* understand.

After you've visited with them for a few moments, you'll see that nice lady who directed you to the vacant house that you didn't rent because it was just a tad too primitive. Smile and speak. And over there, you'll see the owner of the hardware store you browsed earlier. He smiles and waves. Smile and wave back. This is very gratifying for those of us who may not have ever spoken to our closest neighbors back home but does it help you find a house? Yes. Here's how.

You've just demonstrated to a lot of folks that you want to become a part of their community. Mexico is the ultimate model of a networking society. You're on a different footing with them now because you're moving from being a forgettable tourist to becoming a part of their network. Maybe tomorrow one of these people will remember that their cousin's sister-in-law's uncle has a small house that just might be for rent.

After you've been house hunting for several days, if it takes that long, take some time off. Go sightseeing, spend a day looking at crafts or if you're close to a spa or *balneário,* plan to spend the day relaxing in a warm pool.

Relax and relax. If you can, schedule a massage. Most towns of any size will have someone who can do this. In both Pátzcuaro and upper Ajijic I saw signs advertising pedicures and foot massages for diabetics. They won't care if you aren't one. Ladies, find the beauty parlors. If nothing else, just lie around and do nothing.

Rental Stories and Prices

Are you really aggravated that I haven't mentioned rental prices yet? There's a reason for my hesitancy and that's because they'll vary a lot, depending on where you want to live and how diligently you search—and ultimately how lucky you are. Here are some prices, locations and descriptions of places where my friends and I have lived or are now living. These are current as of publication but they'll probably be outdated by the time you arrive.

La Manzanilla

One of my rentals was a small twenty-year-old *casita* high on a hill overlooking La Manzanilla on the shore of Tenacatita Bay, south of Puerto Vallarta. The house had a 15'X32' main room (kitchen, dining room, living room combination) and a 9'X12' bedroom. A terrace ran the full length of the house and down one side. Inside, off the bedroom, there was a big bathroom and at the end of the side terrace and down a half-level, was a large covered area with an outdoor shower. The house sat on a sloping lot set into the jungle and on its lower level was a big unfinished room that I used for locked storage.

My water came from two large concrete rooms called *aljibes*. These were built at each end of the house, one below ground and one above. The water was pumped from them to a large black plastic tank called a *tinaco* installed on the slope above the house. The water in the tanks was rainwater, diverted from the roof into the *aljibes*. I had access to the municipal water supply via a hard rubber hose running from one of my landlady's other houses over the hill. The water supply to the house was grav-

La Hamaca, William Gentes, 1993

ity fed and at the time I rented it there was no water heater although the house was partially plumbed for it. Later I installed both a water heater and pressure system. Like everyone else I bought bottled water for drinking and cooking.

On the roof, I built a *ramada*, like an arbor, where I strung my hammock so I could lie in the shade and catch the breeze off the bay while enjoying the view. Cost to build the *ramada*? About $300 US for a 12'X16' structure.

Rent on the house? About $260 US a month at today's exchange rate, plus utilities. Deposit? $0. I paid the first month's rent and moved in that day. How long did it take to find it? About three hours, but half that time I spent eating a leisurely lunch and talking to folks. How did I find it? A Mexican National I met on the street took me to see the lady who owned it and then to see the house itself. Talk to EVERYBODY.

Galveston, Texas/Puerto Vallarta, Jalisco/San Luis Potosí, SLP

As a reference, a place about the same size, albeit nicer construction and with hot water, across the street from the Galveston, Texas Seawall cost me $700 a month about five years ago. My older place on the beach in Surfside, Texas was $450 a month about 7 years ago. A two bedroom, two bath condo in Puerto Vallarta overlooking the Bay of Banderas cost me $900 US a month three years ago. My one bedroom, fifth story rooftop "penthouse" in San Luis Potosí cost me $350 US per month (without phone and with all bills paid) two years ago. All but the Galveston locations were furnished.

La Manzanilla, Jalisco

There's a house in the village by the bay that rents for $150 US a month, negotiable. Very negotiable. It has one bedroom, a small bath, a fair-sized Mexican-style kitchen and living room combo with no rear wall and a large walled-in courtyard. Before you dismiss this one, a lot of the high dollar *gringo* houses around there are built without exterior walls all the way around. It would need lots of TLC and some repairs, but definitely it's a doable deal—and more private than it sounds.

La Manzanilla, Jalisco

The rental steal of all time was one I found for a friend. She has seven dogs, most of them large, and needed an unfurnished house with a big fenced yard, a difficult feature to find in our price range. What we ended up with was a little fixer-upper. It had three bedrooms, three baths, a small central atrium about 10' X 10', a huge kitchen with a stove and refrigerator, ceiling fans, beautiful tile floors, and a few pieces of furniture that the landlord moved out at her request.

The real appeal though was the walled-in yard. It covered two large city lots and even though it needed a bit of reclamation work it had banana trees, a few papayas, a couple of coconut palms, a mango tree, and several non-fruit bearing trees. In addition it had a concrete pad which had been previously shaded by a palm leaf roofed *palapa*, which is sort of a little grass shack without walls. It also had a telephone line.

Cost? $320 US per month. Deposit? $0. She could have paid the rent and moved in at leisure. How did I find it? The Mexican National who steered me to my rental told me about it and led me there. He helped me find two great inexpensive houses, spent another half day helping me find my way around and I picked up the tab on two meals. I gladly paid his requested fee of $20 US.

Lake Chapala-Ajijic, Jalisco

One of my friends, a realtor, called me one day and asked if I'd stop by the B&B she was managing to meet a disabled Vietnam vet who was staying there until he could find a permanent place to live.

It took us about three hours on a Sunday afternoon to find a place—a small two bedroom *casita* on the grounds of an old Mexican home. The owner's grandfather built the main house so the current owners have had years to nurture and perfect the gorgeous landscaping and grounds. The house is fully furnished with very attractive Mexican furniture—a few antiques, such as a hundred year-old *tortilla* press--a huge carved desk, some lovely rugs, a TV, telephone, and tasteful wall décor. A large kitchen and dining area looks over his ample private patio, a huge bathroom, and another small covered patio.

I've since become friends with the owners and have been invited to their home on several occasions. There's a homey feel to the place and they really care about their tenants. One lady lived there for nearly twenty years.

Cost? $400 US a month plus the monthly cable TV bill (about $30 US), his telephone bill, and about $20 US a month for the gardener. Deposit? $0. He paid the first month's rent and moved in the next day. How did we find it? A small notice posted on the bulletin board at one of the grocery stores. I think the only addition he's made has been to install a bag of sugar, a container of milk, a box of Rice Krispies, and a six-pack of Modelo in the kitchen.

Lake Chapala-Ajijic-San Antonio Tlayacapán, Jalisco

Here are some other rental prices from the budget range. In this well-known *gringo* retirement area I have a friend who rents a beautiful three bedroom, two bath home with a huge storage room, a small rear patio, a large glassed sun room, and a large *sala*, or living room, from a Mexican landlord. The house has twelve foot high walls that support a well-crafted *boveda* ceiling. *Boveda* is a building technique that mortars bricks in arched rows about three feet wide to create a dome. The ceiling arches to a point about eighteen feet high. The floors are tiled which makes the place cool and easy to clean. A solid stucco-covered rock wall surrounds the grounds and there's a fair amount of landscaping. The house is "furnished" and costs $450 US a month. Deposit? None, just first and last month's rent to move in. How did she find it? She and I went to look at another house and a guy trimming the trees on the grounds mentioned that he had a place that he could show us. How did we know to look at the first house? A neighbor told us. Talk to EVERYBODY.

Lake Chapala-Ajijic-San Antonio Tlayacapán, Jalisco

A really adventurous and creative friend rented a small unfurnished, two bedroom, one bath house with a small yard and covered parking area. She's infused the place with the entire palette of bright Mexican colors and turned a dumpy little *casita* into a really cheerful home.

Her garden is filled with dozens of potted plants of various types, textures, sizes and colors. The house is built in a style that's typically Mexican that many of us might not be used to seeing. You enter via a small "receiving room" at the front. To the right is the kitchen. When you enter the kitchen you see that all the rest of the rooms are in a straight row. In other words, you go from the kitchen to the living room, then to a bedroom, then into a narrow hall in front of the bathroom, and finally into the second bedroom. There's also a large storage/laundry room with an outside entrance. Cost? $250 US a month. How did she find it? Through a real estate company. Deposit? $250, plus first and last months rent.

Lake Chapala-Ajijic Area-San Antonio Tlayacapán, Jalisco

When I lived in San Antonio Tlayacapán my maid lived next door. She had a two bedroom, one bath house with a combination living/dining/kitchen area. All the rooms were large. She had no hot water piped to the house and heated water for bathing in an outside cooking area against the front wall of the courtyard. The house was plumbed and had electricity. Her rent was about $70 US per month but she bought the house eventually for about $15,000 which was little more than the land was worth. Is something like this a possibility for you? Yes, you certainly could rent a little place like that and fix it up to suit you and the missus.

Lake Chapala-Ajijic-La Floresta, Jalisco

Another acquaintance has a two bedroom, two-bath home with a small built-in office in the front. The home belongs to a Mexican National but was furnished and decorated by a Canadian couple who owned it at one time. The furnishings are mostly Mexican "*rustico*" style except for an overstuffed sofa and loveseat. It came with a microwave and large appliances. The room-sized covered patio is filled with numerous plants. There's a spiral stairway leading to the flat roof that provides a lovely view of the area. Cost? $550 US per month. How did she find it? Through a real estate company. Deposit? $550, plus first and last month's rent to move in.

Lake Chapala-Ajijic-San Nicolás de Ibarra, Jalisco

I rented a nice modern house in this small village about fifteen miles from Ajijic and about a half mile from the Chapala country club. Inside, the house had five bedrooms, two and a half baths, a two-story dining room with a balcony overlooking the first floor and a huge chandelier. Outside there was a small rear patio with a smaller front garden, a laundry/storage room, and covered parking. A large, second-story terrace provided a spectacular view of the lake and mountains.

Even though I rented it unfurnished the big kitchen had a quality built-in gas stove. The house had closets which some older Mexican houses don't. Lots of closets. Cost? $450 US per month. How did I find it? I found it listed in an English language newspaper. If that house had been located closer to, or in the more desirable *gringo* neighborhoods, it would have easily rented for twice the price. I'm positive that I was one of only two *gringo* households in the entire town.

San Miguel de Allende, Guanajuato

Another acquaintance of mine lives in a small, efficiency-type apartment near the plaza in San Miguel de Allende. She pays about $200 US per month and claims to feel very crowded and displeased. She's also going through a divorce after a long marriage.

San Miguel de Allende, Guanajuato

This is not an area I'm personally interested in and therefore I didn't spend a lot of time researching housing costs. If you want more information, one of the best real estate sections in any Mexican publication can be found at the website of Atencion San Miguel at *http://www.infosma.com*.

Saltillo, Coahuila

In Saltillo I found loads of great housing bargains. If you want to buy a very special house for under $50,000 US then this might be an area to explore. The rentals were also low. An older five bedroom house with two living areas, five baths and laundry room situated on a canyon in the hills at the edge of town was about $350 US, unfurnished. This place had that old '50s and '60s California Cool type of architecture modified by a couple of Mexican touches. It needed cleaning and a few minor repairs and was definitely worth the effort.

Saltillo, Coahuila

An up-to-date, two-bedroom, two-bath house in town with a small fireplace, window treatments, ceiling fans, *saltillo* tile floors, ornately tiled baths and countertops was $450 US. There was secured, covered parking inside the big walled-in yard for three-cars.

Melaque, Jalisco

We recently rented a small place in this lovely beach town to use as a getaway hide-out. A local artist owns it but she rents a larger house on the beach in order to have more room for teaching. The house is small, with one large furnished room and bath, a large rooftop *palapa*, an outdoor kitchen, another *palapa* at ground level, and a beautifully landscaped walled-in garden. We're paying $100 US a month that includes all bills. The place has an air conditioner so we volunteer a bit for electricity, and we offer the house to our landlady when we're not there so she has a place to get away by herself if she feels the need. We're less than four blocks from the beach.

San Luis Potosí, San Luis Potosí

My "penthouse" in this city was a unique little fifth-level rooftop *adobe* plopped atop a huge, beautifully-tiled *terrado* (no misspelling) with meter-high *adobe* walls around it. There was a small bedroom with a closet and a king-sized bed, a good-sized living room, a large kitchen and dining room combo, and a big bathroom. The shower was so large that I could stand in the center with my arms outstretched and not touch a single wall as I turned about—not that I really spent much time spinning around in the shower but I could have if I'd been so inclined.

The view of the city and nearby mountains was breathtaking and so were the evening breezes. There was no telephone and the furnishings were fairly plain but I did have a TV with a cherished remote control.

All the bills were paid and the rent was $350 US a month. How did I find it? I stopped by one of the language schools and asked several of the teachers for leads. They *all* speak English since that's what they teach, and they're *all* on a tight budget since Mexico pays teachers even more poorly than most U.S. states. Several of them knew about the place and directed me to it since it was out of their price range. Talk to EVERYBODY.

My Australian neighbors in San Luis Potosí had a lovely two bedroom furnished apartment two floors below my penthouse. It equaled any very nice apartment in the U.S. and was only $400 US a month including all bills except the telephone. It was light and airy with large picture windows. The furnishings were stylish and comfortable.

A couple of English teachers in Potosí rented tiny, inexpensive apartments in the $125 to $150 US range but neither of them seemed to be too thrilled about the accommodations at those prices. One got evicted just as I was heading back to Texas for a month and I let her stay at my "penthouse" as a caretaker while I was gone. She e-mailed me after a week to thank me and tell me that she felt like she'd moved to Heaven. Maybe that $125 place really was Hell.

If you look in the right places you'll have lots of options.

Improvements to Rental Properties

Earlier I mentioned a realtor's comment about losing your investment if you make improvements to a place. We seem to be a nation of doers and fixers and tinkerers, always wanting to stamp our personalities on the places we live. I've spent time, money, imagination, and labor on every place I've ever lived regardless of whether I owned or rented. Many of my friends down here have too.

If you're a tinkerer, there's good news here South of the Border. In the U.S. if you make an improvement and it's attached to the structure, it stays when you go. In Mexico it goes *with* you. That means I took my water heater and pressure system when I moved from La Manzanilla. And the *ramada*. Which leads me into a story or two for all of you.

I know a lady who, along with her hubby, leased a run down place near one of the major retirement areas. There are probably about one hundred or so other *gringos* in the same town. The rent was very low—about $250 US for a three bedroom, two bath house with several pocket patios and a huge fireplace in the hallway. The two of them set to work with a limited budget and lots of energy and imagination and turned that raggedy old sow's ear into a very attractive silk purse.

At the end of the lease period the landlady raised the rent to $700 US a month. What's wrong with this picture? These folks had installed ceiling fans, a water heater and kitchen cabinets. They'd remodeled bathrooms, patched, painted, planted, and done numerous other things to improve the property at their expense and this was their reward?

Well, our friends got a bit crossways with their operation. True, they did fix the place up. True, they did spend their own money. And true, their lease did not have a "no-sublet" clause. But they were snowbirds who decided to sublet the place while they were in Texas. For how much? Only $700 US per month.

So who set the rental value for the next lease period, landlady or renters? And what happened? At the end of the lease the Texans gutted the place and left, taking all the improvements they'd made, with the exception of the paint on the walls and the kitchen cabinets that the landlady purchased from them.

Another friend paid to have awnings made and installed on the exterior of the place she was renting. Her landlady immediately began telling her that she was going to raise her monthly rent by $50 as soon as her lease was up. My friend informed the landlady that she would move and the landlady offered to buy the awnings since they made the place so much more attractive. My friend failed to get her money before she moved, however, and to this day, more than two years later, has not received one penny. The little house has been vacant since.

How Fixer-Upper Rentals Can Put You Ahead of the Game

A very good friend of mine, a realtor, devised a strategy to make the best use of her money by renting rundown places on a gradually escalating scale and then using the money she saved by fixing them up.

This is how she did it. If a place could be visualized to be rentable at $400 US a month if it were repaired, she might make the following offer to the owner. She'd rent the property for $150 a month for the first year, $200 a month the second year, $250 the third year, $300 the fourth, and then jump up to the full $400 rate by the fifth year. The rent would still be a bargain because she's renting at a four-year-old market rate. In her mind she's saved, over the four year period, $8,400 in rental money, part of which she applied to repairs and remodeling in order to end up with a house that suited her needs and pleased her aesthetically. You'll discover a lot of options here and probably invent a few of your own.

Questions to Ask a Potential Landlord

Here is THE list of questions to ask a potential landlord, *gringo or* Mexican. Don't tear these pages from the book. Xerox, *please*, Xerox.

- Is the rent figured in dollars or *pesos*? This is important because as the value of the *peso* drops your actual rental cost drops. As the *peso* increases in value your actual rental cost rises. Dollars remain constant. Example: If your rent is 3,000 *pesos* each month and the *peso* is at a 10 to 1 exchange rate (US $1=10 *pesos*) your rent is $300 per month. If the exchange rate drops to 9 to 1 (US $1=9 *pesos*) your new rent is actually $327 US per month. If the exchange rate drops to 8 to 1 (US $1= 8 pesos) then your rent is $354 US.

- Who pays the bills? In some cases the bills are included in the rental cost. It's more likely though, that you'll be paying most, or all, of the bills. Often the utilities are left in the name of the owner and you just pay for him at the electric company, bank or neighborhood *tienda* or hand the cash to him directly. I've done it both ways. You can have the names on the accounts changed into your name if the landlord is willing. Again, personal preference.

🐞 Is there a telephone? (If this is important to you.) There may be a telephone line but sometimes the actual instrument is missing. Go buy one. If there is no phone line and you want one I'll tell you later what to do. Also be sure to ask if the last bill has been paid. Sometimes the line is there but *you* can't use it because the landlord got stiffed for the bill the last tenant ran up with long distance calls to Bahrain and Holland and he hasn't been able to come up with the money to pay it. Don't despair, he can use your rent money to pay TELMEX. You'll understand of course if he asks *you* for a telephone deposit.

🐞 Where is the fuse box for the electrical system and where do I buy fuses? Those funny looking things are fuses? Some Mexican fuse casings have screw off tops and when one blows you just insert a new metal conductor. Easy.

🐞 Are the plumbing lines vented? Huh? If the plumbing lines are not vented the gas from the sewer lines seeps back up through your shower drain. Aside from the odor, this is not a major problem and is simple to solve. Just plop a big flat rubber stopper that's available at all hardware stores and many grocery stores, over the shower drain.

🐞 Who pays the gardener? If you have a gardener, which is not a situation I like to get stuck in, make sure that the number of hours he's supposed to be on the grounds, as well as his duties, are specifically listed and understood. Many "gardeners" turn out to be overpaid breathing lawn sprinklers. I'm never happy paying someone a reasonable wage just to stand and hold a water hose. Or even worse, to turn on the water (sans sprinkler) and leave the hose lying somewhere in the yard while they're off at another house doing who knows what with Fulano and the guys. Make sure that both he and the landlord understand that if you're paying, you're assigning duties. As you can tell, this is a sore spot with me. Sometimes the maid and gardener are part of the rental deal and you're stuck with them. My best guess is that you won´t be happy with this situation. The hired help maintain a loyalty to the person who hired them and pays them. If you have to retain them as part of the rental agreement, insist on paying them yourself, and do so face to face.

🐞 Who pays for repairs to the house and its systems? You'll usually be responsible for everything less than $50 US. Sometimes *all* repairs will be your responsibility. It will depend on your individual deal with the owner. Get it cleared up before something breaks.

🐾 What if I need to leave the country or move for some reason before my lease is up?

🐾 Will my rent be raised if I make improvements to the property?

🐾 Do I need to get permission before I make improvements? I always ask anyway as a courtesy.

🐾 Where is the gas tank? Some are large fixed tanks and some are portable cylinders. If you have portable cylinders a truck will come by daily to exchange empty ones for full ones. If you have a stationary tank you'll have to deal with the adventure of calling the local company to come fill your tank. If the latter is the case, here's a tip. Check your gauge occasionally and never let it drop below 30 or 40 percent full. If you do let it run too near empty, you may well end up taking cold showers and eating out because it may take several days for the gas company to get to you. Not that they're necessarily that busy--they may not be able to take your order correctly because you don't speak Spanish. In that case, get help from someone. And buy an electric skillet, hot plate or a portable gas grill. As far as the showers go you're on your own. I *will* give you this helpful hint though. If you have the large portable cylinders, the guy on the delivery truck will change them when you buy a full one. If for some reason you have to change one yourself, or if you're off the regular delivery route, there's a trick to removing the regulator and hose from the tank. When you get your wrench on the fitting, turn right. I know the old righty tighty, lefty loosey rap too, but that doesn't apply to gas cylinders on *either* side of the border. It's a safety measure.

🐾 What's the meaning of life? Hell, your landlord won't know either but it'll get his attention and make him really cautious about coming around and bothering you.

🐾 (Optional) As I buy my own furniture is there a place to use or store the furniture in the house now? And are those things crawling on the cushions dangerous?

🐾 What's that smell? Trust me, there will probably be some kind of odor, either good or bad. If it's bad you need to find out if it's permanent. Few things are worse than living downwind from a hog farm. Or pulp mill. Or tannery. Or soap factory. Or the municipal dump. Or discovering that the place you're looking at was previously used as a flophouse for lepers. *Do not* take this one lightly. If you manage to escape the scenarios above, take note that an awfully large percentage of the population here seems addicted to burning every scrap of plastic they can gather up.

There's no way I know to escape that particularly horrible odor.

☞ How many young children live in this neighborhood and where do they play? Some of you may as well own up to the fact that those shrieking children at play 18 or 20 hours a day just outside your door cease to be cute after the initial 17 or 18 seconds. Find out now if this will be a problem.

☞ Where is the water heater? Are all of the kitchen and bathroom faucets plumbed for and hooked up to both hot and cold water? Do you mind if I just twist 'em all to see how they work? Does the wind constantly blow out the flame on the water heater? In Mexico most, of the water heaters are mounted outside the house. Some are covered and protected, but many are not.

☞ Do you mind if I flush this commode? I'll need to push against it too. I failed to do this once and ended up buying a whole new unit because it tipped over and broke as I stood up. Turns out it was secured to the tiled floor by a thin ring of silicone, no bolts. As long as we're talkin' toilets let me tell you how to flush a commode that has no water running into the tank. You may need to use this technique often. Fill a bucket with water from the shower or a nearby faucet and pour it into the stool. Not the tank on the back, the part you just got up from. It works every time.

☞ How long will it take to get my rent deposit returned when I move? (If this one is applicable.)

☞ How much notice do you require me to give prior to moving out?

CHAPTER 6

MOVING YOUR STUFF

The house you finally decided to rent was chosen according to a number of personal criteria, including the furniture question. If you're debating the merits of moving your NoB household SoB, read and absorb the suggestions throughout this book. There is a wide selection of furniture, appliances and other household items available in Mexico. If you've decided to ship your household goods and furniture to Mexico on an FM-3 with *Maneja de Casa* documentation, your moving company and broker will give you exact instructions and advice about how to do it. Information about that process is in the second half of this chapter.

Bringing a Carload on a Tourist Visa

The advice in this section applies *only* if you're driving down and entering Mexico with a Tourist Visa, and bringing stuff with you.

Before you leave home, write up a list of all your electronics gear. Include a description, serial number, country of manufacture, and approximate date of purchase. Take your list to a local electronics dealer or repair person and ask them to assess the current market value and write it all up on a company receipt or a page of letterhead or something that looks official. Wouldn't hurt to get it notarized, although some would consider that overkill. Mexicans in official or quasi-official positions *love* stamps and official-looking seals. Just wait until you need to get a paper validated here and note the joy and gusto with which the person slams their own personal stamp repeatedly onto whatever document you've presented. It's always an impressive performance. Don't even think about trying to bring in something brand spankin' new, still in the original packaging and expect not to pay duty on it. Even if you're allowed to bring it in duty free, like a laptop computer, be sure it looks used. Let the dog and the grandkids loose on it so that it looks the part when you pack it into a different box. Be sure to keep the styrofoam packing, because there's a very real risk of losing every piece of information on your hard drive if it gets jarred around too much. I lost the entire manuscript of this book when I set my computer on the rear seat of my truck and toted it back from La Manzanilla to San Juan Cosalá.

Here's an abbreviated list of used items you can bring into the country duty-free with your Tourist Visa (FM-T). If you want to see the officially sanctioned and approved list of absolutely everything, go to *http://www.sre.gob.mx/seattle/ing_ser_llevar.htm.*

1. Clothing and shoes (some sources will tell you enough for a two-week stay, but who knows?).

2. One camera and 12 rolls of unexposed film (no one has ever counted my film).

3. VCR or movie camera that can be carried and operated by one person, and 12 blank videotapes.

4. Books and magazines for your personal use, but no pornography.

5. A laptop computer.

6. Used sports equipment for each person. There's a specific list but anything reasonable will get by.

7. Five used toys for each child, or for loony Uncle Larry.

8. If you're an adult, 20 packs of cigarettes, 5 cigars or 200 grams of tobacco if you're a "roll-yer-owner "or pipe puffer.

9. Three liters of wine, beer, or liquor if you're an adult who's inclined to carry coals to Newcastle.

10. Medications for your personal use that are in their original, properly-labeled containers from the pharmacy and accompanied by the prescription.

11. Luggage enough to hold it all.

The customs officials at the border will ask you for the information you've written down. Or maybe they won't. Everyone has a different story about crossing the border and every story is probably true—and contradictory. Border crossing stories range from the mundane, "They just looked in the car and waved us on", to truly epic tales, nay, *sagas*, of Herculean efforts to overcome the intricacies of Mexican bureaucracy and obstinate, corrupt officials demanding (or at least hinting for) "*la mordida*", the "little bite", the bribe.

If you're bringing new items, or items that aren't on the duty-free list, or are exceeding the limits of duty-free things you're allowed, you need to declare them to the customs officials. If you don't and they find them because you've hidden them and are sweating bullets in front of the officials, you'll have to pay the duty and could be eligible for a fine or seizure of both you, and the contraband for not declaring them.

When I crossed at Laredo I gave the customs officials a list of items that required customs duty. They got out a chart showing the percentage of import tax due (on things like electronics, different rates are charged depending on the country of manufacture), I paid it, got into my truck and drove South.

Checkpoint Charlie

About eighteen to twenty miles from the border you'll come to another *"Aduana"*, or customs checkpoint. I say "about" because I've never bothered to measure the distance between them. There are people who travel certain routes fairly consistently who can tell you to the exact millimeter how far a second *Aduana* at *La Frontera* is from any border crossing from Tijuana to Matamoros.

Yes, I *know* they just checked your stuff at the border. They may want to look at it again. On one of my crossings, they did. You can be fairly certain that if you roll up to the 18 mile checkpoint signal light with a Tourist Visa and a truckload of stuff, somebody is going to check you out. My somebody was a brand new *Aduanero,* fresh out of training and wearing a brand new shirt that had gone directly from the store to the seamstress to have all the patches attached and then directly onto his eager little body. Do we sense a potential situation? Hell, I knew they were going to check me out from top to bottom and frankly, I was surprised they didn't give me more than a once-over at the border. This kiddo was gonna remedy that little oversight.

The Customs "Traffic Light"

When you go through customs in Mexico you'll usually see a traffic light mounted on a short stand about head high or car door high, depending on your method of entry. It's a dwarfed version of a traffic signal with red and green lights. On the stand is a button that enters you in the Mexican Border Crossing Lottery!

Green means they're probably not going to check you this time. Red means pull over to the stall where any of seventy-six or seventy-seven uniformed *Aduaneros* or *Aduaneras* are expansively waving. From casual observation, I honestly believe any of them could qualify, without further training or experience, as college-level drum majors or majorettes. They *are* a bit more restrained when you arrive by air. A bit.

Items You Can't Bring Into Mexico

Even though these folks might look like wannabe majorettes, please keep in mind that each one is as serious as a heart attack and has the authority to take pretty well what they want from your load and place it in the "ain't gonna cross the border" stack. Plus, they can confiscate your vehicle and send you home—if you're lucky. Scary, huh? It shouldn't be unless you're transporting illegal drugs, more than twenty thousand undeclared dollars in cash, or a freakish amount of almost anything, or almost any amount of extremely large knives, swords, guns and/or ammunition.

You may call that 30.06 shell a watch fob or a key chain or anything else you want to, but at customs, they may inform you that it's a free ticket to jail. Concerning all the above-mentioned items, *JUST SAY NO!* It doesn't matter that it's your great-grandfather's Spanish-American War carbine that's had the barrel plugged. It doesn't matter that it's a chrome-plated, pearl-handled sidearm captured from a Viet Cong general and mounted on a lovely plaque and presented to you by your adoring troops. *NO!* Leave it NoB. Not even a single shell, even a casing, should be in your vehicle. Am I sounding hysterical? Just believe me on this one, even if you disregard everything else. They really frown on these things. That could be one of the reasons you feel safe walking the streets and *plazas* at night.

Bear with me here, Canadians, because I couldn't find similar information on the Department of External Affairs website but here's what the U.S. State Department says. It will apply to you. There's a list of Canadian Consular Affairs Publications in that you can review at *http://www.voyage.qc.ca*. The U.S. website is at *http://travel.state.gov*.

> "The Department of State warns U. S. citizens against taking any type of firearm or ammunition into Mexico without prior written authorization. Entering Mexico with a firearm or a single round of ammunition carries a penalty of up to five years in jail, even if the firearm or ammunition is taken into Mexico unintentionally."

For the official Mexican word on items not permitted into the country look in Chapter 7.

The Eager Beaver

Anyway, to make a four-hour story a bit shorter, the brand new guy wanted to inspect every item in my truck personally, even though I'd already passed the customs officials at the border. At some point in the inspection more experienced supervisors intervened and it wasn't too bad. My friend Anne, with whom I was caravanning, spent a lot of time and energy schmoozing every honcho in sight and trying to help smooth the way. At the border they'd told me to declare and pay duty on two lamps and the little guy was very interested in seeing them. Where were they, you ask? In the front of the truck bed, among the very first items packed. Then he argued that the value I'd claimed for my copier/printer was just *waaay* too low. I stood firm as he appealed to a couple of supervisors who just shrugged and walked away from the whole situation. Score one for recalcitrance. And evidently schmoozing pays off. Or maybe they just wanted Anne to leave.

Finally he called off his search and told me to load up and leave. At this point people usually cram stuff back into their vehicles as quickly as they can, spin their tires, and spray gravel for a generous distance as they speed away.

While I'd been unloading my stuff, I had stopped from time to time to rest and drink a soda or a bottle of water. I'd also shared drinks with some of the super-visors who occasionally stopped by. A lot of official stops can be made a lot less stressful by offering a cold drink to the officials who are pulling you over. Note: Carry a cooler of sodas and bottled water when you travel.

Anyway, as each item came from the truck I carried any debris, packaging, and wrapping to the trash barrel. *Sloooowly.* I reloaded the truck at about the same rate, tying up about four of the official inspection lanes with all my scattered possessions. Sometime during the re-packing, the young *Aduanero* disap-peared from the scene. Anne got a bit impatient, but I was quixotically making a statement.

Enough border stories, though. The *Aduaneros* are efficient, proficient and courteous. If you prepare well enough, it usually goes very smoothly.

Importing Your Household Goods, and the *Menaje de Casa*
If you decide to import your household goods and have an FM-3, you have approximately a 6-month window from the issue date of your FM-3 to do so. If you want to see the official word on how to import your household go to *http://www.sre.gob.mx/Seattle/ing_ser_household.htm*.

If you decide to bring the farm, be sure to study the instructions for the *Menaje de Casa*. No, *that* French soundin' deal is a totally different story. The *Menaje de Casa* is an official inventory of your household goods.

International Movers and "Breakers"
Movers? Yep, if you're gonna move everything you own to the new place you'll need to hire a moving company that's experienced in gettin' your stuff SoB without a lot of hassles. You can't rent a U-Haul and do this one yourself. It's too complicated and even if you could figure out what to do, you'd be tied up at the border for weeks. Plus, U-Haul won't let you take their trailers deep into Mexico. You *could* buy a small trailer and bring some of your most valuable

possessions down that way, but make sure all of the paperwork for the trailer is aces up and absolutely correct. Be prepared to pay a snout full of duty when you cross into Mexico. All this is usually better left to the professionals. If you do decide to pull a trailer or a boat anywhere on the South side of the Rio Grande, you'd better have it identified and added to your Mexican insurance policy. My policy states that if I'm pulling a trailer that's not listed on my policy and I have a wreck, my coverage for *everything* is voided. That means truck, trailer, legal assistance, third-party liability--in short, *everydamnthing.* As Jerry Lee Lewis told us, "Think about it, darlin".

Back to the pros. To begin the process of pricing and arranging your household move, check out some of these sources: The Pan American International Movers Association at *http://www.paima.com.* One of their members will be close to your state or province.

You might want to check out Transcontainer in Guadalajara. E-mail: *transcontainergd@attglobal.net.* Phone 011-523-3659-4466 or 4440 or fax: 011-523-3639-1563 from the U.S. or Canada.

If it's important to you, you can check out this company, advertised as "The only openly gay moving company in the U.S." at *http://www.gaymover.com.*

My personal recommendation is Strom Moving of Ajijic. Their website is http://www.strommoving.com, e-mail strom@laguna.com.mx. This is a truly International company. Kathy is originally from Seattle, Doug is a retired B.C. firefighter, and now they live in Mexico, just around the corner from me. I recommend them for several reasons; they're experienced, Doug is at the border to supervise every crossing, they're *not* one of the "Breakers," and Kathy is available to answer your questions and offer advice even if you decide to use another company. Like me, they want you to get accurate and up-to-date information so your move will be less stressful and your relocation as smooth as possible. There's much more so check the website.

Or just get out the Yellow Pages and look up some of the local franchisees like Atlas, Bekins, Nationwide, etc.

Refer to the list of Mexican customs brokers at *http://www.caaarem.org.mx.* The brokers are listed by name, city, and phone number.

You'll want to find out if your goods will be stored prior to delivery, whether they'll stay on one truck for the entire trip, what the customs fees will be (this will be a charge over and above the moving fee, usually), and approximately how long the move will take. Good luck. The mover you choose will give you detailed instructions. Do exactly as instructed. *Exactly.*

Household Items You Bring Across the Border Yourself

If there are some objects you don't want to entrust to the movers and are willing to cross the border with yourself, be aware that you could end up paying double duty on them. When you're crossing the border, you are subject to being searched by customs officials just like everyone else crossing with a carload or trailer load of household goods. You'll have to list, and if necessary, declare those items and pay customs on them. If you get the red light you'll have to pull the items out of those carefully packed and even more carefully inventoried boxes anyway. It's not okay to pull up to *Aduana* and tell the *Aduanero* that you don't need to pay the import duty on those items because you've already paid through your broker. It's not okay to argue that you didn't even really need to tell them about the stuff. It's probably not a good idea just to keep quiet and smuggle the stuff in, unless you want to begin your trip by violating the law.

Don't argue, don't explain, just pay the applicable import fee and boogie on outta there. Just remember that you're the one who chose to bring those things --blaming the one who's doing his job is counterproductive. It may just as well turn out that this is no problem at all. Each situation is different.

If you do need to pay, the *Aduanero* assisting you will give you a form to fill out that lists each item to be taxed along with its country of manufacture. As soon as it's been filled out and totalled, he'll direct you to another place to pay.

When you get your receipt, put it with your other papers where you can easily retrieve it. You'll need it about 18 miles or so down the road at the next *Aduana*. In some parts of the country Mexican customs folks also have roving check-points which means you could be stopped *anywhere*.

Hang tight darlin' cause we're just gettin' started.

Chapter 7

Head for the Border

It's time to drive across the border. Get set for a tremendous adventure. Thrills, chills, exotica, joy, intrigue, wonder and awe, aggravation, exhilaration, excitement, exasperation, fatigue, trepidation, relief and quite possibly the vapors. And that's just what you can expect during your brief stay at the border. But don't despair, it gets a lot more interesting as you head South.

Of course, you can't really have memorable adventures unless you actually *cross* the border. Here's a suggestion. If you get to the border any time past noon, plan to get your paperwork processed and then spend the night at a nice hotel or motel on your choice of sides. Have a nice leisurely dinner, re-check your planned route, and relax. Get up early and get a fresh start.

Do not order *tequila* in any form tonight. You're going to be facing a lot of sun tomorrow. Sun and *tequila* are only slightly less compatible than sun and vampires. Trust me on this one. Stop at the nearest 7 Eleven and stock up on travelin' snacks, too. You'll pass a lot of stores on the way but not all of them are gonna be sellin' Vienna sausages and shavin' cheese and saltines.

Or, if you're really, really unfortunate everything will go as smooth as silk and you'll be bereft of a single border horror story to compete with those of your friends and neighbors. *Pobricito!* Poor baby!

The three gauntlets you're going run today are Immigration, Temporary Vehicle Importation, and Customs.

Immigration, *Migración*

Before you left home you should have applied for and received either a U.S. or Canadian passport. Call your local Post Office for the location of the nearest office where you can pick up an application and instructions. U.S. and Canadian citizens don't actually need a passport to enter Mexico but you'll be surprised how much easier dealing with banks and bureaucracies will be with one. If you're a U.S. citizen visit *http://travel.state.gov/passport_services.html* to download a passport application form. Canadians will go to *http://www.ppt.qc.ca*. We covered this material earlier, in Chapter 1.

To get your tourist visa you'll also need a picture ID, like a state or international driver's license or ID card. If you absolutely refuse to get a passport, you can use your notarized birth certificate or a notarized statement of citizenship. Don't complain that you can't cross the border because you've come all this way with your old, beat up birth certificate that you forgot to have notarized.

With your passport and picture ID, you can proceed to *Migración*. Technically the paper you're getting is not a visa, it's a *Forma Migratoria de Turista* (FM-T).

The *Instituto Nacionál de Migración* identifies it as a "migration form or card" although it looks like a thin piece of paper.

A few things can happen at this juncture in your crossing but the two most likely are that you actually find the visa office, or just as likely, you end up wandering around the grounds of the crossing area sobbing softly. Don't worry. The border officials are very experienced at solving problems like yours. Someone, at some point will come out and gently lead you to the correct office. How long it takes them to respond depends on how entertaining they find your performance, and how close it is to shift change. If you're really layin' down a possible award winner, it might take hours or at least until someone senses that you're ready to collapse. It's usually too damn hot at the border to get a volunteer to carry you inside.

Once you're finally rescued and inside the correct office, you're eligible for a lesson in Mexican bureaucratic behavior. You'll recognize it because it's the same behavior displayed by public service drones on the Northern side of the border, except that these guys are usually wearing some sort of uniform.

Dry your eyes, stroll over to the *Migración* counter and stand there for a few minutes. Watch the guy sitting at the desk. He'll probably be reading the paper or clipping his nails—fingernails, if you're lucky—or engaging in some other sort of activity. His interest in what he's doing is far greater than most folks' patience so you may decide to announce your presence by discreetly clearing your throat. He may look up. If he doesn't you might succumb to the idiotic belief that God has lifted the curse of Babel from your tongue, instantly making you fluent in Spanish.

Do not--no, let me re-phrase this--under no circumstances should you say "*Excuso mea, Señor. Needo el visa.*" Speaking gibberish coined on the spot has led more than one potential tourist or emigrant to experience adventures beyond their wildest and most sordid nightmares. If you feel the need to communicate verbally you might try saying, "*Disculpe* (Deece CULL pay) *Señor, quiero una visa touristica.*" This may or may not induce him to put down his paper or clippers. If it does, he may shift his eyes to a point somewhere along the counter or to another one behind you. Despite being completely motionless, staring fixedly, and drooling slightly from the left corner of his mouth, he's not suffering from the onset of a stroke, he's actually signaling you to follow his gaze.

If you pick up on the subtleties of his body language and follow his stare, you'll probably see a pile of pale blue forms. They're blank immigration forms, visas. Help yourself and take one. Fill it out in either black or blue ink with the pen from your pocket or purse that you *always* carry. Getting your hooks on *his* would be more difficult than separating a starvin' Doberman from a ham hock.

Spanish is the official language here and most everything you'll be asked to fill out, read, or sign is printed in Spanish. In this case, the visa form is printed in Spanish first, then English. Fill it out and, yes, there's a space for your passport number. Leave it blank if you've insisted on crossing without one.

Now that you've filled out the form, take it to the clerk. If you're lucky he'll write 180 on it, collect a small fee, and send you on your way with a stamped entry visa good for six months. If he writes any other figure and you think you may need more than the 90 days he's written, just ask "*¿Mas dias, por favor?*" Maybe he'll signal you to fill out a new form or maybe he'll just shake his head. Luck of the draw. It's possible to extend your visa to 180 days after you reach your destination, but try really hard to get 180 days now. If you're not successful, seek out a Mexican *Migración* office or consular office for an extension once you get to where you're going. It's no *big* sweat, except that the government has recently begun to charge for the privilege.

The fee for a Tourist Visa? Less than $20 US. You won't have to apply or pay for one if you already have an FM-3.

If you're truly unfortunate, the following scenario might unfold. A neatly dressed and smiling gentleman nods and waves you to the counter he's standing behind. "May I help you?" he asks in unaccented English. "Yes," you reply, "I need to get a Tourist Visa." He then places a pale blue form on the counter between you and helpfully explains how it should be filled out. "Do you need to borrow a pen?" he asks. "Please use this engraved 18K Cross, a gift from my dear departed mother in recognition of my appointment to my present position twenty-two years ago." He then writes 180 on the form, stamps it, asks for the fee, and hands you your portion of the document. With a big smile, he waves *adios.*

As you turn to go, you notice a squadron of green and orange-striped rhesus monkeys fly from his shorts, up and out the skylight.

That's about as likely to happen as the events I've described above.

Chances are your experience will fall somewhere between these two extremes. If you absolutely have to, you can embellish your actual border crossing story later over drinks and never have to prove its actual veracity.

Now that you have a Tourist Visa firmly in hand, you're ready to face the next challenge.

Temporary Vehicle Importation

This next step is very simple. Especially if you have prior experience in sexing alligators, translating Sanskrit to Latin, or juggling chainsaws and bowling balls. After the monkeys have made their escape, ask the gentleman for directions to the *Hacienda*, where you'll get the permit to temporarily import your vehicle into Mexico. *Secretaria de Hacienda* is the Mexican taxing authority, not a ranch house. You'll need to produce a few more documents at this point.

You'll need a **clear title** to the vehicle you are driving to prove you own it. If it's still subject to seizure by the bank, you'll need a **notarized letter from the bank** allowing you to take the car into a foreign country—where they'll have almost no chance of recovering it if you decide to stay South of the Border without ever making another payment. I don't know of anyone who's ever managed to legally obtain one of these documents but theoretically, it *is* possible. I know folks who have used a bill of sale and a temporary certificate of title. It might work for you if you fail to plan ahead.

You'll need a **driver's license** issued somewhere other than Mexico. I know. As Brother Dave Gardner used to say "Ain't that weird?"

You'll also need proof that you have **insurance** provided by a company that's legally permitted to issue policies in Mexico.

Before you even think about crossing the border, make sure all of your papers are in order and all the names are written exactly the same. If you just got married yesterday, and if that marriage created a name change, and if you're attempting to use your new name on the visa and permits, you may not have made it this far. If you're planning on any kind of legal identity change, get it out of the way long before you hit the border.

If you show up with a Pennsylvania birth certificate reading Wanda Latrice Klotzburg, a California driver's license showing your picture above the name, Riviera Sun Child Deluxxxe, an Illinois car title issued to Fantayzha Laquisha

Jackson because you just bought this van last week in Chicago and the DMV hasn't had time to issue the new papers, a passport issued under your previous married name of Wanda L.K. von Smythingham, a marriage certificate showing that you are now Revera Sun Child Deluxxxe Silverman (nee Klotzburg), and a platinum card borrowed from your mother and issued under the name of Doris K. Yakamoto, you haven't gotten close to this counter. They turned you away long ago.

They don't care if you have a note from Mama giving you permission to use her credit card. They don't care that you have a receipt for the purchase of the van. They don't care about your disastrous first marriage to that weasel Sidney or how delightfully playful and romantic your new hubby Raoul is. They don't have the time or the inclination to play "This is Your Life".

Discount any border stories from people who claim to have crossed with even more garbled and mismatched papers than I've just described above. Some of the stories will be the result of senility or Alzheimer's, some will be absolute bull manure manufactured on the spot, and one or two may have happened years ago when bribes were *de rigeur*. Do you really think you'll find an official willing to take on the task of straightening out a mess you were too disorganized to avoid?

If you're interested in the official word on how to import your vehicle just go to *https://www.banjercito.com.mx/iitv/index_en.htm*.

This page is headed "Temporary import of vehicles". No matter how long you plan to stay in Mexico, unless you naturalize your vehicle it will be temporarily imported. This site will also tell you how much you must pay if you don't have, or don't want to use a credit card or debit card to import your vehicle.

If you choose to get your permit through this website you can avoid some of the aggravations discussed in the next section.

Waiting for Godot's Car Permit
Even though there may be about 7,000 people queued up in front of one of the permit windows, usually fewer than 300 are actually waiting to gain a vehicle permit. The rest are family members, neighbors, beggars, Chiclets sellers, hitchhikers, drinking buddies, and other assorted hangers-on. Your processing won't take more than a few days at most. People have told me about getting in and out in thirty minutes or less but I've also caught them lying about other things. The border operates twenty-four and seven at most crossings so you won't get locked out or turned away. Again, you can make note of the hours each crossing operates *http://www.customs.gov/top/office.htm* and click on Ports of Entry or *http://www.nafta-customs.rq/english/hours-mx.htm*. Seri-

ously, plan on a wait of at least a couple of hours. You may be blessed with *un milagro*, but counting on miracles is a losing proposition.

You'll probably be standing in a very large, very noisy, oven. Expect major problems if you're addicted to chocolate. Border offices aren't air-conditioned and your Snickers and chocolate-covered cherries are now semi-liquids oozing from their paper containers. Laundry and shower facilities will be as plentiful as seating. Your odds of finding a chair in one of these offices are only slightly better than spotting a Yeti patiently waiting in an adjacent line. Some folks bring folding chairs.

Which brings us to the next items. Water. Snacks. Bring a small cooler of extra water or soft drinks to share with anyone who looks the least bit stressed, thirsty, and official. It ain't a bribe, it's a kindness which might be repaid.

Here's another important *regalo* for you. Anytime you enter a building in Mexico where you intend to transact business of any kind, be sure to carry several items. First, a pad of paper, anything on to which you can write messages or take notes. Next, a pen or two since most of the other folks you encounter will not have one and will want to borrow yours. Just as in your hometown, never lend anything that you can't afford to lose. Then, something to read or otherwise occupy your time while waiting. And waiting. And waiting. Depending on the agency you're dealing with, you may have time for a couple of games of Monopoly or Trivial Pursuit.

When you finally arrive at the window they'll want to see your Tourist Visa, your vehicle title, your insurance papers, and small change to pay for the copies you'll have them make for you. They know exactly what you need. There's a list of items taped to the wall or the front of the counter telling you exactly what to present. Do not attempt to convince the clerk that the document you've handed over is really much more official than the one they've requested, the one you don't have, and can't find. Look at the list and then get your ducks in a row before you get to the counter.

If you've presented the papers they asked for, if they were acceptable to them, if you stopped to get legible copies made of each one, if the credit card or bank debit card you presented has the same name on it as all the other documents, then you'll be ready to pay the import fee for your vehicle, about $25 US. You'll sign a declaration stating that you agree to bring your vehicle with you when you leave the country and then finally you'll be issued a sticker (the famed *Solicitud de Importación Temporal de Vehículo*) that will be affixed to your windshield, legally clearing you to drive anywhere in Mexico.

You should be headin' on out the front door by now with a temporary vehicle importation sticker in your hand. A(n) *Hacienda* representative used to go to your vehicle and personally affix the sticker to the windshield. The last time I crossed, border officials were allowing individuals to do this for themselves.

You'll need this sticker whether you're entering the country with a Tourist Visa or an FM-3. You've got to have it if you're going on into the interior, except for the Baja. Many of the rules here don't apply over in that beautiful part of the country, but we're not going to be traveling over there within the pages of this book.

Back to the sticker. Never peel it off the windshield until you turn it in at the border when you decide to permanently remove your vehicle from the country. *This is crucial.* Don't remove it, and don't allow anyone else to either, unless the car is totaled in a wreck, and then you'll need to bring it back to the border if you intend to bring in a replacement. Again, *http://www.bajabound.com/before/vehicle.asp#ban* or *http://www.byhisgrace.com/borderlands/cities/NLaredo/crosshrs.htm* will give you the hours of operation for each Banjercito module or office where you can turn in your auto sticker or offer proof that the vehicle was wrecked in Mexico and cannot be driven back to the border before leaving the country.

Here's another piece of advice regarding the sticker. When you drive to the Banjercito ask an official what the procedure is for returning the sticker at their location. Don't scrape it from the windshield until you ask. Some officials want you to deliver the sticker to them and some want to remove it themselves. Play it safe and ask.

Getting Your Vehicle Permit with an FM-T or FM-3: The Debate
Okay, now it's he-said, she-said time. For how long is your permit valid? If your Tourist Visa was issued for 180 days, your auto permit is valid for 180 days. I've heard stories that some officials are issuing permits good for only 90 or 120 days. The law says that the permit is valid for the term of your visa. Maybe. Here comes the "Who really knows?" section. **What happens to the validity of your Temporary Vehicle Import Sticker if you get an FM-3 while in Mexico on a Tourist Visa?**

You have at least three options to choose from when considering the FM-T vs. FM-3 car importation question.

One, get your FM-3 before you come South. Again, call the nearest Mexican Consulate and find out how to get there and when you should come. I've heard that people have done this over the phone and through the U.S. Mail. I've also heard about people being committed to funny farms after pursuing that particular choice.

A lady from Montana recently told me that a Mexican Consulate representative in Arizona told her that she did not need an FM-3 to move to Mexico because that document was required only for Canadians. That information, if it were true, would come as quite a surprise to the many Europeans, Asians, Canadians, and U.S. citizens, as well as citizens from a hundred other countries, who shuffle down to *Migración* each year to apply for or renew theirs.

In 2001, the cost for an FM-3 was only 913 *pesos,* around $100 US, so why not get it? Keep in mind that a new administration just took over in Mexico so a lot of officials are learning plenty of new *migración* rules, regulations and responsibilities. Just go armed with knowledge and patience.

Two, do it the way I did. Come in on an FM-T and get your FM-3 once you settle in. Your sticker will be valid as long as your immigration status is legal. If you do this you should also go to a bookstore or *papelería* and buy a copy of the *Ley Aduanera* and photocopy pages 60, 61, 62, and 63 and carry them in your vehicle with your other papers. Highlight *Artículo*106. If you want to download and print it from the Internet go to *http://www.cddhcu.gob.mx/leyinfo/pdf/14.pdf.* 87 pages. In Spanish. This may or may not help you to explain the law to any cop who stops you. One friend tried it and was told by the cop "I am the law today". Three hundred US bucks lighter he was soon on his way.

Here's how it should work. I entered the country the last time on a Tourist Visa and got my FM-3 after I arrived. I drove on my original vehicle sticker, issued under my Tourist Visa until I crossed the border two years later when I had to get a new one. In Puerto Vallarta I was stopped in the parking lot of the airport by the *Policia Federal de Caminos* because I wasn't wearing my seatbelt. In the PARKING LOT. Anyway, the officer asked for my license and I handed over a photocopy of my Texas license.

"This license has expired."

"Si."

"No, this license has expired."

"Si."

"Your license is expired. No good. Not valid."

"Si."

Suspecting, I'm sure that he was dealing with a nut case, the officer looked at my vehicle permit that was also expired, and asked if I had an FM-3.

"Si."

"May I see your papers?"

"Si."

I normally get semi-cooperative when I sense a free ride to any municipal building looming, so I got out the envelope holding photocopies of the rest of my documents and handed over all the copies of my FM-3. He looked them over and handed them back, turned, got back into the cruiser with his partner, and drove away.

The point of this story is that he considered my expired vehicle sticker to be valid as long as my FM-3 was current. Or maybe it dawned on him that I wasn't going to offer up some sort of settlement agreement. What will the next guy say? Who knows. Here's the exact wording from the website of the Mexican Consulate in Seattle: "Your permit is good for 6 months. This period cannot be extended, unless your immigration permit is extended." They're at *http:// www.sre.gob.mx/seattle* if you wanna take a look for yourself.

In an earlier ramble you *did* notice that I said copies didn't you? There must be a reason. If there is any way to avoid it, never give the original of a document to anyone who stops you along the road, either in town or on the highway. Once they have your original document in their hand, the balance of power tips completely to their side. When this situation arises and originals are demanded, I explain as well as I'm able, that I don't carry originals when I'm traveling due to my fear of highway robbery and the difficulty of getting replacements. It's worked so far.

The State of Jalisco has published a wonderful little booklet printed in 1999 called *Practical Guide to Security for Tourists Visiting Jalisco.* This booklet states that your vehicle may legally stay in Mexico "as long as you are in Mexico legally if you are a foreigner". There's about a ton of really good info in this publication and you might be able to get your hands on one if you write to:

SECRETARY OF TOURISM of the State of Jalisco (SETUJAL)
General Technical Direction, Division of Procedures and Verification
Paseo Degollado 121, Level 3
Plaza Tapatia
44100 Guadalajara, Jalisco
Mexico

Your third option is to drive back to the border after you receive your FM-3 and apply for a new permit. If you cross the border and return with the sticker you got with an FM-T they may insist that you buy a new one. That's what happened to me.

They Own That Sticker

There may be a big problem if you get a vehicle stolen while you're in Mexico. By law, you must return that auto importation sticker to the Banjercito when you exit the country for good. Supposedly that proves you actually took the vehicle from the country and didn't sell it to your neighbor in Veracruz, which is illegal under current Mexican law, except in limited instances of older vehicles that have been nationalized.

Everybody has heard stories about blowin' across the border headed North and never even thinkin' about returnin' that sticker. I've done it myself on several occasions. There are just as many stories about Honest Johns (and Joans) who tried to return the stickers, but were rebuffed. Evidently, the age of computers has changed all that.

One friend who attempted to bring in a replacement for her vehicle that had been stolen was told that she must return the import sticker from the other car before she could be issued one for the new vehicle. Impossible to do, of course.

Then Ms. Yossarian presented the police report of the stolen vehicle. No dice. Then the copy of the insurance check. No dice. Still Catch *Veinte y dos*.

"Under your FM-T or FM-3 you're allowed only one vehicle in the country at a time."

"But I'll only have one vehicle. The other one was stolen."

"Well you must turn in the import sticker before you will be permitted to enter the country with another vehicle."

"But the sticker is on the windshield of the stolen car."

"Perhaps you might try this..."

I won't tell you what was suggested, or whether it worked. It might be illegal.

The U.S. State Department says if you bring a letter from the Embassy stating that your car was stolen while you visited or legally resided in Mexico, everything will be taken care of very easily. "Here's a note from my Uncle." *Buena suerte!* I've also heard that a new permit can be attached to your birth certificate instead of your FM-3 number. Try everything.

See why you need to retrieve that sticker and the chunk of windshield it's attached to from the junkyard where they towed your vehicle after that bus totaled it out?

Customs, *Aduana*

If you've looked at the choices of entry lanes into Mexico and you're confused, welcome to the club! If you exchanged your dollars for *pesos* at a *casa de cambio* just before crossing, you could have asked someone which entry point to use. At the smaller crossings the answer will be "That one there, the only one." At the larger crossings, you may need directions that are more detailed. In some border towns, you may find, on the U.S. side of the border, someone who actually speaks English. If not, go to the closest Wal-Mart. Chances are nobody there speaks a word of English either, but at least you'll be having your nervous breakdown in somewhat familiar surroundings. It's better to get an accurate measure of your frustration quotient now, rather than 643 miles South of the Border in the small dusty village where your fuel pump cratered.

Each crossing, even at the exact same location, at the exact same time of day, with the exact same *Aduanero* (customs agent) on the exact same day of the week, will be different. This statement is so statistically accurate that it almost counts as an absolute. Boy Scout it and Be Prepared for anything.

If you've figured out the lane that will get you to the *Aduana*, roll on through, take your turn-off into one of the inspection areas, hand the official your immigration and vehicle importation papers, and press the customs light as instructed by the officials. If you get a red light pull up beside the table you've been motioned to, turn off the engine, and wait. Uniformed *Aduaneros* will then ask you several questions. Rapidly. In Spanish. Unless you're fluent, your response should be "*No entiendo. No hablo Español.*" If you do happen to be fluent in Spanish, your reply should be "*No entiendo. No hablo Español.*" Sometimes it doesn't pay to tell everything you know.

Yes, they probably do think it's strange that you're entering their country without a working knowledge of the language but it happens hundreds of times a day and the old hands are used to it.

(If you've been reading straight through, you'll recognize that the information in the next few paragraphs was covered in Chapter 6, Moving Your Stuff. Skip over it if you've already been-there-done-that.)

If you get the green light and you have very few items in your car, you might be waved through. Whatever the color of the light, though, you can still be asked to pull over for inspection.

What the *Aduaneros* or customs agents want to know is what you have in the vehicle that you need to pay the import duty on. If you're loaded up like the Joseph Smith exodus heading West in Conestogas, you may have to suffer through a fairly thorough inspection of the cargo. If you have that big desktop computer lashed to the roof or cleverly hidden under a blanket in the back seat, now is the time to declare it.

If you do have something to declare, tell the *Aduanero* so you can pay the appropriate fees and scoot on out of there. The *Aduanero* who is assisting you will give you a form to fill out where you'll list each item to be taxed along with its country of manufacture. As soon as it's been filled out and totted up, they'll direct you to pay at another window. It may be at the other end of the counter or it may be in another room. Just go where they direct you and pay your import fee. In *pesos.* The ones you got earlier on the other side of the border. See how well it's all working?

When you get your receipt, put it where you can easily retrieve it. Remember my earlier statement that you'll need it about 18 miles down the road at the next *Aduana* ?

You'll know what to expect at the next *Aduana* because it looks like a big multiple toll booth complex off to the right and it usually has a Highway Patrol car parked there so they can run you down if you fail to stop. As you approach it slow down because you're going to have to pull over and pass by the go/no go signal light. Remember? Push the button and watch for a signal from the attending *Aduanero*. If you get a green, you'll probably be waved on through at which point you'll drive on down a bit and pull back onto the highway and scoot on toward your destination.

Items You Can Bring Duty Free
Again, the list of items you can bring into the country duty-free with your Tourist Visa (FM-T) is at *http://www.sre.gob.mx/seattle/ing_ser_llevar.htm.*

More Items You Can't Bring Into Mexico
La Secretaria de Turismo has published a brochure titled *Bienvenido A Mexico, Amigo Turista Si Visitas Mexico Por Carretera Recuerda* which is intended to help you with a few things you need to know before you cross the border. If you can't translate the previous sentence, the brochure won't be of much use…unless you continue reading. Here's an abbreviated version of what SECTUR wants you to know.

1. Don't carry weapons, cartridges, or dynamite into Mexico. You can be jailed from 5 to 30 years if you fail to heed this order.

2. If you are a hunter, you will need a special permit to carry a gun.

3. Do not carry, transport, deal in, sell, supply, export, or import any narcotics. The punishment for these activities runs from 10 to 25 years in jail.

4. Do not assist anyone without proper documentation in entering or leaving Mexico. Jail again, for up to 10 years.

5. If you are carrying cash in excess of $20,000 US you must declare it at Customs. If you fail to do so and are discovered, you face having the excess impounded and paying a fine. If you attempt to cross with more than $30,000 US and fail to declare it, you have committed a crime and can receive up to six years in jail.

The Customs booths are installed by the General Police Department (PGR) to help guarantee personal safety, and to control illegal drug traffic, the movement of illegal aliens, the transport of drugs, and to assist anyone who has been kidnapped. If the PGR agents stop you, please show them all the documentation they request. You must allow them to search your vehicle if they ask, and you should answer all of their questions truthfully.

If You Get Hassled

This is not a one-way street though. The SECTUR wants you to know that you have certain rights. First, you may request that any agent show you their official ID. Any search of your vehicle should be conducted without damaging your property and the agents have the responsibility of putting things back the way they were. You may prefer to do this yourself, however. The officer(s) should "obey a good, kind, and respectful conduct."

In the rare case that you feel you have been treated unfairly or disrespectfully, there is a formal complaint procedure. A form is printed inside the brochure but the chances of you ever seeing it are about the same as winning the Poker World Championship out in Vegas. Not likely.

Here's a rough reproduction of the *PGR/Secretataria de Turismo* form.

```
COMPLAINT FORM

Name:

Age:                              Gender:

Place of Birth:

Address in the Republic of Mexico:

Telephone Number:

ACTIONS

Place:

Time:

Date:

(This all pertains to the incident being reported)

Name and Position of the Agent (if known; if not,
give a complete description)

Recount the event:

WHEN THIS FORM IS RECEIVED, AN INVESTIGATION WILL
BEGIN. WE THANK YOU FOR YOUR HELP IN KNOCKING DOWN
CORRUPTION.
```

```
Send the completed form to:

Controller, Internal Department of PGR

Av. Paseo de la Reforma No. 752

Planta Baja

Col. Guerro

Delegatión Cuaútemoc, C.P. 06300

Telephone numbers are (55) 5529-9500 and 01-800-70-
700 (I know it looks strange, but that's the toll-
free number).
```

Once you've dispensed with border issues and customs, you can relax and turn your attention to the road.

A really good site to check out before you leave home is *http://www.kmbykm.com.* You'll find articles by David Eidell as well as Dan "Mexico Dan" Clark and other experienced OMHs. Explore a bit and you'll find a great deal of useful information about driving in Mexico, as well as a few specific trip logs with detailed driving directions.

At *http://www.mexconnect.com.mx_/quickguide.html* is *Driving in Mexico-A Short Practical Guide.*

One last item and I'll let you go. The Ministry of Finance of the Government of Mexico has printed a booklet titled *Driving to Mexico.* Among other things it lists the operating hours for all the Banjercito Modules in Arizona, California, and Texas, and offers up some other useful information about crossing the border. This is the official word so you might want to call 1-800-446-8277 or contact your nearest Mexican Consulate for a copy.

Contrary to what you may have heard or read, the Mexican authorities really do want to help you. Now, let's get you back on the road.

CHAPTER 8

DRIVING AND OTHER DARING PURSUITS

Mexico's Toll Roads

The very good news is that on your journey from the border you'll travel an excellent highway system. You'll more than likely encounter some construction work but you'll survive it. The roads are extremely well marked and it's almost impossible to get lost if you stay anywhere close to civilization. You should have in your hand at least one very accurate road map and you'll be good to go.

The best road maps are the large *Guia Roji* books. Take time to study these maps--they hold a wealth of information. They're updated annually so find one with the year of issue fairly close to the year of your trip. Look on the U.S. side of the border in Wal-Mart or in some of the local bookstores. If you've truly planned well, your local Border's or Chapters or Walden Books has ordered it for you.

You may also want to join the American Automobile Association (AAA). They publish a fairly good set of travel guides and can provide you with some cultural information. I've discovered several things in their texts that I personally disagree with because I know better from practical experience, but there's nothing on the pages that'll hurt you. Contact them at *http://www.aaa.com*. The Canadian Auto Association is at *http://www.caa.ca* if you're that far North.

You can get a Mexican driver's license once you're here if you choose, but your U.S. or Canadian license will be honored throughout the country as long as it's not expired. In Appendix 2 I tell what you can expect if you choose to get a license here.

While you're on the *autopistas*, the "*cuota*" or toll road system, there will be restrooms and small *tiendas* at most toll booths. Or at least a soft drink machine. Many of the tollbooths will be near a PEMEX (*PEtroleos MEXicano*) gasoline station and mechanical help is often available. On the "*libre*", or free roads, just pull over and pee anywhere, like the locals do. Ladies, one word: bedsheet. Get someone to hold it up as a privacy screen.

If you wonder how much it'll cost you to take the trip South via the toll roads you can look at *http://www.sct.gob.mx/autotransporte/index.htm* for a listing of all the charges from city to city. The site is in Spanish but it won't be difficult to figure out. The names of the cities will look familiar and all you'll need to do is figure the *peso* conversion rate at the time of your trip.

To find the distance between Mexican cities look at *http://www.trace-sc.com/distance.htm*.

Travel Information

Once you're in Mexico you can get travel information by calling INFOTOUR at 01-800-903-9200. There will be someone there 24/7 and they'll be able to converse with you in English. I called them at 4 a.m. just to make sure this information was correct. They'll send you brochures and other tourist information about any area you wish to visit, but they explained that it might take as long as 30 days for you to receive their mailings.

In the bookstores you'll also find a series of magazines titled *Guia Turistica* or *Tourist Guide.* These are annual bilingual publications that provide excellent in-depth travel advice and recommendations about Mexico's individual states. The 2001 cost for these publications is about $10.00 US and well worth it.

Free sources of travel information are the Mexican airline magazines if you can find them. They often provide very good information about interesting sights and cities, and they're well written.

Don't Bring the Volvo

If this is your first trip to the interior by car, and you're at the border in that Swedish import, you've already made a major mistake. Yes, I know Volvos are finely engineered and precisely constructed touring machines, but you'll play hell trying to find parts or get repairs.

In most fair-sized towns and every city, you're likely to find dealerships for Ford, Chevy, Dodge, Chrysler, Jeep, Nissan, and VW. Lucy, do I need to 'splain that this means you'll be able to service your car with factory parts? You'll see all kinds of autos here. Jag X's and J's, a bunch of Caddies, a few Lincolns, Suburbans, and other assorted road yachts. My advice is to stick with something you can buy parts for and something that a mechanic out in *El Oeste*

Nowherelandia might have a passing acquaintance with and therefore a chance of repairing. That normally means the majors listed above. However, I must also add that even that isn't a sure shot. The mechanic doing repairs to my Chevy 350 c.i.d. couldn't find a set of radiator hoses in Guadalajara in spite of going to three different places, including a dealership. Maybe they'll be there tomorrow. Oh, well.

Here are a few reasons why bringing a large and/or low-clearance car to Mexico is something to avoid: highways, city streets, village streets, and dirt roads. As long as you're on the *autopista* toll-road system, you're traveling on some of the finest highways anywhere. (Maybe—it depends which part of the *autopista* you're on.) Many of them are relatively new, well-maintained, multi-lane super-highways with wide grassy dividers. Some are not. If you have a problem with the roads or any government personnel associated with them you have a method of informing officials of your dissatisfaction.

The Federal Toll Roads and Bridges and Related Services folks, CAPUFE, have recently begun to put "Complaints, Reports, and Suggestions" forms in boxes attached to the sides of tollbooths. The forms are bilingual so motorists can report problems in either of two languages and make suggestions to the agency. If it's important, get a form and file your story. You can call them at 01-800-990-2900 or e-mail them at *contraloria@cafufe.gob.mx*. If you need to report a problem by mail, use this address:

Administración de Correos No.6

C.P. 62130, Cuernavaca, Morelos

Be sure to include a full description of your complaint or suggestion, including date, time, persons involved, your address and telephone number, the location of the incident you're reporting, and the names of any witnesses or officials with whom you may have dealt. They're trying to help you as much as possible.

Impediments to Pleasure Cruisin'
Although I'm very suspicious, I can't actually prove that the Public Works Director of Houston, Texas attended the same School of Public Inconvenience as the Director of Federal Highways for Mexico, but there are certain similarities in the way they schedule repairs and new construction.

Somehow they find out exactly where you're planning to travel, as well as when, and then they tear the living hell out of as much roadbed along your proposed route as they possibly can. There are a lot of highway demolition teams in Houston and Mexico, and I suspect they're the same guys--crossing back and forth across the border, traveling from place to place and totin' lunch buckets, picks, shovels and dynamite.

Besides "construction", there are other impediments to pleasure cruising.

Topes

"We didn't know what the hell happened," he said, his voice rising as he related the story of a two-day trip from Puerto Vallarta to points South along the coast in a rented VW bug. "We were just cruising along about 50, and WHAM, it felt like the bottom of the car had been torn off! Richard was belted in but he still hit the dash because his seat ripped loose from the floor, and Cathi came flying in from the backseat and landed on top of us."

"We thought we'd hit a cow," Richard chimed in.

"Or someone on a bicycle," Cathi added.

These three young college grads had just been re-introduced to a traffic control device that they were not prepared to see out on the open road. They're up where you live too. You call them "speed bumps" or more euphemistically "traffic calming devices". We call them *topes*, or "sleeping policemen". Their function is the same in Morelia as it is in Memphis or Mozambique or Montreal— to make you to reduce your speed. Or else.

You're accustomed to seeing them in parking lots or on some residential streets back home, but in Mexico, they're everywhere. Most of them are marked by black and yellow signs (kindly supplied by the government) that show the word *TOPES*, or a small graphic of a washboard, below which the distance to the hump is indicated—*a 200 m* or *a 300 m*, or whatever. In Spanish, "*a*" means "to", so *a 100 m* means it's 100 meters to whatever you're being warned about. Whether you remember that "*m*" means meter, and whether or not you can do the conversion quickly enough to know that 200 m is about 656 feet, *do* slow down immediately. You might be interested to know that your Mexican insurance policy will not pay for damage to the undercarriage of your vehicle if you run over a *tope* or a pile of rocks. Read it.

If the government hasn't been out to post an official sign, a small homemade sign leaning against a signpost, or a fence post, or the side of a building, or even against an old paint bucket set up for the purpose is all the warning you'll get. Be alert to any possibility. I once saw an old table turned on its side, with the warning painted on the tabletop. Anything close to the roadbed could be a warning sign. Be alert.

Some *topes* are very benign. In Mezcala, I saw long strips of tractor tire tread spiked to the road. Very gentle. In some places, they're high and steep enough to tax the skills of even the most experienced Sherpa.

Occasionally, I've crossed a relatively gentle little rise only to drop off into a small arroyo on the other side of the mound. Some of the more timid (or sane) drivers slow to a creeping roll and don oxygen masks and crampons before making the push to the top. It might take one of these daredevils anywhere from two or three minutes on up to a time period rivaling the third Ming Dynasty to ascend the *tope* in front of them. If you get behind one of these drivers just plan to pull over at the next *restaurante* or *cantina* and stop.

During your Mexican driving career, you're gonna smack at least one *tope* at a much higher speed than would be prudent. Don't fret. You'll see a lot of shops near these things advertising "*mofles*", mufflers.

That's another reason I wouldn't show up at the border in a Corvette or a Jag or anything else with low ground clearance.

Dr. Frankenstein Needed Spare Parts, So Will You

Before you pass the city limits of your present home town make sure you get Cloyd and Leotis over at the neighborhood Gulf station to check out the whole vehicle before you load up to shag off to Mexico. Make sure they look at the brakes, the suspension (shocks, struts, springs), and the universal joints. The roads may play havoc with certain parts of your vehicle. Spring for a new set of tires if you have any questions or doubts. I also carry a couple of cans of some sort of aerosol tire inflater and sealer along with my spare.

Put spare hoses and belts in the trunk. If your vehicle does not have an in-line fuel filter, have Leotis install one. Have him show you where it is and how to change it. Toss a spare one, or the replaceable filter element, if applicable, in the trunk with the other stuff. Carry an extra air filter. This may sound like over-kill again, but in the past I've had to clean my old worn out clogged up one several times until I could get to a Jeep or Chevy dealer. Might not hurt to throw in a new fuel pump or two. Or three. Keep reading, I'll explain shortly.

I also carry a big canvas bag containing a nylon tow strap, a siphon hose, lots of flashlights, emergency reflectors, a small floor jack, and a two-foot long, two-by-twelve board. On a lot of these highways you're not going to have much room to pull over to change a flat, or a solid surface to set up your jack. The joke your auto maker gave you isn't to be trusted.

Delco makes a collapsible four-way lug wrench. Read carefully. Go to the local auto parts store and buy one. Next go to the hardware store and buy a three-foot length of galvanized pipe that will slip over each of the four bars on the wrench. Put both pieces of equipment in the trunk. Why? Well, if you don't have these items the chances of successfully changing a tire on the side of the road are almost nil. The guys at the tire shops back there in Vicksburg and Vancouver love to cowboy with those pneumatic tools. Your lug nuts are snugged down tighter than a freshly used noose. You have equal odds of loosening either without assistance.

Hence, the four-way and the cheater pipe. Now they'll unscrew easily. Which they will not if you attempt to use the 89-cent, zero-leverage, toy lug wrench given to you by Ford, or Chrysler, or GM, or Nissan, or Volkswagen. Or Volvo.

See if I'm not right on this one. Take a minute to go out in the driveway to try to break a lug nut loose. I'm not responsible for hernia repair.

Don't waste space carrying a spare gas can. If you run out of gas just hitch to the nearest PEMEX, buy two gallons of water and pour them out. DO carry a funnel with a long flexible tube so you can push down the little trap door in the fill pipe of the fuel tank. Stick it where you can easily locate it. Does this sound like the voice of experience? To avoid repeating some of my mistakes I always fill up when my gas gauge reads half full. Or in this case, half empty. There's really no excuse for running out of gas in most parts of Mexico, especially if you stay on or near the *autopistas.*

Medio Dia en Sonora, William Gentes, 1992

You should also have a roll of toilet paper where you can get to it. Many Mexican bathrooms do not supply paper. The PEMEX stations and OXXOs (Mexican-style convenience stores) usually do, but there's always a chance that one of the prior users took it all when they left. You'll notice that many, if not the overwhelming majority, of Mexican commodes have no seats. Folks tend to liberate them. If you absolutely need to have one you're advised to carry your own. That's not a joke.

Car Trouble
If you have car trouble along the way, just sit tight. The "Green Angels" will be by to offer free labor assistance. These are government-employed mechanics who can effect small repairs and have you on your way in short order if you have the parts they require. Remember those extra belts and hoses? If you have a cellular phone that will work in Mexico, or if you're on a "*cuota*" where roadside phones are usually within walking distance, you can call 91-800-90392 to the Green Angels Hotline.

Keep something in mind. These "phone booths" are actually two-way direct communication systems. When you pick up the handset and press the button you'll be speaking to a person who can dispatch help. The stations are numbered and all you do is look at the number and tell the dispatcher what number you see. Many of these stations have been vandalized and don't function.

After they show up to help, offer sodas to the guys, as well as the universal gift of love, friendship, and appreciation—chocolate. And a nice tip. They'll refuse. Insist. Gently. They'll accept.

If you can't get to a phone just raise the hood and sit tight. The Green Angels patrol from dawn to dusk and make their complete circuit twice a day. During some holiday periods they may patrol a bit later, it all depends. At any rate, they'll find you.

In the past, I've heard stories about people staging breakdown situations to induce you to stop and render aid so they could rob you. Use your own judgment. Same deal with hitchhikers. I usually pick up anyone who looks like a working man. Most folks are a bit apprehensive about stopping for a group of guys walking down the road carrying long sharp machetes. In Guadalajara or Mexico City I would be too, but in the countryside these guys are just hoofing it home carrying the tools of their trade. Do whatever you're personally comfortable with. Well-dressed hitchers will never get close to my vehicle because every Mexican carjack story I know begins, "There was this well dressed man just standing there…"

I also never pick up identifiable counter-culture types. If you get stopped and searched and one of your passengers has something on their person they should have smoked, snorted, or injected last night, or even worse, something he stuffs into the crack of the back seat so the cop's dog can sniff it out, you probably just lost a vehicle and gained access to one of the fine Mexican prisons.

Car Repairs

If you have car trouble in Mexico chances are good that the cause will be diagnosed as fuel pump failure whether it's the real cause of the malfunction or not. *No funciona, la bomba de gasolina*. Everydamn *mecánico* in Mexico who's worth his salt can not only change any fuel pump in less than 85 seconds, he can produce the exact tools to do it from his back pocket. This may be the single exception to the "don't drive an exotic car to Mexico" rule. I'm willing to bet that every *refaccionaria* in the country stocks a full range of gaskets and fuel pumps for everything from an Alfa-Romeo to a Hudson Zephyr.

I bought three on one trip from the border to Guadalajara. At the second stop I patiently explained that no, I didn't need a new fuel pump because the guy back up the road just installed one about two hours ago. The *maestro*, equally patient, explained that Mexican fuel pumps were manufactured under very poor quality control standards and that I evidently had been blessed with one that should have been rejected. I opened my wallet, again. My next stop was at a clean, well-equipped Jeep/Chrysler dealership in Lagos de Moreno. You guessed it! *Numero tres!*

That one got me as far as the tollbooth for the "next stop, Guadalajara" leg of the trip. Or rather, close enough that the freelance *mecánico* who stopped to offer his services (No, *gracias*, I'm not buying another damn *bomba de gasolina* ever again, even if I live to be 384 years old and am forced to drive a succession of deteriorating, fuel-pump-eating Rolls-Cahnardlies.) agreed to drive me to the nearest tow truck. (Ask for a *grua*.)

I rode back to the Jeep in a clean, late model flatbed car carrier. The driver loaded me up, asked me where I was headed and when I replied, "Puerto Vallarta" he nodded, popped the clutch, and sped away South. We whizzed past the tollbooth and toward Guadalajara.

It was a bit past dusk when we pulled up in front of a house in a residential area that I later discovered was Tonalá, one of the five main sections of Guadalajara. It's a city suburb and they're cheek to cheek. The driver stopped, got out and began releasing the binder chains. I bailed out, protesting loudly that I wanted the Jeep taken to a Chrysler dealership. "Oh no, señor. Está bien aquí." I wasn't buying.

Then from the shadows came a slightly accented voice; "Señor, I speak your language."

"Can you fix my Jeep without replacing the damn fuel pump?"

"Sí, I think. If you wish."

That was my introduction to Don Carlitos. He and Andrés repaired my Jeep—without replacing the damn fuel pump. I had business to attend to in PV so I caught the bus and after two weeks came back to claim my completely repaired vehicle. It seems the timing chain had been defective. There were also new plugs and wires, a rotor and distributor cap, and filters. They'd changed the oil, added new transmission fluid, overhauled the carburetor, done a brake job, replaced some fuses—"Now the radio plays, Señor"—put in a new flasher for the turn signals, repaired the door latch, and replaced a few screws...

"No charge Señor, for the wash."

"Y cuanto cuesta por todo, *Don Carlitos?*"

"Ssssssttt!" "Joven, tequila, Squirt, ándale!" *he commanded, as he handed a teen several crumpled bills and sent him scurrying to the corner* tienda. *There was small talk, stalling, more small talk, and more stalling, along with another inspection of the Jeep and numerous reminders that the wash job was free. "We did much work, many things needed attention." My sphincter was puckered, my breathing was strained and labored, and my anxiety level was teetering precariously on a tiny ledge just below hysteria. Don Carlitos's words, meant to be soothing and reassuring, were anything but.*

Would I be able to pay for all of this with the few thousand pesos *left in my pocket? My mind began to torture me with visions of paying for some of the repairs but not having enough to redeem the Jeep, and then, flat broke, hitching back to PV, or to the U.S. without money or the Jeep. Then, even more lurid misfortunes flashed through my mind—my tortured body lying on the side of the road, mercifully released from misery by a* machete *whack to the throat.*

Luckily, Don Carlitos was even more apprehensive than I was. Andrés had taken himself somewhere out of sight. The boy returned and set a couple of bottles on the desk in the office into which I had been ushered, handed some change to Don Carlitos, and backed from the room to join Andrés in his hiding place.

Bottles were opened and drinks were poured and consumed. Bottles were reopened and drinks were again poured and consumed. It seems that Mexican working men, used-car salesmen, me and a rowdy little red-haired waitress up in Galveston, and nervous South of the Border mechanics all drink tequila *straight up, with just a hint of citrus chaser.*

"Don Carlitos, por favor mi amigo, cuanto cuesta *?"*

Again, the bottles were opened, drinks were poured and consumed. "Momentito " *he muttered as he began to dig through the piles of paper strewn carelessly about the desktop. I foolishly believed that he was actually searching for my bill, but that fantasy was shattered when he uttered a satisfied "Aaah!" and held up part of a dirty broken pencil as though he were showing me a Mayan artifact.*

About that time I began opening the bottles and liberating the liquids and wondering if the missus was a good cook and how comfortable this dirty sofa might be when used as a bed.

Mercifully, Don Carlitos began diligently putting the pencil to use after a few more minutes of searching for a piece of paper with enough blank space to figure my charges.

Now that he was actually making an attempt to release me from my miserable state of anxiety I felt it best not to disturb him, so I again opened the bottles, poured the drinks, and attempted to place the bottles back on the desk. Finding my coordination insufficient for such a daunting task, I carefully placed them somewhere in the vicinity of where I believed the floor might be.

I'm sure that long years of experience had taught the Don *the exact moment to present the bill to the victim. As calmly and fearlessly and cleanly as the matador places the blade, Don Carlitos set the scribbled bill on the arm of the sofa.*

"Cuanto?", I croaked, just before another great gulp, sans chaser.

He made a gesture in the direction of the paper, then paused, and with a distressed look on his face and with a catch in his voice, squeezed out, "Two thousand, three hundred pesos, Señor. *We did many things, but if this is too much, perhaps....".*

Even in my near comatose condition I knew that Don Carlitos had just told me that I had gotten one hell of a lot of work done for much less than it would have cost me in the U.S. Moreover, I now had a functioning radio and had been gifted with a free car wash. I could drive away from Guadalajara with the radio blaring, completely free from worries of bandidos *wielding rusty* machetes.

I intended to say, in the gravest manner I could muster, "This is much money for such a small amount of work. And of course, I did not request much of the work you did. Perhaps we can reach a more reasonable accommodation if we discuss this matter."

What actually came from my mouth was loud, manic, relief-driven hysterical laughter fueled by cheap tequila. *Tears rolled down my cheeks and my breath came in gasping chokes between churning fits of uncontrollable and unrestrained howls and yelps. When I finally regained my composure enough to sit up straight again, Don Carlitos was uncapping the bottles.*

No, I didn't drive until late the next afternoon. Don Carlitos sent me home with the cop who lived around the corner and I ended up sleeping on a much cleaner couch.

Life should be a lot easier for you because I'm guessing you're a bit more responsible than I am, so you've had your vehicle checked out and serviced prior to any long trip. If you do have mechanical problems on the way down most mechanics will be able to get you fixed up and on the way within a reasonable time. You may need to front some parts money, and it might take a day or two to get those parts, but regardless of how shabby the shop might look, the work will usually be up to standard.

In July 2002 I had work done on my 1996 Chevy V-8 truck at a very well equipped shop in Chapala. Here's how it broke out:

Replace serpentine pulley belt	280 *pesos*
Replace tension pulley	900 *pesos*
Replace gas filter	60 *pesos*
Flush radiator	30 *pesos*
Add coolant	110 *pesos*
Balance four tires	200 *pesos*
Align suspension	100 *pesos*
Lubrication	40 *pesos*
Align lights	50 *pesos*
Bleed brake lines	80 *pesos*
Complete tune-up w/ new parts	850 *pesos*
Labor	300 *pesos*
Total:	3,000 *pesos*

The days of on-the-spot parts manufacture by resourceful mechanics in dusty, ramshackle Mexican garages have pretty much gone the way of factory in-stalled Holley four-barrels. Most of these guys are good but as in all other aspects of life, modern auto engineering has almost made this practice obso-lete. That's why I told you to bring spare parts.

In September 2002, Teresa contracted repairs to her 1993 Chrysler Concord in a small Ajijic shop. The mechanic had to modify parts from another vehicle to repair the heater. This is her bill:

Replace radiator	1,600 *pesos*
Fabricate heater core	900 *pesos*
Replace brake linings - wheels	220 *pesos*
Turn 2 brake drums	60 *pesos*
Replace 6 spark plugs	100 *pesos*
Replace oil filter	98 *pesos*
Replace air filter	80 *pesos*
Add 5 liters oil	195 *pesos*
Replace fan belt	70 *pesos*
Replace battery and terminals	680 *pesos*
Labor (includes checking all systems)	900 *pesos*
Total:	4,895 pesos

Small Change and Gasoline

If this is your first SoB road trip, this little *regalo* can save you a lot of stress. If you hand a storekeeper or street merchant money and they wander off with no further word, don't panic. They've gone to find someone with change. Or, they're very casually stealing your money. Either way, don't panic.

And in Mexico, Chiclets are often small change. If you make a purchase that comes to, let's say, twenty *pesos* and you hand over a fifty you should receive thirty *pesos* in change. If there are only twenty-five *pesos* in the change box you'll get them, plus five *peso's* worth of packaged Chiclets. Do not refuse the proffered change. Do not growl, glower, giggle, grin, grimace, grunt, or gripe. Accept your "money", nod, smile and be on your way. For a long time each time they were offered up I thought the shopkeepers were presenting me with a *regalo* because I was such a fine fellow and a welcome addition to their wonderful country. Even the truth is cool down here, just not as charming as personal fantasy or self-delusion.

Anyway, keep as much small change and as many small bills on hand as you can manage. Offer to pay with a large bill, but if this is not possible drop to the next smaller, and work your way back down the ladder. Pull your cash out one bill at a time. If the shopkeeper sees that you have a pocket full of change, he may try to work the exact amount out of you regardless of how much change he may have.

You're going to need yours in case you break down in *El Desierto* and want to buy a semi-cool soda at the only *tienda* in the village, which may have a daily cash sales total of less than three hundred *pesos*. You'll discover the secret of cold fusion long before you pay for that soda with a two hundred *peso* note.

You can always spend your big bills at the PEMEX station when you gas up. I *strongly* suggest that you spend your big bills at the PEMEX when you gas up. I also strongly suggest that you buy a locking gas cap for your vehicle. In order to insure that it is actually serving its intended purpose you must personally twist it back on after each fill up. Many attendants don't twist gas caps all the way on, either from lack of knowledge or for some other more sinister and nefarious reason. Check it yourself. If you're too embarrassed to do it at the station just pull over a few miles down the road. You also need an anti-theft device that will attach to your brake pedal. Lots of folks use steering wheel locks, but they're easily foiled. Alarms are almost useless since everyone here is used to hearing them go off at all hours of the day and night. As Don Carlitos told me when he advised me to take the one off my Jeep, "You have insurance, don't you?"

PEMEX is modernizing and expanding at a remarkable rate in anticipation of the free-market assault of, and competition by, foreign fuel companies. Most service stations will have modern gas pumps which will re-set the register to zero when the nozzle is removed from its storage niche, so the old practice of not clearing the pump and overcharging for gas purchases is a thing of the past. However, short-changing is not.

Look at the pump before you pay. If the pump registers three hundred and twenty *pesos* and you hand over a five hundred note you should receive...let's see, six times four carry the nought, divide by 17.2... 180 *pesos* in change. Count the change while the attendant is there. You should have figured the correct change before you ever released your grip on the cash. If the amount is incorrect, bring it to the attendant's attention immediately. The problem will be corrected post haste, unless paranoia has grabbed you in a stranglehold and cut off enough blood flow to your brain to cause you to see larceny rampant in every transaction. The lack of blood has led you to leap to the erroneous conclusion that you've been cheated, when in fact his or her math skills are far better than yours. In that case, a ten *peso* tip and a heartfelt *lo siento* or *disculpe* would both be appropriate. And civilized. I usually tip a bit anyway—a couple of *pesos*—or more on the rare occasions that someone actually washes my windshield with a reasonably clean rag. Some guys have squirt bottles. Few have clean rags. There's a lot of heat and smoke generated over the issue of whether these guys should be tipped. If you think tipping a low-paid National twenty or thirty cents isn't appropriate, don't. But don't even think about speaking to me or coming over to sit at my table if you see me out somewhere. You deal with your good reputation and I'll try to protect what's left of mine.

A lot of these guys have highly developed special talents and skills. I'm sure that somewhere, high in the mountains of Mexico, or far out in the middle of the desert, PEMEX has a secret training facility that does nothing but instruct attendants on how to squeeze the last seven drops into an already dangerously full gas tank. Unless you specify an exact *peso* amount, you'll be treated to an exhibition of precision pumping literally intended to get every drop possible into your tank. When you say "*lleno,* (YAY no) *por favor*", full please, that's precisely what you'll get. You can attempt to stop them before the eighth or ninth time the gas gurgles back down the fill tube before they squeeze the handle again. You can also attempt to stop an avalanche midway down the mountain. Same result.

I've also pulled up and confidently said "*Hielo,* (YAY low) *por favor.*" Now the pump jockey knows I don't want a tank full of ice, so he just nods and fills the tank with *Magna*. Usually though he'll ask. "*Magna?*" *Si.*

Magna sin is regular unleaded. *Sin* means "without" or "none". Lead in this case. 87 octane. Pull up to the green pump. Premium is 93 octane. Pull up to the red pump. They're right there side by side. The diesel pump will be over out of the way somewhere. In some stations on the busier highways there will be many diesel pumps. You can also purchase octane boosters, fuel additives and injector cleaners, as well as oil, transmission fluid, and brake fluid. There's usually a sign above the locked cage on the fuel island where all these good-ies are stored. Sometimes the cage is empty. I suggest using the fuel additive about every third fill-up and injector cleaner every fifth or sixth. Don't plan on finding windshield washer fluid at a PEMEX station or many other places, ei-ther. A friend reported seeing some at Wal-Mart in Guadalajara for somewhere in the neighborhood of 60 *pesos* a gallon, which is about $6 US.

One thing you'll notice is that there are a rapidly increasing number of facilities with signs reading "*Carburacion*". These are places where you can buy LP gas to power your vehicle if you've had the fuel system converted. The price of fuel will be about half the cost of gasoline but I have no idea how efficient your fuel use becomes. Depending on where you are in Mexico the conversion can cost from around six-hundred to a thousand dollars US.

I'm not recommending this, just alerting you that LP gas is available here.

Road Snacks, MIB, and Young Soldiers

Let's say you're rolling along the autopista with a full tank, the CD player blar-ing and a cooler full of travel drinks. It's not essential that you carry a lot of stuff though, since there are approximately 78 million little roadside *tiendas*, Pemex stations, and cafes along most of the routes you're likely to be taking.

And, there will be OXXOs, the Mexican 7 Elevens, and in some places you'll find *real* NoB 7 Elevens. Stop and shop; they're all safe.

When I'm gonna be out for extended peri-ods, either for a border run or for cross-coun-try sightseeing, I do carry a cooler of cold stuff. Ice is in refrigerated boxes labeled *hielo* (YAY low). The boxes look just like the ones in front of the 7 Eleven back in Tulsa, except they read *hielo*. I also carry snack crackers, Vienna sausages, fried pork skins and shaving cheese--the stuff in a spray can. And chocolate, inside a ziploc bag in the cooler.

I'm always ready to share the contents of my cooler with the young guys holding the locked and loaded automatic rifles, along with their buddies manning the light machine

BANDIDO, WILLIAM GENTES, NO DATE

guns behind the sandbagged bunkers. They're not *bandidos*, just Mexican Army troops on standard training exercises. Those of you who have raised kids know you need to keep them busy to avoid problems with their behavior. Nice folks. They're not going to be a threat unless you insist on dressing for travel as a North Korean Navy Admiral, or Stallone as Rambo. Some things are better restricted to the privacy of the bedroom.

For some reason, these guys stop me frequently. I've never met one that spoke English. You're usually in pretty good shape if an officer is running the show because the young enlisted men in charge seem to be much more curious about what's in your bags. And your portable CD player. Especially your portable CD player. There will be many questions. About your portable CD player. They'll do a fine display for their *amigos.* Of your portable CD player. This is when I casually flip open the ice chest to retrieve a cold Coke.

That focuses attention on me and away from the portable CD player. It also gives me the opportunity to nod toward what is soon going to become an empty ice chest. It seems to be impossible to shake down or inconvenience someone who's just given you a cold beverage out in the hot middle of nowhere. So far, I've never lost a CD player, or a nice knife, or anything else. Only a few cases of sodas. And crackers. And two or three cans of shaving cheese.

However, I do *not* offer to share goodies with the MIB. The Men in Black. PJF. Federal Judicial Police. They're armed, dangerous and serious as a Hong Kong whore shortage. And very polite. Many of these guys speak English as well as you do. And trust me on this one guys, they've had some training. They tend to make me nervous. If they want a cold Coke they can take one. I try to stay silent and cooperative and non-threatening.

In 1876, Porfírio Diaz installed himself as dictator of Mexico. To solidify his position and to discourage dissent, he formed a national police force called the *Rurales*, who were recruited among the thugs and *bandidos* of the country. The main perks for this group were showy uniforms, good salaries, and the authority to shoot on sight, no questions asked. No reflection on the modernairres, just a brief history lesson.

He glanced back at me from the driver's side of the station wagon in front of me that he'd just signaled to stop. Evidently, I looked a lot more suspicious. He slapped the roof of the dented, smoke-belching wagon and as it rolled away, he motioned for me to pull off the road and onto a large graveled area.

Another one was standing about thirty feet from the roadbed and he signaled for me to drive to him. I did. Slowly. With both hands in full sight on the top of the steering wheel. I'd shifted into low when I slowed and stopped on the highway and I had no intention of reaching down to shift or do anything else at that point. In my peripheral vision, I was aware of the first MIB walking along beside me from the road. Black fatigue pants bloused over black paratrooper boots. Black T-shirt stretched tight over a fit torso. Black mirrored shades beneath a black baseball cap. And, a blue steel 9mm semi-automatic in a black nylon holster strapped around his waist and secured to his thigh by another strap. Deep South County Sheriff meets Military Special Ops.

'Buenas tardes."

I nodded in reply. A quick question in Spanish. I silently looked at him. This was no time to create a problem for myself with a wrong answer to a misunderstood question. In English, "Do you speak Spanish?". I shook my head.

"Would you turn off the ignition and get out of the car?" Don't expect any jokes here because this was not a humorous situation. I was somewhere just north of Aguascalientes, headed for Texas. Hot, tired, needing a shower, a shave and a haircut, and driving a high-clearance, big-wheeled dark blue Jeep with blackout windows and no chrome. I'd have stopped me if I'd been looking for potential arrest material. I have no idea why they were in that particular location and I didn't ask.

Of course, I was very happy to comply with the request. I stepped down from the Jeep and walked about 15 feet away from it. MIB numero dos kept an eye on me while numero uno leaned in and looked around. He then walked to the back and raised the hatch and opened the tailgate. After poking at a black bag or two, he motioned me closer. As I approached, he asked "May we put the dog in the car?" I nodded and motioned to the open door with an empty handed wave.

He turned and gestured to the dog handler standing nearby to bring over the huge drooling German Shepherd that was straining at a short leash. He was up onto the driver's seat for a quick sniff and then back out. Then around to the back, with a big hop into the cargo box. He gave a cursory sniff or two, and jumped out.

Uno was to my right, dos to my left and neither took their eyes off me while the dog was working. As soon as the animal was released, Uno spoke. "Thank you. Have a good trip."

I again nodded and got back into the Jeep, started it up, and pulled slowly away with four shaded eyes on me for a loooong way.

When a lady friend of mine was stopped by the MIB they instructed her to stand close by and observe them to insure that they didn't plant anything in her vehicle. Whatever the drill, you should *always* be cooperative.

Let me enter one more observation into the record. On an average day of highway and small town travel you'll probably see more weapons here than you'd ever expect to find anywhere outside the gates of Fort Benning or maybe downtown Jerusalem. Cops, bank guards, private security guards, military. It seems as though everybody is packin'. Except you. Now, contrary to dozens of wild stories I've heard and read, I have seldom had a weapon pointed at me, either on purpose, or due to someone mishandling one. In Mexico, I mean. Texas barrooms and hostile foreign countries fall into categories all their own. The times I *have* had a weapon pointed at me were when I drove up to one of the military checkpoints. They sometimes place a light machine gun in a sand-bagged position in order to set a field of fire encompassing the highway. You'll definitely be in their sights, but you won't be threatened. I've never observed anyone who was carrying a weapon handle it in an unsafe or threatening manner.

Most of the *"and then he pointed it at my head"* stories seem to be barroom BS manufactured and distributed by the members of the elite *Gringo* Goober Group. Some OMHs might have a believable story left over from the old days, but things are a lot less Wild Westy now. Except in certain areas along the coast from Mazatlan to the border, and a couple of areas in the nearby mountains. Don't go there unless you're prepared for adventure. *And* a couple of places farther South that we're not considering in this book.

Yes, it is disconcerting to see or be stopped by young men in flak jackets with automatic weapons or shotguns. Yes, it may be a bit nerve-wracking to have to walk past a weapon-totin' guard at the bank or *casa de cambio,* jewelry store, or even some of the travel agencies. You'll get used to it.

There's another group to be aware of. In random locations, especially near tourist areas, folks dressed in regular civilian attire may flag you down on the highway. Male and female folks. Males usually in accepted male fashion, females in accepted female fashion. This is not a requirement as far as I know, but it usually works out that way. They'll normally have a white pick-up parked perpendicular to the roadbed. On the door of the truck will be four letters. Two lines. SH above CP. Surrounded by a blackline square. *Aduana* again, the ones who really make me nervous. Customs. Dangerous as a hedgehog in your gym shorts. These are the folks who have legal authority to seize your vehicle and all of its contents, including you. Do not mess with these folks in any way, shape, form or fashion.

The first time they stopped me was near Bucerias. Your worst stereotypical nightmare approached the Jeep. I had the top off and several passengers aboard, headed for class near PV.

The guy was about five ten with three hundred pounds of excess gut barely restrained by a tautly stretched shirt and low-slung pair of trousers. He glanced at the sticker on the windshield and brusquely demanded my papers. I handed over a copy of my passport and my tourist card. No. He wanted the papers for the vehicle. I attempted to explain that the papers were in my apartment because I had the top off the Jeep and didn't leave anything in it.

No esta bien. He ordered me out of the Jeep but immediately an older man approached and waved me back. I settled back into the seat as the older guy spoke to me in broken English. *El Gordo* stared, scowled, snorted, and pouted behind him. That's when I learned about the necessity of understanding the rules. You are required by Mexican law to carry your vehicle importation papers in the vehicle. Make copies now. No, the import sticker is not sufficient proof that you own the vehicle you're wheelin' down the road.

I was released with instructions to carry my papers in the future. I immediately drove the few blocks home to get them. That's the only near-negative experience I've had with the *Aduana* even though I've been stopped several times. Now my papers are in order.

Pit Stops

We'd stopped at a big roadside *restaurante* somewhere near Copala for lunch. I asked for the *baño* and was directed to a small building out back. Two openings faced me, each doorway covered by a plastic shower curtain. I pushed one aside and saw two commodes divided for privacy by another shower curtain. I did my business, tried to flush and discovered that there was no water in the tank. Oh well.

As I stepped out, I noticed a small bucket sitting on the walk. I bent down to rinse my hands and started back into the restaurant. That's when I noticed folks washing their hands at the sink attached to the rear wall of the restaurant.

I didn't need to because I'd just freshened up in the bucket of flushing water. I should have poured it into the stool.

Pit Stop Particulars

Most places in Mexico have signs in restrooms asking you not to throw paper into the commode. At one B&B on the coast, a sign read "If it didn't pass through your stomach, it doesn't belong in this commode."

One evening I was sitting in an open-air Jacuzzi high above the Pacific with a gorgeous German lady who looked at me with sparkling bright blue eyes and tenderly announced, "We don't have honey wagons in Mexico." Is this a clue as to why I say my romantic life has turned to crap?

She was partially correct though. They're available in the cities and larger towns, but not in many of the villages. And not where bright-eyes and I lived. Mexico has septic tanks, but few honey wagons. It's the Roach Motel school of waste management. The poop checks in but it never checks out.

At any rate, don't throw paper into the commode after you've used it unless there's some indication that you should do so. Like the absence of a trash container in the stall you're sitting in.

And when you go into the bathroom, unless it's your own, at a friend's house, or at a hotel or B&B, be sure to carry your own paper. If you're on the *plaza*, or in the market, or the bus station, or anywhere you have to pay a fee to pee, the attendant will hand you two or three sections of toilet paper when you pay. I mean the little squares. The-sections-between-the-perforations. Lots of folks carry small packs of Kleenex. Or stenographer's notebooks. Or dictionaries. Just don't sit down until you have a supply of paper of some kind in your hand. Some places will have lots of paper. On BIG rollers. Unfortunately, you're usually not sitting in one of them.

Now gird your loins girls, this has to be done. I know it's your first time and I'll try to be gentle. Here's how you manage.

Do the deed then take your paper and tear off a strip long enough to double over. Those three sections the attendant gave you won't help at all right now. Use it and then neatly fold the paper to cover what's inside. Pray that your selected paper is very absorbent. Deposit the tidy little package into the trash can. And before you leave, make sure you wash your hands. With soap. *Jabon*. Twice.

Now at home, in your personal bathroom, you'll want a can with a lid. A can that's just the perfect size to hold one of the plastic bags you've been saving from the grocery store. Change bags every day or wait until the cat faints as he tries to race past the bathroom door. Your house, your choice. I've discovered that leaving the same bag in there for extended periods actually helps keep the bathroom clean. After a few days, you can't force your visitors in there at gunpoint. But now let's get back out in the fresh air.

All About Road Signs

If you want to see what some of the more common road signs in Mexico look like, go to *http://micasa.yupi.com/jet_liera/VIAL.htm*. This site may get you a bit more acclimated to the small differences you're going to find. If you ordered the *Guia Roji* map collection the signs will be shown there too. Anyway, as we're wheeling along reading road signs in a foreign language, eventually even the most dense among us may begin to wonder if things would be safer and easier if we could actually understand what the signs were announcing. Probably. Here are rough translations of a few of the more common signs. These are in alphabetical order.

Aduana	Customs
Aeropuerto	Airport
Aeropista	Secondary Airport (Local, not international)
Alto	Stop-also means "high,"
Altura Libre	Vertical Clearance (Height)
Anchura Libre	Horizontal Clearance (Width)
Auxilio Turistico	Tourist Aid or Assistance
Avenida	Avenue or Boulevard
Baje Su Velocidad	Lower Your Speed (Seldom Seen)
Bajada Pronunciada	Steep Hill
Basura	Trash
Brecha	Unimproved
Calle	Street
Camino	Highway
Camino Derrapante	Slippery Road
Camino Dividido	Divided Highway
Camino Sinuoso	Winding Road
Campo Militar	Military Base
Campamento	Trailer Park Campground
Carreterra	Highway
Ceda El Paso	Yield Right Of Way
Cerrajero o Cerrajeria	Locksmith or Lock and Key Shop
Ciclistas	Bicyclists
Circulacion (with an arrow)	Keep Right
Conceda Cambio De Luces	Dim Your Lights When Signaled By An Approaching Car
Con Raya Continua No Rebase	Do Not Pass Where There is a Solid Stripe
Conserve Su Derecha	Keep Right
Continua	Continuous Turn - Right Turn on Red
Continua Con Precaucion	Right Turn on Red

Cruce De Caminos	Crossroads
Cruce De Ferrocarril	Railroad Crossing
Cuota	Toll Road
Curva	Curve
Curva Peligrosa	Dangerous Curve
Deposito De Basura	Deposit Trash Here
Derecha	Right
Derecho	Straight ahead
Despacio	Slow
Desviacion	Detour
Disminuya Su Velocidad	Reduce your Velocity - Slow Down
Doble Circulacion	Two Way Traffic
Empieza Camellon	Median Divider Begins
Entrada	Entrance
Entrada y Salida los Camiones	Entrance & Exit for Trucks and Buses
Entronque	Junction - There are several types
Estacion	Station
Estacion de Autobusses	Bus Station
Estacionamiento	Parking
Estrechamiento A Un Lado	Road Narrows on One Side
Estrechamiento Del Camino	Road Narrows
Ganado	Cattle, livestock
Gasolineria o gasolinera	Gas Station (PEMEX)
Gaseria	Natural Gas, LP Gas, Butane
Glorieta	Traffic Circle
Grava Suelta	Loose Gravel
Grua	Tow Truck
Hombres Trabajandro	Men Working
Informacion Sobre Carreteras	Information About the Highways
Inspeccion	Inspection
Inspeccion de Ganado	Cattle Inspection Station
Inspeccion de Zoosanitaria	Animal/Bird Inspection Station

Izquierda	Left
Lago	Lake
Laguna	Lagoon
Libre	Free, No Toll
Llantera	Tire Shop, Tire Repair
Luz	Light
Maquina	Machine
Modulo de Suguridad	Security Office
Mofles y Escapes	Mufflers and Tailpipes
No Deje Piedras Sobre El Pavimiento	Don't Leave Rocks On the Highway
No Hay Paso	Road Closed
No Doble Fila	No Stopping
No Prenda Fuego En El Pavimento	Don't Build a Fire on the Pavement
No Rebase	No Passing
No Tire Basura	Don't Throw Trash (Don't Litter)
No Use El Claxon	Don't Honk Your Horn
Paradas Continuas	Frequent Stops (You'll see this on buses)
Peatones	Pedestrians
Peligrosa	Dangerous
Playa	Beach
Poblado Proximo	Town Near (You're nearing a town)
Posada	Hotel
Presa	Dam, Ditch, Trench
Prohibido Vuelta en U	No U Turn
Prohibido Estacionarse	No Parking
Prohibido Seguir De Frente	Do Not Enter
Prohibido Vuelta A La Derecha	No Right Turn
Prohibido Vuelta A La Izquierda	No Left Turn
Proximo	Near or Approaching or Next
Proyecto	Under Construction

Puente	Bridge
Puente Angosto	Narrow Bridge
Puente De Cuota	Toll Bridge
Puente Movil	Drawbridge or Moveable Bridge
Radar En Operacion	The Cops Have Radar Guns
Refraccionaria	Parts Store
Muelles	Springs
Retorno	Turnaround on a Divided Road
Rio	River
Salida	Exit
Semaforo	Traffic Signal Light
Servicio De Grua	Tow Truck Service
Solo	One or Only
Solo Izquierda	Left Turn Only
Superficie Irregular	Bump or Bumpy road
Suspensiones Para Automoviles	Auto Suspension
Taller Autoelectrico	Auto Electrical Shop
Taller Mecanico	Mechanic Shop
Taller Soldadura	Welding Shop
Telefono	Telephone
Termina	End
Termina Pavimento	Pavement Ends
Terraceria	Dirt Road
Tope	Speed Bump
Transbordador	Ferry
Un Solo Carril	One Lane
Vado	Dip, and can also indicate an area prone to flooding
Velocidad	Speed
Velocidad de Salida	Exit Speed
Vibradores	Small Speed Bumps
Vuelta	Turn

Zona de Acampar	Camping Area
Zona de Derrumbes	Rockslide or Landslide Area
Zona Escolar	School Zone
Zona de Tolvaneras	Dust Storm Area

A quick word about bridges in Mexico. They all have names. Even the ones that don't have names will have a sign saying *Puente Sin Nombre*, Bridge With No Name. I'm telling you this to reduce your level of confusion as to what type of bridge it might be. Just a plain old bridge. With a name. Or without. Unless of course, it's a *puente movil.*

Passing

Even though knowing what all those signs say does take some of the fun out of driving, there are still plenty of adventures waiting. Simple things like passing, for example. Normally if you want to pass someone you just wheel out and floorboard it. Not here. Many of the roads are so curvy that you often have to wait for a signal from the driver ahead, usually a wave to encourage you to come on, but sometimes a flash of the turn indicators. A flashing left signal means you can come on around in comparative safety. Maybe. Sometimes you'll get two or three at once.

The funniest commentary on this practice I've ever read was written by Harriet Doerr in *Stones For Ibarra.* After you've read the book, Chuy Santos' taxi will always be on your mind as you drive through Mexico. Anyway, pass at your own risk. At night I've signaled that I was going to make a left turn only to have someone misunderstand and try to pass as I began my maneuver. Use a hand signal as often as you can, and you'll be a lot safer.

As long as we're on left turns you need to know that while "a kiss is still a kiss" a left turn in Mexico is much more than just a left turn. Pay attention here, unless you really enjoy causing auto collisions. There may also be a question about this on your driver's license test. The answer is "Pull to the right before making a left turn." Huh?

There are a number of ways to make a left turn in Mexico. Most of them involve making a right turn first. Here's how it goes. If you're driving down a two lane highway and want to turn left and, if there is traffic coming to meet you, pull to the right shoulder of the road. There's usually a wide spot built for this maneuver. After the meeting and following traffic clears, make your left turn from the far right shoulder.

If you're driving in town and there's enough room on the street, follow the same procedure. Unless... If you're driving on a nice four-lane divided street and need to turn left, look to the right. There should be a one-way road running parallel to the one you're on. Pull over onto it. Be careful! (Some are marked by a *Ceda el paso* sign that means merge after the traffic clears.) Many drivers believe that the speed limit on these side roads is somewhere in the mid triple-digit range. They also apparently believe that it is illegal to use their brakes on that road. The folks who have already taken possession have the right of way and protect it much better than Lincoln's bodyguards.

If you manage to safely get onto this side road, you'll eventually come to a cluster of traffic lights. The signal you'll be most interested in is the one far-thest right. It'll be set up this way.

- Red lens on top or to the left
- Yellow lens below or to the right of red
- Green lens below that or to the right of yellow
- Green arrow on the bottom or to the far right
- A sign displaying a curved arrow and the words "*Con Flecha*".

Most of the time.

The green sometimes starts flashing (three times) and then turns to yellow, then red. Red usually gets the opposing drivers to stop. At this point, you'll get to make a decision. You have two choices. If you managed to get to the left side of the lane you're in, you can turn left when the green arrow comes on. The green light means you can proceed straight ahead ONLY!

Let me repeat. DO NOT attempt a left turn until the green arrow signals you to do so. It's illegal and dangerous. Obviously this does not apply in the instances where the signal light, *semáforo*, has only three lenses.

Now it's time for another decision. If you want to drive back the way you just came, you'll need to turn back onto the road as soon as you pass the first divider. If you want to pull into the parking lot of one of those stores, or the hotel on the far side of the road you'll need to drive on across the main road and turn left onto the parallel road on the far side. The opposite match of the one you just left. Easy when you learn how.

As you're cruisin' down one of the *cuotas* you may suddenly remember that you left your wallet on the counter of that OXXO back in León. *No problema.* Look for a sign on the side of the road reading *Retorno*. Then ease into the left lane and when you see an extra traffic lane to the left, pull into it. It will allow you to U-turn and head back the way you just came. Yes, you'll have to pay the toll again. Both ways.

Another type of left turn involves turning right onto a long sweeping curve that will lead you back to a position perpendicular to the highway you just turned off. Stop, look, listen, and proceed straight on when it's safe to do so. It'll make sense when you see it.

Earlier I said "most" of your left turns involve turning right first. One that doesn't occurs when you're driving down a divided boulevard. When you come to a break in the center divider, just turn left. Up North you're used to swinging wide to the right to maintain the standard traffic flow, but down here you'll hug hard to your left. Unless…you see that the lanes of the divider are marked and indicate that you should keep to the right. It's always one contradiction or another, isn't it?

One more quick tip. If it's broad daylight and someone flashes his lights on and off, or if it's dark and you get a similar signal, slow down and pay very close attention. There's some sort of situation ahead of you. Be prepared for anything. If this happens as you approach a narrow bridge, stop. The other guy just told you he's comin' on.

And a lot of folks caution against driving at night. Actually, nobody in their right mind would even want to consider this. Usually it's just me and the truckers flying through the dark, although you'll usually find a pretty active level of traffic on the *autopistas* connecting the major cities.

Nighttime Road Hazards

In some areas away from the *cuotas*, the highways will have two major characteristics. They're narrow, and they're a treasure trove of potholes and washouts. Like regular nightmares or bed-wetting, either one can cause you great nocturnal distress. Drop a tire off the edge of one of those washouts and kiss the Volvo *adios*. Smack one of the holes at anything exceeding a crawl and kiss a tire or the suspension *adios*.

Another nighttime driving hazard is reflectors, like the ones truckers should put out when they break down. About 37 drivers in Mexico have a set. Do you? So what do they do to keep you from crashing into a stalled vehicle if they break down on the highway? They carefully and artistically place rocks on the road to alert you to danger. There are no warning signs indicating that there are rocks on the roadbed. *Adios* oilpan. Or transaxle case. Or Volvo, as you madly swerve to avoid the rocks and slam into the front of the Dodge pickup cruising along towards you without lights so the driver can save the battery and the bulbs.

I know some of you are still dealing with the trauma over Santa Claus and the Easter Bunny, and I hate to add to your disillusion, but regardless of what Mom told you, there really are things in the dark that will hurt you. Especially on Mexican highways. And other war zones. That's why I have huge spotlights mounted on the grille guard on the truck. When I flip those babies on I can see for ten or twelve miles down the road at night. I usually pick up some interesting sights.

Like the large animals who wander onto the roadbed. That's one reason why folks advise against nocturnal traveling. I've never felt particularly stressed about it having grown up in rural Texas, but it can be dangerous. Those big critters can bring you from sixty to zero in nothing flat if you broadside one.

If you are ever unfortunate enough to have this happen, and your vehicle is still drivable, do not hesitate to drive it. Fast and far. You'll probably be either dead or badly injured, though. Get away from the area and the animal if you can, even though by Mexican law the owner of the animal is at fault, and liable for damages. Good luck finding him. I've never hit an animal but one day I smacked a buzzard as he was gettin' airborne up by Saltillo. He hit the window post on the passenger side of the Wrangler but didn't do any damage. At least not to the Jeep.

Other Hazards

Almost as bad as whackin' a bird is getting caught behind a slow moving truck in the mountains. One hauling large hogs to market. I've been around hogs for years so don't try to tell me all that nonsense about how clean they are. They stink. And the ones on the way to market are really pissed off. It's prudent to know they've got nothing to lose, hatred in their hearts, and possess full bowels and bladders. Trust me on this one. Do not get close to the back of that truck. Yes, I've seen the commercial for the Ronald McDonald Circus that shows all the cute pigs doing their tricks. I've even seen "Babe". I'm not inferring that pigs are stupid, I'm just telling you not to get too close to those that are on the way to the slaughterhouse.

And speaking of getting close, this is the ideal time to talk about Mexican flagmen. At the edges of road construction sites, seemingly placed about fifty miles apart, these *muchachos* can make your *viaje* a riot.

These guys used to be fairly dangerous to deal with because they had no means of communicating with each other. They are *now* dangerous to deal with because they *do* have means of communicating with each other.

Let me explain. You see the signs warning you about construction ahead so you slow down. As you approach the actual work site, you see a flagman. It's time to be alert and mentally prepared so you can collect data, process it, and determine its meaning while you plan a course of action. You may see some fairly standard signals in addition to a creative display of the flagman's individuality.

First, if he's just holding the flag straight out so that you can see the entire thing, that means stop. Usually. It could also mean he's overwhelmed by too much responsibility and his entire central nervous system just headed South. Play it by ear.

If he's waving the flag around his head or shoulders, it may mean you should proceed. It may also mean he's being attacked by killer bees on their way to terrorize St. Louis. Or, that he has the earphone of his Walkman plugged in and is jivin' on. Play it by ear.

Occasionally you'll see him standing there with the flag between his knees, his head bowed, and hands clutched before him as if in prayer. This means that he's not yet gained full walkie-talkie proficiency and believes that the handset will function only if he's staring at it. It's always fun to keep creeping forward to see what happens.

He'll probably panic and start patting the air in front of his waist. That means slow down. Or stop. It gets even more interesting if the flagman on the other end starts asking questions or giving instructions. Some of the expressions will stay in your memory forever.

Sometimes he'll forget that he has a flag and he'll revert to hand signals. It may look as though he's shooing you away, but he really means for you to come on. I'm sure that extensive psychological studies have been undertaken in an attempt to explain this display.

I've also seen them stand relaxed and unconcerned as traffic flew by. On both sides of the border. It's pretty much all a gamble so keep your wits about you.

Some drivers actually survive these encounters. A few of us really enjoy them.

Accidents

In 1995 in Mexico, the leading cause of death among people 15 to 64 was accidents. Forty percent of those accidents were related to motor vehicles. Be careful on those roads!

One morning in San Luis Potosí I ran into a peddler. Even though I was fully focused on the task and driving responsibly, I was blinded by the sun. Never mind that my son Matthew's version was that I was jabberin' to beat sixty and had no idea where I was.

Piedras por Pancho, William Gentes, 1990

Fortunately, the Jeep had a high bumper. I was going slow and could respond to Matt's shouted warning. Not quickly enough to avoid hitting the peddler, but enough to prevent a real disaster. What do you do in a situation like that?

What I did was sit him down on the sidewalk. I told Matt to get the old fellow a Coke or cigarette or whatever, and keep him sitting away from other people until I returned. Then I walked up the street to an ATM and withdrew money.

When I got back and after we determined that he had no injuries, I paid him several days wages, put him in a cab, sent him home, and cleared out of the area. That was the right thing to do.

Cops are not required at the scene of an accident unless there's death or blood. Neither occurred in this case. It's both legal and encouraged to work out a mutually satisfactory agreement between the parties involved. You should avoid police intervention as much as you would exposure to anthrax. Why? You're a foreigner (read: you have money) who is probably not fluent in the language, nor acquainted with anyone in town who will be able to assist you. Chances are there may be some doubt as to actual liability. At the first opportunity you should get out of the area and back onto the road. It's not illegal in all cases, and it can be smart. Yes, Virginia, there are adjusters. Use them only when you have no other option. There's a wonderful book put out by the University of Texas Press written by Bob Burleson and DavidH. Riskind. It' s called *Backcountry Mexico--A Traveler's Guide and Phrase Book.* These guys have the same attitude about haulin' ass as I do.

The preceding has been my personal opinion but here's the official scoop, direct from the *H. Ayuntamiento Constitutionál de Colima, Dirección General de Tránsito y Vialidad.* That's the State Department of Colima, General Department of Transit. In case any of you believe that I've actually translated any of these brochures and booklets, please let me set you straight. Most of the translation was by the lovely and talented Veronica Martinez of Roma Property Management in Ajijic, Jalisco. Since Spanish and English do not translate word for word, what you're reading is my interpretation of her translations.

Here's what the State of Colima says to do if you have a motor vehicle accident (MVA). The items in parentheses are my comments, not theirs.

- Other than your company adjuster, avoid using an intermediary when dealing with the General Department of Transit. (You may need to find an interpreter but restrict your comments to supplying basic ID info and avoid any discussion of the incident until your adjuster arrives. This is based on my years of experience as a licensed adjuster in Texas.)

- Avoid moving your vehicle until the police have been notified and they have noted the circumstances and damages, regardless of how great or small. (This will be contradicted in just a few lines. If you do move your vehicle you should take photos from different angles and locations beforehand. If skid marks are visible, shoot them too.)

🐾 Remain calm and show copies of your insurance and registration papers to the police officer. (He or she will also want to see your FM-T or FM-3. Do you remember that I advised you to make copies of all your official papers? You should also have a copy of your insurance papers to give to the authorities. In other words, make copies of everydamn piece of paper you have that concerns your stay in Mexico, and keep the copies some place different from the originals.)

🐾 If you and the other driver reach agreement as to fault and the amount of damage done, and if nobody has been injured, you may settle up and go on about your business. But if your car is not driveable a wrecker must be called. (Keep in mind that many drivers will not have insurance, just like many drivers NoB.)

🐾 If you and the other driver can't reach an agreement, you must contact the police to investigate and assign fault. If the decision of the police officer is not acceptable to you, you have the option of going before a judge. (I'll tell you how to deal with this in just a minute.)

🐾 If there were personal injuries as a result of the MVA, the case will be sent to Public Court where the matter of fault will be decided as well as the legal standing of all the parties involved. Each driver may also be required to undergo a physical examination.

🐾 If you are responsible for damage to municipal or state property, your vehicle may be impounded until you pay for damages and present a release letter from the affected institution. If you damage federal property you must deal with the Major Department of Transit.

🐾 If either driver involved in the MVA is found to be drunk or under the influence of any other drugs, the case goes directly to the Public Court for adjudication.

🐾 In any MVA, the officer on the scene should make note of the actions taken, and if a settlement was reached.

🐾 If you are involved in an MVA, your insurance company can intervene on your behalf. (You should carry in your purse or wallet a card with a toll-free phone number to call to report your dilemma. Wait for the adjuster to arrive before negotiating your way out of any situation. It may take awhile and on rare occasions, you may find yourself in a cell overnight. Don't panic, I've been locked up more than once and lived to tell about it. Not SoB, but if you have money they'll get you food, and that bedding probably isn't as dirty as it looks. When you're dealing with the authorities and your linguistic proficiency is almost nil, silence really is golden. If you have to, get someone to call your insurance company every thirty minutes or so. Some of the local adjusters may have other jobs and you'll need to wait until they can be reached. DO NOT just leave a message with someone and hope for the best. If all else fails, call the nearest consular office or official.)

One more thing. The Mexican court system has so far remained uncontaminated by the presence of U.S.-style plaintiff's attorneys. Your insurance coverage need not reach the seven-digit range to provide adequate protection for you, and fair compensation to anyone who might be injured or lose property due to your negligence or bad fortune.

If you're interested in a re-cap of your legal rights following an auto accident in Mexico, check out *http://www.drivemex.com/Your_Legal_Rights.htm*.

Even if the worst occurs, as long as you're not physically injured or killed, insurance will usually be enough to take care of any disastrous situation.

Who Can and Who Cannot Drive Your Vehicle

Here's a brief list of those people who may legally drive your car in Mexico: your spouse, your children or other descendants who are licensed, your parents, your siblings, or a Mexican or another *gringo* if you're in the car with them. You can't loan your vehicle to another *gringo* unless they have the same immigration status. If you do, and they're stopped or if they're involved in an MVA, your vehicle can be taken from you and you can be fined. The folks named above will need to be able to prove their relationship to you, or be able to prove their immigration status. My insurer assured me that any legally licensed driver with an FM-3 or FM-2 would be covered while driving my vehicle in Mexico.

In the event that you require repairs, the employees or owner of the repair shop may drive the vehicle without you being aboard as long as they are testing the repairs and if they can prove that the vehicle legally entered Mexico. The shop must be registered with the tax authorities, the mechanics must be able to show that they've been legally and properly retained to perform the repairs, and that the test drive is being done on a normal working day during normal working hours. In certain places, in certain shops, that means 24/7/365.

Aside from those folks, you may not legally loan your vehicle to a Mexican citizen to drive, but again, any licensed driver can legally drive your vehicle if you're in the car with them.

People You *Wish* Wouldn't Drive Their Vehicles

Many of the auto related aggravations you'll have to deal with involve the new breed, the teens with toys. Kinda like back where you came from. You're wheelin' across the desert floor at a sane and sedate sixty or seventy when you glance into the rearview mirror and see what must be the highway patrol rollin' up on you at about a hundred and eighty-five miles an hour. As he draws closer, you see it's a red Corvette. With a dwarf at the wheel. As he tears past, you see that it appears to be a ten year old boy, eating an ice cream with one hand, stroking his passenger with the other, and steering with God-knows-what. Disconcerting. You spend the rest of the day in morbid anticipation of topping a hill and seeing car and body parts strewn over half the state you're trying to get through.

But these kids are true amateurs compared with the terror-inducing behaviors of Mexican bus drivers. On one trip along the Devil's Backbone on the road between Durango and Mazatlan I decided the best trauma defense was sleep. My traveling companion reported later that many of our fellow passengers spent portions of the trip heaving up breakfast and lunch.

This guy's cousin, and I'm basing this assumed relationship solely on the identical lack of driving skill, put me through a fairly sickening travel experience on the ride from Colima to Manzanillo. That's a fairly straight route compared to many, but he managed to find curves never imagined by the road designers and builders, as well as potholes and washouts never put there by the forces of Nature. And for some reason he thought he should jerk the bus from lane to lane every seven hundred yards, accompanying each lurch with a lead-footed tromp on the brake pedal.

One night I was sitting just a few seats back from a driver who was chatting away with an apprentice and almost missed a curve high in the mountains. Conversation continued to flow as he wrestled the speeding bus off the dirt shoulder and back onto the road and through the turn. I nearly wept.

Recently some cities and municipalities have been running random drug tests on public bus drivers. Several have been fired or suspended and laws have been changed to enforce criminal consequences for dangerous bus drivers. In 1999, the Mexico State Congress ratified Article 61 that legally redefined a driver's responsibility and liability in the event of death caused by his or her negligence behind the wheel. Before that time, if a driver ran over someone and killed him the charge was accidental homicide. Now the charge is first-degree murder and carries a punishment of five to fifteen years in prison without the possibility of parole.

Regardless of any existing law, here's my advice about buses. Start hittin' every church service you can right now, because if one of these guys comes cruisin' up behind you on the downhill side of a mountain, you'll definitely want Jesus or Mohammed to recognize your voice as you scream for help and mercy. Jesus Saves.

RVs and Converted School Buses

Now we're gonna get into the area that I know the least about, but had the most fun researching--RVs. Land yachts. And school buses. Cool stuff. One of the big advantages to considering this option is that you can just drive your house down to Mexico instead of having to hunt for housing. Lots of folks turn to it for permanent as well as temporary situations. If you know anything about RV life, this might be an option for checking out the country. Hell, even if you don't, you can learn.

Someone who does know something about both RVs *and* Mexico is David Eidell. If you go to *http://rversonline.org/RV4Mex.html* you'll find a mini series of articles he's written about his RVing experiences in this country. At *http://www.mexonline.com/amigonews/june/01june.htm* you'll find his article, "First Aid Tips & Suggestions". Check it out too. I'm going to be presumptuous enough to add one thing to his tip on removing a fish bone stuck in the throat. David recommends using a small chunk of banana to help swallow the bone. If a banana isn't handy, you can get the same result with a wad of bread. Tear the soft center out of a *bolillo* or wad up a piece of white bread.

To his information about scorpion stings, I'd like to add that you can treat your animals with Benadryl, too. Adjust the oral dosage to match the size and weight of the animal, and don't worry about spraying too much on the affected area. In one single weekend an acquaintance of mine lost two hounds, one stung on the nose by a scorpion, and one to a hungry 'gator who snatched him when he went to the lagoon for a drink.

You'll find a lot of helpful information in a book written by an adventurous Canadian couple. JohnandLiz Plaxton wrote *RVing in Mexico, Central America, and Panama* which can be ordered at *http://www.ogopogo.com/rving/index.html#Welcome*.

At *http://www.sunseekerpub.com* you'll find another book that will be very be useful. Information about ordering *Mexico by RV* can also be found by e-mailing *info@sunseekerpub.com* or by calling or faxing your order to 866-743-9624. Kathy Olivas did a fantastic job on this book and I believe you'll enjoy reading it.

Traveler's Guide to Mexican Camping by MikeandT erri Church is subtitled "Explore Mexico and Belize With Your RV or Tent". The book is published by

Rolling Homes Press in Livingston, Texas and you can contact them at *http://www.rollinghomes.com*. Besides giving you a great guide to many campgrounds and places to visit, they include a good section on border crossings that spells out how to find them, what the facilities are like, and what the routes are like heading south.

Check out *http://www.sanbachs.net.cgi-bin/mexico/mexicot.cgi* for a list of RV parks in Mexico from Acapulco to Zihuatenejo.

Yadda,yadda,yadda. Here's the fun part guys, school bus conversions!

If you can't afford to buy a nice, or even not-so-nice, professionally constructed RV, you may want to break out the toolbox and power toys on a used bus. Ready?

First, run through these websites to see some of the things that are available to you: *http://www.orisus.com/sbc* or *http://www.rv-busconversions.com*. You can also look at *http://www.iv-busconversions.com* to find out how to buy a book on bus conversions.

At *http://www.bobsokol.com/bus.html* you'll find out how to order Bob Sokol's *How to Convert a School Bus to a Motorhome*. Go to *http://www.busconversions.com* or call 714-799-0062, fax 714-799-0042 to order Bus Conversions Magazine. Is this great stuff, or what? Now that you've actually gone crazy enough to build a rollin' home you're gonna need to insure it. Miller Insurance Agency, Inc. advertises that they'll help you out. Go to *http://www.millerrvinsurance.com*, call 800-622-6347, or fax 503-699-9348. They say they'll let you pay by Visa, MC, or debit card. You can also try the bunch I've mentioned before, International Insurance Group, Inc. of Flagstaff, AZ. Contact their RV division at *rvinsurancepro.com*. Call toll free at 888-467-4639, or call 928-214-9750. The fax is 928-213-8476. Mail can be sent to them at 1300 S. Milton, Suite 218 in Flagstaff, AZ 86001.

Other sites worth a visit are *http://www.rvadvice.com* and *http://www.hikercentral.com/rving*.

Take Time to Smell the *Cacti*
Do yourself one more favor. Take plenty of time driving down so you can stop to smell the cacti. Most folks make the trip to their new home as though their speedy arrival was of utmost concern to someone. It ain't. Relax, enjoy the scenery, take a side trip or two along the way. Have fun.

Long Distance Buses
Some of us, even though we own vehicles use the long distance buses for traveling around the country, although occasionally a routine trip *can* turn into a real adventure. The fares are reasonable and the first class and executive

class buses are very comfortable. Most have VCRs that show movies, are air-conditioned, and have restrooms and reclining seats with foot rests. Your fare even includes a light snack. As I mentioned earlier, I suggest sleeping as much as possible. Just stop by a terminal sometime and have a look at what's available.

The schedules are posted in military time, the 24-hour clock. Departure times will be listed like this: Mazatlan 13:30. That means the bus will leave the terminal headed out for Mazatlan at 1:30 in the afternoon. 12 noon plus an hour and a half equals 13 and 30. From midnight to noon the hours are preceded by a zero. 04:15 is 4:15 am. If you get confused just ask an old sailor. Wait, bad advice. Stay completely away from old sailors. And young sailors. Ask one of the friendly looking people sitting around the waiting room. You'll eventually find someone who speaks English.

Are the stories you've heard about riding a bus and sittin' next to an old lady totin' a bunch of squawkin', tied-together chickens and leadin' a pig on a string true? No. Yes. It all depends. If you're on one of the new first-class or better long distance runs, probably not. Once on a particularly harrowing trip across the Devil's Backbone from Durango to Mazatlan, I *did* sit across the aisle from an ancient *señora* who was traveling with a small bird in a ventilated box. The chirping bird didn't bother me at all but the gagging and vomiting of some of my fellow passengers did. Remember my advice about sleeping? This is the rare situation where being close to one of us old sailors is actually beneficial. We're used to those rough rides. Leaving the driving to someone else has its risks.

If you develop an overwhelming desire to ride a bus south from the border or if you want to travel around the country in relative comfort, you can find links to many of the bus companies at *http://www.mexconnect.com*. When the page opens, locate the box that reads "Site Search". Type in "bus schedules" and you'll be zipped onto a discussion thread where people have posted contact information.

An absolutely fantastic site has been put up by "Steve". If you look at *http://www.magic-bus.com* you'll find an explanation of the classes of buses, some humorous travel advice, tips for Canadian travelers, and links to the schedules of the larger Mexican bus lines.

A book, *Bus Across Mexico* is available at *http://www.geocities.com/busacrossmexico*. Lots of other good info too.

At *http://www.mexicolaw.com/Tourism.htm* you'll find an extremely complete and helpful guide to Mexican buses. This is the site of Attorney Vernon Penner and he's offered up a section written by Gabriel Alejandro Martinez Ramirez that gives you the scope of the bus system and links to bus websites. Mr. Penner can be reached at vpenner@mindspring.com.

Local Buses

The larger and more populated towns and cities normally have good local bus systems that run on a regular basis. They often shut down at nightfall or shortly thereafter, and in many places, you won't be able to catch a bus after 10:00 p.m. Cabs in cities operate twenty-four hours a day but they can get to be expensive if you depend solely upon them, even though the rates are low compared to those in the U.S., Canada and much of Europe. The buses will have a fixed rate, usually just a few *pesos*. For example, a ride from Chapala to Ajijic, a distance of about five or six miles will cost about 8 *pesos*. A ride from La Manzanilla to Melaque, a distance of about eleven or twelve miles costs 8 *pesos*.

Taxis

Warning! Anytime you contemplate taking a taxi ride in Mexico make sure that you negotiate the fare before you get in the cab, and make sure that you and the driver are clear that the fare is being given in *pesos* or U.S. dollars. I'm sorry, Canadians, you'll have to juggle three currencies. This is one of the times that a pad and pen come in handy.

Cruisin' the Streets

Drivin' around any one of these quaint little Mexican villages, or for that matter, old sections of the cities is a bit more complicated than you might imagine. These are old, old places. That means the village streets were in place before big old Detroit iron was ever thought of. Sure, you say, but there were wagons and surreys and horses crowding the streets then. Right, and horses and versions of those wagons and carts are still running those same streets, but now they're competing with you and your bigdamn Buick for ridin' room on a very narrow strip of dirt or cobblestone roadbed. And that's a roadbed that will usually be narrowed by cars and trucks parked on one or both sides of it.

So here's the next thing to think about. How are you gonna navigate these narrow straits? Like we say in Texas, "Drive Friendly". Leave your attitude at the house, get yourself on a testosterone thinner, and keep yourself out of any situation that could lead to getting' your head stuck where it shouldn't be. Pay attention out there! Here's a likely scenario. You´re cruisin´ down one of those little lanes and meet a car comin' toward you. The road is normally wide enough for two cars to pass, except there are a bunch of cars parked next to one of the curbs. What to do? *What to do?*

If you intend to get along, assess the situation to see who has the best opportunity to pull over. If it's you, let the other guy continue on. Find a spot where you can pull over or just stop dead in the road to let the other driver come on through. He'll be lookin' to do the same for you if the situation is reversed. Whoever yields to the other will normally get a smile and a wave in thanks for the courtesy. Unlike NoB, waves of less than two fingers are very rare down here.

Another situation arises at crossroads, where obstructions turn them in to blind intersections. Drive slowly unless you enjoy the dented fender look. You're retired now and probably don't need to follow that breakneck schedule anyway. I've heard several versions of how to handle simultaneous cross-street arrivals so I'll just share them all with you. One version is that the East/West traffic always has the right of way at intersections. The theory is that the folks traveling in those directions will at some point have the sun shining directly into their eyes so they get the yield. Sounds good to me. Then again, there's the NoB idea that it's correct to yield to the vehicle to your right when both cars are on streets of equal importance. This rule is also part of the Mexican traffic law. Yet another school of thought says that the vehicle on the larger thoroughfare has the preference. I prefer to follow the advice of Alberto, The Kissing Cop, who told a class of prospective Mexican driver's license holders to always slow down and prepare to yield, because "maybe the other driver don't know this law".

Bigdamn Cars on Littledamn Streets

Too many drivers spend a lot of in-town driving time backing and cutting the wheels of their vehicles to extreme angles in order to jockey around the tight corners at narrow intersections. If your vehicle of choice requires an area about the size of a soccer field to execute a 360 degree turn, you're not going to enjoy driving in the villages here. Trust me on this one.

For years I drove a Jeep Wrangler. A significant other of one of my past lives convinced me that someone of the higher social standing into which she was determined to drag me should dress better and drive something more respectable. That turned out to be a Chrysler convertible. With a six-centimeter ground clearance and the security of a screen door, it was hardly perfect for Mexico. Luckily, I thought at the time, my dear sweet daughter had gotten past her cowgirl phase and could trade me her bigdamn extended cab Chevy half-tonner for my breezy little cracker box. Well, I was half right. Still stuck with the big Chevy, I long for my Wrangler and take some comfort in knowing that I had sense enough not to bring the damn Chrysler.

Parking and Other Ordeals

Here comes one of my pet peeves. I've left notes on windshields, enjoyed up close and personal discussions, tossed out dirty looks, and have often wished that I had a stronger bumper so that I could leave a dent or two for the thoughtful folks who park in the yellow zones close to intersections. The law says that even if the curbs are not marked, you must park at least 6 meters, about 19 feet, 8 inches, from the intersection. This is important because the streets are usually going to be very narrow and very crowded. You can cause some really interesting traffic jams if you're rude enough to park in such a way that cars and trucks have to stop and jockey back and forth in order to make a simple turn.

And as long as we're on the subject of parkin', be absolutely sure to park as close to the curb as you can. The law states you must park no more than 50 cm, roughly a foot and a half, from the curb. Here's my advice: get as close as you possibly can, and once you've parked, fold in your rearview mirrors on both sides of your vehicle. The sidewalks and roadbeds are usually very narrow and the chance of having a mirror crumpled and removed by pedestrians or passing traffic is fairly significant.

One more word about curbs and then I'll get off the subject. A lot of them are very high. This allows for efficient runoff of heavy seasonal rains, but it also means that, in a lot of places, you won't be able to open the door once you've parked. Some of the less mentally facile park an abysmally great distance from the curb, thereby guaranteeing that other drivers will be either totally blocked, or at least inconvenienced. They do it so their passengers can easily disembark after the parkin' is done but the brighter among us let our passengers out beforehand.

Shootin' the Breeze

You'll also encounter situations where the driver in front of you has stopped dead in the middle of the road to shoot the breeze with someone, either a pedestrian or another driver. Here's what you should do. Sit there. Do not honk your damn horn. Give them a reasonable amount of time to finish the conversation, and if it begins to look like they're going to spend the entire afternoon or evening visiting, you can then gently tap the horn to let them know it's time to move on. Here's the reasoning behind all this. There are very few parking spaces along village lanes. Mexicans (and *gringos* who have been SoB for a while) take care of a lot of business out on the street. Lots of folks don't have phones, so if you happen upon someone with whom you need to discuss business and you don't see a parking place, just stop for a minute and get things done. It's not rude--it's smart and often necessary. Practice patience, because I guarantee you'll find yourself in the same situation someday.

Objects Below Your Radar

You also need to be aware of stealth bicycles, sneaky pedestrians, and anything else that might be able to zoom near and below your personal radar.

Everybody Else is Walking

One thing you'll notice when you come to Mexico is that the great majority of the people in the villages walk, as opposed to the NoB custom of driving everywhere. Many people can't afford a vehicle so walking is their main means of transportation. You'll want to acquire this habit too because you'll gain much from it. You'll get a lot of good exercise and you'll become acquainted with the townspeople and learn the country while you're dealing with people, places, and situations on a face to face, hand to hand basis rather than through a windshield. It's perfectly safe to be out and about on the same streets your neighbors are using.

CHAPTER 9

INSURANCE

Two California-based companies provided quite an interesting experience for a friend of mine. She had two insured vehicles stolen in Mexico. The claims settlement time for the first vehicle was about four months. The claims settlement time for the second vehicle was only about four months. It would have been longer but she was able to enlist the aid of someone higher up the company competence chain than the local agents/adjusters who repeatedly assured her that they were doing everything within their power to effect a satisfactory settlement.

The local agent, a woman, told her on one occasion that since it was my friend's birthday, it was her "sincerest birthday wish" that the claim be paid that very day. This was a woman who had evidently suffered many birthday tragedies. Each time my friend prodded, the agent reminded her that she was "a good Christian woman". A written complaint to the California authorities provided no relief or assistance whatsoever.

My insurance is written by a company in Arizona. Regardless of the state your company operates from, you'll probably find a disclaimer somewhat like this one:

Arizona Statute A.R.S. 20-422 © requires that you be given the following notice:

> "This policy is issued by an insurance company that is not regulated by the Arizona Department of Insurance. The insurance company may not provide claims service and may not be subject to service of process in Arizona. If the insurance company becomes insolvent, insureds or claimants will not be eligible for protection under Arizona law."

Interesting, huh?

Another friend decided that the smart thing to do would be to purchase insurance through Lloyd in Mexico. You can contact them at *http://www.lloyd.com.* Their e-mail is *sucesoros@lloyd.com.mx.*

She understood that Lloyd guarantees to have your claim settled and paid by the thirtieth day after the loss is reported to the company. She thought that in addition to a fluctuating currency exchange rate, there is some difference in the way time is calculated here that's unique from the rest of the world. Her claim was settled in a blazing three months.

Actually, what the policy said was that the company would *decide* within 30 days whether to accept liability for the loss, not that they'd pay that quickly.

A doctor I know in Mascota, a *gringo* from Texas, had his vehicle stolen in Guadalajara and the claim was paid within thirty days, so it can happen. However you need to keep in mind that he is a graduate of the University of Guadalajara Medical School, fluent in Spanish, married to a Mexican citizen who is a business owner, and is currently practicing in Mexico. It could make a difference.

Who Ya' Gonna Call?

There is, however, a bright light at the end of this very short tunnel. There are companies that will settle your claim via English speaking adjusters and pay the actual value in U.S. dollars. Again, I get no compensation or consideration from either of these, but here are two companies I've used and feel comfortable with. You can contact them before leaving home and they'll mail your policy to your U.S. or Canadian address. Or if you're passing through one of the towns along the border where their offices are located, you can stop by and pick it up in person.

Sanborn's has been doing business in Mexico for more than forty years. "Mexico" Mike Nelson has either written or been a major contributor to the entertaining and informative Travelog books that provide detailed travel information. These large paperback classics use detailed driving instructions to get highway travelers smoothly from Point A to Point B, as well as border crossing tips and instructions. Many other Mexico travelers have contributed to these books so they're extremely accurate and up to date. Written in English, each volume provides a wide range of general and specific travel information. I'd advise you to buy one covering your proposed route whether you purchase Sanborn's insurance or not. They will give you sections of the books free of charge if you insure through them and tell them which route you'll be taking. The people I've dealt with have all been very polite and professional, both on the phone and in person, although recently their rates have been a bit higher than many of us feel is necessary.

Some Mexican customs stops, *Aduanas,* are located SoB and these guides tell you exactly where they are. The Sanborn's web page address is *http://www/sanbornsinsurance.com.* You can e-mail them at *info@sanbornsinsurance.com.* Their toll free number is 1-800-222-0158.

If you purchase insurance through Sanborn's, ask them about the possibility of filling out your Tourist Visa application and your vehicle permit application in their offices. They speak English. This may save you a lot of time and stress, but it could also deprive you of a passel of good border stories. They're authorized to offer this service.

I just recently heard that a couple I met and shared several day trips with had finally settled their stolen vehicle claim with Sanborn's. Nine weeks from loss to settlement. However, he admitted that part of the delay was his fault, and some was the fault of the police. His advice was to check all the forms you submit carefully to ensure that the information was properly taken down.

In this particular case the VIN was improperly written on the loss report--two digits were transposed, and as an additional impediment to smooth claims settlement the folks had to return to the frozen North. So figure in a change of location. They ended up with a lot of lost time because they had to re-submit and mail an additional set of documents. Nine weeks ain't bad for all that. And the folks are satisfied with the service although they said the adjuster was a bit lax about returning phone calls. As a former claims adjuster, I might have a different opinion about claims time, but that's a whole other dogfight.

My current carrier is International Insurance Group, Inc. of Flagstaff, AZ. Their toll free number is 1-888-467-4639. The group consists of three entities that can be contacted individually or through the Unit Manager, Nancy Hicks at 928-214-9750 or by fax at 928-213-8476. Their web pages are *http://www.internationalpro.com* for International Insurance Group, Inc; *http://www.mexpro.com* for Mexico Insurance Professionals; and *http://www.rvinsurancepro.com* for RV Insurance Professionals.

In a 1999 issue, Baja Life magazine (*http://www.bajalife.com*) carried a column by Hugh F. Cramer who wrote about problems encountered by some drivers who believed themselves to be properly protected by Mexican insurers, but due to financial problems within the companies ended up with no coverage. I was pleased to see that the travel clubs through which the policies had been sold immediately turned to more stable companies. One of the companies they turned to was Mexico Insurance Professionals, my company. Their prices are competitive and their service is excellent. I highly recommend them.

No matter which company you choose for your insurance, you should do several things once the policy is in your hands. First, read it. All of it. There are terms and conditions different from what you're used to. Second, make copies of the policy. Keep one copy of your papers in the vehicle and keep another copy in a safe place while you're traveling. When you get to your destination keep another copy somewhere in your home.

Go to *http://www.mexicoautotravel.com* for a clear look at Mexican insurance requirements. You'll hear stories from some who pooh-pooh the idea of buying insurance SoB, but keep in mind that Mexican law follows the Roman and Napoleonic models. That is, you're guilty until you prove your innocence. If you've ever been involved in a motor vehicle accident anywhere, you know how difficult that can be. Use your head and get good coverage.

You'll probably encounter someone who claims to pay an unbelievably low premium for coverage and ridicules your higher premium cost. Take those bargain stories with a grain of salt and diligently seek information about the stability and dependability of your prospective insurer. Go to *http://www.mexpro.com/ mexproranking.htm* for a look at major Mexican companies.

Why Do You Need Insurance?

Go to *http://www.hispanicvista.com* and look for the article dated March 26, 2001 by Patrick Osio, Jr. titled "Mexican Tourist Auto Insurance: buy right or face consequences". You can contact the writer at *hispanicvista@home.com* if you can't find the article on the site. Incidentally, if you're the proud possessor of an FM-3 and plan to live in Mexico forever, and as long as you drive a U.S. or Canadian-plated vehicle you'll be insured under a Tourist Automobile Insurance policy. It's much cheaper than any of the alternatives and it's federal law.

Keep in mind that your hometown policy is absolutely no good in Mexico. Before you cross that border be certain you have a valid Mexican insurance policy in your hand. There's a policy rider that you should request if your agent doesn't automatically add it to your new policy. It's the "Legal Aid" coverage. The premium on my policy was only an additional $20 US and it provides bond money if you're involved in a serious automobile accident that involves bodily injury to the other person(s). As a guide, my policy covers a declared vehicle value of $15,000 US and provides the following coverages:

🚗 Collision, with a 2% glass breakage deductible and a 2% or $500 US collision or total loss deductible, whichever is greater

☞ Third party liability of $50,000 US

☞ Bodily injury liability of $50,000 US per accident, $100,000 US total

☞ Medical expenses for my passengers of $2,000 US

☞ Legal aid

☞ Travel assistance

My premium in 2001 was $271 US and in 2002 was $276 US. At renewal, in July of 2002 I upgraded my coverage to include the newly offered vandalism and partial theft options along with a couple of other minor changes for a total premium of $515.27 US. This may seem high to some, but International Insurance Group, Inc., has a proven, long-term track record of excellent claims settlements. Here's something else you need to know. If you buy insurance within the country, from a Mexican company, you may pay a much higher rate. Just like where you live now, it pays to shop around. One question you'll need to ask is if your policy has a time limit on keeping your vehicle in Mexico. I've heard stories, totally unconfirmed, that some policies require you to remove the insured vehicle from Mexico at certain intervals. Mine never have, but you need to make sure about your coverage. You also need to make sure you're covered for driving throughout the entire country.

If you failed to read your policy and are about to be the recipient of a major league screwin', you might be able to get some relief from the National Commission for the Protection of Financial Institution Clients (CONDUSEF). There are things added to or omitted from some policies that are totally alien to your NoB coverage. One scam to watch out for is a clause that states you're not covered for repairs, just *legal advice.* The Guadalajara Colony Reporter reported that CONDUSEF had received twenty complaints about this kind of scam in 2002. (September 7-13, 2002 issue.) Their website is at *http:// www.condusef.gob.mx.* It opens in Spanish but most sections have English translations. E-mail can be sent to opinion@central.condusef.gob.mx. The site lists 35 offices with toll free numbers and addresses.

When You Drive Back to Visit

When you drive back North to visit the kids or to stop by the old neighborhood to gloat a bit, you're gonna need temporary coverage. Over in Flagstaff the folks at Mexico Insurance Professionals, my guys, can write this for you if you contact them at *http://www.mexpro.com/mexpromexusa.htm* for a free online quote. On my last trip I was rather rushed and bought coverage locally. The cost for a 30 day policy for liability only was $80 US. In some areas you can contract for a short-term policy with a local agent. You'll have several options available.

CHAPTER 10

SU CASA ES MI CASA

Now that we're at the house after all that road time, it's time to settle in. Before you roll up your sleeves, open your wallet, and start heading off to the hardware and furniture stores, the first thing you need to do is take inventory. If your rental is unfurnished this shouldn't take too long because there's probably not much here aside from the basic structure. There may be no light fixtures, light bulbs, toilet paper holder, drain plugs, ceiling fans and very possibly no water heater, almost certainly no stove, or refrigerator—*nada*. None of the *very* basics that you're likely to take for granted. The last tenant took them. Not *stole* them, took them, because he bought that stuff just like you're going to. Enough about unfurnished for right now. Let's assume for a moment that you're renting a furnished place. Ready?

"Furnished" covers a lot of water in Mexico just as it does up North or in Tasmania. You may have scored a nice, pleasantly decorated place with stylish furnishings and china, good silver, a microwave, outdoor furniture, scads of house plants, excellent crystal, a coffee maker, blender, a full selection of

EN LA PLAYA EN MELAQUE,
WILLIAM GENTES, 1993

cookware, and beautifully crafted rugs on the tile floors. You've probably also exceeded your housing budget.

Here's a more likely scenario. One furnished house I rented had four plastic plates, four matching saucers, four matching cups (all in stark institutional white), two clear plastic drinking tumblers, twelve or fourteen assorted pieces of cheap table silver, a blender, a scratched and dented Teflon frying pan, a small aluminum sauce pan, a spatula, a dull butcher knife, two ice trays, and an old broom.

There was one light bulb for the entire house. The structure itself was nice. It was about two years old and had a large kitchen with new appliances. The furnishings were fairly decent but cheap (one night my bed fell apart), and there was no décor of any kind on the walls. In one of the two bedrooms the only piece of furniture was a large armoire. This rental cost $450 US in San Antonio Tlayacapán in the Lake Chapala-Ajijic area.

In contrast, a friend rented a place just around the corner that had been used as a weekend home by a couple from Guadalajara. It was a small, two-bedroom house that was nicely furnished with *muebles rustico*, the Mexican handcrafted rustic furniture, and local arts and crafts. The kitchen was completely furnished with good quality glazed earthenware dishes (probably enough to serve twelve) and accessories, fairly nice appliances, and a good selection of pots and pans (including two sizes of my all-time-favorite cooking pot, the wok). It didn't have a shower curtain or sink drain stoppers. The folks *did* leave a nice selection of spices and seasonings though. Now this friend thought her little dollhouse was just *waaay* too crowded with furniture and decorations for her taste. It left her no place to add her own stuff. Hmmm. This one cost $425 US a month and had been listed with a realtor.

Here's another likely scenario. Four to five rooms with sixty-one kazillion types of furniture arranged in crazed configurations interspersed with built-ins. Concrete built-ins. *Large* concrete built-ins. For instance, this was what I found inside the place in La Manzanilla.

- Small gas range, four burners, no oven, Fraga brand
- Small refrigerator, small freezer compartment, two ice trays, Acros brand
- Good quality plastic outdoor furniture, with a glass-topped table and three chairs
- A 19"X39" varnished wood table with two drawers, locally produced
- Three small round occasional tables
- A lower-quality king-sized mattress
- Two lower-quality twin mattresses

- A china cabinet
- Three plastic lawn chairs, like you get at Ace Hardware or Wal-Mart for $6.00
- Nine houseplants in various-sized pots
- Two very inexpensive, painted pottery representations of the moon and sun for the walls

Un-furnished rentals normally do not include a stove or refrigerator. If you have to buy one or the other they're fairly reasonable. The stove should be in the $100 to $150 US price range and a suitable Mexican-made refrigerator might be from $250 to $350 US.

In the event that you have a furnished rental but don't love your appliances, you can go to Sears, Wal-Mart, Sam's Club, CostCo, Comercial Mexicana or Mega Mercado in one of the larger cities and buy a foreign-made or up-scale Mexican stove and refrigerator at a much higher price. There are also "*bazars*" or second-hand stores in areas where both Nationals and *gringos* live that sell used appliances. Some folks denigrate the quality of the Mexican manufactured products but I've found that the refrigerators keep food from spoiling and that the stoves allow me to cook the unspoiled food. It's possible that I've missed something somewhere along the line, but I'm fairly certain that those are the primary uses of the aforementioned appliances. Several of my more domestically-inclined female friends tell me that Mexican manufactured refrigerators have inferior insulation and that sometimes the ovens don't seem to get very hot or to have accurate heat regulators. I defer to their experienced assessments. Since most of my cooking takes place topside I *can* offer a warning about stove burners.

Some Mexican-made stoves appear to have burners that look like every other burner you've ever seen. This can be deceptive. A blue flame from six inches to a foot high can shoot straight up from the center of the burner—a little like the one Durwood Lambert ignited just before he blew up the science lab during your junior year at PS 187. If this happens, don't panic.

Just go to the outdoor market and buy a heat diffuser for each burner. It's a round, lightweight metal implement that you lay on the wire racks already in place on the stovetop. It's actually two pieces of metal that look like extremely shallow pie tins that have been turned inside to inside and attacked by a five year-old with a power drill.

Stuff You'll Really Need
Now for the things you'll really need. Light bulbs for sure. Candles, flashlights, or a kerosene or oil-burning lamp for when the power fails, which it will. Relax,

the same thing's gonna happen here like it did when the lights went off back home. It gets dark. Except in the daytime when all the fans go dead.

Don't lug a glass lamp down here or a bunch of candles that'll be demolished in transit. Buy them here. Ask at the hardware store for a *quinque,* pronounced KEEN kay. They'll probably show you a portable butane container with a Coleman-type-mantle for about 37 or 38 bucks US or a traditional glass oil lamp with a fragile chimney for around 14 to 18 bucks.

You'll also need a few rubber drain stoppers. You can buy several kinds— those sized for specific openings as well as the big flat ones. These can be easily found at the *tianguis* (the outdoor market*),* a *ferreteria* (hardware store), or where you buy *abarrotes,* general groceries. You can also pick up toilet brushes, shower mats, trashcans, buckets, mops, and cleaning brushes there. Stores that specialize only in plastics are common.

CON TARUGOS A BAÑARSE, QUE HASTA EL JABON SE PIERDE,
WILLIAM GENTES, **1982**

Bathrooms in budget rentals probably won't have medicine cabinets or towel closets. Hanging organizers go over the showerhead in a hurry and metal shelving units over commode tanks cost about $20 to $30 US. Look for them at furniture stores or in one of the larger, more up-to-date hardware shops.

Beds with box spring foundations are not traditionally used here. The average Mexican bed is a wooden platform, with or without legs, that sometimes sports built-in drawers. The platform provides excellent support and stability. I'm sure the Mattress Police would rather have you buy both a box spring and mattress but you don't have to and it makes things easier if you're into the gypsy life. One thing you'll discover is your king-sized sheets won't fit your bed if it's a Mexican one. They make the mattresses about 3 inches shorter here.

If you want a tad more comfort in your sleeping arrangement, eggcrate foam pads and quality mattress covers are available in the cities at Sears, Wal-Mart, Costco, Mega Mercado, Carrefour, Comercial Mexicana and at some furniture stores and the *tianguis.* Shop around, though. A king-sized eggcrate foam pad cost me about $22 US in Guadalajara. In Manzanillo they wanted $82.

Getting Into Hot Water

Now that you're actively setting up house what if you come across some things that need to be repaired before you settle in? Remember the realtor who told you emphatically that "You don't want to rent from a Mexican landlord, we know how to protect you"? Well, let's see how one company backed up that one.

A friend who rented through a realtor had a water heater that wouldn't stay lighted. Remember reading that you'd probably be responsible for any repairs costing less than $50? That doesn't apply to pre-existing conditions that are brought to the landlord's attention within a reasonable amount of time, usually a month, but it's better if you report any problems as soon as you discover them.

Anyway, she reported the problem to the realtor and he kindly explained to her that the owner lived in Guadalajara and he wasn't sure he'd be able to get her permission anytime soon to have someone look at the problem. After an inordinately long period of time, filled with daily phone calls to this protector of renter's rights, he finally, after more than a week and a half *did* manage to get someone to come solve the problem.

She now had hot water. Just not to the kitchen faucet. Remember the questions on the Landlord Quiz that asked, "Where's the water heater? and "Are all of the sink, bath and shower faucets plumbed for both hot and cold water?" This place had only a cold water pipe running to the kitchen.

Back to the protector of renter's rights, who this time refused to return phone calls. We may as well get this one out of the way right now, ladies. You'll probably need to be a bit more insistent down South because females might not be taken too seriously otherwise. At any rate, my friend asked for my assistance so I visited the office but the realtor wasn't in. I asked to speak to the owner but was told that there was no owner. I then asked to speak to whoever was in charge. I was told that no one was in charge.

After politely offering to stand in their parking lot with a large florescent sign warning off other possible customers, he finally agreed to contact the wayward realtor and get something done. Don't set your heart on true turnkey services here, you might get it broken. Save a little heartbreak and use the Landlord Quiz in Chapter 5.

In With the New, Out With the Other

Do you remember that one of the other questions you asked the prospective landlord was about storage—a place to put his furniture as you began buying your own? Here's why you did.

When I moved into the place in La Manzanilla I wrestled the existing tables out and had others built more to my liking. In the living room two small built-in daybeds served as sofas. Each had a cheap mattress and a frilly bedspread on top of the concrete foundations. Guess where I chucked the mattresses and frilly spreads? Right, into the storage room downstairs.

Build Some Stuff

The place in La Manzanilla came without a lot of useful furniture and very little storage in the living area. So, in the dining-living room I had the carpenter build a long narrow table to fit a niche where the window looked out over the village and provided a gorgeous view of Tenacatita Bay with its beautiful, protective mountains. That was my "office" although watching the Bay and listening to the surf often interrupted an otherwise productive day and prompted me to grab my walking staff, whistle up the dogs, and go to the beach for awhile.

The place had no kitchen storage either. Many Mexican houses don't have kitchen cabinets or drawers. What I *did* have was a very nice built-in bar dividing the kitchen from the living-dining room. It was a curving L shape with a shelf built below the serving surface. I had a carpenter build a wooden shelf to sit on the floor beneath the existing shelf and two more to be attached to the kitchen wall to hold spices, glasses and cups. I bought hooks to hang utensils and under one shelf I attached a paper towel holder. One of the items I hung was a woven bag that held fresh limes because regardless of where I'm living, I usually mix up at least a quart of *limonada* (limeade) every day. One reason you see people squeezing lime juice over their food is to kill bacteria. Make this a habit. One of my maids used to make me rub cut limes on every cut and scratch for the same reason.

A large pottery bean pot stood on the small counter beside the sink to hold wooden spoons, ladles, a chocolate stirrer, and other cooking tools. The coffeepot and blender were on a table beside the refrigerator and my microwave was on top of it. The 'fridge-microwave arrangement was convenient since I had to unplug the 'fridge when I wanted to use the microwave. Using both plugs at the same time caused huge showers of electrical sparks that tended to scare the hell out of me.

Electricity, Surge Protectors, and the Mexican National Extension Cord

Down here you'll encounter rolling brown-outs and power fluctuations on a fairly regular basis, and when the carnivals and vendors who follow the festival and *fiesta* circuits show up, you can almost bet on at least one power interruption due to the use of the Mexican National Extension Cord. The MNEC is an OSHA examiner's stroke inducer, a wonder of dare-deviltry, and as dangerous as datin´ your wife's sister.

Here's how it works. When these guys roll into town to set up their individual booths, they need power for the fifteen or twenty million lights they'll string all around them. Up North, similar set-ups would normally involve the use of por-table generators. Down South they very often involve the use of the MNEC.

From their booths the guys will run two long electrical wires with the insulation stripped from the ends and bent back to form hooks.

When they're ready to hook up the power they take each wire individually and, using a long wooden pole, raise the wire and look for the nearest overhead power line. Each wire hangs from a different line and if the installer manages to avoid a public electrocution, the lights begin to glow. If this maneuver is performed incorrectly someone usually gets the corpse out of the street so the rest of the guys can get on about their business.

Most of the craftsmen who require electricity to complete a job at your house will use the MNEC or a variation. Sometimes they'll just plug directly into your wall sockets with bare wires, or hook up to the meter box the same way. The squeamish or sensitive should not watch.

If you're bringing a computer (or some other piece of expensive electronic gear) get the best Uninterruptable Power Supply (UPS) you can find, prefer-ably one that will allow you thirty minutes to shut down after a power loss so that you don't damage your equipment. You can get them here but the choices are limited and it may take a few days to get one ordered. This is an item you might consider buying before you come down. Will you really need it? Oh yes! Definitely!

And once you're in your new home hire an electrician to come out and install at least one grounded receptacle where you'll use your computer. In budget rent-als nearly all the plugs will be two-pronged. While he's there have him test your circuits too. It's a smart idea to use a surge protector and power regulator for your microwave and for your TV and stereo. You can find suitable ones here that will be just fine for those appliances.

Send a Photo of Your Place to Christopher

If you don't like the looks of the joint you moved into you need to get a little creative. My walls in the beach house were a pale tan and I decided to follow a friend's lead and use some color. In the kitchen I painted new shelves Royal Blue and had them mounted above the tile on the walls, about five and a half feet high. Above them I painted a deep pink stripe, Mexicali Red, nine inches wide along the length of the shelves and downward to the floor at one end of the kitchen and along another wall to the door.

Three inches above the pink line, I painted a thin John Deere green stripe to keep the Mexicali Red one company. My nearest neighbor was an artist who painted vines and birds around the lines. In Melaque some friends and I found a platter painted with slices of fruits in colors echoing the stripes. I hung it up. In front of the bar, facing into the dining room-living room, I had a bookcase built and I painted it Lime Green. *Serapes* with some of these colors were sewn into new cushions for the sofas. Aahh, it was a real Christopher moment. You do watch Christopher, don't you?

In the bathroom above the tile I "washed" the walls with Foam Green paint and my neighbor painted seaweed, octopi and starfish on top. I glued some ceramic fish, real seashells and starfish to the wall to make it look a little like the part of the Pacific I saw at the bottom of the hill.

The rest of the decor consisted of lamps, personal items, Mexican crafts, and Oaxaca rugs that I really like. And geckos. Lots of geckos. Live geckos.

This is by no means meant to be a gotta-do-it-this-way spiel, just an example of what a fifty-year-old wannabe Blues legend could do on a limited budget. The subject I'm really *most* interested in comes up next. Read on.

Chapter II

What Do You Reckon Manna Really Is?

Aaaaahh! Food. Some of us love it for different reasons at different times. Sometimes it's festive and celebratory. Sometimes it's sensual and seductive. Sometimes it's soothing medicine for the mind and body. Sometimes it's fuel for that lagging metabolic generator. Sometimes it strikes a deep chord of satisfaction with its taste, texture and presentation. And sometimes it's just a damn tuna salad sandwich.

If you're nervous about ordering food here there's a nice little book put out by S.L. DeChoisy titled *Know What You Eat In Mexico: all the secrets and misteries (sic) of the Mexican Cooking in 800 words.* Costs about 20 *pesos,* a couple of bucks. It's quadra-lingually written in French, German, Spanish and English. Contact them by e-mail at *decoisy@arrakis.es.* They're in Spain. Or wait 'til you get here and buy a copy at a local newsstand or bookstore.

Restaurants

You might be surprised by the diversity of restaurants you can find here in the larger towns and cities: Oriental, including Chinese, Thai, Japanese, and Vietnamese; Italian, which is very common, and pizza parlors including Dominos and Pizza Hut; East Indian, Argentinean, Polish, Indonesian, local fried chicken in addition to Kentucky Fried Chicken; German; French; fast food such as Burger King, Dairy Queen,Whataburger and McDonald's; Lebanese; Cuban; an occasional Tex-Mex or Arizona-Mex place; and upscale Mexican places where you can order traditional dishes as well as continental fare like Chateaubriand and bananas flambé; Spanish; Brazilian, Portuguese, Mediterranean; Arabian and Swiss. And Sirloin Stockade with all those buffets. And Outback Steakhouse. Even a New Orleans-style restaurant. As astounding as this may be, there are also British and Dutch restaurants in some places. Dutch. Brother Dave again…"Ain't that weird?".

I'm *Fonda* Eatin'

In every town, usually on or near a *plaza* or marketplace, there will be small, simple restaurants called *fondas.* You'll also see them in the neighborhoods. A lot of these might remind you of an old-style drugstore diner with a counter fronted by spinning stools. Others will have a few small tables, and you'll find some in living rooms or on patios. These places are not big on fancy décor or ambiance. They're set up to provide you with a quick, relatively inexpensive, meal and get you on your way with a minimum of hassle. The menu of each place is usually very limited but there are often enough places nearby, each with a distinctive food, to give you a choice of meals. You'll also probably get to watch Spanish language TV as you dine. Go ahead, it can be memorable.

Another Mexican eating place is a *cenaduria. Cena* means dinner and *ria* is the suffix that means shop or store. Just like *panadería,* bread shop or bakery; *ferreteria,* no, not a ferret shop, a hardware store; *paleteria,* ice cream store; *licorería,* liquor store; *taqueria,* taco stand; *lavandaria,* laundry; *carniceria,* butcher shop; *zapateria,* shoe store; *muebleria,* furniture store; *pasteleria,* pastry shop; *frutería,* fruit and vegetable store; *tortilleria,* tortilla shop.

So a *cenaduria* is a place that serves only one meal a day, dinner. Some are dedicated buildings or storefronts, but many are set up in someone's front room or out in the street where folding tables are arranged next to the curb. Sure the food's good, and the level of hygiene is acceptable. Earlier I told you to eat where the locals do and you're not likely to find tourists at a *cendaduria*. The cost for a meal is usually from $2.50 to $4.00 US. It's good food, comfortable seating, a great way to meet the folks in the hood and best of all, *no mucho dinero.* Cenadurias are often open as late as two in the morning. I've found that *costillas de cerdo, arroz* and *frijoles* sopped up with *tortillas* after midnight are wonderful fuel for my crazed writing frenzies.

You might see places advertising *comida economica,* bargain food, or *comida corrida,* food on the run. The element they share with *cenadurias* is that they serve a limited and fixed menu at a single price. You might stumble over one or two places serving a more ambitious range of dishes but most have no printed menus at all, except for the occasional painted sign. One of my favorite meals can be found at a little place in Melaque where the Japanese owner serves up delicious German potato pancakes.

Street Eatin'

Eating on the street is one of my favorite entertainments. I'm always surprised at how few *gringos* seem to take advantage of it. Plus it's so simple. And you meet interesting and influential people. How simple is it? Just walk over and see if they're cooking anything that looks good to you. If they are, just hold up the appropriate number of fingers to order what you want. If there is a variety of options, just point to the one, or ones, you want.

Yes, I *did* say entertaining too. For example, one evening a lady and I were sitting at a little sidewalk place on our first, and come to think of it, last meeting. Cheapness may not be any more appealing in Mexico than Minneapolis or Montreal. Anyway, the local soccer team had just beat the snot out of all the other competitors in a big tournament off somewhere. Did they stop by our table to tell us? No, they cruised up and down the main drag in a number of vehicles whose drivers were blowing the horns while the boys in the beds of the trucks laughed, shouted, waved, and raised high both the two big trophies they'd earned, as well as the spirits of all of us sharing in their pleasure.

And later that evening we met a local *vaquero* who had his horse, *Lucero,* perform for us. And then tried to persuade one of us to buy the talented steed.

I know, everyone warned you not to, but... you might find a little lady selling small bags of popcorn on the plaza. That tub sitting in the wheelbarrow is full of *elotes*, ears of boiled corn. Or you may want to try some roasted corn from that other lady. If you want it smeared with *mayonesa* and it's early in the day, go ahead. If not, don't dare, unless they just came out for the evening traffic. That stuff has the potential to put you on a prolonged Pepto-Bismol binge. You may just choose to go with *limón, sal,* and *chile en polvo* or *salsa,* although that's a gamble too.

On another corner of the plaza is a guy cooking hot dogs. Some of them are wrapped in bacon. Let him doctor one up for you and when he asks, *"Todo?"* (that's a one word phrase that asks, "Do you want me to load up this dog for you?"), the correct answer is "*Sí!*".

And here's a *señora* with a folding table selling delicious homemade cakes and *pays* (pies), including my personal favorite, *pay de queso,* cheesecake. My friend Judy has been here for years and is enamored with the *pastel de tres leches*. It's moist and heavenly and not always readily available, but you're depriving your taste buds if you never try it. You can buy it in a mix but it's a pitiful way to be introduced to such a heavenly delight. Incidentally, the mix is a liquid.

In case the idea of eating dinner while roaming the distance of, say, a soccer field, seems strange, think about a county fair. There used to be a floor of the old Jax Brewery on Jackson Square in New Orleans that had a set-up similar to Mexican *plaza* eating. There were dozens of food booths, each selling something different. Get a plate of red beans and rice here; go there for a big hunk of *boudin*, over there for a bowl of gumbo; and over there for a roasted turkey leg. Places like that, and *plazas* like these are omnivore nirvanas. Except that nirvana is less expensive here.

Even though I'm enthusiastic about street eating I do draw a few lines. I don't drink the *liquados* or *agua frescas* prepared by street vendors unless I see them being prepared from bottled water. A bad *jamaica agua* in Old Town PV once sat me down for a day or two. And I have no problem watching the guys grilling sausages for *tortas*, but I do draw the line at innards. Intestines. *Tripas. Tripas de puerco.* I don't go there.

I'm also wary of those containers of *salsa* and *guacamole* that have been sitting out. My doctor in Jocotepec recently ran several lab tests after I complained of stomach problems and found that, "There was a zoo in there". She and her husband, who is a pathologist, carry their own *salsa* when they eat out. Bacterias, fungi, and saliva end up in those communal dishes. The August 3, 2002 issue of The News reported that researchers from the University of Texas at Austin, ran tests on restaurant *salsas* in Houston and Mexico City. They found that two-thirds of the *salsas* from Mexico were contaminated with one of two types of E. coli. Forty percent of the Houston *salsas* were contaminated. The really bad news is that the level of contamination in Mexican *salsas* were *one thousand times higher* than those found in Houston.

It's also not uncommon to visit the *farmacia* once a year to ask for tablets to kill the latest batch of stomach parasites we've picked up. When street eating, stay with the very fresh, the chilled and the freshly heated food, like the good stuff below.

Over here a lady is using a plow disc to cook up beef stew. The stew isn't like what you're used to; it's a bit drier, fried, and delicious because she's using a bit of bacon, some sausages, onions, and peppers. I don't know for sure, but logic tells me that someone saw one of those cast off discs layin' out somewhere on a *rancho* and decided it would make a great skillet. One of my BBQ grills is made from a tire rim. Not much goes to waste In Mexico.

Just smell those roasted chickens. You'll find them cooking in the *rosticerias*, in the tall Boston Market-style stainless steel rotisserie cookers. *Pollo asado.* Depending on the individual place, an order gets you a chicken and a side dish or two for $4 to 5.00 US. It seems like in a country full of street-runnin' *pollos* that it'd be cheaper but this price seems to be pretty consistent over most of the country at present. Sides? Oh, maybe a kind of slaw salad, small chunks of potato, or a big scoop of rice.

A friend's favorite *rosticeria* is the one on the left as you're facing the front of the Chapala Market, on the square. If you're asking a local for directions they'll know which direction to point if you say "*Donde esta La Plaza* (or *El Centro*)? Either of the two will get you headed in the right direction. Anyway, one day when my friend failed to call me or drop by and share the bounty, she and another friend bought a chicken and were given some incredibly tasty potatoes as a side. Evidently they'd spent quite a long time lying on the bottom of the rotisserie cabinet soaking up hot chicken grease. The potatoes I mean, not the ladies.

They both still fondly remember the exquisite flavor and delightful greasiness, and can describe the texture and aroma in great detail. I, on the other hand, cannot. I'm still pouting over missing that one.

Want to know how chickens taste cooked on those grills made from 55 gallon drums? They're a bit drier, sometimes tougher and stringier, but still great. The flavor is different because of the open charcoal cooker, I guess, or else because of the *pollo*. Chicken fat is very yellow here and someone tried to convince me it's because they're fed marigolds. I shudder to think that Mexican "Tysons" and "Pilgrims" might send flowers to their chickens.

Let's go see the other *taco* guy. Hhhmmmm. *Res* (beef), *pollo* (chicken), *lengua* (tongue), and *cesos* (brains). Brains. See those little light-gray things about the size of a tennis ball? They're kept whole because it keeps 'em from dryin' out. Along with intestines, tongue and brains are two more lines I don't cross.

And over here are fish *tacos*. Chunks of fish are fried in a tempura-style batter and are *muy rico*, very delicious.

Now, do you see how inexpensively you can eat if you let yourself relax a bit? And if you need something familiar, this lady is cooking French fries. And this old man is roasting peanuts over that small brazier.

Oh, here's another place serving *pozole*, the soup of the Aztec gods. It's inexpensive, filling, delicious, and addictive. Without a doubt, it's the best soup in the world despite what Julia Child or Emeril or anyone else might try to tell you. The base ingredient is hominy, usually with pork and red *chiles* added.

And here they're serving *birria*. It's either goat (*chivo, cabrito)* or beef (*res*) or pork *(puerco)* or lamb *(cordero)*, cooked with some *maguey* leaf maybe, a *chile* or two, and a little *jitomate* for seasoning, and served in its own juicy broth. Unless you're used to goat, you might want to locate the *baño* first and make sure you have correct change before ordering. *Chivo* is a bit rich and greasy and can have rapid and startling effects on the digestive system of the uninitiated. I scored a bonus one day when a female friend gave up her dish when she discovered it was full of goat. Until my full disclosure she was blissfully enjoying her meal.

Keep It In Your Pants; Your Money That Is

Comida corrida, *fondas*, *cenadurias* and the whole street-eating scene are bargains for us NoB types who have been tutored to shell out bigger and bigger bucks for snacks, coffees, and drinks as part of our social hanging out. And this might be obvious, but if you need to stay on a daily food budget (that's how a lot of us figure living expenses) and want to eat out, be careful. Here's how to do it. Make your selections, figure the math and then stick with it. Here's why.

Scenario Number One. You and your friends are sitting at a table in a restaurant. While you're studying the menu a waiter brings you chips and *salsa*, or a saucer of citrus sections with slices of cucumber and *jícama*, or some other free *botana.* What you get depends on your geographical location, the day of the week, the time of the year, the phase of the moon, the mood of the cook, and probably what was bought at the market that day.

While you were deciding on your entrée you sipped a cold (*frio*) Corona. (I'm a Pacifico man, myself.) You select the *chuleta de puerco* (pork chop, my personal favorite) and hand the menu back to the waiter—which means you've already spent $7 US for the chop and $1.00 or $1.50 or even as much as $2.00 for the beer. As the waiter takes your order he may ask *"Algo mas"*? Something else? The correct answer is "No". When you've finished the chop and beer he may return and ask *"Algo mas?"* which is his way of asking you, are you ready for something else? This is where you have to squelch the urge to prolong your evening by ordering more food.

Drinks and desserts, the two D's. If you want to stay on budget and have more enjoyable evenings *later in the month*, it's time to stop. You tend to lose track of *margaritas* and *cervezas* while you and your friends wait for food and discuss the events and places of the day. The two D's will romp through your budget like Sherman's Pyromania Tour of the South.

Scenario Number Two. One evening I got into town late and stopped at one of the nicer places to grab a hamburger and fries. That's not a sacrilege, by the way. Sometimes you need to enjoy the fare you grew up with. Anyway, another expat stopped by to talk and during a long meal and conversation I had three beers with the burger and fries and ice cream for dessert. After he left, and I was preparing to leave, a couple at the next table spoke. She commented on Pirata and asked what kind of dog he was. So I sat down to talk with *them* for awhile, ordered a glass of wine and after an interesting late evening of food, spirits and great conversation, I'd spent about $19 US. It'll sneak up on you.

ACARAJAS, BRASIL, **WILLIAM GENTES,** *1989*

Scenario Number Three. The next night I had two beef tacos and three beef and cheese *quesadillas* for about $2.80 US, and walked three doors down to the *licorería* and bought two *Pacificos* for about $1.45 US. I ended up spending $4.25 or so for a very satisfying dinner.

Why Won't He Bring the Bill?

After you've eaten, and had your drink, and conversed, and are ready to leave, you must say *"Por favor, la cuenta"*, (la KWEN tah). That means you want the bill. Or hold up your palm and act as though you're writing on it. It's best if the server is looking at you when you do the latter. The waiters are much too polite to give you the impression that they think it's time for you to leave. Manners or not, the longer you wait to ask for the bill, the bigger the chance that you'll have just one more Pacifico.

In spite of all the great dining experiences available to you, there will be times when you just want to bunker in and not have to deal with anything more complicated than a good book or a TV show. You'll still want food, so you need to know how to get your own supply.

Grocery Shopping

Recently I saw a cost of living comparison chart at *http://www.expatriate.com* that showed a basket of groceries sold in the U.S. for $100 that cost $112 in Mexico. Let me suggest several reasons for that. American brand-name foods have to be imported to Mexico, which means import costs will be added to the price of the item. Plus researchers probably didn't account for the change in buying habits among expats from frozen, canned or otherwise prepackaged foods to fresh foods purchased at the market. There's another reason, too. It's amazing how many less-than-knowledgeable travelers write travel articles based on little or no investigation, which is why you need to get out and check things for yourself.

When we talk about grocery stores most of us think about those huge super-markets where we can buy everything from apples to zirconia jewelry. You're not going to find many of those here, although in the larger cities and towns you can find Wal Mart, Carrefour, Gigante, Mega Mercado, Comercial Mexicana, Costco, and some other locally-owned stores that are nearly as large. How-ever, they may be more expensive than you're used to, especially if you've moved to Mexico from the U.S.

If you live in Monterrey, Veracruz, Mexico City, Guadalajara, Morelia or any other large city, it might be worth your while to patronize the big supermarkets especially if you love the hustle and bustle of big cities and you buy in suffi-cient volume to garner a considerable savings. You'll find lots of the products you're used to back in Joplin but it won't take you long to notice that most, if not all of them, are as high as a giraffe's ass, price-wise. *Imported*, don'cha know.

To get an idea about the U.S., Canadian, and international brands and prod-ucts that are available in a medium-sized village, I walked around Melaque, a Pacific beach town where many Nationals spend school and family holidays.

The items on the following list were not stocked by all the stores, nor were some of the products exactly what you might find in the U.S. Take Del Monte brand corn as an example. A lot of U.S. brands serve the Mexican market with products that are packed in familiar cans and boxes but are labeled in Span-ish. Name brand products labeled in English cost more than the same brand labeled in Spanish.

In Leon, in the State of Guanajuato, several foreign food companies own pro-cessing and packaging plants. Among them are Campbell's, Danone, Green Giant, Celanese, Kraft Foods and JC Penney. Under NAFTA many major com-panies like these expanded their markets into Mexico so that Mexicans could buy a box of Nabisco brand Honey Grahams for a quarter of the price the same box imported from the U.S. would have cost them a few years ago.

But back to Melaque. Keep in mind that this list came from a small town about 140 miles from the closest *gringo* retirement/tourist area.

Adams Gum

Afrin

Ajax Cleaner

Alberto VO5

Alka-Seltzer

Ammens Powders

Appleton's Special Rum

Aqua Net

Aunt Jemima Pancake Mix

Austin Snack Crackers

Bacardi Rum

Ballantine's Scotch

Band Aids

Bayer Aspirin

Betty Crocker's Cake Mix

Bic pens and lighters

Bold Detergent

Brut Cologne

Brylcreem

Camay Soap

Campbell's Soup

Canada Dry Ginger Ale

Caribe Wine Coolers

Charmin tissue

Chivas Regal

Clairol Shampoo

Clorets

Clorox

Coca-Cola

Coke Light

Colgate Toothpaste

Crest Toothpaste

Curity Baby Products

Danone (Dannon) Yogurt

Delaware Punch

Del Monte Vegetables

Delsey Tissue

Doritos

Dove Beauty Bars

Downy Fabric Softener

Dr. Pepper

Dramamine

Duracell Batteries

Easy-Off Oven Cleaner

Ecko Aluminum Cookware

Evenflo Baby Products

Eveready Batteries

Fanta

Finlandia Vodka

Folger's Coffee

Fresca

Freshen-up Gum

Fuji Film

Gatorade

Gerber Baby Food

Gillette Razors

Grecian Formula

Hall's Cough Drops

Head and Shoulders

Heinz Vegetables

Heinz Catsup

Hellman's Mayo

Hershey's Chocolate

Huggies Diapers

Hunt's Catsup

Jack Daniel's Bourbon

J&B Scotch

Jell-O

Jergen's Lotion

Johnson & Johnson items

Karo Syrup

Kellogg's Cereals

Kleenex

Knorr Bouillon Cubes

Kodak Film

Kool-Aid

Kotex Sanitary Pads

Kraft Macaroni & Cheese

Libby Vegetables

Lipton Tea

Listerine Mouthwash

Lysol Disinfectant

Maalox

Maggi Seasoning Sauce

Maruchan Instant Lunches

Mexsana Powder

McCormick Mustard

McIlhenny & Co. Tabasco

Mennen Powder

Milky Way Candy Bars

Mr. Clean

Nabisco Products

Nescafe Instant Coffee

Neutrogena T/Gel

Nivea Beauty Aids

Nutrasweet

Off! Insect Repellent

Old Milwaukee Beer

Oral B Toothbrushes

Palmolive Bath Soap

PAM Cooking Spray

Passport Scotch

Pedialyte

Pepsi & Pepsi Light

Pepto-Bismol

Pert Shampoo

Pond's Hand Cream

Pringle's Potato Chips

Pro Toothbrushes

Q-Tips

Quaker Oats and Cereals

Ragu Spaghetti Sauce

Raid Insect Spray

Rayovac Batteries

Reach Toothbrushes

Reynolds Aluminum

Selsun Shampoo

Sensodyne Toothpaste

7 Up & Diet 7 Up

S C Johnson Products

Scotch Brite Pads

Similac Baby Formula

Slim Fast Diet Drinks

Smirnoff Vodka

Smucker's Jams	Trident Gum
Snickers Candy Bars	Vaseline
Solarcaine Cream	V-8 Juices
Spam	Wildroot Hair Tonic
Sprite	Windex Glass Cleaner
Squirt	Wonder Bread & Buns
Sweet 'n Low	Zest Soap
Tang	Not a Single Zirconia
3 Minute Oats	

You can see that you're not contemplating a move to some poorly provisioned outpost on a dusty road to oblivion. When you get to the tourist areas, retirement gulags and larger cities, the selection increases dramatically to include many more international products such as a wider selection of spices and seasonings, cake mixes, crackers, canned soups, candies, and specialty foods.

Smokers will find these brands along with Mexican and Cuban brands:

Benson & Hedges 100's	Marlboro Lights
Benson & Hedges Menthol 100's	Marlboro Menthol
Camels	Raleigh
Camels Filters	Viceroy 100's
L & M Filters	Viceroy Lights
Marlboro 100's	Viceroy Menthol

Since the time of Sir Walter Raleigh on up to the days of the brown snuff rivulets running down my grandma's chin, you dippers have had to make do with that powdered stuff. You'll find the new and improved Copenhagen and Skoal brands here in many places. Your girlfriend and I don't know why you'd want to hunt for 'em, but they're here.

So what else do you really need to know about shopping in Mexico?

As far as canned goods, cleaning products and most grooming aids are concerned, the Mexican brands are less expensive and just as good, if not better, than what you get back in Quincy or Quebec. If you employ a maid she'll tell you what to buy as far as cleaning supplies go. Fabuloso and Clorolex usually top the list, but Clorox *is* available. Even if you clean for yourself, and you *are* retired, with plenty of time to do it, you can ask around or experiment to find the local products that work best and which ones you prefer. For instance, Ajax

Expel added to mop water or other cleaning water, will kill most bugs in cabinets or on the floors. You can do two chores at once.

Get Over It!

Uh, oh, I feel a rant coming on. The one thing that I hear many expats (women expats actually) complain about is that they can't find peanut butter. It's only available in *every damn* grocery store in Mexico except for those in the high elevations of the Sierra Madres Norte south of Durango, parts of the Yucatan, and a few other places you probably don't want to move to anyway. What they don't have is Holy Brother Waldo's Organically Grown and Personally Blessed, Totally Virgin, Gently Roasted, Twenty-two Freakin' Dollars a Jar Chunky Peanut Wonder. As far as I'm concerned the best brand is Pronto's Aladino con

TIENDITA AJIJIC,
WILLIAM
GENTES, 1988

Trocitos (pieces). I've also found Peter Pan *crema de cacahuate extra crujiente* (extra crunchy), as well as Skippy. Peanut butter is here and easily available, as are several kinds of jams and jellies, honey, and syrup. You ladies stop that whinin'.

The Veggie Life

If you're a practicing vegetarian you might want to learn a phrase not commonly used by we hoi-polloi carnivores. That phrase is: "*Dame, por favor, un plato de verduras crudas.*" Bring me please a plate of raw vegetables. You might need to name them. Le*chuga, jitomate, cebolla, zanahoria, rábano, pepino, apio.* Lettuce, tomato, onion, carrot, radish, cucumber, celery. You can also say "*verduras crudas picaditas*" and Marcel Marceau the "chopped" part. If this is a neighborhood place where you might be eating often, ask the cook if you can demonstrate how you wish it prepared. Folks can be mighty accommodating. And once you gain access to the kitchen, put on a real show. The other diners are watching to see what the hell is going on. You may become a local celebrity.

Get used to ordering raw veggies because a Mexican salad usually looks like this: a piece of lettuce, a slice of tomato and two or three rings of white onion. It's more or less the same idea as a McDonald's hamburger; it has all the elements of the real thing but it falls just a bit short of being what you expected. Some restaurants in or near the *gringo* stalags are beginning to serve excellent salads. Usually *ensalada verde* will be a variation of the above described plate. But if you see *ensalada de la casa* listed on the menu, *el menu* or *a la carta,* be sure to inquire because it's sure to be more elaborate.

Speaking of chopping; if you're doing your daily shopping and decide you need only half as much cabbage as that head will provide, just ask the storekeeper "*La mitad solamente?*" as you point to or hold up the cabbage. They'll usually divide things for you and this will save you money.

And of course for your dining pleasure there's always cheese (*queso) tacos,* cheese *quesadillas,* and a fair selection of soups *(sopas),* rice *(arroz),* and beans *(frijoles).* Be creative with your ordering. Steaming is part of Mexican cooking so you'll be able to order steamed vegetables by asking, "*Vegetables al vapor?*"

In larger towns you'll find vegetarian restaurants if you search a bit.

So the *very* good news is that if you're a vegetarian or a frequently fasting monk you can survive for next to nothing here. Fresh produce is both inexpensive and plentiful. Unless you eat a lot of apples or Peruvian grapes. Imported, don'cha know. Even Mexican grapes can get pricey at times because the Mexican wine industry is picking up steam right now and producing some nice reds.

The local veggie shops and markets usually get fresh produce on Wednesdays and Saturdays. If you want something special, or something they don't normally carry, you can let them know by Monday or Thursday and they'll order it for you. Today I bought 25 new potatoes, three ribs of celery, a head of cauliflower, a stalk of broccoli, a medium-sized purple onion, 23 limes, a small white onion and a large avocado for 29 *pesos,* or about three bucks US. Recently a 14 pound watermelon, two large onions, 14 new potatoes, a large head of cabbage, 16 *Roma* tomatoes, and a kilo of green beans cost me about six bucks.

You'll have a selection of bananas, papayas, mangoes, pineapples (*piñas),* watermelons (*sandias),* squash and squash blossoms, green beans, lentils, both white and purple onions, *chiles* (peppers), green, yellow, orange and red varieties of the bell pepper, corn, Brussels sprouts, grapefruits, oranges, prunes, raisins, dates, strawberries, blackberries, blueberries, lettuce, pumpkins, cucumbers, purslane, sunflower seeds, pomegranates, tomatoes, cabbage, a great variety of beans, peas, snow peas, yams, parsley and *cilantro,* beets, eggplant, both red and white potatoes, mustard or spinach and other greens, bean sprouts, alfalfa sprouts, pears, nectarines, kiwi fruit, leeks, garlic, asparagus, *avocados,* cauliflower, *tomatillos,* okra, quince, zucchini, walnuts, pecans, almonds, pistachios, peanuts, turnips, figs, coconuts, limes, Asian pears, celery, tangerines, Mandarin oranges, a variety of radishes, several types of melons, carrots, olives, peaches, plums, garbanzos, guavas, mushrooms, and exotic items, depending on where you are. You will almost never see russet baking potatoes.

There are also *chayotes,* a bland squash called Christophenes in Louisiana; and *pitayas,* the very sweet, very messy cactus fruit that's eaten by squeezing it and slurping the meat, seeds and juice from the reddish-purple skin. Just a warning, though, don't leave them lying on your dashboard unless you want a sticky glue capable of soldering I-beams. You'll also find *tunas,* another cactus fruit, but of the *Nopal* cactus we call prickly pear cactus in Texas; *nopales,* the "de-thorned" and sliced leaves of the same cactus that are used raw in salads or cooked with herbs or other vegetables; *jícama,* a truly ugly tuber that looks like a rough-skined brown turnip that has a crisp, almost sweetish taste that can be fried or eaten raw in salads or with lime juice; *nances,* a plum-like fruit that the Mexicans eat either green or yellow; and *mamey,* a large brown, sweetly tart fruit resembling an *avocado* that wraps around two large interior seeds. A green thorny-looking thing, called a *guanabana,* tastes like a citrus banana. Brown raggedy things that look like giant bean pods are *tamarindos.* Shuck 'em out of the shell, peel off that sticky skin, drop them into water to soak until the beans float, and then throw the beans away. Add sugar to the water and you'll have a wonderfully tasty drink, or a cure for constipation. You'll discover other treats as you go adventuring. And if you're lucky you may meet someone who owns a passion fruit vine and will share the fruit, called *maracuya,* with you. They're hard to find in the stores.

You'll also find yogurt, a wide world of domestic and imported cheeses, different pastas (spaghetti, noodles, macaroni), eggs, cream cheese, sour cream, cottage cheese, molasses and other syrups, popcorn (even *microonda*—for the microwave), wheat germ, pickles and rice, although it may be difficult to find brown rice in some areas, and the pickings on the pickle aisle may be a bit slim.

For my fellow omnivores, there's plenty to sate our voracious cravings. Pork, beef, chicken and other fowl; rabbit; fish and other seafood; goat, lamb, ostrich and occasionally, wild game, can be purchased in the *carnicerías*, butcher shops, and larger grocery stores. The greater part of these meats, with the exception of seafood and some poultry, are quite taxing in their texture—I guess the correct word would be "tough".

By no means are you going to find all these foods in every town or village on every single day of the year. This is meant to illustrate the variety of foods that are available in the local markets in many places, most of the time.

How to Shop in a *Frutería*

Here are a few pointers to help you avoid looking like Fulano's half-wit sibling when you walk into a *frutería* for the first time. Once you enter you'll see a stack of small, round, plastic dishpans sitting around, although this, as everything else, varies from place to place. The big corner store in Jocotepec, a village on the Northshore of Lake Chapala provides some very nice woven baskets laced with rawhide bottoms. They're hanging all over the store. Another place just off the plaza in Saltillo has plastic buckets. Those are your shopping baskets. And yes, some places do have actual wire shopping baskets and carts. It varies. If they're not in sight just ask for one. Pantomime if you need to, just get your hands on one and act like you know what you're doing.

Thump those melons and squeeze those peaches, just the same way you do to drive Harvey berserk in the produce section of the Safeway back in Phoenix.

Here's where you discover the difference between Harvey and Jose. If you see something new and wonder what it is and what it tastes like, or if you wonder if that *sandia* is really as sweet as the color and texture of that split one would lead you to believe, just ask, or pantomime, for a small sample. Harvey never would, but Jose will oblige your request. Or just taste a grape, you're not going to get arrested. You're not shop*lifting*, you're shop*ping*. I suppose you could occasionally cop a free meal using this approach, but when they get wise to you you'd better move to another market

"Mangos Ocho Pesos, Mangos Ocho Pesos, Mangos Ocho Pesos..."

There are also vendors who come right to your door. Not if you live in a really, really *gringo* neighborhood or gated community, but you wouldn't do either of those things would you? You'll know they're coming because they have speakers mounted on the roofs of their vehicles and they blare out their sales pitch as they cruise the neighborhoods.

Last year I was driving in from San Juan Cosalá toward Chapala and got caught behind one of those mobile entrepreneurs as he slowly chugged along in an old Subaru station wagon. Twin speakers mounted on the roof were blasting out his message as a really manic and stressed-out monkey, chained to the car, leapt from one of the speaker supports to another as though his sanity could be preserved. Yes, I thought the same thing. There's a sight you're not likely to see in Ottawa or Omaha.

Street vendors bring all sorts of things: fruits and vegetables, freshly baked breads and pastries, and in certain little towns, even clothes, hardware and furniture, mops, brooms and cleaning supplies. It doesn't matter if you can't understand what they're saying, just go out and see what all the hubbub is about.

What'd I Say?

Speaking of understanding what the vendors' speakers are spewing, one problem you'll encounter unless you're fluent in Spanish is the realization that you've often initiated a conversation or negotiation with a few words of Spanish that led you briskly to the linguistic pool you later found yourself drowning in.

A friend explained it to me once. She said that once I initiate the conversation in what sounds like fairly fluent and passably pronounced Spanish, the listener naturally assumes that my vocabulary exceeds the thirteen words I actually know. I've gotten better, but not by much. I still have trouble with numbers in any language so I've learned something that I'll pass on as a little *regalo.*

Carry a pad and pencil. You can get by with pantomime and pointing, gibberish and gesticulation up to a point, but you better make damn sure you're crystal clear about money matters. Sometimes Mafia moneylenders can be easier to deal with than some Mexican merchants. I recently wrote out a construction estimate on the back of an old clay floor tile. Use what you've got at hand and save yourself a lot of misunderstandings.

And no, the street merchants usually do not have a pen or pencil, unless that's what they happen to be selling.

Forrest and Bubba Knew Shrimp, I Know Bread

Let's spend a few minutes on the fascinating subject of bread, or *pan.* That's pronounced "pahn". The two most frequent brands that look like what you're used to are Wonder and the Mexican brand called *Bimbo.*

I know what you're thinking. A lot of tourists think it's quite humorous and I'd be willing to bet there are at least four or five bazillion souvenir photos stored away somewhere showing goofily-grinning *gringas* grouped beneath a *Bimbo* sign.

Both of these brands offer regular white bread that's no better for you here than it is there. A weak imitation of whole wheat bread is called *pan integral,* hamburger buns are *bollas*, and hot dog buns are called *medias noches,* or midnights. Why they're called *medias noches* is a regular mystery among us *gringos.*

A lot of folks haunt the local *panaderías*, the bakeries, until they learn the schedule and routine. Usually they bake in the mornings and have their product ready for sale in the early afternoon. One storeowner I know brings fresh bread back when she re-opens the store after her *siesta.* Some *panaderías* offer special items on special days, sometimes even in the early mornings, and most have a huge and tempting selection of *pan dulce*, sweet breads, i.e. pastries, tarts, cakes and cookies ready for sale. In some places, you'll find *panadería* operations in large grocery stores and pharmacies. Wherever you see them, they all operate about the same. When you go in you'll see a stack of large aluminum or plastic trays, like round serving trays or baskets, and lying around somewhere, sets of tongs. Grab a tray and tongs and let loose the *dulce* demon. Everything is there, so tong away. Buy lots. Pastries in Mexico are inexpensive. When you're loaded up, head for the cashier's counter where a clerk will either bag or wrap your purchase.

Pastelerías are shops that sell cakes, pies and other similar confections. One year while on vacation in San Felipe in Baja Norte I made the mistake of discovering a fantastic *pastelería* close to my hotel and sharing the knowledge with my partner. I'm definitely not a morning person but my bride of the moment insisted that I get up each morning to stagger off and pillage the bakery. Luckily, it was neither complicated nor expensive.

I have no clue what those Baja goodies cost but it couldn't have been much. I'd dribble a few *pesos* onto the counter, the smiling and sympathetic lady would sort through them, take some, return some to me, and send me on my way with a huge bag of diabetic triggers. Even in a semi-comatose fog, they were delicious. They still are.

Donuts

You'll even find donuts in Mexico. As a matter of fact some places have Dunkin' Donuts countertop display cases although I believe I'm safe in saying that the Philadelphia Police force or the Moose Jaw Mounties, after a taste test, might argue something about false advertising. Plus those are too expensive anyway. Remember the cars that drive through the neighborhoods? About a fourth of the price as DD or other specialty shop products—about one and a half to two *pesos* each for *bolillos* (boh LEE ohs) and most sweets. The coffee shop stuff sells though, because *gringos* love to congregate and drink coffee and lie to each other about how cleverly they pick stocks and how poorly whoever is in any elective or appointive position is doing. The majority of us are too "mature" for our sex lies to be taken seriously anymore.

A lot of the more "high-strung" ladies strongly encourage their spouses to join one of these informal groups as often as possible with the advice, "Go early, stay late."

Back to the *Bolillos*

But the subject under study is bread, not BS, so let's get back to it. Many of my friends are simply enamored with *bolillos*, probably the most common bread throughout Mexico. They resemble a small roll of French bread. In some places, they may be called *pan blanco*, the same as the packaged stuff. Play it by ear until you know for sure. They normally cost between 15 to 22 cents US depending on where you live and who you buy them from. And, like every individually produced item, quality varies. The best ones are light and easy to eat. The worst are identical in looks to the best, but usually suffer from a tendency to get harder than Chinese calculus or more rubbery than your brother-in-law's inflatable date. Find a good supplier and stick with 'em, even if you have to walk a few extra blocks to get a fix. And don't plan on stockpiling to save yourself a trip to the store. They're not loaded with preservatives and they'll go bad quicker than a catfish on the Kalahari. Do yourself a favor and buy fresh daily.

In nearly every *abarrote* in Mexico there will be a box or basket of bread on or near the front counter. The locally made *pan* and *pasteles* will be in it, usually covered by a cloth. Sometimes the whole shebang is inside a huge plastic bag. If they're in a bag, look for the open end (which is usually neatly tucked under) and root your way in. But wait! First ask for a smaller plastic bag (*una bolsa, por favor*), slip it over your hand, pick up what you want, and pull the bag off your hand, from the wrist edge first. If you're dexterous you've just flipped the bag around your selection and freed your hand. If things didn't go quite that well, then go ahead and pay for all the stuff you just scattered across the floor of the *tienda*. Sometimes you'll be spared and have tongs to snag your goodies. You'll still need to request "*una bolsa, por favor*".

Are *bolillos* economically feasible? Several little neighborhood restaurants in most Mexican towns think so, as well as nearly every roadside or sidewalk vendor worth his salt. *Tortas* (sandwiches) with a variety of fillings are sold very inexpensively—about a dollar or so in many cases—by many Mexican cooks. They'll pack that thing with almost anything you'd put on a regular old white bread sandwich: ham (both fresh and processed into a tidy little meat-like luncheon loaf), chicken, beans, fried or grilled pork, cheese, sausage, fried potatoes, eggs, or combinations of these ingredients.

Tortas, just like the white bread sandwiches that you find in bus stations and other shrines of gastronomic delight usually have been garnished with at least a bit of the ubiquitous *chile jalapeño.* If you're not acclimated yet, consider this your heads-up. *Tortas* are definitely a bargain; they're inexpensive, tasty, and filling.

A growing number of shops, stores and restaurants are learning to prepare U.S.-style sandwiches, both hot and cold, and to charge U.S.-style prices. You may be dying for a BLT or a Reuben but compare the cost of it and a *torta* if you're watching your *pesos.*

But don't confuse these sandwich *tortas* with other pastries and main dishes called by the same name.

A few places are actually coming up with bagels and cream cheese. And count on those bagels being frozen. There *are* New York style bagel bakeries advertised in Mexico City and Guadalajara. Now *that's* something I'd brave the cities for.

Buying *Tortillas*

You can go to the *tienda* in some *gringo* areas and buy them there or you can go where your neighbors go, the local *tortillería.* You buy them by weight, by the *kilo* or a fraction thereof. Just announce, *"un kilo, por favor"* as you walk up to the counter. Or *"medio kilo"* if you want half a kilo. Or *"un cuarto",* one quarter, if you really just want a few. How many tortillas are there in a *kilo*? About forty to fifty.

As a monument to dying traditionalism, Wonder sells ready-made flour *tortillas.* Flour--as in northern Mexican cuisine, Arizona, Tex-Mex and Taco Bell. Harfi brand offers ready-mades of both *trigo* (wheat) and *integral* (mixed grains). Tia Rosa brand sells them as *"tortillianas"* and Milpa Real sells a corn variety that will stay edible for 30 days, if refrigerated.

Since the time of the *conquistadores* wheat *tortillas* have been the choice of the moneyed and/or cultured classes. Corn is regarded as lower class. Some restaurants will offer you a choice, but usually you're going to be served corn *tortillas* or white bread.

Huevos and Other Misunderstood Orbs

Let's go back to the grocery section again and discuss eggs. *Huevos. Blanquillos.* Folks may tell you to avoid the former word as it also has reference to male anatomical parts. I say that no company would print the word *"huevos"* on a box of their product if they really believed that people would think the box was full of testicles. They *do* serve testicles in toney Yupraunts in Colorado so I'm sure they must have a reputable supplier. We used to save 'em and fry 'em up in batter after we worked calves each spring. But we were discussing eggs, weren't we?

In some stores, you'll find them in cardboard cartons with lids. In others, they'll be packed in styrofoam. In the smaller shops they'll be sold by weight, just like *tortillas*, where they'll be carefully placed in plastic bags before they're weighed. Or you'll see them stacked neatly in the cardboard trays on the counter. Unrefrigerated. *Huevos,* I mean. Not testicles.

Just to be on the safe side, smile when you ask the grocer, *"No tienes huevos?"* Everyone gets the joke. Ladies, you can say, *"No tienes blanquillos?"*

I don't know how long they'll last, perhaps several days. I've never had any go bad on me. If I find that I'm not using as many as I'd planned, I put them in the fridge after a couple of days. Or mix them into the dogs' food. Figure about 17 or 18 medium-sized eggs to a *kilo*, and you can buy just one or two if you wish.

The corner restaurant that serves the $2 US ($2.50 with *jamón or tocino*) breakfast (*desayuno)* offers *huevos al gusto* (as you like them). You may like them fried (*frito)* or scrambled *(revueltos)* but I'd wait until I was more fluent to try to explain anything else, although you may, on occasion find a place that can poach *(escalfar)* one for you. If the menu offers *huevos a la Mexicana,* I'll bet you can figure it out—scrambled eggs with *chiles, cebolla* (onion), *jitomate,* and sometimes garlic and *cilantro.*

You may want to further refine your fried egg order by specifying *huevos duros* (hard), or *estrellados* (sunny side up). I always pantomime for over easy (hand held out and quickly flipped, followed by the "just a little bit" sign with thumb and forefinger) because I seldom remember *estrellados volteados.* Sounds like you're asking for an electric star or something. *Estrella* means star and *sol* is the sun, so it seems to me it should be *huevos sol* something or other.

Do not panic if your order of ham and eggs comes to the table as a plate of eggs with chopped bits of chopped ham cooked in. That's how it's usually done. If you want them the way you usually get them back home, specify *separado.*

Toast? Easy, *tostada.* You can even buy this at the grocery store. *Bimbo Pan Tostada. Huevos, tocino o jamón, salchicha* (sausage), *and papas fritas (*fried potatoes) ought to get you by for breakfast, but you can also order an *omelet* (you got it) with any of the above ingredients plus *cebolla* (onion), *queso (*cheese), and *pimento morron* (sweet, or Bell pepper). *Hot kakes* (sometimes with a "c") are offered in some places. And you get real butter and jam. If they don't bring it, ask for *mantequilla y mermelada.* Or if you prefer, you can also get *margarina.* French fries are called *papas a la francesa* and you might get them instead of hash browns or country fries. You'll usually find beans on the plate if you order a Mexican breakfast of *chilaquiles.* Actually, I wouldn't be too surprised to find beans served with almost anything, including dessert. *Chilaquiles?* They're strips of leftover *tortillas* that are too dry to serve. I don't mean to infer that they're spoiled or stale, just a bit dry. They're cooked with eggs and bits of beef or chicken and a nice spicy sauce. They're much tastier than this description would lead you to believe.

I know that all this skipping back and forth between Spanish and English is disconcerting, but if you're sitting in a little eatery out on the blazing sands of East Nowherita, looking at a page full of Spanish and wondering how to get a meal, this might be useful. Or, the owner *could be* a retired Harvard linguistics professor who will be glad to help you order. Just as soon as he finishes pulling a five-carat diamond out of that goat's butt.

Here's a final tip that seldom works but it's always worth a try. Many Mexican cooks seem to believe that bacon is not fit to be served if it's any color other than dark brown, tinged with black. If you order bacon you might say "*no muy frito*" or "*termino medio*" or any phrase that someone might teach you, that you hope will induce the waitress or waiter to ask the cook to ease up a bit in the crematorium. This over-cooking mania may stem from the fact that many *gringos* still persist in the idea that *any* pork eaten South of the Border is 100% likely to blind, cripple or kill you.

And finally, *pimienta* is pepper and s*al* (sahl) is salt, which offers an opening for another side trip...

Salt on the Tale

I was heading back North from a trip to San Felipe, a hot, windy little village on the Sea of Cortez, in the Baja, almost due south of Mexicali. I kept noticing large patches of white off in the distance to my right. Those who know me can tell you what happened next. The next dirt road I came to became my new destination. I went adventuring in that little San Diego based rental car. Aside from a Jeep Wrangler, my favorite Mexico car is any rented one.

I bounced through ruts and washouts. I slid, spun and skidded through loose sand and powder, testing the mettle of that little rental until I happened upon the coolest business operation I'd seen since Uncle Rayford opened up that goat-gland "transplant" clinic in Matamoros.

Right in front of me were several eighteen-wheelers, a forklift, a few front-end loaders, and a swarm of laborers with shovels. The ground was covered with salt and the loaders were scraping and piling the stuff into huge ten and twelve feet mounds. The laborers were shoveling salt into big bags and loading pallets at a fair clip. The forklift loaded the pallets onto the flatbeds. That salt was just money laying there for the taking. I'm sure someone was paying for the privilege, and I was very impressed.

Years later, I saw a similar, but more labor-intensive operation near Manzanillo. On May third I came wheeling around a curve and there to my left was what I recognized as some sort of salt-making operation. At the next road I turned left and followed a dirt road a short distance to a cluster of houses where one hell of a party was underway in the middle of the afternoon. I saw *Mariachis*, food, drink, women and children, and what I assumed to be salt workers. They were. *Happy* salt workers.

I drove past the party and down toward the edge of the shallow lagoon where I saw a uniquely simple method of harvesting salt. As I was leaving, a young lady waved me down and in perfect English asked, "Do you have questions I could answer?"

Yes I did.

She explained that water from the Pacific was pumped into holding tanks. The tanks were pits about a foot deep, ten feet wide and twenty feet long, dug into the soft earth and lined with black plastic sheeting. The seawater was drawn into the pits by portable gas-powered pumps and allowed to evaporate for several days. The partially evaporated sludge would then be pumped across the road into shallower pits about four or five inches deep. There the evaporation process continued until all that remained were damp salt crystals. The salt was then swept out of the pits into piles and later bagged for transport.

Who was the young lady? Her name was Connie, or Consuela, born in the nearby town of Santa Rita and transferred to the U.S. about the time of her fifth birthday. She grew up in Oregon, attended school, and now, after ten years had been back in Santa Rita for a year. She was one of the nominees for Queen of the upcoming festival scheduled for the next Saturday and did I want to come? Did I want to stay for the party today? "It's for the construction workers", she said. It was with great regret that I had to decline.

You may be wondering how I remember that this happened on May third when I'm usually totally lost when it comes to time. The party. Lest I give the impression that I know more than I do, I'm going to let an expert explain the festival held each May third. The following is paraphrased from *The Cross in Mexico* by Virginia B. de Barrios. It's available in most bookstores here and I highly recommend it.

The Day of the Holy Cross, or El Dia de la Santa Cruz (May 3) is celebrated throughout most of Mexico. This day is dedicated to the *albaniles*, the masons, and now, in more modern times, all construction tradesmen. A colorful and elaborately decorated cross tops any building under construction. This is a day for the men to really celebrate. Feasting, drinking, fireworks and the day off are vital components.

If you ask any of the workers why they're being so honored, the chances are that you'll get a shrug for an answer. Here's what Virginia B. de Barrios says.

Emporer Constantine charged his mother, Santa Elena, with the task of traveling to the Holy Land to search for the Nativity of Christ, and if found, to supervise the construction of a basilica there. Successful in finding the site, she searched for relics and objects relating to Christ's crucifixion. She asked the masons under her supervision to assist in her search and they eventually found The Nails, but no part of The Cross.

After a year of labor and searching for the cross, Elena had exhausted both money and hope. As she was preparing to return home, disappointed and disconsolate, the masons approached her with a unique and generous offer. They acknowledged her kindness toward them and were grateful that she'd paid them well for their work. They offered to work an additional day without pay. She accepted their offer and the masons went back to work. Within a short time, on that day, May third, the workers found and recovered the Holy Cross, as well as two others.

Santa Elena appreciated the kindness and the efforts of these workers and arranged for them to be remembered and honored each year on the day of the discovery.

When the fireworks start blasting on the morning of May third, you'll know why.

Nice story, huh? Here's another one about Huixtocihuatl, the Aztec patron goddess of saltmakers.

It was told that Huixtocihuatl was the sister of the rain gods. As siblings often do they had a quarrel and she left home to live alone in the ocean, where she developed a method of extracting salt by exposing shallow vessels of ocean water to the sun. Because of this, she became the goddess of salt.

Chapter 12

Household Help

Now that you've found a home, stocked it, and figured out how to find your groceries, other things will begin to creep into your consciousness like, "Should I hire a maid?" I can imagine several scenarios that might justify such a move.

- You've managed to find a huge filthy old *casa* at a ridiculously low cost.
- You and your spouse have both been rejuvenated by the fresh Mexican air and you spend massive blocks of time making love both day and night.
- You drink yourself into a stupor by noon each day.
- You're as lazy as a Missouri mountaineer.
- You want to impress the folks back home.
- You have way too much money.
- You can't stand to clean the litter box.
- You've gone temporarily insane.

Do what you want, but keep a few facts in mind. First and foremost, a full-time employee has many more rights in Mexico than you might imagine. As an employer you have at least as many responsibilities, if not more, than you would in the U.S. or Canada. For instance, there's a Mexican minimum wage here. There are also seven holidays each year when you are required to pay your employees for taking the day off.

Common Holidays

1. January 1st New Year's Day
2. February 5th Constitution Day
3. March 21st Benito Juárez Day
4. May 1st Labor Day
5. September 16th Mexican Independence Day
6. November 20th Revolution Day
7. December 25th Christmas Day

Let me just mention that if you're employing a male in certain parts of the country you probably won't see him on Mother's Day. I haven't figured this one out yet, but you need to find out if he's gonna be at your place workin' or if he's gonna be sittin' out somewhere with Fulano and the boys, emptyin' *tequila* bottles and carryin' on about how much they love Mama. Trust me, and check it out if having him show up is important to you.

You'll be required to pay, by December 20th, a Christmas bonus of a least fifteen days pay. You'll be required to pay vacation pay, plus a 25% bonus during the vacation period. After one year's employment it's six days. Two years, eight days. Three years, ten days. Four years, twelve days. After that you get a breather and the time only increases two additional days for each succeeding five years of employment. Unless your employee is dismissed for good cause you'll also be required to come up with severance pay. And just like in the U.S., you'll pay into the Mexican Social Security system. For a brief look at some of your SS responsibilities you can go to the English language version of http://www.ssa.gov/statistics/ssptw/1999/English/mexico.htm. This info is a bit out of date but it's the best available on the web.

You need to know that if your employee has been on your payroll for less than six months and becomes ill or disabled, you'll be required to continue paying the salary for up to a month. If they've worked for you for more than six months, you're required to pay the salary for as long as three months. In the event that your employee dies, you may be responsible for the cost of the funeral. Here's some really obvious advice. If you decide to hire domestic help, use your head. If an applicant stumbles and falls when entering and leaving the premises or exhibits any tendencies toward unusual non-coordination or spastic actions, interview someone else. If an applicant exhibits any indication of past multiple major injuries or a tendency towards illness or disease, interview someone else. Freshly healed wounds, a mass of open sores, a hacking phlegmy cough, or unevenly dilated pupils might be a few warning signs that you're in danger of hooking up with a potentially expensive non-productive employee.

If you're determined to go ahead and hire someone, and yes, in spite of all my ranting I usually do, there are a few more things to consider. If you hire live-in help, the room and board you provide is considered equal to 50% of their pay. Many if not most full-time blue-collar employees work at least five and a half days a week. If yours do, they're entitled to a full seven days of pay. And Sunday is traditionally considered to be the official day off. If you require your employee to work on Sunday, you'll be required to pay an additional 25% of the daily salary. Even if you only require your folks to work five days a week, you're responsible for that extra 25% if one of those days is Sunday.

There is *some* good news though. If you hired someone and discovered that the gem you thought you had was actually secondhand costume jewelry, there's a 30-day "get out of the situation free" card right on top of the deck. If your employee doesn't fit your needs you can let them go without having to prove a problem or having to come up with severance pay—providing you do so no later than day 29. If you're not using a contract for employment, and nobody I know does, your employee is considered hired after 30 days. If you need to terminate them after that, the severance pay is three months salary. Automatic, no appeal, pay up, that's it. If they quit, you won't owe the severance. Or if you fire them for justifiable reasons you won't owe severance. Justifiable reasons? Stay tuned, here come a few.

- If an employee fails to show up for work for three consecutive days (some lawyers say four days) without good reason (health, injury, incarceration, etc.) and fails to notify you, they are considered to have quit.
- You may release an employee if they have misrepresented their work experience or skills, or
- the employee threatens or performs acts of violence, or offers up threatening remarks, or
- they perform any sort of immoral or illegal act while working, or
- they steal from you, or
- they sabotage or purposefully damage your property or belongings.

Keep in mind that if you decide to terminate an employee for any of these reasons you'd better be damn sure you can prove your accusations beyond a shadow of a doubt unless you enjoy being the target of a lawsuit—which you're gonna lose. One way to chronicle accusations is to keep a dated, detailed written account of every single infraction your employee has committed and have someone witness each entry. If an employee quits or is discharged you need to report it in writing to the labor authorities and get a stamped acknowledgement. If you fail to get official verification the ex-employee can come back at any time and claim a later discharge date. In that case you may wind up paying for periods when the person was not on your payroll. Do not take this lightly. It's a relatively common occurrence. Mexican law strongly favors the employee in cases of labor disputes. It doesn't matter what documentation you have or how many witnesses you come up with; you're very likely to lose. The folks I know who have been involved in these disputes wish they'd just settled up with the ex-employees before the hearing.

Here's something really important: if you rent a place or buy a house where the maid and gardener have been employed for a considerable length of time and you replace them, you may be responsible for shelling out severance pay. Check this out before signing a contract because it could amount to a significant chunk of money.

Here are the obligations you're going to assume when you hire someone. You must:

- Follow all labor laws. I don't know all of them, and you probably won't either. Good luck to all of us.
- Pay all salaries and any required severance.
- Treat your employees respectfully. If you're like any one of several Texas school superintendents and principals I know, this may be a challenge. I tried to train some of 'em but they're tougher to deal with than my Special Ed kids ever were. But just to be semi-fair, so was I.
- Provide any tools and materials required to do the assigned job.
- Allow your employees time to vote on election day.
- In the event that the poor misguided souls belong to one, you must allow them to attend union meetings. No, I did not belong to a teacher's union, although I was president of my local non-union independent statewide teacher's organization.

Here's a short list of the main things your employees are required to do while working for you.

- They must follow the labor laws. They probably don't know them all either.
- They must follow and adhere to any reasonable work orders and requirements.
- They must let you know if they're going to be unable to come to work, but they must not miss work unless it is unavoidable or justified.
- They must not report to work under the influence of drugs or alcohol.
- They must not show up for work carrying a gun. Having looked down

the business end of a weapon on a couple of continents, I'd have to say that this is one situation you'll want to handle very carefully.

🛠 They must store all tools and materials carefully, and care for them well.

🛠 They must not steal from you, or borrow items without permission.

Paying for National Health Care and a Pension Plan

Many people, including Mexican homeowners and some businesses, pay nothing into the IMSS system on behalf of their employees. Since 2001 the government has made a concerted effort to encourage them to do so. Encourage in this sense means "force". Some *gringos* are really upset about this, suspecting that it's a ploy designed to get us to help take up some of the financial burden of healthcare in Mexico. Other than the IVA (sales tax) and obscenely low homeowners taxes, very few foreigners pay much into the government coffers at all.

If you're serious about leaping into the churning vortex of employing domestic assistance, you may want to stop by a bookstore to purchase a copy of the Ley Federal del Trabajo, the federal labor laws. You won't be able to comprehend much of it. It's written in legalese. Spanish legalese.

It will be easier to go to *http://www.mexconnect.com/mex_/laborlaw.html* where you'll find many of the provisions of Mexican labor law in English. The American Chamber of Commerce of Mexico, A.C. has provided this information for the benefit of large-scale employers but you too can benefit from their kindness.

Maids and Other Mixed Blessings

If you do decide to employ a maid you're embarking on an unknown adventure which may enable you to safely navigate the waters of an alien sea or cause you to end up shattered on the harbor rocks. This one's always a toss-up and a roll of the dice. Remember that in Mexico, working as a maid is a respected vocation. Treat your maid with respect.

One part-time maid that I employed never spoke to me after the initial interview, not even a *"gracias"* on payday. Another one showed up to do her work, unannounced and at irregular hours. One evening when I was doing the drip-dry after a shower and standing naked at the ironing board pressing a shirt I turned to find her standing in the doorway. Thankfully, she had all of *her* clothes on.

The good ones though, will make all the difference in the world. One used to show up in the evenings with cakes and pies and sweet corn *tamales*. She taught me to make *aguas frescas* to drink instead of soft drinks. She brought cat's claw from a tree in her yard to brew a cancer-fighting tea for me to drink.

VESTIGIOS, WILLIAM GENTES, 1978

I was invited to all the family functions and parties. She even managed to teach me a bit of Spanish and a lot about the daily ebb and flow of life SoB.

I really have mixed feelings on this subject, as you can probably tell. This is one you're just going to have to work out for yourselves. I've never needed a full-time maid so I'm giving you hourly prices for a part-timer here. In 2000, in the Chapala/Ajijic area, many of my friends were paying maids $1.25 to $1.75 US per hour. I paid Maria $2.00 an hour because she came each evening after a long day at her regular job at one of the local hotels, where she's worked for more than twenty-five years. One of the cost of living charts I refered you to earlier shows $5.00 a day as the wage for a full-time maid. Not only do I not believe that, I'd be ashamed to admit to paying someone 60 cents an hour. Of course, it's a different situation if she's a live-in and takes all of her meals at your expense. I'm currently paying Rosa 20 *pesos* an hour out here in San Juan Cosalá. She comes three times a week for a four-hour shot and carries out her duties like a pro.

If your Spanish is almost non-existent, get your hands on the following gem. RuthM. Dietz wrote a book called *Spanish-English Housekeeping*. It's a bilingual treasure chest of illustrated descriptions of many Spanish words. For instance one illustration shows a drawing of a pitcher with the label "Pitcher (water)", and written below that, *La Jarra*.

The book also has a list of phrases for you to use while communicating with your maid. "Never put grease down the disposal. *Nunca eche grasa en el desechador.*" Doesn't that look simple? Chances are good that you're never going to see a garbage disposal in any house you'll live in here, but isn't it nice to know you'll be able to toss out instructions about one if the need arises?

Instructions and explanations are offered for each room of the house--the children's nursery, the laundry, the patio and yard. Emergencies, general conversation, the metric system, and many other subjects are covered in this valuable book. It can be ordered from the publisher, Eakin Press. Look on *http:// www.eakinpress.com* or write to Eakin Press, P.O. Drawer 90159, Austin, Texas 78709-0159. The phone # is 800-880-8642 and the fax is 512-288-1771, or you can e-mail to *sales@eakinpress.com*.

Gardeners and Other Ways to Piss Your Money Away

The same legal factors apply if you decide that cutting grass and trimming plants SoB are only slightly less complicated than teaching chess to cockroaches and that a highly skilled and tremendously efficient gardener must be employed to ensure that the job be done correctly.

First, nearly all the highly skilled and tremendously efficient gardeners in Mexico already have jobs. The ones hoping you'll hire them seem to be mostly proficient at loading twenty meters of old water hose into a rusty wheelbarrow, pushing it around town searching for a gringo who'll pay good money for him to unload the hose, hook it up to water the lawn, unhook and load it back into the wheelbarrow, and then jollyfrock on down the trail with a pocketful of dubiously earned *pesos*.

Or the variation. "I'm a master of the secret and sacred mysteries of ancient Aztec plant care and cultivation." This one claims he's a master gardener but can't seem to figure out how anything works or what needs to be done. Unfortunately your *jardin* does not contain a single ancient Aztec plant. You, of course, consider this quaint and cute so you're going to show him how modern tools and techniques can transform your barren plot of sand and weeds into a tropical Eden.

Every day. Same lesson. He just can't seem to grasp the concepts presented. But he can water. While you're "teaching".

Congratulations, you've just volunteered to be your own gardener. "Patsy" means the same in both English and Spanish. How smart is it to pay someone to do something that you have to personally supervise minute by minute? Keep in mind that you just bid *adios* to spontaneity. You're tied to a schedule—set by the gardener.

Yes, it is possible to find a reasonably proficient *jardinero*, but from observing and listening to the trials and tribulations of my friends and neighbors I suggest that you hire someone to do the gardening for you on a trial basis. If he's going to be hired full time, remember you have 29 days to move him on down the road if he's unsuitable.

Temporarily Hired Hands

Your water storage tanks, the *tinaco* on the roof and the *aljibe* underground, will require cleaning and disinfecting on occasion. You can do it yourself but why not pay one of the locals $10 US or so to drain the water, clean out the sediment and wash everything down with *Clord*?

Even if you enjoy gardening why not hire one of the locals to stop by to do the mowing for you? I grumble about hiring a full time gardener but using occasional help makes good sense. You don't have the obligations of a full-time employee and a local has the opportunity to pick up a few extra *pesos.*

Use Your Head, Be a Good Employer

I've seen too many *gringos* allow their employees to take advantage of them. Many of us seem to believe that lax punctuality and responsibility should be overlooked or tolerated because somehow we've been convinced that those are Mexican characteristics. Nonsense! I owned a landscaping company in Ft. Worth a few years ago and can assure you that my Mexican employees showed up on time and did their jobs.

As an employer you should require that your employees do what is expected of them within the time frame they agree to do it. There is nothing mystical or magical about laboring in Mexico. It's the same all over the world.

Also, do not loan money to any of your neighbors or employees. If they're in a bind or if you feel you need to assist in some way, either pay for the service they need the money for, or just give them the money as a gift. If you loan money, in the overwhelming number of cases you'll never see it again. Or the person to whom you loaned it. (Just like where you live now.) Teresa says she's always followed this rule: loan money to women but not men. The women, if they understand it is a loan, will always pay you back.

By the same token, never pay for a job in advance. There's a Mexican saying that I've heard from several Nationals, in one form or other, that explains this caveat. They say, "If the musicians are paid in advance, the music is never as sweet" or " A paid musician plays poorly". Think about it. Since many Mexican tradesmen work at a low profit margin they may ask for half of the cost of the job up front so they can buy materials. This is an exception to the earlier statement. You do it NoB and it's common practice SoB.

Consumer Complaints

There is a mechanism in Mexico that allows consumers to complain about faulty products and services. If you feel that you've been taken advantage of or that the product or service you received was not what you contracted for, and the businessperson won't work with you to arrive at a satisfactory settlement, you can go to PROFECO. PROFECO is the Mexican consumer protection agency with main offices in Mexico City (DF) and branch offices in many cities. From Mexico you can contact them at 01-877-868-8722 or check out their website at *http://www.profeco.gob.mx.* Click on the bar that says "For foreigners" and you'll be able to file your complaint in English, right on the web. If you call, have a Spanish speaking person nearby to assist you. PROFECO has a few bilingual staff but don't count on always being able to reach one.

You'll be much more successful with complaints you bring if you have a contract to refer to, copies of receipts to show, or the testimony of a witness. Just think back on the difficulties you may have had in dealing with business and trades people where you live now, where you speak a common language and share common customs and experiences. Then triple it. A word of advice. Be very prepared.

For a list of government entities and private organizations that are set up to listen to and act on your complaints, check out *http://www.tomzap.com/legal.html.*

A Differing Point of View

One bad habit that many *gringos* fall into is to undervalue their employees. Working as a maid is a respected way of earning a living, and your employee deserves to be treated as well down here as you treat your employees NoB.

Some folks tend to be either condescending or overbearing toward their employees. They assume their employees would end up on the street if it weren't for the largess bestowed upon them by a benevolent foreigner. What a crock. I know of a few maids and gardeners who haven't been happy with their employers and quit. This is an old culture, a proud culture, a self-sufficient culture, and many of the people are perfectly accepting of the way things are. It's a whole other way of thinkin'.

As soon as I walk out onto the terrace he catches my eye. A quarter mile or so to my left, big and solid; the buckskin is slowly pulling a plow down the rows of green, but he doesn't seem quite right for that particular task. This is not a plodding draft animal, but...

LA FAMILIA DE GABRIEL, WILLIAM GENTES, 1982

My attention turns to other things, other thoughts. Straight ahead lies the lake, and behind it, only meters back from the far shore, the mountains. A pale blue haze hangs over them as it usually does this time of year, draping itself over the high hills and the small villages along the shoreline.

The villages. I count ten. A short distance apart from my raised and faraway vantage, but a long journey on foot for those who live in them. Tonight they'll come alive for me, sparkling, twinkling, speaking to me of life in rural Mexico. But now they're out of place somehow. Artificial, and too real. Too perfect in their shapes, yet imperfect in their places. Out of place, unreal, the symbols of rural life.

In the dusty lane at the far side of the first pasture between mi casa and the lake, are the first of five tiny plots. Alberto slowly, patiently urges his small herd to move from one dry grazing ground to another. All day he sits astride the horse or occasionally drops to the ground to walk a bit or perhaps to catch a brief rest beneath one of the yellow-bloomed primaveras. Long days. It's close to dusk now and I heard the clatter of hoofbeats crossing the highway just after dawn. Maybe not the sounds of Alberto's horse, but another observing the same daily ritual. Long days.

Here, only a few short yards from mi casa, they come ambling down the shoulder of the road. I had seen them earlier as I drove back from town. Something at the far side of the road catches their attention and they turn to determine it's worth. Deep red flowers are deemed suitable fare and quickly devoured. As I watch, a fire is set by someone just below the rise of the roadbed, just out of sight, just beyond where the three are grazing. The gray wood smoke wafts up, accenting the feeding animals, staging another sensory delight. The larger cow, broad-hipped and heavy-bagged, is the first to turn away, followed by the young bull. The smaller heifer takes the remains of the red flowers left by the other two. The bull stops at the gate of my neighbor's land, his tierra. When I leave the terrace later, he still stands there. The others are gone.

...my attention returns to the field of green and my earlier thoughts about the buckskin are confirmed. The older man is removing his harness. The plow is on it's side near the horse's rear hooves. Now his task completed, a boy leads the horse away from the man, from the plow, from the harness, down the rows of green and toward the lake. He stops only a few meters from the man, adjusts the rope harness on the horse's head, tosses a rein across his neck and leaps astride the tired beast.

The buckskin's head comes up, his tail raises, fans out in a soft wind-whipped banner and he begins to prance. Now he becomes what he's meant to be. No longer a beast of burden, no longer bound by iron and soil, he is once more a proud and equal partner with the rider on his back. The boy lightly bumps his *heels to the stallion's flanks and the response is immediate. They bounce down the crop rows in a dance of tightly restrained exuberance, the horse barely held in check by the boy, but prancing and twisting, quivering with the desire to GO! The boy, mindful of the often-heard warnings of the father, keeps control until the horse is settled and unlikely to trample the young plants. Neither can wait a second longer. The boy lessens the pressure on the reins and the buckskin, with no further urging, lunges quickly, almost unsteadily forward. Within a heartbeat he regains his stride and gracefully springs into a full gallop, with ears back, neck outstretched, and mane and tail flying as he sprints between the long rows of crops. I can see and feel the pair's joy in the freedom of being released from the drudgery of the field. Boy and buckskin are of one mind, one soul, one spirit, and one desire; to run, to be cleansed of the menial work of the day.*

They race to the end of the unfenced field and at the dusty lane the buckskin spins smoothly to the left, east, away from the setting sun, and carries the boy toward the foothills, toward the high ground, toward freedom from the oppression of the field of the lowlands. Now they reap their reward. This is their pay for long, hot, boring hours in a dusty field beneath the blazing unblinking eye of the Mexican sun. This is a pay more precious than a purse full of pesos. *Right now these two are kings, warriors, the least fettered and most noble of those who have ever been. Tomorrow, real life returns, but now...*

Real life for the campesinos *is barely evolved from the most fundamental of existences. Real life. Where home is a crudely constructed stone or adobe brick shelter, built, or more correctly, being built by the resident owner. Mexican houses are in a constant state of ongoing construction. Bricks are purchased a few at a time if money is short. Concrete is purchased a bag at a time if money is short. Only enough wire to carry electricity to one room is purchased if money is short. Money is always short.*

CARIÑO MATERNAL, WILLIAM GENTES, 1978

Real life. A mean existence for the women of these houses. The women who carry water in pails. The women who scrub clothes on a concrete rub board or a stone. The women who cook over open fires. The women who bear children and care for them until at last they mature to barren blessedness and the young are grown. The women who work the small fields alongside the men when it becomes necessary. It s often necessary.

Real life for these men of the Mexican earth. Mi Tierra, *regardless of how unyeldingly it gives to their needs.* Mi aldea, *my village, regardless of how poor or how isolated. Some are drawn away to* El Norte, *to the cities. But* mi tierra *remains within them no matter where the body is. The heart, the soul, the spirit, are always in* mi tierra. *And many return. The soul of* El Norte *is not the soul of* mi tierra. *Real life is here. The women are here. The children are here.* Mi aldea *is here.* La vida *is here.*

Chapter 13

Communications

Telephones

Nearly everyone complains about the telephones in Mexico. In some quarters, rumors of folks having a new line installed are fables that should be prefaced with "Once up a time" or the Navy version "Now this ain't no bull". Let me gently dissuade you from these thoughts.

In La Manzanilla I applied for residential telephone service on the 4th of the month and on the 11th I had two live usable lines. Would have had them on the 10th but even though several of the villagers told the installer where I lived, he looked at the tire tracks and didn't believe that anyone ever really made it past that big pile of construction sand in the road. He evidently spent a good portion of the afternoon searching for the shortcut to India, which does not route through that village, so by the time we made connections it was too late for him to do the job right then. *Mañana*.

Like a teen-age girl going home after a summer at the shore, I was afraid I'd never see him again, but then I fell back on a tried and true method of persuasion. *La propina*. The tip. Accompanied by a matter-of-fact sounding, but extremely hopeful, *hasta mañana*.

Mañana came and so did he. Two he's. They got the deed done, collected another round of tips, and were outta there. End of myth. TELMEX, and the folks down where the rubber meets the road can definitely get the job done when they want to. I'm now officially a fan.

Typical? Oh hell no! If you doubt the power of chocolate and tips, just sit there and wait for thirty days or more like your shy or self-righteous cohorts. In most places, you can reasonably expect to wait at least a month on up to never for new service, or you may want to buy the line and number that someone is advertising for sale. That's a fairly common transaction and a quick and easy way to get a line.

If you do manage to get a phone, you'll need to know how to use it. For local calls it's a fairly simple operation, just like in Hog Joint Junction. I didn't make up that name. I saw it in the PV bus station on a jacket from an auto body repair shop in one of those strange Midwestern states where they let the village loonies dress up in three layers of clothing in the middle of August and sit on city park benches for days at a time, luring pigeons.

The problem comes when you need to call Hog Joint Junction from Hermosillo to register a complaint about their disreputable Senator carryin' on with that little intern. Since I believe there's nothing worse than trying to deal with the anguish of an unrequited gripe, I'll tell you what to do.

Call em. Raise hell. Dial 001-area code-phone number. Easy. Unless you have no idea what the area code or numbers are. If you don't, then dial 090 for International Information. Don't panic if a nice Spanish-speaking lady starts talking. She's just alerted you to the fact that the line is busy, and that piece of information will be verified as soon as she quits speaking, when you hear the familiar beep, beep, beep of the international busy signal. Try again later. If you're having trouble finding area codes, you can always go to the TELMEX website at *http://www.telmex.com* to locate the info you need.

There may also be a Hog Joint Junction, Mexico. If there is and you know the area code and someone's number, here's how to call them from Mexico. Dial 01-area code (regional number)-phone number. If you need to ask for the number, dial 040 for National Information. I doubt seriously that there's a Hog Joint Junction, Israel, but if there is and you need to speak to someone there, and you have the country code and phone number, you can dial 00-country code, area code (regional code)- phone number. 00 works for anywhere other than the U.S. and Canada, where you'll use 001. If you need help finding that international number, just dial 090 for the International Operator.

There are certain hours during which you can receive substantial LD discounts of 33% and 50%. After you get here you can stop by a local TELMEX office and pick up a current phone book to get the specifics. Maybe. Sometimes they run out of them.

If you've just absolutely got to buy Licensed Personal Trainer Antwahn Llewelyns Underarm Flab Buster from the Flim-Flam Network, you can easily call the 880 number on your screen. 800 numbers are changed to 880 prefixes when calling from Mexico, and the 888 prefixes are changed to 881.

I don't know about those 1-900 numbers but you can reach the International Operator at 090 and ask her what to do, but don't mention my name. She thinks I'm in one of the Equatorial Africa rainforests teaching pygmies to pole vault.

Here's a list:

If you're in Mexico:

020 LD within Mexico, with operator assistance

030 Correct time

031 Wake up calls (But why would you do this to yourself?)

040 Directory assistance for Mexico

050 Telephone repair

060 Emergency- Fire, Police, Ambulance. This will not automatically bring help. Be sure to ask your neighbors what numbers to dial before you depend on this number.

090 LD international information

01   plus area code and number for Mexican LD

001 plus area code and number for LD to Canada and the U.S.

00   plus country code, then area code and number for other international LD

001 plus 880 for U.S. and Canadian 800 toll free numbers

001 plus 881 for U.S. and Canadian 888 toll free numbers

01   plus 800 for Mexico toll free numbers

If anyone NoB wants to call you, then all they need to do is dial 011 52 plus area code, and your new number in Mexico (011 52 000-000-0000). Keep in mind that only Mexico City, Guadalajara and Monterrey have two-digit area codes. All others are now three. Moreover, some cities like Guadalajara have four-digit prefixes. That means instead of dialing a seven-digit local number you'll have to dial eight numbers. From the states to Guadalajara it's going to look like this: 011-52-33-300-0000. Again, if you need area codes in Mexico go to *http://www.TELMEX.com*. If you have other questions about phones and service, you can call TELMEX toll free at 01-800-123-2222. You can also try 01-800-123-2020, but be prepared to speak Spanish.

If you can't manage to get a phone installed at your house, you can always use a couple of other services. In almost every town you'd consider living in, there will be at least one local business advertising *Servicio de Larga Distancia*, usually along with *FAX International*. Just walk in, write the number you want to call, followed or proceeded by the letters E.U. and give it to them. Don't put parentheses around the area code. *Estados Unidos.* United States or Canada, if applicable. They'll dial it for you.

While you're waiting, look around the room. When your call has been connected the operator will point to one of the booths along the wall. Head for it, pick up the receiver and chatter away. Briefly. Rates are high.

After you hang up, go back out to the operator and find out how much you spent. What are the rates like? It varies depending on the service you use. Here are some prices from a service in one of the retirement towns.

Local calls	1.50 *pesos* per minute
Mexico LD	4.50 *pesos* per minute
U.S. and Canada	14.00 *pesos* per minute
Collect calls	No charge

50% discount on Mexico LD all day Sunday, and from 8 p.m. to 10 p.m. Monday through Saturday

33% discount on LD calls to the U.S. and Canada all day Saturday, 7 p.m. to 10 p.m. Monday through Friday, and on Sunday until midnight.

This is another situation where it pays to shop around. You might want to check the time when you walk into that booth, too. Sometimes clocks run fast.

Be extremely cautious about placing LD calls from your hotel or at any service that advertises that you can use your credit card to call the U.S. or Canada. You might have to take out a bank loan to pay for those calls.

Luckily, some options are available. You can use certain U.S. and Canadian calling cards if someone NoB will let you use their card, or if you're snowbirdin' it, or if you're maintaining a residence with a phone in it NoB, you can use your own card.

The access numbers for NoB LD providers are:

AT&T	001-800-462-4240	For some reason this number violates the 880 rule I just gave you. At least it did in February 2002.
MCI	001-880-674-4000	
Sprint	001-800-234-0000	is another aberration. It rings through just fine but the Sprint operator may answer in Spanish. If you use the 880 instructions you may end up talking to someone at Applied Research Technology. I just got their answering machine, but it *was* after regular business hours.

001-800-877-8000   will get you in touch with Sprint-Global One also. *Another* variance from the 880 rule.

You can check out Canada Direct at: 1-800-561-8868 from Canada to see how the service works, or visit their website at *http://www.infocanadadirect.com.* It could save you a shilling or two if you qualify for service. Look at this before you leave home if you have a child or a relative you intend to call often.

You can also save money by using a call-back service. These are companies set up to allow you to call internationally at reduced rates. Currently the rates seem to be hovering in the 19 to 22 cents US per minute range. The company issues you a number that you dial. After a single ring you hang up the receiver. Within a few seconds your phone will ring and when you pick up, you'll dial the area code and number you're trying to reach.

Or you may want to buy a Mexican phone card. It's about the size of a credit card and they're available in varying denominations, depending on the company that produced it. They're available in 30 *peso*, 50 *peso,* 100 *peso* and 200 *peso* denominations. In some places, you might even run across a 150 *peso* card. You'll see signs everywhere, at *farmacias, tiendas*, and even some souvenir shops that will have a graphic of a telephone above the word Ladatel. There are also other card producers, but Ladatel seems to be most common in the areas we're discussing in this book. You can also buy TELMEX calling cards at your local office, assuming you're in a locale that actually has an office nearby.

There's a slot on the front of the phone into which you insert your card. There's an arrow on the card showing you how it should be inserted. Leave it in the slot until you hang up. There's a little digital display on the front of the phone and it'll tell you how much value is left on your card. If you hear a bell while you're talkin' it means "finish up fast cause were shuttin' down". You can use the card for local or LD calls within Mexico, as well as for international calls. For long distance calls be sure to buy a fresh 200 *peso* card, and talk fast.

If you have a cell phone NoB you may be able to use it to call home from Mexico. Some service providers can give you instructions that include a special code or a company-provided reconfiguration of your existing service. It'll be expensive to use this option but it could be a good temporary solution. You can purchase cell phones here with different options and plans. Avoid any plan that asks you to rent the phone and pay for air time.

Bookstores, Newspapers, Magazines, and the World Wide Web

Turn to Appendix 1 for the mother lode of information on books, newspapers and magazines in selected Mexican cities, and websites on the Internet.

Semi-Real Bookstores

If you're a voracious reader you're soon going to miss the giant bookstores you're used to NoB. Toughen up. This is going to take some getting used to.

In most towns, the bookstore will be more of a newsstand operation with magazines, newspapers and a small selection of books in Spanish and a very few in English. If you're in a tourist area you'll probably be able to get a couple of different U.S. and Canadian papers but don't count on it in the small villages. In Appendix 1, you'll see how to use your computer to access worldwide news sources including the electronic version of your hometown newspaper. You'll need to drive into one of the cities to find much of a book selection in *any* language and I can almost guarantee that you'll have only a very limited offering in English. Bring lots of books. If you live in a *gringo* community of any size you'll always find someone to trade with or to borrow from. If you use a computer you can order books from Amazon, Barnes and Noble, or Chapters, have them sent to addresses in Canada and the U.S., and then ask friends to bring them along when they come to visit. In a few of the larger towns and cities you'll be able to find a local bookstore through which you can order books from major Canadian and U.S. distributors. Should you have books sent through the mail? Keep reading...

In September of 2001 the *Guadalajara Reporter* printed an article highlighting the expense and difficulties one local resident encountered when he ordered a book through Amazon.com and had it delivered to Mexico via one of the very visible international private mail delivery services. The book was ordered online on August 1, 2001. The book was finally delivered to the customer on August 8, 2001. Here's a breakdown of the costs associated with the delivery:

Book:	$6.75 US
S&H:	$3.99 US

Now we'll see what the mail forwarding company tacked on.

Service charge:	3.85 *pesos*
Shipping:	10.36 *pesos*
Handling:	52.61 *pesos*
IVA (sales tax)	10.02 *pesos*
Tariff:	0.49 *pesos*
Total fees:	76.84 *pesos*,

or an additional $8.40 US for a final cost of $19.14.

If he'd used a local Guadalajara bookstore, Sandi Bookstore, which you can reach through their e-mail address *sandibooks@vinet.com.mx*, or at their website at *http://www.sandibooks.com*, the cost would have been $8.60 US with about the same delivery time. This is how I get my books, although some areas will offer other options. You just need to check around.

If you maintain a monthly mailbox contract with one of the private mail services to receive book shipments, figure an additional $30 US per month or more. My neighbor in La Manzanilla received packages of books from Germany through the Mexican post office in San Patricio Melaque on a fairly regular basis and paid absolutely nothing when she picked them up. I told you earlier how to get your own Mexican post office box. If you decide to use one of the private mail services, be sure to ask questions about the cost of shipping and receiving parcels.

Once you get here you'll find some familiar names in worldwide shipping, such as FedEx and UPS. In many areas they offer only one-way service. In other words, you can send parcels out, but you can't receive them. Check around in the area you're considering to find out who *will* receive those packages for you.

Bringing Your Computer Across the Border, or Not

There's a lot of conflicting information out there about bringing a computer across the border. I brought a desktop Compaq and a big printer/fax machine/copier combination across on an FM-T but a query to the Mexican Consulate in Austin, Texas got me a reply saying you could only bring in a desktop computer on a *menaje de casa* with an FM-3.

If you choose not to lug your magic box down with you there are several options you can consider. TELMEX offers a couple of interesting plans for purchasing a computer. Many Mexican families can't afford to shell out several hundred dollars all at once for a computer, so TELMEX offers two plans that allow you to pay the cost of a new computer over a two year period, plus you'll be provided internet access through their Prodigy service. Although plenty of high-speed techno types lament the shortcomings of Prodigy in some areas, I used the service in La Manzanilla and had no complaints. The main thing you need to know is that regardless of their claims of having English-speaking technical reps who can help you hook up to the system, don't count on ever getting one on their tech support line. If you wish to avoid a nervous breakdown ask a Spanish speaker who knows about computers to help you with this.

The TELMEX plan requires an initial payment of around 1000 to 1500 *pesos* and a monthly payment of either 399 *pesos* or 499 *pesos* for twenty-four months, depending on the computer you choose--either Acer or Compaq. It's worth looking into if you need a new computer. It goes without saying that you need to be connected to the TELMEX phone system.

In the cities, you'll be able to find Compaq computers for just a bit more than NoB prices, but it could be worth buying one here to avoid the hassle and expense of bringing one with you. By the time you figure in the import tax and having to lug it around, it's about a wash.

A friend recently ordered a Dell computer to be delivered in Mexico and he reported that everything went smoothly. All the machines come from Texas, there's a Mexico-based distributor, and the thing was delivered with no problems. Check out their deals at *http://www.dell.com*.

A final option is to have a local tech build you a low-cost custom rig. I had this done, and spent a small fortune, enough to have bought two or three good factory-built units by the time I finally got the majority of my technical problems solved. I'll never take that route again.

Supplies
You can get your printer cartridges here. I use the Hewlett-Packard Mexican equivalent, which is called HQ, that's compatible with HP, Canon, BX3, Lexmark, Olivetti, Xerox and Epson. Some places are even able to refill them for you.

You'll also find many of the same items you buy NoB including printer paper, zip drives, speakers, and other toys and accessories.

Chapter 14

Buying a Whole New Enchilada

What's Available SoB?

If you've not settled the question of whether you should lug your household SoB or buy new, knowing what's available to buy in Mexico might help you decide.

- TVs (Philips, Zenith, Panasonic, RCA, JVC, Daewoo, Aiwa)
- stereos and CD players
- blenders
- coffee makers
- hand mixers
- bread makers
- microwaves and toaster ovens (and microwave popcorn)
- telephones and answering machines (Bell phones)
- computers, printers, surge protectors, paper, printer cartridges, etc.
- plastic containers with snap-on covers
- hand and power tools of all types and descriptions (Black and Decker, Makita)
- paint, rollers, brushes, thinner, polyurethane, etc. (Comex and Sherwin-Williams)

- building materials of all kinds
- rugs and carpets in all price ranges
- furniture in a range of styles and quality
- all toiletry items, including feminine health and hygiene products
- towels and bed linens, although it *is* difficult to find 100% cotton
- clothing and shoes (although my size thirteens are sometimes difficult to find)
- BBQ grills, gas and charcoal, and outdoor cooking tools
- pet foods, both canned and dry, as well as birdseed and other pet needs
- medicine, first aid supplies, etc. (NC Johnson & Johnson)

I can find my Zest soap, although I'm slowly moving over to the Mexican brand *Lirio*, and my Crest toothpaste but not my MG217 shampoo. Of course even in the U.S. I've only been able to find it at Walgreen's but that's an easy one to work around.

In larger cities you'll find Sears, Wal Mart and Sam's. And Compaq computers. And McDonald's, Burger King, KFC, Dunkin' Donuts, and Pizza Hut. And Chevrolet and Ford dealerships. And Goodyear, Firestone, and Bridgestone tires. And Pennzoil and Quaker State motor oils at the places that change your oil and lube your car. Windshield washer fluid is very difficult to find, although Wal Mart and Costco usually have it, at a premium price. *Tequila* is less expensive and probably just as effective.

Get Flexible About Brands and Quality

The big thing to remember is that you won't always find the brand you want, even though you'll see quite a few familiar brand names. For those items you deem essential to a civilized lifestyle, be prepared to undergo shopping forays into the big cities. Many Mexican families have no TV, no refrigerator, no car, or no computer, but it's because they can't afford them, not because they're not available. Even though many parts of Mexico are still rural, the stores in the major cities are *loaded* with consumer goods.

Shopping, Mexican-Style

Then again, you may not get exactly what you want even though you're in Sears, Wal Mart or Sam's Club . These stores gear their merchandise to the Mexican population. Clothing and shoes for the bigger *gringo* are perfect examples. It might help to remember that you're not only going shopping, you're going "adventuring".

For example, I wanted some square-shaped handles for my faucets. I visited several hardware stores in a couple of towns. One day while driving through a small town I spied a store selling plumbing fixtures and supplies. On a whim I pulled in and checked out the place. There they were, dozens of boxes of exactly what I needed, little chrome, square-shaped handles. *Now* it seems that everyone but the lady pushing the ice cream cart is selling the shiny little things. You sometimes need to be patient and inquisitive. And in the right place.

One thing you'll find about the stores is that they're usually not at all what you're used to up North. For one thing, they're often tiny. The reason for this is that they specialize, after a fashion. For instance, one store sells plastic wares of all types--dishes, wastebaskets, storage containers, china and glassware, and pots and pans of all sizes for home and commercial use. The store next to them sells furniture, TVs, portable stereos and small appliances.

But then again, don't be surprised if the place you go to buy a garterbelt also sells automobile batteries. Small businesses flourish here and they can be as unique as their owners.

Nearly one hundred per cent of the small stores, the neighborhood *tiendas* (grocery stores, the sign painted over the door will probably say *abarrotes*. *Tienda* means store, *abarrotes* are groceries, so the place is actually a *tienda de abarrotes*, grocery store.) will usually open packages to sell you one item, a single roll of toilet paper or a few cigarettes. Ask, because that's how a lot of the locals buy and sometimes you just don't need or can't afford a whole package of something.

ROSCA DE REYES, WILLIAM GENTES, 1995

Shopping in the Outdoor Markets

Here's a good tip for buying a lot of your smaller cooking and decorating items. Most towns of any size in central Mexico have a weekly outdoor market called a *tianguis* (tee-AN-gees), or generally, *"mercado"*. You'll be amazed at the offerings.

Kitchenware, from pots and pans to china. Lots of plastic utensils and waste-baskets and such. An amazing variety of food. Clothes, shoes, socks and hosiery. Tools and plumbing parts. Stoves and blenders and their repair parts. Furniture. Toys, bicycles and tricycles. Places to eat. Watches, charms, jew-elry. Herbs, spices, natural medicines. Puppies, kittens, birds. Beautiful pot-tery, weavings, baskets, paintings. Honey. CDs and audio and video cassettes. Small appliances such as irons, hair dryers, and coffee makers. Potions, lo-tions, unguents, and salves. Shoe polish, strings, and saddle soap. Knives, *machetes*, pitchforks and axes. Candles, light bulbs, lamps, batteries, and light-ers. And previously-owned treasures of all kinds mixed in with the new.

A while back I read a guide to one of the retirement areas where the writer referred to these as "local flea markets". They're not. Remember the word *tianguis.* Okay, the one in the *Santiago* section of Manzanillo does have a sign that says "Flea Market". They're playfully poking fun at us. It's a *tianguis,* or just plain ol' market, *mercado.*

You may save some money at these places if you're a real bargainer. Watch the locals to see what kind of transactions take place. A lot of merchants set a fair price and don't haggle much, if any. The exceptions are usually handcrafted items, used items, or large purchases. In other words it's still a fair method of shopping but don't get your shorts in a wad if the person doesn't want to haggle. Some do, some don't. Plus, are you really going to enjoy that *mango* more after haggling over it to save a few cents? Done properly though, haggling is a social activity, and some little operators are in business as much for the per-sonal contact as for the few *pesos* they might make.

If you plan to spend a large chunk of money my suggestion is to bargain like a Turkish rug merchant or a Vietnamese peace negotiator. That's the time to get serious, not over a ten or twelve *peso* purchase.

Here's a quick bargaining story.

A rather persistent and personable young man was out on the streets of Barra de Navidad selling hammocks. Nice hammocks, well made, colorful. Two hun-dred and fifty pesos each. My friend wanted one and began the bargaining process after an initial refusal. After a spirited and good-natured back and forth the price finally agreed upon was only two hundred pesos. Both parties were happy with the transaction and we resumed our short walk to one of the local waterfront watering holes. As we passed one of the many stores on that street I glanced to my left and saw across the street a large stack of identical hammocks laying on the sidewalk beneath a hand-lettered sign reading, "180 pesos".

Oh well, the entertainment was worth the other two bucks or so.

At any rate, you're missing out on a great experience if you don't visit your local *tianguis* occasionally. You might see a group of *Huichol* Indians, dressed in their traditional white garb decorated with intricate, colorful, embroidered trim, working on their beadwork or yarn art. Or a craftsman selling his or her one-of-a-kind creations. There's often a strolling musician or two playing for donations.

In Patzcuaro there's a special weekly pottery market where you can buy one-of-a-kind original pieces not available in the stores. The ladies bring their work and sell directly to the public. And the *tianguis* is where you'll meet a lot of people, fellow expats from your town as well as from the surrounding areas, locals, and interesting visitors from all over. More than just a venue for getting supplies, it's also a lot of fun.

Have People Tote Stuff Down

And one more thing on the subject of getting what you need SoB. Friends and relatives are always asking what they can bring. So far I've asked folks to bring a bamboo steamer, my shampoo, a new pair of Topsiders, a cookbook and a particular Dr. Seuss book.

Ask your visitors and other expat friends to bring things back for you from their travels too. You'll do the same for them.

Can't Find It? Get it Made

While living at the beach I loved cooking outside in the open air. The food tasted better and cooking wasn't so tedious when I had a great view of the bay and mountains, and it seemed a bad idea to heat up the house with open fires when it was already hot as Hell. Go rent Night of the Iguanas and watch the heat drive Richard Burton loony. It was filmed right up the road from my house, near Puerto Vallarta.

I knew where to buy the outdoor cooker I wanted—Mexican-made, inexpensive, sturdy, and simple to hook up to my gas tank. The problem was that the place that sold it was a five-hour drive away. Problem? Nah! I just walked down the hill to the ironworker's shop, showed him a drawing of what I wanted along with the approximate dimensions, and then appealed to his artistic side. I soon had a beautifully designed custom-made gas grill on my patio.

CHAPTER 15

HOW MUCH IS THAT PERRITO IN THE WINDOW ?

Other than your future bride Esmeralda, or Savage Jake the Stalker, are there animals in your life? If so, do you plan to bring them SoB?

Fido Needs Papers, Too

Here we go then. Call the veterinarian and ask if he or she has a blank U.S. Interstate and International Certificate of Health. If so, arrange to take Fluffy or Jacque's Golden Queen Canadien in to get a check-up and clearance just before you leave town, headed South. Theoretically this paper must be issued within 72 hours of the time you reach the border. I've been unable to find anyone who admits to having been asked for it, but never anticipate variations from the written word.

You're also supposed to have a pet vaccination certificate showing that Ginger and Snuffy have been inoculated against rabies, hepatitis, pip and leptospirosis.

The long festering scratches on your face and arms will not prove to the Customs officials that the animals were actually inoculated. As a matter of fact they may cause you problems when trying to cross the border. Some *Aduana* officials might feel that anyone crazy enough to try to restrain a cat while someone else pokes it with a needle is way too unstable to be let loose in Mexico.

The law says you're supposed to have proof of these inoculations. Once again, I recommend erring on the side of caution, *and* using a vet who has a sack to stick the cat in during torture.

The U.S. State Department says that you'll be charged a fee when you and the menagerie hit the border. I've never had to pay. Load 'em up, head 'em out.

A Rolling Zoo

You may have a pet carrier or cage. You might let them run wild in the car as you're hurtling down the highway hoping they don't distract you at an inopportune moment. Or maybe you have them attached to a long rope so they can run alongside the car for the exercise. Perhaps you've strapped them across the hood so you can keep your eye on them. From past experience I can assure you that your pets will, without fail, do all they can to thwart your most earnest attempts to move them over great distances. Pirata, my one-eyed canine companion is a good traveler and some friends claim the same about their pups, but unless you've already taken extended journeys with your pets and know their travel habits, I suggest you devise some way to restrict their movement.

As far as cats are concerned, I have only two words. Tranquilizers. Strong. Actually I have a couple more.

Some folks may try to convince you to sneak off and leave Ratty and Boots when you move because they won't adjust. It may be that you have an abnormally sensitive cat, in which case I also encourage you to abandon the little psycho, but assuming yours are no more behaviorally unbalanced than the average, they'll adapt just fine. Max lived on the hill in the jungle behind the La Manz house for about a month when we first moved. He came down to eat, but not to sleep. Mona believes herself to be a human so we can't really judge cat habits based on her actions. Both of these guys have moved four times with me. Now they roam the rooftops of my current neighborhood and come through the window to sleep on the down comforter every night. They're more stable than a lot of the folks who claim to understand their behaviors. And much better company.

Birds

The bird? *No problema.* I read somewhere on one of the official U.S. government websites that you can legally bring four canaries into the country. If you're planning on transporting four canaries into Mexico I suggest that you first go to bed in a very dark room for several days and reassess your entire life. Or move to somewhere in Sonora. I won't be living there.

You know you're going to let Tweety have free run of the interior. That's how you bird people are. One of three things may happen. Your bride lets the window down for just a sec to shoo an insect away and you react to her scream and look over just as Tweety's tail feathers make their last appearance in your life through the sliver of open window. You slam on the brakes as you're look-ing over your shoulder to see which direction he flew, your right front tire slips off the pavement, and the Volvo flips end over end twenty-three times.

Or, Tweety's flitting about the interior, enjoying the trip, when suddenly he tires. Oh look! Here's a perch, right on Dad's face. He's just a small parrot, this rare Egyptian Speckle Headed Asp Killer, but his talons are long. And sharp. As he lands gently on the bridge of your nose with his claws fully extended for a good grip, you swat wildly to alleviate the torturous pain and you swerve just a bit to the right. Your right front tire slips off the pavement, and the Volvo flips end over end twenty-three times.

Or as you're hurrying through that miserably hot strip of desert real estate near the Mexico-U.S. border Tweety falls into a swoon. Quickly you snatch him up to administer avian CPR because your spouse of thirty-two years is rhyth-mically screeching, "Do something! Do something!" and as you bend to the task, something both the AAA and the CAA advise against at any speed above zero, your right front tire slips off the pavement and the Volvo flips end over end twenty-three times.

What to Expect Once You're Here
Assuming you actually get those little darlings down here, what can you ex-pect? Let's run down the list. You've probably heard the stories about how, at worst, the Mexicans mistreat animals, and at best, are apathetic towards them. Sometimes. Maybe. It all depends. There are two sides to this issue and the *gringos* don't always fare too well either. We'll talk about this a bit more in a minute but right now let's just concentrate on what's available to you and Scaly and Scabby and Tweety. In most towns of even moderate size you'll have at least a couple of vets, and maybe a groomer or two. If not, the vets usually shampoo and clip.

Sometimes the cuts look a bit odd. Sometimes they even embarrass the dogs. The vet is never embarrassed. His hair usually looks great because he can shop around and can afford to pay for a decent cut, but you're stuck with whatever his skill level may be. Just as in the U.S. or Canada or Taiwan or Ethiopia, skill levels and dedication vary. Ask the locals who they use and make your decision accordingly. If you see a really hilarious styling job make damn sure you find out who committed the crime.

A CONAIR Haircut Kit for about $20 US might come in handy if you have the inclination to groom your dogs yourself. Ms. T recently found a pro set in a small hardware store in Guadalajara. $25 US. If you stop by a pet store or vet's office in Mexico to buy a pair ask for a *recortador, para mis mascotas.*

Veterinarian Services

Plenty of medical services are available. I've had animals spayed and neutered and have had friends who have taken both dogs and cats in for dental work. I personally know three dogs that have received chemotherapy here and many other surgeries are routinely performed. Pirata had one eye surgically removed after it had been displaced and damaged. One friend had a carcinoma cut from her Whippet.

If you and your vet speak a common language ask if he is a large animal doctor or a small animal specialist. It can make a difference. All the standard medications are available and be sure to understand the dosage instructions if Stumpy needs a round of pills. My critters are all Nationals and get their vaccinations locally. Sometimes I'll even ask the vet to give me one too. Hey, hepatitis is hepatitis.

Critter Chow

As far as food is concerned, it all depends on where you live. In various places you'll find Iams, Science Diet, Waltham (Whiskas and Pedigree), Alpo, Purina, Diamond and Hagen, as well as several other Mexican brands. And there are plenty of *carnicerias. Higado* is liver. *Hueso* means bone. You can also further explain yourself if you're paranoid. Say, *"Para mis perros"*, if you suspect the butcher thinks you're really going to use them for dinner, which I've done. Some butchers will strip that bone cleaner than a surgeon's fingers, but others will leave enough to feed three dinner guests. Just don't brag about the low cost of the main dish. If you do ask for dog bones and the *carnicero* barks, smiles, and goes to the back to retrieve a different slab of meat, flee. And never return.

Otro Supplies

You'll be able to find kitty litter SoB although the next person who says anything close to "Is it clumping?" within my range of hearing had better be wearing track spikes. Get a grip, people. A cat is gonna poop and pee in this stuff. Period. If you're concerned about clumping capabilities you should probably stay a lot closer to your therapist.

You'll have a choice of leashes, choke chains, whips, quirts, harnesses, muzzles, collars and other assorted goodies and they're available in a variety of colors and materials. They also make the same types of products for your pets.

Fleas are *pulgas* and ticks are *garrapatas.* Flea and tick sprays shampoos and powders are widely available, although I've never understood why anyone would want a *pulga* or a *garrapata* for a pet.

If you insist on bringing a bird, and keep in mind that his brain is smaller than the average teen's most heart-breaking pimple, you'll find cuttle bones, seed, water disinfectant drops, toys, cages, mirrors, bells, the whole nine yards. Just don't plan on legally taking a bird back North. Not the one you brought down, not the one you might buy down here, not the one you found in the yard and nursed back to health, *nunca!* It can be legally done but unless that little bundle of fluff lays golden eggs, is talented enough to open for Wayne Newton, or is a close blood relative it might not be worth the effort and expense.

If you're determined to bring Screechy with you, and if you return North for some reason and want to bring him along, go to the U.S. Customs Service website at *http://www.customs.ustreas.gov/travel/travel.htm* and to the U.S. Department of Agriculture website at *http://aphis.usda.gov/oa/pubs/ petravel.html* for the official rules and costs. There seem to be only two places that are equipped to deal with the processing of your birds and there appears to be a considerable investment of time involved. Check it out. Canadians will want to look at the Canadian Food Inspection Agency website at *http:// www.inspection.qc.ca*. At present there are fees for bringing your animals and birds back into Canada as well as a minimum forty-five day quarantine period for birds. You might as well look at *http://canadaonline.about.com/cs/customs* for even more bad news.

Mexican Pet Stories

Are animals mistreated here? Are they mistreated in Casper, Coos Bay, Carson City and Columbus? Animals can be mistreated anywhere. Before you decide anything about this touchy subject, read a few stories.

In La Manzanilla I had a dog that actually belonged to what many of the pet owners I've talked with define in very uncomplimentary terms. I won't report the epithet they normally use, but they apply it to anyone, usually a "snowbird", who comes down and adopts a dog or cat for the six months they're here and then abandons them when they leave. In some areas, such as San Miguel de Allende, they can just drop them off downtown or call the authorities and the pet will be taken and destroyed. No sweat, we'll adopt another one next year, Marge.

Unfortunately, this snowbird stuck my La Manzanilla dog with a really horrible name, "*Cosa Cochina*". "Thing, sow, or slattern". She was used to hearing the first part, so I changed the last. She loved to chase birds and *mariposas*, but- terflies, so she became "*Cosa Mariposa*".

In restaurants, from humble to swank, I've seen plenty of Mexican pets that were well behaved and content to have been allowed to accompany their hu- mans to dinner. Every day I see well-cared-for little critters in and out of the houses in different towns. They have nice collars and are happy, friendly, clean and healthy. There *are* a lot of street dogs in some places and dogs whose jobs are to guard rooftops and lots. Are they regarded as tools? Sometimes. Does the care of dogs, cats and other pets vary widely? Yes.

My vet at the beach spoke almost no English. His is a very Mexican town with few *gringos* around. He owns one of two well-stocked pet shops in town. People who ignore their animals rarely spend enough money on their care to justify two pet stores in one small town. Nearly all the big variety stores have a pet department and pet shops are quite common in the cities and larger towns.

Kids and Pets

To educate children about dogs and their care, Mexican companies have set up a couple of websites. One is *http://www.perrosdemexico.com.mx* and the other is *http://www.mascotanet.com*. They're in Spanish, but then that's the language of the targeted audience. By the way, *perro* means "dog". *Pero* is the conjunction "but". This illustrates the importance of learning to trill those double r's.

And, if you want to visit those sites or any others in Spanish, go to one of these translator sites and type in the URL, or web address and they'll translate for you. There are two things to know about these translators; first, they're free and second, you won't get a word-for-word translation of the text. You'll be able to figure out most of what's happening, but it'll look strange to you.

These three addresses all take you to the same translator. Use *http://www.world.altavista.com/tr* or *http:www.babel.altavista.com/tr* or *http://www.babelfish.altavista.com*.

Take Spot to Dinner

In many places you'll see animals in the restaurants. The owners may have cats, dogs, chickens and ducks wandering among the diners or parrots, song-birds and squirrels housed in cages on a patio close by. One place had a small *coatimundi* chained within view of the patrons.

One night I tied Pirata's leash to a tree across from one of the beachfront eateries in La Manzanilla and Pedro, the owner, told me when I sat down that my dog was welcome.

If animals in restaurants bother you, there's good news! In any town where we expats gather, some of the tonier and more pretentious *gringo* enclaves have pressured a few of the local restaurants to post signs stating that due to "Health Department" regulations dogs are not allowed in their establishments. I don't go to them because I don't feel it's our right to come down here and impose our values on these folks.

Well, They Started It!

As far as mistreating dogs goes, I have to admit to attacking a pit bull on the *plaza* in Ajijic. And then there were the two ugly episodes with Ricardo's pit bull bitch. They were *both* at fault. Honest.

On the *plaza* a snarlin' little bastard came barrelin' out to get P boy, but I managed to snatch up my pup and deliver a splendidly-timed kick that sent the pit bull ass over teakettle, and skitterin' off under a park bench where I proceeded to trap him and kick his mean little ass until the older Mexicans begged me to stop. I think anyone who feels the need to own a vicious dog should be required by international law to be chained genitals to genitals with the damn thing, twenty-four and seven.

The first time Ricardo's bitch went after Pirata she got him down with the intention of ripping large chunks out of his back. I waded in to separate them and Pirata, in his terror-stricken confusion, took a hunk out of *my* right calf.

The second time, she came rippin' out of the shadows and grabbed him by the head on the side where his only eye is, I panicked and did the first thing that entered my mind. I jerked her mouth open. It *can* be done if you're scared enough. Pirata cut a trail outta there the second he was freed from the maw.

I, on the other hand, was standing there with a double handful of open pit bull mouth. Which quickly became a double handful of closed pit bull mouth. Which just as quickly became a double handful of nothing as she released me to take out after Pirata. As she shot past I managed to grab her tail and hoist her up off the ground. At that point, Jose, Ricardo's brother, came running out onto the street to beg me not to tap her against the telephone pole I was headed for.

I surrendered the dog to Jose and I went off in search of Pirata. All the neighborhood kids joined in and I'm sure I looked like a cross between Henry the Eighth's blade man and a shell-shocked Pied Piper. We found him six blocks away in the candy store, scared, trembling and bleeding, but managing to eat scraps of cake fed to him by the owner's young son.

We stumbled home together. And I do mean stumbled. He was bleeding, which concerned me, and *I* was bleeding, which *really* concerned me.

Here's what happened next.

Chapter 16

Is That a Stethoscope In My Pocket, Or Am I Just Glad to See You?

So here I am, bleedin' like a cactus juggler, shocky, and without a clue as to what to do. Then it hit me. I'm a guy, I'll do a guy thing, something really stupid and dangerous. I'll drive to the store and get some stuff. Gotta have some kind of stuff.

Whoops, wait a minute. Blood. Everydamnwhere. Can't get in the truck with all this blood. I know, I'll just walk to the store. It's two blocks away, but if I continue on this shortcut it'll only be four and a half blocks.

I stumble in and manage to ask for hydrogen peroxide in Spanish. Have no clue how I knew. Agua Oxigenada.

Now things become really critical. My hands are bloody, numb, and swelling. And my jeans, which I rarely wear, are extremely full of ass and big thighs. Even half in shock I have my wits about me well enough to know how danger- ous it would be to try to convince that young female Catholic clerk to dig into my front pocket for enough change to pay for my purchase.

I pick up the bottle between my wrists and mumble 'Mañana". She nods, re- lieved I'm sure that she wasn't going to be forced to touch anything that would put her religious training in question. Out into the street, I open the bottle and wash down.

Maybe I should just lie down. If I don't take the shortcut it's only two blocks to the house. No, I should probably get to a doctor if I knew where one was. I'll call my amiga at the B&B, she'll know. Uh, oh. Line's busy. Stay here Pirata. I'll drive to her office, it's only five miles. Seems like all this should really be hurting. Okay, here we are. The door's open.

"I need a doctor".

She looks up from her computer and speaks, compassion in her voice, concern in her eyes.

"Red Cross, down two blocks, right three. Can't miss it." Aw hell, Sarge, wave off the medevac chopper, I still have one leg left. I can hop the 40 klics to the aid station.

Down two, right three. She was right, I don't miss it. Gotta love a woman with a sense of direction.

By steering with my wrists I'm able to lurch into the parking area of the Red Cross, Cruz Roja, *where the ambulance drivers look really pissed that I've almost run them over. But when they see the situation they run to the truck to help me out. Once in the door we're met by a very attractive young nurse who takes over.*

"Sit here" and boom, boom, boom. Clean this up, jerk the rest of that nail off, and let's get a dressing on this finger, "You won't need stitches I think, we'll leave the big puncture wounds open to drain". Then an even more gorgeous doctor comes in. "Tetanus? Four years ago, I think. In PV. It's good for seven isn't it?" Then comes a gringo *med student from U of G to write it all up and tell me I'll survive. "How much? Okay."*

In the hallway there's a big metal box with a slot in it. Everyone discreetly disappears and I stuff a few bills in it. 'Gracias y adios".

After that episode you can bet your ass that I know where the nearest doctor's office is, not to mention the location of his house. And where his mother lives. And how to get to every *Cruz Roja* clinic within a hundred mile radius. You might want to do a bit of planning too.

If you're an extremely cautious and responsible planner—and I once read somewhere that some people are—here's a treat. If you want to avoid some of the befuddlement I experienced, there's an organization called the International Association for Medical Assistance to Travellers, which may be able to help you. Yep. Travellers. Even if the spellin' is a bit different the service is free and the information they provide is extremely good. They'll clue you in to medical information and warnings to heed throughout the globe. They'll tell you when and where you might need certain immunizations and will send you a packet of information that includes directions for contacting English-speaking doctors when you're out of the country.

You can register on-line at *http://www.iamat.org* and information will be sent by overland mail. There's a box on the site you can click to alert them that you're willing to make a donation to help offset their costs, but it's not required. Just like when you take the flirtin' babysitter home; let your conscience be your guide. It took about three weeks to receive my packet from Canada.

Stab Me or Oil Me Down

A lot of folks seem to believe that injections and the ingestion of substances concocted by brilliant people with spotless lab coats and questionable social skills will protect them from illnesses. I personally believe that Alka-Seltzer, Pepto-Bismol, and an attractive young witch waving chicken feathers through the smoke of a dried goat scat fire and rubbing hog fat over my nude body will cure just about anything I'm likely to catch. Except hepatitis, rabies, and tetanus. And this really bad rash I'd rather not discuss.

Anyway, if you really want to get inoculated you can call the Centers for Disease Control at their international travelers' hotline at 1-888-232-3228.

They're also at *http://www.cdc.gov*. They'll tell you what you want to know. You can also call them at 1-877-394-8747.

State Department Info for Alla Y'all

I really must refer you to this website even though you should be warned that if you followed their travel advice you'd never leave your bomb shelter, much less your hometown. But if you want to find out who sells travel insurance or who can load you in an airplane and haul your hurtin' carcass out of the country, go to *http://travel.state.gov//medical.* Lots of insurance companies and medical evacuation services are listed there. My Canadian friends can take advantage of this information, too.

Does Your Health Insurance Cover You in Mexico?

First, check with your insurance carrier to see that your coverage is valid in Mexico. Some is, some ain't. Medicare and Medicaid are in the "ain't" category, as are many of your Canadian government-sponsored plans.

Next, inventory your medical needs. For instance, do you require supplementary oxygen on a regular basis? This will affect your choice of places to live because smaller towns may not be able to provide it.

What I'm gonna suggest again is that you go to the U.S. State Department website but this time look at the list of healthcare insurers and do some preliminary research about coverage before you ever leave Sioux Falls or Saskatoon. There are insurance carriers in sizeable Mexican towns where agents are available. I'm not going into specifics because this is a complex area and advice needs to conform to individual requirements. You'll be able to get homeowners, renters, health, income protection, medical evacuation, and auto insurance with no real problems. You can easily protect yourself and your possessions. CASA Liberty is a full-service company with offices in most of the places we're discussing. They have a bilingual staff and can be reached at 011-800-112-2222.

In Appendix 1 you'll find publications and websites specific to certain areas. If you have an idea where you might want to move I strongly suggest that you order books and newspapers from that area. The ones I've listed will be in English. Newspapers and magazines display advertisements from doctors, dentists, clinics, hospitals, alternative health care practitioners, and pharmacies. All have phone numbers and some have e-dresses and websites.

Treatment for Chronic Conditions

Do you require any type of ongoing therapeutic treatment such as dialysis, transfusions, or physical therapy? Again you can arrange for many of these things, but be sure the services will be available near your new home.

If you're diabetic you'll be able to get test strips, as well as Glyburide and Glucophage. In some towns you'll find doctors who specialize in the treatment and care of diabetes because it's prevalent here. Your medications will probably be a bit less than what you're paying now, but the test strips may be a bit higher. You'll be well served if diabetes is a problem you have to deal with. In 1996 diabetes was the 4th leading cause of death in Mexico among adults, with 36.4 deaths per 100,000. If you need more information about traveling as a diabetic you might want to go to *http://store.diabetes.org/adabooks/ product.asp?pfid=763* and check out the info on *The Diabetes Travel Guide* by DavidaF. Kruger, MSN,RN,CS,CDE. In addition to medical advice, it contains *The Diabetes Travel Foreign Phrase Translation Guide*. You can also order it through a local bookstore, or online from *http://www.amazon.com.*

Link Up With a Mexican Pharmacist

Are you on any cutting-edge, newly developed, or limited-access drugs for your medical condition? You'll probably have to bring them with you and have a responsible party get them to you on a regular schedule. If you do your preliminary planning well, you'll find a good English-speaking pharmacist who can assist you with your medications. This is good advice for both sides of the border, especially if you're being treated by more than one doctor. A good pharmacist can save you a lot of misery if you take the time to discuss with him or her all of your treatments and prescriptions. NoB doctors sometimes recommend against this.

If you want to see what some of the more popular prescription drugs sell for here go to *http://www.maztravel.com/maz/retire.html#assist* where you can find info on drugs and much more.

You cannot legally send drugs through the mail to Mexico. Your supplier in the U.S. or Canada will not do this for you. I do know folks who swear that they have friends mail prescription meds to them regularly. In the long run, this method is likely to be undependable.

Medic-Alert Bracelets

In case you have a chronic condition or allergies to medications you definitely should consider wearing a medical warning bracelet or necklace, something a rescue worker can see immediately. A card in your wallet or purse, or a nice note from your doctor will be totally useless, especially if you're unconscious. Check out Medic-Alert in the U.S. at *http://www.medicalert.org* or in Canada look at *http://www.medicalert.ca.*

Disabled U.S. Veterans

If you're a disabled veteran you absolutely, without fail, need to contact the U.S. Department of Veterans Affairs at:

VA Health Administration Center
    PO Box 65021
    Denver, CO 80206-9021 U.S.A.
    Phone: 303-331-7590 or FAX 303-331-7803
    E-mail: hac.fmp@med.va.gov
The web site is *http://www.va.gov/hac/fmp/fmp.html.*

These folks will give you information about the Foreign Medical Program, as well as other benefits to which you might qualify. My buddy Bill told me about this program. Not married Bill, Happy Bill. They'll reimburse you for any expenses incurred while treating your service-connected disabilities while you're outside the U.S.

Mexican National Health Care: IMSS

Once you're here you may want to sign up for the IMSS, a Mexican Social Security Institute program which, among other functions, administers the national health care system. Senator Clinton did not help with their program so it's actually up and running. They have clinics and hospitals all over the country. You can apply for coverage in person once you get here but be sure to take a Spanish speaker with you. The cost at present is around 1,533 *pesos* per year per individual. That's less than $170 US at the current exchange rate. There are also plans for couples and for families at low rates also.

There's a short waiting period before coverage goes into effect and certain pre-existing conditions will have a longer waiting period or will not be covered at all. I've heard of cases where a person with a pre-existing problem was denied coverage completely. Don't trust anyone's opinion on this vital matter unless they're an accredited representative of the IMSS in the geographic region where you are applying for benefits.

Here are some of the highlights of their terms and conditions of coverage from their publication. Verify this information personally when you apply.

℞ Pre-existing medical conditions including, but not limited to, malignant tumors, chronic degenerative diseases, diabetes, obstructive lung disease, degenerative diseases of the central and peripheral nervous system, vascular cerebral disease, drug and/or alcohol addition, AIDS, and mental disturbances, are excluded from coverage.

℞ The waiting period for coverage of the following conditions are as follows:

> Benign breast tumor -- 6 months
>
> Birth -- 10 months
>
> Surgery for gynecological diseases, varicose veins, hemorrhoidectomy, rectal fistula, rectal prolapse, hernia, among others -- one year
>
> Orthopedic surgery -- two years

These time limits begin on the day of registration and in some cases *may* not limit your access to other medical services. **DO NOT** depend on my advice or the advice of anyone other than an IMSS representative for the final word on any matter concerning your eligibility for coverage or treatment. Check it out for yourself.

The IMSS Family Health Insurance program does not cover:

℞ aesthetic surgery

℞ eyeglasses, contact lenses, vision correction surgery

℞ treatment for self-inflicted injuries or attempted suicide

℞ sports injuries, or those related to high-risk undertakings

℞ preventive or screening exams

℞ treatment for behavioral or learning problems

℞ surgical or medical correction treatment of fertility alteration

℞ dental treatment, except extractions, oturation and cleaning.

Your IMSS coverage must be renewed every year within 30 days of expiration. If you fail to do so you must then re-apply as a new subscriber. During the first year of coverage, if you request treatment for any of the diseases for which there are pre-existing limitations without having declared them on your application form, your coverage *can and might* be discontinued.

This is serious. If you decide to use IMSS, make sure you get approved for coverage before you dump any other policies you may have.

Will you receive good care through the IMSS? What about the doctors? Hell I don't know. Gotta be as good as the group in the U.S. who told me ten years ago that I had less than a year to live after being diagnosed with a serious disease. Just like everything else, there are folks who have had good experiences, and those who have had bad ones. The people who report good experiences probably have a more positive outlook in general. What's the best way to use IMSS? Middle class Mexicans who use it say they reserve the IMSS for the really big emergencies. For checkups and minor mishaps they just pay the fees from their own pocket and go to private physicians. Using IMSS for every minor procedure often means standing in endless lines and dealing with annoying red tape.

Mexican Health Insurance Plans
There are also good and relatively inexpensive health care policies available from insurance agents in Mexico and from a few Mexican hospitals. Shop around. Here's a site you can check to get some idea of costs. This is not an endorsement, merely another resource in case you've yet to visit the U.S. State Department site.

Insurance Services of America

> http://www.immigrationhealth.com
> e-mail: health@immigrationhealth.com
> phone 1-800-647-4589

Will You Get Good Care From Mexican Doctors and Clinics?
Judging by the few doctors who have treated me, my guess is that you'll receive excellent care. You just need to figure out how to pay for it. It's rarely as expensive as what you'd expect. A bone scan in Guadalajara would have cost me about $450 US when I was referred by one place that caters to *gringos,* but through my small-town MD it cost roughly $250 US. Plus the MD wanted a set of X-rays and didn't charge me for them. In the U.S.? At about the same time I had my scans done in Guadalajara, a *gringa* nurse in La Manzanilla returned to California and had a similar CAT scan. The same procedure there cost her

over $2,500 US. About ten times as much. I recently had X-rays of three views of my nasal sinuses done in Chapala, Jalisco. I had no appointment, walked in at 4:15, and left at 4:50 with my films. Total cost was 400 *pesos*, about $45 US. A CAT Scan in Guadalajara cost me $80 US. In addition to being much less expensive, I also find that Mexican MDs are less likely to lose sight of practicing the art of medicine in order to pursue the business of medicine.

Por ejemplo. I had stopped by the doctor's office in Manzanillo about six in the evening to set an appointment for some minor dermatological work. The appointment was for the next Monday, five days away. I walked outside and sat down at the sidewalk café next door to have a coffee before I drove the fifty miles back to the house. I had just finished stirring *azucar* into my coffee when a gentleman approached.

"My daughter said you needed an appointment. I'm free now if you wish."

I *did* wish, as a matter of fact, so I dropped the spoon, tossed a few *pesos* on the table, and slid on in. Nothing malignant. Anesthetic. Electric zapper. Nine small growths removed. 500 *pesos.*

Did we exchange meaningless chatter and reams of paper? No. Did I get a receipt? No. Did I get done what I wanted done? Yes. Am I satisfied with the work? Yes.

The same doc cut out a fatty cyst from my back. 700 *pesos.* Office visit to remove four stitches ten days later: 50 *pesos.* Plus he gave me one of the waiting room magazines that I asked for.

"I can't cure your cancer."

"I know that, I just need you to keep me mobile and pain-free for the next twenty years or so."

"I can do that."

See how easy they are to work with? The U.S. guys who condemned me to death are still trying to convince me to let them perform a seriously disfiguring surgery that each one guarantees will not cure me or make me feel one bit better. You do what you want to, but I can tell you that the docs here will listen to you and work with you.

And if they don't, maybe their wives will.

I had developed some sort of chest congestion and a horrible cough one summer in PV. My landlady was a petite blonde Canadian who had been living in Mexico for most of her life.

"My husband will kill me if he finds out I told you this. He's totally switched from allopathic to holistic health care, but this works fast. Go to the farmacia and ask for (No, I'm not telling.) and get three doses and three syringes."

I knew about buying your own syringes. The year before I'd cut a big hunk out of my heel on the beach one evening, just like in "Margaritaville".

The next day at school I got to thinkin' about the horrors of tetanus so I stopped at the nearby pharmacy. They didn't have the tetanus vaccine in stock so a friend called to have some delivered. I bought a syringe and on the way home after class I stopped to have a doctor give me the injection. I'd already used a steak knife to perform my own "this chunk here ain't never gonna grow back where it belongs" surgery the night before.

For the chest congestion and horrible cough, though, not one but three injections would be required. I had two students planning to travel to South America after they earned their TEFL certificates. When I explained what valuable medical training they could receive absolutely free of charge the guy took the bait and agreed to take a stab at it. She was more cautious. I could have done it myself but they were to be flank attacks. I felt as though I could use some assistance.

It worked out well. I showed him how to draw up the vaccine, where to stab me and after a bit of nervous hesitation he did a fine job. Twice. She thought that since we'd already committed what she thought was a breach of medical safety, she might as well try it too. On the third day I took my customary position on the bed, drawers down to expose my bare butt, and waited. He was not prepared to surrender the syringe. I heard the thud, but by the time I looked over she'd already dropped the object she'd hit him with and was bent over picking up the vial and syringe from the floor.

She did a damn fine job for a first effort.

And Hospitals?

For information about hospital facilities and services check out the sites and addresses for these hospitals SoB. Their website will give you an idea of what you can expect.

United Medical Services
    Royal Pacific Yacht Club Local #E
    Marina Vallarta
    Puerto Vallarta
    011-52-322-221-2827
    e-mail: *Unimedical@Medical-Hospital.com*
    attn: Dr. Humberto Alcalde

http://www.Medical-Hospitals.com

Hospital Americas
Av. Americas 932
Guadalajara, Jalisco, Mexico 44620
011-52-33-817-3141 or 817-3004
e-mail: *americas@megared.net.mx*
attn: Dr. Moises Hernandez Gutierrez

This hospital advertises that they will accept and process claims for U.S. insurers. They were unwilling or unable to attempt to file my claim to the VA's Foreign Medical Program because the $450-500 US charge was not sufficient for them to bother with. This actually worked to my benefit because I got the same diagnostic testing done for half what they would have charged. You really do need to shop around. Lots of folks swear by them.

Hospital del Carmen
Tarascos 3435
Fracc. Monrraz
44670 Guadalajara, Jalisco
011-52-33-813-0025 or 813-0042
e-mail: *hdcarmen@saludangeles.com*
http://www.mediks.com

A friend recently had orthopedic surgery at del Carmen and was very impressed with everything about the place. His private suite cost about $100 US per night and he reported that the nursing care was first-rate. Another local had a hip replacement operation and recommends the facility.

I recently hired Dr. Badial to correct my severely deviated septum and, while he was at it, to straighten out my nose. While I was under anesthesia Dr. Jiminez performed minor cosmetic work on my eyes and cheeks. The combined cost of the two doctors, the anesthesiologist, the OR Nurse, and all associated hospital charges was about $3,500 US. There were a few extra expenses for medications and follow-up visits.

The surgery was first-rate, the doctors were incredibly good, and the hospital facilities were clean, well-equipped, and very modern. Very impressive.

For care in Mazatlan, Puerto Vallarta, and Los Cabos you might check out

Balboa Hospital and Walk-In Clinic
Plaza Balboa, Suite 4-16
Ave. Camaron Sabalo 4480
e-mail: *balboahospital@touristmedicalassit.com*
http://www.touristmedicalassist.com

A lovely lady friend of mine had a cosmetic surgeon tighten up the skin on her eyelids and below her eyes. The cost was 12,000 *pesos,* about $1,300 US, and she could have had more work done for the same money. She's very pleased with the results and had no qualms about recommending her doctor to me.

Home Health Care

Some of you may need Home Health Care, and I'm happy to tell you that it's available even in some of the smaller towns. MediCasa de Guadalajara is an example of one of the larger companies. They also have a branch in Mexico City. Here's an abbreviated list:

Specialized Nursing Care for

Cancer

AIDS (SIDA)

Cardiology

Special infusions

Respiratory therapy

Peritoneal Dialysis

Physical therapy and rehabilitation

Home Health Aides on a 24 hour basis:

Clinical laboratory services,

Disposable medical supplies, and

Medical and therapy equipment including,

Volumetric ventilators

Pressure ventilators

Inhalation therapy

Oxygen tanks

Infusion pumps

I.V. poles

Apnea monitors

Oximeters

Phototherapy

Liquid oxygen containers

Manual and electric hospital beds

Orthopedic frames

Pneumatic and egg crate mattresses

Wheel chairs

Crutches

Commode chairs

They advertise that they will bill your U.S. or Canadian insurance company directly. Let me advise you to *confirm* that your insurance company will cover your needs while you're in Mexico. If not, use that U.S. State Department website so you can contact insurers who *will* provide SoB coverage. They're at *http://travel.state.gov//medical.* Be careful when it comes to your coverage and make sure you understand all the possible restrictions and exclusions. If you sign up for IMSS coverage be sure to check that these services are covered.

Again, I'm not recommending the folks at MediCasa, but you can contact them in Guadalajara at 011-800-711-2182 or 011-52-33-616-0684or 616-0685 or fax 011-52-33-616-0490. In Ajijic call 011-52-376-766-2126 and in Mexico City call 011-52-55-264-0158 or fax 011 52-55-584-3374. In case you've noticed, Mexico City has a two-digit area code (55), as do Monterrey (81) and Guadalajara (33), but all other geographic locales have a three-digit code. This changed on November 17, 2001. You can check out the TELMEX website *http://www.telmex.com* to find a listing of all the new area codes.

Long Term Care

If you want someone else to take care of things for you and the spouse you might want to look at a place in Mazatlan. It's called The Melville. Evidently Herman Melville, the author of Moby Dick, spent time in Mazatlan at some point in the distant past. D.H. Lawrence spent time in Chapala in the '40's and some locals trumpet the fact, not realizing that Lawrence despised Mexico and almost everything about it, in spite of the exquisite beauty and grace of his descriptive prose. Don't make an important decision about care just because a place sounds good. Check it out thoroughly, ask questions, be smart.

Anyway, their website is *http://www.themelville.com*

Assisted Living Facilities

There are some assisted living facilities in the Lake Chapala-Ajijic region of Jalisco in case you need to bring an older or disabled relative who needs daily care and attention. Alicia's and *La Casa Nostra* are near Chapala. Contact Alicia's at *aliciascovelescente@hotmail.com.mx* telephone 011-52-376-766-0721 or 011-52-376-766-3087.

You can contact *La Casa Nostra* at *lanostra@prodigy.net.mx,* phone 011 52-376-765-4187. Beverly Ward is the Owner/Administrator and has a beautiful facility near Ajijic in the Riberas del Pilar area.

A young Canadian entrepreneur has teamed up with a Mexican Doctor and a very experienced Canadian Nurse/Administrator to open an assisted living place in Ajijic. *Mi Casita* is an attractive and homey facility. They provide for special diets, offer cable TV and phone service, and have regularly scheduled visits by the doctor. Contact David at 011-52-376-766-0050.

Small operations have begun to spring up to care for the elderly. You or your loved ones will be well taken care of.

The Pharmacy Deal

If just walking into a pharmacy and selecting what you want without benefit of a doctor's note surprises you, please realize that in Mexico many folks don't immediately go to a doctor's office for all their aches and pains. You can usually walk into a *farmacia* and tell the pharmacist what your problem is, and get the medicine you need right on the spot. *Farmacias* are owned and/or operated by licensed physicians and it's not uncommon to walk in while the doc is examining a patient right there in front of the counter.

Danza de los viejitos, William Gentes, 1982

Dr. Polo on the square in Ajijic, Jalisco has a small room at the back of his pharmacy where he gives me my semi-regular hip-load of B-12, but many examinations and procedures are done more or less out front. If you're asking for advice about drugs or have questions about your symptoms make sure that the person you're talking with is the doctor because pharmacies also staff non-medical employees.

Don't let me leave you with the impression that you can walk in and get controlled substances just for the asking. For those, you'll still need a doctor's prescription.

It's Your Responsibility

You may also be surprised to discover that you'll be the caretaker of your medical records. This means that you'll carry your x-rays, lab results, doctor's charts, notes, and other documents with you from place to place.

I Came to Heal and to Learn, I Stayed to Teach

Sick, tired and fragile; looking for a place to move was the farthest thing from my mind when I planned the vacation my friends said I had to take. The previous few years had been difficult. I had cared for my fiancée at home during his battle against two primary cancers. It was almost a year after his death that I finally realized I was ill. The toll his illness and death had taken on me was an incurable, debilitating disease. By May of 1990, I was so ill with Fibramyalgia and Chronic Fatigue Syndrome that I nearly canceled the vacation that changed my life.

I still don't know why I thought it would be easier to go alone to Mexico on vacation. My entire experience had been lunch in Rosarito Beach, and I spoke no Spanish. When I considered being in Boston or San Francisco or Chicago alone, I sobbed. When I thought of Mexico, I imagined colorful flowers and the sun, warm on my cheek.

Armed with the Sunset Mexican Travel Book, *I pored over the myriad of cities, places and sights. I sensed the altitude, crowds and pollution of Mexico City would worsen my condition. No way could I climb pyramids, cope in subways or be that street smart. I was breaking sick fever sweats dozens of times a day in cool Southern California, so I knew*

JUDY KING, WRITER, SPEAKER, PUBLISHER,
AJIJIC, JALISCO, MÉXICO

I wouldn't be happy in the heat and humidity of the beach resorts.

I kept returning to the well-thumbed section on Guadalajara that was billed alternately as the "City of Roses", the "City of Eternal Spring" and the "City of Fountains". I read that the area around Guadalajara produced all of the images that I consider as "Mexican"—Tequila, Mariachis, the Mexican Hat Dance, and the handsome Charros with those tight fitting, silver-studded outfits. I was attracted by descriptions of the colonial and European emphasis in Guadalajara's architecture, dance, music, food and attitude.

There was a sentence about a nearby North American retirement colony at Lake Chapala—I already lived near Leisure World and had been to Sun City—so I promised myself I wouldn't go there. I would stay in the city.

I arrived on a Monday afternoon in May. I spoke no Spanish; few of the Guadalajarans I met spoke English. My hotel was just a couple of blocks from the downtown walking plazas. I spent my days walking the beautifully clean streets, exploring buildings, people watching from benches near shoeshine stands and listening to marimba musicians. I ate the street vendor's watermelon, found and ordered a chocolate ice cream cone, and communicated with my phrase book and smiles. It was heavenly. I felt free and light and warm.

Midweek, with a jolt, I realized that I was forgetting to take my pain medications. I was not in pain for the first time in months and I was functioning without daily naps. I felt stronger and was thinking more clearly. I couldn't imagine how on earth I could be so much better in just a few days. Maybe the doctors had been right, perhaps this was all in my head or maybe, just maybe, living in a world of plastics, synthetics and chemicals was keeping me sick. Less than a month before, I had tried and failed to write a check because I couldn't remember how. I had given up reading books because I couldn't retain the story line. One day I sat in my car for nearly an hour before I could remember to drive home from my neighborhood Target store, then found I couldn't summon the effort required to describe these events to the doctor. I had spent whole weeks of that winter in bed, too weak and feverish to do more each morning than shower and dress. When I rested all day, I could go to the kitchen and heat a can of soup for my dinner before I fell back into bed, exhausted, but unable to sleep.

Maybe, I was as crazy as the doctors had indicated. Here I was, alone in a foreign country, walking the downtown streets, ordering and eating foods I didn't know, surrounded by strangers speaking a language I couldn't understand and still I felt safe, protected, secure and well. I felt like I was finally home.

You know the feeling. You're driving home from work in the late afternoon dark of winter. It is cold outside. You're tired and alone in the car. You have laundry waiting, but haven't a clue what's for dinner. Lights are on in the houses along your route and in your mind's eye Ozzie and Harriet are having dinner with Donna Reed and Jim Anderson and everyone inside the house is happy...and not dysfunctional.

In Guadalajara I felt like I was inside the house, sitting in the warm lamp glow at that happy table. For the first time of my life, I felt really at home.

Synchronicity took over my trip and my life when a tour group from California checked into my hotel. Joining them for lectures about living in Mexico and whirlwind trips to Tlaquepaque and Ajijic, I confirmed what I already knew. I needed to be here. It was possible for me to live in Mexico.

In six short months, I had sold my furniture, traded my car, settled my daughter in her first year of college and was relaxing on the terrace of my home at Lake Chapala. I had a maid to do the housework and laundry and I had gained strength and contentment. Then, one day I looked up and down my street. I waved to the Los Angeles couple in their home on my left. I chatted with the Dallas folks of the house on my right. The new owners parked their California-plated car in front of the house across the street.

Suddenly I realized how surrounded I was by gringos. In the distance I could hear faint music from the oom-pah town band and the pop-pop-pop of skyrockets. The shame hit as I remembered my solemn promise to myself—I had planned to learn about Mexico and to learn Spanish, just as my ancestors had put aside their Danish, German and Dutch to learn English. I had the grace to blush as I remembered how disdain-fully I had viewed the Asians and Mexicans who clustered into tightly-knit exclusive communities when they moved to California. I had done exactly the same thing when I bought an American-style house surrounded by other foreigners. I shopped in stores catering to Ameri-cans. I even worked with other for-eign real estate agents in an office helping Americans and Canadians find housing. I had come to a for-eign country and immersed myself...in the English-speaking community. I might as well have stayed in the United States.

I vowed then and there to begin liv-ing the life in Mexico I had planned for myself. Soon, I left the house on the hill and moved into the village of Ajijic. Mind you, the house was still more American than Mexican, but I started going to the weekly street market. I bought sodas and bread at the little corner store. And when I heard bands and skyrockets, I walked to the plaza *to see what was happening. I asked questions and read everything I could find to learn about the saints and virgins in the local churches. I pieced together random bits of information and took notes so that I could remember how each* fiesta *was celebrated along with wedding, baptism and 15th birthday traditions.*

I began a program of learning Spanish that worked for me—I learned just three Spanish nouns each day. I didn't even consider worrying about verbs for a number of years. I immediately started using those nouns as often as possible.

As soon as I could ask questions in Spanish (and understand the answers) I started reading Mexican newspapers, magazines and books and then pumped my Mexican friends for details. I wanted to understand it all, and it was frustrating to repeatedly ask "Why," and always hear the same answer, "Por que eso es el costumbre." *Because it is the custom!*

As I learned to live the adventure of Mexico, I began sharing the joy and warmth and knowledge I was accumulating. The details of the adventure fascinated me, and I found wonderfully interesting bits of trivia in the religion, language, culture, history, food, traditions and customs of Mexico. I found special ways to incorporate the information into my spiel as I showed houses. I looked for any op-

portunity to speak to groups of newcomers. The "Focus on Mexico" groups even called me "The Ajijic Storyteller".

As I learned about Day of the Dead and Christmas celebrations in Mexico, I designed altars to honor my own dead and started incorporating a traditional Mexican nacimiento, *nativity scene, into my Christmas decorations. What a joy to see Mexican families inspired by my example to rebuild family traditions.*

There is no doubt in my mind that my Mexican life has evolved just as it was planned by a power greater than me. I believe I am right where I am supposed to be. I was supposed to "come home" to the middle of an enormous foreign city and then to find my life and my passion while healing from a difficult disease and a difficult time. I am so grateful to have been in the right place at the right time to find my passion and purpose—learning and teaching the Adventure of Mexico.

JUDY KING,
http://www.mexico-insights.com
judyking@laguna.com.mx

Dentistry

I've never had any amateur dental work done here, although years ago a guy in Long Beach tried to set me up for dentures. Luckily the bartender was large enough and quick enough to stop him before he did any major remodeling.

The dental work I've had here has been first-rate. A retired dentist from Michigan visited my dentist in Ajijic on a busman's holiday and was extremely complimentary about the Doctor's operation and his advanced training. His office and equipment were more up-to-date than that of my dentist in Texas. In Barra de Navidad, just as in other small towns, dentists have small operations. You'll most likely see a small waiting room open to the street with a partition dividing the waiting room from the operating room.

One of my absolute favorite set-ups is the young lady whose operating room has a large window in the wall dividing her office from the walkway of a small shopping mall. Go shopping and then stop by to watch someone get a cavity filled, or tooth extracted.

Prices vary, skill levels vary, equipment quality varies, and office spaces vary. Just like back in Thunder Bay or Tulsa. Shop around.

The Witch May Be Busy, Keep a First-Aid Kit Handy

And just as a matter of common sense keep a small first aid kit/medicine box handy. Many Mexican pharmacies sell small plastic kits that contain many of the items you'll need and the cost is usually under $5 U.S. Here's how my personal kit is stocked:

sterile gauze (*gasa)*

clean cotton cloths (*algodon esterilizado)*

adhesive tape (*tela adhesiva)*

alcohol (*alcohol de caña*)

Alka-Seltzer (same name in Spanish)

Advil (ditto)

aspirin (*aspirina)*

hydrogen peroxide (*agua oxigenada)*

antiseptic soap *(jabon antiseptico)*

sulfa powder (*sulfatiazol polvo)*

a variety of elastic bandages (*venda elastica)*

Band-aids in a variety of shapes and sizes

moleskin

Anbesol

individually wrapped hard candies (for diabetics)

Q-tips (Same name in Spanish, they'll know what you want)

Neosporin antibiotic ointment

Maalox tablets *(Melox antiacido* if you buy it at a Mexican *farmacia)*

Pepto-Bismol (same name in Spanish)

Desitin diaper rash ointment (Yeah, you'll use it.)

dental floss (for sutures)

Benadryl capsules

Benadryl spray (Benadryl spray isn't available in some places)

packets of *Electrolitos orales polvo* (electrolyte replacement mix)

an assortment of needles in different sizes (in some areas the doctor won't have one)

pair of small scissors

nail clippers, one large, one small

tweezers (*pinzas*)

reading glasses (*lentes*) and a hand-held magnifying glass (*lupa*)

safety pins (*seguros*)

a metal mirror (*espejo de metal*)

thermometer (*termometro*)

a small flashlight (*cricket*)

a rubber squeeze bulb (like one you clear a baby's nose with) (*perilla*)

assortment of elastic wraps

The American College of Emergency Physicians First Aid Manual

The Medical Guide for Third World Travelers

After my son Matthew was badly injured in a motorcycle disaster years ago I took an EMT course. I suggest that you take a first aid class of some kind before you come. You'll be a lot better equipped to do more than stand and wail if someone is injured or has a medical emergency. In some cases knowing what *not* to do is as important as knowing what *to* do.

Finally, you'll encounter volunteers in the streets and highways carrying cans or small boxes asking for donations for various charities or institutions. When the Red Cross, *Cruz Roja*, does their fundraisers they have banners and windshield stickers and lots of volunteers. **GIVE THEM SOME MONEY!** These hardworking people will be your Emergency Room and ambulance service so it's to your benefit to support them as much as you can. Under Mexican law this is the only organization allowed to render emergency medical assistance to anyone injured in a motor vehicle accident or as a victim of a crime.

It doesn't matter what your opinion of the Red Cross in the U.S. or Canada might be, or what your opinion is of the obscene salaries paid to their upper echelon employees and directors. This is different situation. Most of the *Cruz Roja* staff are volunteers and they deserve your respect and support. They don't charge for their services, so they rely heavily on your donations.

Now as we all know, regardless of how generous you've been, the quality and quantity of medical care you received, the potency and efficacy of the drugs you've taken, your personal genetic makeup, and just pure luck, at some point you're scheduled for the big check-out. Jesus, Buddha, Zoroaster, Mohammed, or one of those other guys is gonna come for you. If your personal savior or whoever is covering for him on that particular day comes for you while you're in

Mexico here's how to ease the burden for your beneficiaries.

First, if you have an idea that your demise is close at hand and you're ambulatory and coherent, it would be smart to get back across the northern border. If that's not an option and you do your last laydown in Mexico, your survivor(s) will get a death certificate from the Mexican authorities. Unless you want to be a pain-in-the-ass-memory for your family forever, you should sign a statement saying that you wish to be buried or cremated in Mexico. This is the simple way to take care of your remains.

If you're a particularly mean-spirited SOB or want to get revenge on your surviving spouse for some real or imagined slights in the past you can insist that your corpse be returned to Canada or the U.S. to be properly worshipped prior to disposal.

If that's your choice you can go to *http://www.usembassy-mexico.gov/ GeRemains.htm* for a complete rundown of regulations and laws, as well as a list of the people who can embalm and bury you, or cremate your remains and ship you north. A shorter, easier to read version of the laws is at *http:// travel.state.gov//return.html.* Canadians can get official information from Consular Affairs Canada at *http://www.voyage.gc.ca/Consular-e/Problems/deaths-e.htm.*

If you find yourself lying out somewhere in the middle of the street bleedin' to beat sixty, or you're clutchin' at your chest at the onset of a really attention-getting heart attack you'll be able to summon help and delay your demise if you can...

Chapter 17

Habla Like the Locals

If Arnold Can *Habla*, So Can You.
When trying to warn a National that he was about to step into a roadway hazard, a lady I know shouted, "*Cariño, cariño*" when she meant to say "*cuidado*", look out! He froze anyway, either from fear or in anticipation of the delights to be enjoyed with the *gringa* who was calling him "darling, darling!".

Luckily Mexicans treat us and our halting attempts to communicate much more magnanimously than we do them and theirs NoB. Everybody has a bucketful of stories about their fumbled attempts at language and will be pleased to bore you to thoughts of homicide given half a chance. But learning the language does more than save you from being the evening's opening act on the *plaza*.

It's Essential
You're going to be a lot happier and thoroughly more independent SoB if you learn at least some Spanish. I hadn't thought about it much until someone brought it up a few days ago. Until you become fairly fluent in the language you're going to be in a state of constant frustration. You'll develop a phobia about picking up the telephone to call anyone other than your *gringo* friends. Need a taxi at 4 a.m. for a trip to the airport? How about calling for services like gas deliveries or needing a doctor to come if Aunt Bullie collapses after the clinic closes? It'll be hard to understand the basic terminology on your deeds, tax statements and bills. You'll have difficulties telling the clerk or repairman precisely the item you want or need fixed. Perhaps the saddest thing will be your inability to develop meaningful relationships with the Spanish-speaking

people around you and you'll end up an isolated and bitter casualty in Paradise. It happens. You're going to need your neighbors and you'll soon discover that pointing and miming won't cover all the things you'll want to convey. Yes, it's harder to learn another language when you're older, but you're going to be older anyway, so you might as well use your brain to assist you in your new life.

You can start lessons before you come. Many Community Colleges offer Continuing Education classes and with a little looking you might find a tutor for a reasonable price. One of the things I did was to purchase a set of language tapes. The method I chose is the Pimsleur Language Program put out by Simon & Shuster Audio. I bought the set of 30 tapes at Barnes & Noble several years ago for about $50 or $60 US.

Or, you can learn Spanish online for free. Check out Learn Spanish Online. Their website is *http://www.studyspanish.com*. The basic program is divided into three sections: Grammar, Vocabulary and Verbs. There are almost 160 lessons available on the free version, and you'll need to enroll using your Yahoo or Hotmail account so you can continue your lessons after you move SoB. You'll be given a code number to access your individual chart. In Appendix 1 I've listed a few more free programs you can check out.

There are also plenty of books available. One of the best, in my opinion, is *Madrigals' Magic Key to Spanish* by Margarita Madrigal. It points out that you probably already know more Spanish than you thought and the author shows you how to increase your vocabulary, quickly and easily. It's logical and simple. The 1989 edition, which I believe is the latest, cost $11.95 US and is available at any good bookstore. The original copyright date is 1951 so it's had plenty of time to prove itself.

Eakin Press offers two nice little books that you might enjoy. *Vocabulary Tutor: Vocabulario Tutor* by Dr.James E. Reveley is a dictionary-type paperback that shows you that you already know over 2700 Spanish words. This complements Madrigal´s book well.

Eakin also offers *Mexican Sayings: The Treasure of a People* by OctavioA. Ballesteros and Maria Carmen Ballesteros. This book gives you some insight into the Mexican mind. You can order these two books using the information given earlier for Mrs. Dietz´s household Spanish book.

A good workbook format that some teachers use here is *Spanish Now!* published by Barron´s. It's another one you can find in any good bookstore.

If you just need to brush up on your rusty language skills there's a company that provides an on-line refresher for you. They offer a year's worth of weekly lessons for approximately $120 US. Check out *http://www.CultureID.com* for more info.

Interested in Teaching English as a Second Language?

This is the flip side of learning Spanish. If you're interested in this, read on.

Teaching English in Mexico by Mark Farley

Teaching English in Mexico is an exciting and rewarding experience. There's no better way to learn about another culture than to live in it. It's one thing to vacation in Mexico, and quite another to work there. When you wake up in the morning and you get ready to teach your first class, you realize that you have blended into another culture. This is an amazing accomplishment-one that will be with you for the rest of your life.

There's a great demand for English teachers in Mexico and jobs are plentiful. Many Mexicans receive higher salaries if they speak English. For example, a secretary at Aetna Seguros Monterey (an insurance company) will receive an additional 1,000 or more *pesos* a month if he/she can speak

English. There are many American companies with branch offices throughout Mexico. The employees are Mexican and need to speak with their American counterparts. Overall, the general consensus in Mexico is that if you can communicate in English, your economic status and position will increase at a faster rate. Mexico Busi-

MARK FARLEY,
Author of the Teach
English in Mexico
Employment Guide;
Director of the Guaranteed Placement
Program of Internet-
Works; contributing
writer, The Teach English in Mexico Newsletter (http://www.teach-english-mexico.com).

ness Magazine (MB) recently stated that learning English and computers is more important in Mexico than getting an MBA.

Most Mexicans learn English grammar and vocabulary throughout their formal education. Unfortunately, they lack the opportunity to practice conversation (especially with a native English speaker). This is true of most schools where classroom attendance is high. Students may be competing with 30 or more students for their chance to speak. When Mexican students finish their education, many find that they cannot speak English well enough to hold a simple conversation.

As a teacher or private tutor, you'll be hired to help the student learn to speak correctly. You will also help build the student's vocabulary. Mexicans prefer hiring a native English speaker because of the need to pronounce words correctly. You should be skilled at the art of conversation and know your grammar rules! Being outgoing, animated, motivated, and full of energy are important qualities for an English language teacher.

Mexicans are looking for native English speaking teachers who are friendly and vivacious. They are looking for teachers who are engaging. It's a bonus when your student can practice conversation and learn something interesting at the same time. Your private students may not

be concerned with your credentials, but you should have an excellent command of the English language. Schools and language centers that can possibly hire you will be concerned with your credentials. Having a college diploma will help...having a college degree in English is better...and having a college degree in English and a TEFL Certificate is the best. You will have more opportunities and possibly more jobs to choose from. Teaching experience is a must too - even if it means volunteering at a local literacy program in your hometown. You do not want to walk into a classroom cold. The last thing you want to do is freeze up-no pun intended. It's good if you have public speaking experience or made presentations to a group. Don't forget to put all that down on your CV (resume). Schools will look for all your teaching experience on your resume and every little bit helps.

You do not have to know Spanish in order to teach English. In many cases, it may be more beneficial that you don't speak Spanish. It forces the student to speak only English with you. If you know Spanish, refrain from using it as a crutch. Some of the most successful language schools in the world insist that only the language being taught be spoken.

Some schools offer training, as they want you to teach their method. They sometimes like to hire those with no experience so they can mold the new teacher. Therefore, if you are one of those with no classroom experience or training, one of these schools may be right up your alley. They usually do not pay as well as other schools but if money is not a big concern for you then you may find yourself right at home. "Newbies" take these jobs to get started and then move on to higher paying schools once they have a sufficient amount of teaching experience. Keep in mind that training is usually not paid so be prepared for that. Normal training periods can run anywhere from two to six weeks.

Teaching English is fun. Yes, that's right-fun! It all depends on your approach. You can use teaching games to make the class something your students will look forward to attending. Learning another language can be intimidating and frustrating. If you make the experience a positive one, not only will your students enjoy it, but they will also learn more quickly. Textbooks are necessary, but can become monotonous. Therefore, it's important to be creative and look at alternative ways of teaching. If you obtain your TEFL Certificate, you will have plenty of classroom games to pull out of your hat.

You will find Mexicans extremely warm and friendly. It's not uncommon for your students to become your friends. They will enjoy showing you their country and their customs. You'll be invited to birthday parties, festivals, weddings, and the like. Don't hesitate to go. It's a good opportunity for you to learn Spanish and your students to practice their English. You'll enjoy learning from your students while teaching them. Many teachers return to Mexico again and again to visit with former students.

The best part about teaching is that you can be your own boss. You set your own schedule and decide on how much you want to work (if you teach privately). Most teachers schedule classes Monday through Thursday so that they can have Friday off. This allows for a three-day weekend-enough time to travel to other interesting sites or see special events. For the adventuresome, there are jungle retreats...for the culturally inclined, there are pyramids, museums, and theater...and there's year-round beach weather.

In conclusion, if you're looking to spend some time in this amazing country and want to get paid while taking a break from your usual routine, this is an opportunity worth exploring. It's truly an experience that will change your life forever.

MARK FARLEY

Here's more on the subject from an article published on *www.mexconnect.com*.

Teaching English in Mexico by Don Adams

It may be true that religion is the last refuge of the scoundrel, but it's just as true that teaching is often viewed by some as the last refuge of the rudderless and unqualified.

As an undergraduate in a North Texas Cow College School of Education I had many classmates who were *really* going to be doctors or lawyers or engineers, but were working toward teaching certification "just in case". At the risk of getting a bit evangelical here I advocate the position that classroom teachers should be those people who have a desire to teach, coupled with the requisite skills, training, abilities, and attitudes to allow them to be successful. I'm doing a bit of sermonizing here, and you'll see more as we go along, but you'll also get a true picture of what you need to know about teaching English and other subjects in Mexico. There are no free lunches, and no free advice, so the cost of tuition here is to read on.

Okay, you've decided that teaching English in Mexico sounds a lot more interesting than any other prospect you have so you're ready to head South for a job. You need a guidebook my friend, and here it is. Read it, analyze it, and take whatever action you deem appropriate.

As a teaching professional one of my concerns is that both instructor and student benefit from their classroom encounters, and to that end we look at your responsibilities, because in the end, that's all you can control. Do the best job of preparation and implementation that you're capable of and both you and your students will be successful.

THE AUTHOR TEACHING ENGLISH TO MAIDS IN A STOREROOM OF THE MAYAN PALACE RESORT IN NUEVO VALLARTA, JALISCO, MÉXICO, 1997

Many folks feel that having spent a lifetime speaking the language, and earning a passing grade in high school freshman English automatically qualifies them to be a teacher in a foreign country. Here's good news for some of you. In a few places it does. There are any number of schools in Mexico that will give you a job based entirely on your ability as a native speaker. These are usually not jobs you want to accept.

Low pay, disappearing or non-existent paychecks, poor working conditions and facilities, high student and teacher turnover, and almost debilitating stress levels are commonplace. Both you and your learners deserve better. You need to develop a higher degree of qualification and competence, and there are a number of ways to do so.

There are schools set up to provide you with introductory and advanced instruction. There's a veritable laundry list of certifications offered by these schools, and a confusing array of acronyms to identify the various certifications and skills. Here's a list of some of them.

- ESL—English as a Second Language
- EFL—English as a Foreign Language
- CELTA—Certificate in English Language Teaching to Adults
- TEFL—Teaching English as a Foreign Language
- TESL—Teaching English as a Second Language
- TESOL—Teaching English to Speakers of Other Languages
- CTBE—Certificate in Teaching Business English
- CELTC—Certificate in English Language Teaching to Children
- CALL—Computer Assisted Language Learning
- DELTA—Diploma in English Language Teaching for Adults
- COTE—Certificate for Overseas Teachers of English (UK)
- TOEFL—Test of English as a Foreign Language
- TOEIC—Test of English for International Communication
- ESP—English for Special Purposes

Which school and program should you choose? It depends on

- your personal educational background and qualifications
- your financial situation
- your geographical location and/or ability to travel
- how you intend to use your training
- employer needs

and various other factors germane to your personal situation.

Some schools have almost no entrance qualifications past determining if you have sufficient funds to pay tuition. I've seen high school dropouts earn ESL certificates, sometimes in the same class with college graduates. This is not meant to be a criticism since I've also seen some dropouts who were much better teachers than a lot of their better educated peers. However, I must stress the importance of gaining a good understanding of what is required of good language teachers, and most of these schools provide an excellent introduction to the field.

Which training school you choose may also be influenced by how much you have to invest, as well as how close or how far away a particular school is. Additionally, some schools have more restrictive entrance requirements, so you need to shop around. In some cases you can take a course via internet, from the comfort of your own home or the local public library, or even by correspondence. You have a lot of options, and I list a few for you, so check out those that look interesting. Costs, time, and qualifications vary, so be careful with your selection. For the sake of convenience I refer to all schools as "TEFL" training facilities. This is only a partial listing and I neither endorse nor recommend any of them.

Instituto Mexico-Americano de Cultura, A.C.

www.spanish-school.com.mx

Guadalajara

Worldwide Teachers Institute

www.worldwideteachers.org

Guadalajara and Puerto Vallarta

Vancouver Language Centre

www.tefl-mexico.com

Guadalajara

Teach and Travel Inc.

www.teachandtravel.com

Progreso, Yucatan

Via Lingua

www.vialingua.com

Guadalajara

International Teacher Training Organization

www.teflteslmexico.com

Guadalajara

The British Council Mexico

www.britishcouncil.org/mexico/english/english/cote.htm (COTE)

Mexico City

International House Teacher Training

> *www.ih-usa.com*

> Portland,OR and San Francisco, Santa Monica, and San Diego, CA

Midwest Teacher Training Program

> *www.mttp.com*

> Madison, WI

Transworld Schools

> *www.transworldschools.com*

> San Francisco, CA

The Boston Language Institute

> *www.teflcertificate.com*

> Boston, MA

St. Giles Colleges

> *www.stgiles-usa.com*

> San Francisco, CA

School for International Training

> *www.sit.edu/tesolcert*

> Brattleboro, VT and Northhampton and Boston, MA and Santa Fe, NM and San Francisco, CA and Chicago, IL

International Language Institute

> *www.ili.ca* or *www.celta.ca* or *www.TeachEnglish.ca*

> Halifax, Nova Scotia

Teach and Travel Inc.

> *www.teachandtravel.com*

> Vancouver, BC and Calgary, AL and Ottawa, ONT

The TEFL Center

> *www.teflcenter.com*

> Toronto, ONT

Vancouver Language Centre

> *www.studyvec.com*

> Vancouver, BC

International Language Institute

www.celtc.ca

Transworld Schools

www.transworldschools.com

Passport TEFL

www.PassportTEFL.com

American Business English Internet School

www.bizenglish.com

ICAL

www.teacher-training.net

Open Learning International — TEFL/TESL as well as the Certificate in Management of TEFL/TESL Centres

www.olionline.com

The TEFL Center

www.teflcenter.com

Worldwide Teachers Development Institute

www.bostontefl.com

i-Venture

www.i-to-i.com

Norwood English

www.norwoodenglish.com

Canadian Global TESOL Training Institute (correspondence)

www.canadianglobal.net

Teach and Travel Inc. (correspondence)

www.teachandtravel.com

I don't believe that this is the best way to get your initial training but any training beats none at all, so if this is what fits your schedule and pocketbook go for it. Once you've gained some experience you can also further your education via some of these sources. One caveat however. If you choose an online or correspondence program arrange for some practical classroom teaching experience. Some courses require it, but others don't. Find a local language program where you can volunteer to assist the staff. In areas with high immigrant populations this will be easy. If you live in Whitebread, South Dakota you may need to volunteer in a local adult literacy program, or as a teacher's aide at one of the local schools. You may find a solution to the problem by looking on *www.esldirectory.com*. This site lists ESL programs worldwide where non-English speakers come to learn the language, so chances are you'll find one close to you. These places will give you an up close and personal look at working in the field, and will probably allow you to observe or volunteer. Regardless of what you choose, you absolutely must see how a teacher plans, prepares, and presents. It's more difficult than it looks.

This may be a bit confusing at first. Hang in there, it's much easier to deal with befuddlement while you're still in your hometown than trying to figure it all out in an alien culture. Here are a couple of **required resources** for your introduction into the TEFL arena. Take time to gather as much information as you can and study it well.

- Dave Sperling's ESL Café is a treasure trove of useful information and worldwide referrals. If you're seriously considering the TEFL field you need to know this site. Look in at *www.eslcafe.com*. There are links to hundreds of other sites which are very informative and up-to-date.

- InternetWorks has two publications that are invaluable in helping aspiring teachers understand what they need to do to survive in the Mexican TEFL/TESL market, as well as where to look for jobs. First is the *Teach English in Mexico Employment Guide* that includes a thirty minute video CD ROM that shows teachers at work in Mexican schools. The second is the *Teach English in Mexico Newsletter.* The monthly newsletter supplies names and contact information for employers in many towns and cities. Each issue highlights a different area. Each newsletter provides information about housing, travel, shopping, and a myriad of other tips to help you make a smooth and stress-free transition. An archived set of the newsletters is available on CD and is a good place to get a feel for the country and the job market. Contact them at *www.teach-english-mexico.com* or e-mail *info@employnow.com*.

For those who have inquiring minds, which I sincerely hope means all of you, here are some sites for you to explore. When you go to the ESL Cafe site there will be many more links, so you can productively surf for weeks and weeks.

- *www.tesol.org* — This is where you should begin your information search. You can find a considerable amount of information about the profession on this site.

- *www.transabroad.com* — Transitions Abroad magazine owns this website. I've read this publication for years and always found it useful and interesting. A lot of the editorial content comes from people just like you, so it's valid and relative to the situation.

- ✒ *www.Spanish.about.com* — This is a "must visit" site containing information on employment, training, ways to use the computer in your classroom, teaching resources, and lesson plans.

- ✒ *www.onestopenglish.com* — Here are lots of lesson plans as well as stories from ESL teachers. There's also a discussion forum and tips on using the Internet.

- ✒ *www.asahi-net.or.jp* — Yuki's EFL/ESL Bulletin Board is a place where teachers from secondary schools around the world can exchange information and help each other. It provides a good insight into the problems and concerns of classroom teachers.

- ✒ *www.handsonenglish.com* — A paid newsletter is available from this site.

- ✒ *www.inside-mexico.com* — If you want to see what it's really like in a Mexican school, visit this website written by a classroom teacher. Lots of additional information about the culture, customs, history, and country adds to your understanding of what to expect. This is a cool site and something I wish more teachers would do.

- ✒ *www.TEFL.com* — Jobs available throughout the world are listed here and you can post your resume online.

- ✒ *www.TEFL.net*— Sign up here to receive the free TEFL.NetInspire!Magazine.

- ✒ *www.englishclub.com* — Another free online magazine, *Progress*, is available along with a good selection of lesson plans, games, quizzes, and much more.

- ✒ *www.eflweb.com* — The listings here offer job information, teacher resources, and referrals to other useful sites.

- ✒ *www.teachandtravel.com* — Teach and Travel Inc. offers information about jobs that are available overseas and has several sections that answer many questions.

- ✒ *www.cambridge.org* — The website for Cambridge University Press will guide you to many of the books used by TEFL teachers worldwide.

- ✒ *www.teflfarm.com*— The Language Fun Farm is teacher written and packed with great ideas and activities for classroom use. This is a definite "must visit" site.

The website of Southwold Primary School in the UK is at *http://atschool.eduweb.co.uk/southwold/links2001.htm*. This is a treasure trove of information for the classroom teacher. Visit this site gratis to find:

☞ encyclopaedias, dictionaries, thesauri

☞ online story books for children and young adults

☞ lessons plans for —

o geography

o artists and paintings

o museums

o music

o settlements

o volcanoes and earthquakes

o religions of the world

o science

o history — including the Aztec civilization and culture

o weather

o rainforests

o environmental issues

o maps

o math

o rivers

Most of the places you'll be teaching will not provide access to a fraction of the information you can access at this site. Spend some time exploring what they make available to you, and use your own imagination and teaching skills to modify the materials to suit your particular situation. I predict you'll soon consider this to be the single most important teaching resource you have.

By the way, you can easily modify these lessons for adult learners. You should consider sending a note to thank these folks and let them know what you think of their site.

At some point you're going to have to submit a resume or a CV. Curriculum Vitae is the European way of asking "What have you done with your life and how are you qualified for the position for which you're applying?" If you didn't already know that you can catch up with those who did, and pass those who don't, by checking out *http://www.englishcv.com*.

Josef Essberger wrote *CVs,Resumes, & Covering Letters* for folks who are just as lost as you. It's a downloadable ebook that costs about $15.00 US. You may be able to find much of the same information if you pay attention to the websites I laid out earlier, but I personally believe that the wheel has been properly invented. Many of the TEFL training courses also have a brief introduction to this skill.

You'll find that most employers in Mexico will want to see you in person before they hire you. That doesn't mean you won't need a CV, but many other factors will come into play. Earlier I referred to the video that accompanies the InternetWorks *Employment Guide.* The CD shows teachers talking about their teaching experiences and presents information about what to expect at a job interview as well as how to prepare for your move to Mexico.

Here's a short interview with Mark Farley, author of the *Teach English in Mexico Employment Guide* and Director of the Guaranteed Placement Program which provides participants with a guaranteed job, access to a personal representative for up to a year, arranged accommodations in the area where you teach, teaching materials, and a few other helpful items.

DA: Mark, aside from the things listed above, how else are you qualified to offer assistance and advice to prospective teachers?

MF: I have taught in Mexico on and off for eighteen years and our company (InternetWorks) is in the 6th year of providing information and resources for those interested in teaching English in Mexico.

DA: Based on your experience what do you consider to be the most important characteristic of a successful EFL teacher?

MF: The most important quality a teacher should possess is enthusiasm. The teacher should be motivated to teach and have an intense desire to help others learn. It is also important to know grammar and to know how to present the material in a fun and exciting way.

DA: So what do you think are the *minimum* requirements for a successful teacher?

MF: You should have classroom experience. You should be confident and outgoing. If you've never presented material to a class, then you may find yourself freezing up. Schools in Mexico are looking for outgoing, motivated individuals who can take control of a classroom. Some schools have even suggested receiving drama students or theater majors, as they can be lively and they know how to communicate to an audience. This is not a job for the shy or quiet. If you have never taught a language before, it is a good idea to volunteer at a local literacy or ESL program. Schools in Mexico are looking for teachers with at least some teaching experience. Having a BA is important too if you plan to teach for more than a couple of months. It is a necessary requirement to obtain the work permit, along with other items.

DA: Are there personality types that might not be happy or effective as teachers in Mexico?

MF: Yes, again, if you are shy or introverted, then teaching English is definitely not for you. You must be a good communicator. Keep in mind what I said earlier – some schools have even requested theater majors. If you have a hard time getting your point across or being heard, then you are probably not a good candidate for teaching English in Mexico.

DA: How do you feel about the recent trend toward online TESL and TEFL certification courses?

MF: I feel that these can be effective if they are coupled with actual classroom experience. If the student can take what he or she learns online and apply it in an actual classroom setting (again, possibly volunteering for a literacy or ESL program), then I feel this can be beneficial for an actual teaching assignment. "Live" experience is always necessary as I have seen a few inexperienced teachers freeze up and have to return home as they were just too frightened or too shy to teach.

DA: What one piece of information would you offer to a prospective teacher?

MF: My advice to others interested in teaching in Mexico is to treat this as a serious endeavor. If you go there expecting to have a full-time vacation you will be in for a big surprise. Schools are serious about providing their students with quality teachers who handle the job with professionalism. Showing up to class like you are dressed for the beach is a good way to lose your job.

DA: Any other warnings for these folks?

MF: I would warn prospective teachers that teaching in Mexico is not as easy as they may think. It takes dedication, patience, flexibility, cultural sensitivity, and a lot more. It is not for everyone, and not everyone has all the necessary qualities to be successful.

DA: A couple of years back I ordered the archived CD of your newsletter and found it to contain an amazing amount of useful information. How and why did it come about?

MF: The newsletter was created to provide up-to-date information on teaching jobs in Mexico. And more importantly, it was developed to provide job information for destinations in Mexico less traveled. For example, we have uncovered opportunities in such wonderful places as Orizaba, Toluca, Xalapa, Colima, Morelia, Chihuahua, Poza Rica, Queretaro, Zacatecas, Playa del Carmen, Los Mochis, and Cuernavaca - places that one would possibly discount as having a lot of teaching opportunities.

DA: I know you use teacher correspondents in the various areas to gather information but do you have other sources?

MF: We receive information for our newsletter in many forms. One way we receive information is from our teacher correspondents. These are teachers who actually work in the city they are writing about. Another source is our roving reporters, of which we have quite a few. These individuals will visit a particular city and uncover every possible teaching job in that city. They will also locate inexpensive hotels and investigate local housing options. And lastly, we receive information directly from schools who have discovered our website and realize that we would be in a good position to assist them in locating quality teachers via our newsletter.

There you go, guys. Mark offers a good overview of some of the more important considerations when it comes to teaching in Mexico. For more help you can to go to *www.teach-english-mexico.com*. Let's finish up here by looking at several things that will help you become a happy and effective EFL teacher in Mexico.

I know that the thought of either teaching *or* learning grammar strikes fear into the hearts of many. In the list of websites I gave you is the address of the Cambridge University Press. Some of the books there will be extremely helpful. One set is by Betty Azar. The primary text is *Fundamentals of English Grammar* and it has an accompanying *Teacher's Guide* for your use in teaching, as well as correcting assignments. The third book of the set is *Chartbook- A Reference Grammar-Fundamentals of English Grammar*. These three books will get you through any situation that's likely to arise. I suggest getting them, or a like set, before you ever begin your TEFL training course.

Another book, easier to use than Azar's series but not as comprehensive, is *Creative Grammar Practice- Getting learners to use both sides of the brain* by Gunter Gerngross and Herbert Puchta.

Both of these choices provide you with plenty of lesson plans and classroom activities. They can be ordered through your local bookstore, and are well worth the time and effort required to master them. If you're a bit hazy about phrasal verbs, adjective clauses, modal auxiliaries, and verb tenses you definitely need to invest in a good grammar book. Just to boost your anxiety level a bit, you need to know that some employers require you to take and pass a grammar test before they consider you for employment.

Also, just for fun you may want to pick up a book on idioms. I have an old copy of *101 American English Idioms* by Harry Collins. The illustrations are by Mario Risso and they go a long way toward helping explain terms such as "pay through the nose", "kick the bucket", and "bury the hatchet".

Those of you who plan to teach children or young adults might want to look on the Continental Book Company website at *http://www.continentalbook.com* . They offer a variety of teaching materials, many with a Mexican slant. Another good source is *http://www.deltasystems.com* .

If you wonder why I've included the above, you'll soon find that some schools supply a curriculum that they expect you to follow. Other schools insist on teacher input for lesson plans and presentations. Be prepared for either requirement. And you also should know that the individual schools usually insist on retaining full rights to any lesson plan or classroom activity you develop.

Some teachers realize they must find private students to make enough money to survive. If you find yourself in this situation you'll definitely be writing your own lesson plans, so these books will be tremendously helpful. Be ready for any eventuality. Especially in regard to finances .

You may look at teaching SoB as a great adventure, but as all of the world's great adventurers know, cash is essential to success. What's all this going to cost you? It varies. As you research your options you'll find training courses ranging from a $399 US online course on up to nearly a couple of thousand dollars for a program that offers intensive small class instruction somewhere in Mexico. That's one of your first decisions when seeking qualification.

Next, you need to consider travel and job hunting expenses. As I said earlier, most employers are going to want to see you for a face to face interview before they offer a job. Once you arrive in the area where you plan to work you have to secure housing. In the interview Mark mentioned the city of Colima. As an example of housing costs, I recently saw classified ads in the *El Mundo* newspaper offering "student apartments" for 700 to 800 *pesos* per month in that city. At the current rate that's about $77 to $88 US. At my advanced age and carefully cultivated comfort zone I shudder to think about living in one of these, and I assume you're in about the same shape. A note of caution, however, you're not likely to find deals like this in the more popular and well-known areas. Some schools provide housing for single teachers so check it out before you come. You'll also find that young teachers tend to share housing, so you may wind up moving into a place that a departing teacher is vacating. Where you choose to live and teach is a personal matter; here's one of my favorite places.

In my opinion Colima is one of the cleanest small cities in Mexico, and an excellent introduction to life in Mexico. Colima is a university town so there are facilities and entertainment venues that you won't find in smaller places. There's plenty of acceptable housing, an active social scene, internet cafes, good transportation, excellent shopping, friendly and helpful people, a tiny *gringo* presence of three hundred or so residents, a high percentage of English-speaking Nationals, a variety of language schools, many reasonably-priced restaurants, and modern and traditional grocery stores. Plus you get to live in a gorgeous and ecologically diverse area, and you can write to your friends back home that you work near an active volcano. And you're only a two hour bus ride from the beach at Manzanillo. The only problem for some folks is that at certain times of the year it's only about nine degrees cooler than Hell.

Regardless of which area you choose, there are a few minor expenses you need to be aware of if you rent an apartment. Many furnished places have few of the amenities you're used to. Again, plan on buying light bulbs, cleaning products, personal items, toilet paper, groceries and possibly, sheets and pillows. You need to consider laundry expenses as well as some transportation costs for job hunting.

Here's the fatality report from my TEFL training class of twelve people. Two went to South America and I have no idea how they fared. Three wandered around Central America for a couple of months until one returned to her home in Georgia without ever finding a job. I have no clue about the couple, but he had a knack for picking up short-term employment in the area so I'm sure they did well. One moved to Guadalajara and is still a wildly popular teacher in that city. Another, who is married to a Hispanic man taught for awhile and then moved on to other things, and the rest went home without trying to find a job.

You probably expected to find information here about salaries. Anything I write on that subject will soon outdated.

To find accurate and up-to-date salary information. Look at the *http://www.eslcafe.com* website job listings or the *http://www.teach-english-mexico.com* website for information about how to subscribe to the *Teach English in Mexico Newsletter.*

One additional area to consider is teaching accent reduction. My beautiful friend Melody Noll has written two books to help you in that enterprise. Look on *http://www.ameri-talk.com* to get more info about American Accent Skills. Use both Book 1 and Book 2 to teach Intonation, Reductions, and Word Connections to help your students lose their native accents and learn American accent, pronunciation, and communications skills. E-mail Melody at *Melody@ameri-talk.com* or call 510-655-8439, fax 510-655-6179.

The mail address is:

P.O. Box 8632

Oakland, CA 94609

To Become a Success You Need At Least These Few Things

- an outgoing personality
- flexibility and a sense of humor
- a bit of classroom teaching experience
- information,information,information
- a specific plan of action
- good training
- cash and an ATM card
- passport
- very little luggage
- a good grammar book

Some of you are degreed professionals with teacher certification and classroom experience in your home state or province. You have more options and better prospects than beginning teachers in most cases. You still need to get the TEFL training, but you already have a very qualified foot in the door. Here are a few sites you can explore to get a sense of what your options are.

- *www.state.gov/www/about_state/schools/oteaching.html* — The US State Department's list of International Schools.

- *www.riverdale.k12.or.us/rim/mexico2.html* — Lists American Schools in Mexico.

- *www.isk12.com* — This site offers links of great value.

- *www.Montessori.org* — This is a list of a few Montessori Schools in Mexico.

- *www.iss.edu* — International School Services provides employment assistance to teaching professionals and administrators. They offer a *Directory of International Schools* for about $55 US, including domestic shipping.

- *www.teach-english-mexico.com* — Your subscription to the *Teach English in Mexico Newsletter* is worth its weight in gold.

You also need to look in the classified section of your professional journals. I served as president of my Texas non-union teacher's association but I read the NEA union publication each month, and I suggest you conduct your research the same way. See what everybody has to offer.

Chapter 18

Gittin' Your Ashes Hauled: Guys, Gals, and Gays

We'd driven over to Melaque to buy groceries and on the way out of town Ruben asked if I'd mind stopping by one of the local centro botaneros *so he could see if a friend of his was working. Some* centro botaneros, *from what I can gather, are establishments that open in the afternoons to feed alcoholics, as well as provide a place for really poor voluptuous young girls to escape the midday sun.*

I followed Ruben into the place and we selected a table and sat down. One of the poor, probably homeless young ladies immediately came to take our order. Pity filled my being as I surveyed her clothing, what there was of it. A skirt and a blouse, both sized too small to encase her amazingly supple and curvaceous honey-hued body. The apparent lack of any kind of undergarment only served to accentuate the incongruity of the shiny spike-heeled shoes she teetered about on. In spite of her apparent state of poverty, she nonetheless generously offered to bring food to our table. Embarrassed to eat in the presence of her impending starvation, I declined.

"It's free", Ruben boomed, "get something." Oh hell, when in Rome. In just a few seconds steaming tacos *and* cervezas frias *were delivered up by the young waif who was so weakened from hunger that she could barely navigate the rough, wood-planked floor on those high heels. I noticed that there were a number of sympathetic and generous souls at other tables who were freely*

sharing food and ordering up drinks for some of the other pitiful young señoritas. My heart swelled with pride and admiration to see such generosity and self-lessness and I immediately vowed to begin a clothing drive so that these poor maidens could experience the small luxury of clothes that didn't cling and bind and compromise their modesty—and sensible shoes to lessen the danger of tripping on the uneven flooring.

As soon as we finished our food and drinks, Ruben suggested that we look at a place across the street since his friend wasn't in this charity ward. We left a generous tip and jumped in the truck for the drive out of the walled-in com-pound to a spot next to Junior's strip club.

After parking in front, I led the way since Ruben had stopped to speak with the guy that I later discovered was the owner of the place. As they spoke the owner dumped an unidentifiable, but viciously vile-looking liquid into a shallow, stagnant artificial lagoon close to the entrance of the establishment.

As I entered the small alcove leading into the main room, I saw a stunning young thing walking toward me. Blue eye shadow, long, dark mascaraed lashes, bee stung lips brightly and generously spread with a crimson, creamy paste, short, jet-black hair moussed to the max and combed straight back on the sides. A glitter-dusted chest showed through the generous opening at the neck of a tailored silk blouse. It occurred to me we'd left Tobacco Road and were now evidently traversing the Yellow Brick Road.

I walked on into the large palapa-roofed main room, leaving behind a gaudily painted and gilded six-foot-high plaster replica of the Sphinx, and a large col-lection of vintage '40's black and white photos of scantily clad señoritas in provocative poses. Everything was accented by silky, filmy wall hangings art-fully draped and swagged.

The decor of the main dining area was more restrained. Another palapa roof peaked over an open room and hanging from the wall of an adjoining building, the pillars supporting the roof and the wall behind the bar, were more photos of the provocative señoritas, as well as a sprinkling of color photos and post-ers of Marilyn Monroe. The owner must be a movie fan, I thought.

Open-air dining was being enjoyed by a couple of vaqueros sitting at a table across the dirt-floored room where they'd been joined by an elegantly coiffed and tastefully dressed young companion. At a table near us were three truck drivers clad identically from head to toe in heavy, lace-up work boots, faded denim jeans, sleeveless T shirts, and baseball caps. Chain-drive wallets were securely clipped to each individual's belt and partially jammed into their rear pockets.

At the table next to ours sat three women. One was a conservatively dressed and carefully made-up but remarkably unattractive mid-forties type. Another was a very young and semi-attractive woman who appeared to be about ten or eleven months pregnant. The third one turned and spoke to Ruben as soon as he sat down. As she talked and laughed I noticed that there was a wide space in the front of her upper gum where at least four teeth should have been.

A few minutes later Ruben told me that she was Iva's sister. Iva was the young woman I had hired to help me clean the house I'd recently moved into. The ID was superfluous since I'd noted the facial resemblance and the same genetic dental deficiency immediately.

Without asking, another employee, this one clad in a simple cocktail dress and stylish flats, delivered two saucers of tropical fruit slices to our table and took my order for a cerveza, *and a* ron y coca *for Ruben.*

The jukebox at the back of the room blared out a corrido, *a sad, tuneful tale demanding a response from the listener, one quickly and loudly complied with by one of the truckers. With ball cap tipped back and both hands gripping her bottle of* cerveza, *she rared back with eyes closed and head tilted to Heaven to deliver up the traditional anguished wails and yelps of appreciation and*

empathy demanded by the heart-wrenching sorrow immortalized in the grooves of that little jukebox 45.

Our server came from a spot behind the bar to caution the wailer to tone down both her emotions and her volume. At that point I personally wasn't bothered by much of anything that might transpire because I'd realized that the owner, the two vaqueros, *one of the three* camioñeros, *Ruben, and my own big pretty self weren't the only males in the place. That's right, we were outnumbered by transvestites and bull dykes. Big bull dykes. Eighteen-wheeler drivin'*

CABALLOS, PISTOLAS Y MUJERES INFIELES,
WILLIAM GENTES, 1983

bull dykes. Most disconcerting was the fact that the best looking people in the place, aside from me and possibly one of the vaqueros, *were the trannies. It was all a bit disorienting until the sortin' out was done.*

Suddenly the beer and fruit seemed less than compatible mates and I signaled for our server. Tequila, por favor. Dos. Y mas frutas. *This was a situation that required both a double dose of brain sedative and a sense of humor. I've discovered that things are either a hell of a lot more dangerous or a hell of a lot more amusing after* tequila *enters into the equation. Following earnest conversation that established the subjects in the photos as local transvestites and brief biographical sketches of some of the "girls" in the place, I had enough information to develop a minor thesis. Such was the expected price of hangin' out and bonding with our "waitress" over a few drinks. Maybe it's true and maybe it ain't, but judging by appearances, in Mexico, both workin' conditions and earning potential are better for cross-dressers than they are for whores.*

Yeah, they're here. Guys are here, gals are here, and gays are here. Some are single, some are married, and some are out there wondering.

Guys

Down SoB it's fairly easy to find a young agreeable *señorita.* If true love or any type of reasonable facsimile is on your shopping list, you shouldn't have too much trouble connecting with someone, either *gringo(a)* or National, from the local community. Just be aware of one thing, guys. Mexican daddies and brothers will introduce you to the unpleasant world of barbaric and brutal beatings if they even suspect you're trifling with the affections or delectables of their daughters or sisters. If you discover that you've been dallyin' with a married Mexican woman just go ahead and hang yourself. Don't even risk trying to get out of the country without bein' caught. Pre-conquest Aztec abominations pale in comparison to some of these workouts. I've known a particularly sturdy individual or two who actually survived one of those encounters, and I always pray they won't show up any place I'm trying to get a meal down.

I know some SoB *gringas* who meet guys on the Internet and induce them to come down and visit. There are dating services and bone fide escort services available, as well as houses of ill repute. Publications are out there with "Lonely Hearts" sections, too.

And there's always those married friends who can't stand to see a happy single person so they insist on introducing us to someone who will be "just perfect for you". When the subject rears it's ugly head I usually disconnect my phone, keep the lights turned off, and live on the huge store of canned goods and saltines I keep for just an emergency. It's not safe out on the streets when one of 'em gets in a match-makin' mood. Sometimes it takes months for things to finally cool down enough to venture out, and I ain't *that* great a catch. It seems that in some places, breathin' without wheezin' and bathin' occasionally zip you right to the top of the desirability chart.

I've also seen some good friendships ruined by "love". Most of us need friends a hell of a lot more than we need lovers, so there's always the option of cold-blooded, hot and steamy intimacy without all the forced emotional involvement. If any of you single ladies bought that bill of goods, you be sure to call when you get down here.

Let me just mention that some of the NoB perks that cause guys to accept, or at least submit to semi-permanent domesticity are trumped down here SoB. It doesn't cost much to hire someone to shovel out our lairs occasionally, massages are very inexpensive, and we're usually in the gender minority by a substantial margin so that we get a certain amount of ego-boosting attention without expending much effort. If it's company you're after, somebody is bound to give you a dog after a few days with roughly equal social skills and IQ with whom you can converse, and, thanks to a good selection of TV channels, you can enjoy stateside shows and sports without any fear of having to share the remote. Hell, satellite TV can bring you a full menu of porn channels. Heaven might be better, but I'm at a loss to figure how. In case you lose your head and decide that finding a permanent companion who doesn't bark or meow might be a good move, let me take you by the throat and lead you to *http:// www.bergli.ch* where you'll find books on Switzerland. We all know that the Swiss are world-class romantics and lovers so you need to search their catalog and find the book on inter-cultural marriages. I just can't bring myself to help you any more than that. Oops! Cancel that. My editor just informed me that I should tell you that the book you need is titled *Cupid's Wild Arrows*. Pay attention, guys.

One thing I've noticed and am surprised to find that no reputable researcher has looked into is that some of us of rather advanced age and equally advanced physical deterioration seem to be miraculously transformed into sex symbols as soon as our saggy, baggy asses land SoB.

For instance, you may see a doddering old geezer with a young *seña* and two or three rug rats gnawing at his ankles. Nope, they're probably not his grandkids.

Just as Henry Kissinger remarked, when starlets flocked to him while he was Secretary of State, "Power is the ultimate aphrodisiac." So too is money. I don't mean to sound cynical, and I do hope that true love is really the driving force behind all of these relationships, but I gave up on certain fairy tales and myths long ago.

And, since affairs of the heart and pelvic region work both ways, you may see a rather "mature" lady being squired about town by a handsome young man who could be mistaken for *her* grandkid. Last week he was the *jardiñero,* but this week he's the Lord of the Manor, *El Jefe,* the Khan, the Big Kahuna *del Casa*.

Ain't love grand?

Don't we all have our little desires and fantasies that we'd indulge if we could? One of mine is to absolutely enchant an easily corruptible and totally gullible middle-aged blonde with huge assets, long shapely legs, and a willingness to let me loose with her debit card and Range Rover.

Gals

Ladies, there are not a lot of Mexico-related websites specifically for you but here's one that's currently (as of September, 2002) trying to get up and running: *http://www.mexirover.com/mexirover.htm*. The short version without the *mexirover.htm* is not working yet but go to the longer. Their E-mail is *info@mexirover.com*. Another website is *http://www.womanabroad*.com. This site offers information about single women who travel or live abroad. Not many articles are specific to Mexico but their "survival tips" could make your transition here easier.

And now for something completely different.

Someone who really does know almost everything about single women moving to Mexico is Blue. She's written *Midlife Mavericks: Women Reinventing Their Lives in Mexico*. Here's a little bit of what she has to say.

KAREN BLUE, AUTHOR, PUBLISHER, AND RESIDENT, AJIJIC, JALISCO, MEXICO

From a Single Woman's Perspective…by Blue

In 1995, I attended the first "Retire in Mexico" conference put on in Guadalajara by International Living. There were 5 single women in a group of about 130 attendees. At age 51, I figured I was the youngest in attendance. During one of the "mingle" parties, I asked a female realtor who lived in Ajijic, "What's it like for single women there?"

She answered me in her deep southern drawl, "Why honey child, if you-all are comin' looking for a man, don't. If they're not already married, all the men at

Lakeside are either gay, 90, or gone by Sunday."

Well, looking for a man hadn't even made it to my list of needs and wants. What I was really asking was whether it was safe, whether a single woman is accepted into married society, whether there were interesting, single women living there that I could become friends with and whether the Mexican people would accept me.

The Realtor was right about the men, though.

I've lived in Ajijic six years now, and when Don asked me to write about my experience, I thought about my question to that realtor again.

One day, during one of our "Living at Lake Chapala" seminars, a man asked me if it wasn't harder for a single woman to make the move. Without hesitation, I answered, "Yes. Of course it is. It's harder for a single woman to make a move to the next county, let alone a new country. There's only one person to do all that has to be done. I don't have my best friend with me, like couples do, to share the joys, help pump me up when I'm emotionally overwrought, move the heavy furniture or kill the scorpion in the bathtub."

Obviously two people, any two people, cut the workload in half. But then, I've been divorced for 33 years, and over the years I've moved many times and become fairly adept at compensating for brawn with brain.

On the other hand, it's much easier being single here than it was in Silicon Valley. For one thing, I don't have an 80-hour job, struggling to find time to handle the myriad of other responsibilities that go along with managing a house, raising kids, and having a semblance of a social life. Here, I'm semi-retired. My business partner and I publish a monthly on-line magazine and provide weekly seminars on "Living at Lake Chapala." I have a maid and a gardener who come three times a week for three hours each. I can't remember the last time I've cleaned a toilet or ironed clothes.

My life is much easier here. The weather is beautiful and I live 90% of the year with my doors open, smelling the fresh air and listening to the birds and the bees outside. I have two constant companions, my miniature black schnauzer, Max, and a miniature white poodle, Maurice.

Socially, I have friends who are couples and singles, straight and gay, young and old, *gringo* and Mexican. My life is enriched greatly through these friendships. I don't know why it is, but there are many more women than men who move here alone. I wrote a book about the women, *Midlife Mavericks: Women Reinventing Their Lives in Mexico.* One single man asked me when I'd write one about the men. I responded by saying, "When I know more than three who have moved here alone." I had talked to hundreds of women, interviewed 39 and included 17 of their stories in my book. I literally know only three men whose stories I could write up and one of them is the author of this book.

Ajijic is a small village. I believe there's a common thread that goes through folks who up and leave their own home in the second half of their lives to settle in an emerging country. They have to have a bit more moxie, be more resilient, be more accepting of differences and perhaps, take a few more risks than the average Joe...or Joan.

All this makes for friendships with very interesting people. I've a wide circle of friends who share at least some of my interests and I've converted several into sharing an interest or two. Realistically, there is no pool of datable men. However, I feel safe here and if I want to go to the Little Theater alone, I don't hesitate. I'll always run into people I know and can join for intermission. I prefer not to go out and eat alone, but sometimes, in the middle of a busy day, my stomach demands that I stop for lunch. Generally, someone is there who asks me to join them. That never happened in Silicon Valley.

I've been an expat once before, when I worked for Hewlett-Packard in Germany. We "foreigners" tended to band together and help each other out. I find that same phenom-enon here. People offer help. "I'm going to Costco tomorrow. Do you need anything?" I'm learning how to ask for help for the first time in my life, too. If I need someone to house and dog sit, I've three friends who are more than willing to help out.

And the Mexicans, by nature, are very kind and helpful. They live in the present and always want to make whoever is with them happy. (Of course, that's not always good. Especially when you ask them for directions and they give them to you whether they know them or not!) My garage mechanic is a phone call away (now that he has a phone). If my car's broken down, he'll come right away, either fix it on the street or tow it into his shop, taking me home along the way. When it's done, he'll bring it back to my house. Mind you, I always have to wipe grease off the steering wheel, but it's worth it. If I go grocery shopping and don't have enough money, they say, "Bring it tomorrow."

I have a handyman I trust. He has my keys, so I can call and say, "Pablo, the fountain pump isn't working," or "One of my phone lines is dead," and he'll come fix it. I don't need to wait for him.

On the down side, most Mexican men don't like working for women – Mexican or otherwise. When I first got here and was gutting and remodeling my house without a working knowledge of Spanish, I found it to be very difficult. Communication wasn't clear, my frustration showed and getting frustrated or angry is the worst thing you can do. I've had to learn a lot of cultural lessons, give up my need for control, and modify my Type A personality.

All these things, I believe, are very good for my health and my attitude. Friends back in California say they've seen me change. I'm calmer, have more patience and have adopted, for many situations, the Mexican *mañana* attitude. Things will get done, maybe not when we want them done, but they'll get done.

And that's probably the bottom line about being happy living in Mexico as a single woman. Or a single man. Or a married person. If you're not happy with yourself, Mexico is not going to make you happy. It's an inside job.

KAREN BLUE
http://www.mexicoblue.
homestead.com

Gays and Lesbians

Let's kick open *that* closet door. I'm not an expert on the subject, but I know folks who are, and they report that life here is as full and rich for them as it is for everyone else. Sounds just like "regular" folks, huh? You don't see the kind of mindless hate and prejudice here that you do in many NoB communities. A lot of the snowbird enclaves have very active gay contingents whose members seem to move easily from one group to another as they make their way through the local social scene.

An acquaintance from Houston makes regular trips to Puerto Vallarta to enjoy the very active and non-judgmental atmosphere of the beach community there. Guadalajara has a very extensive network of clubs catering to all tastes and inclinations, both gay and straight, male and female. If you want to check things out for yourself, here's a list of websites. For PV, *http://www.pacopaco.com* will get you hooked into the site of one of Puerto Vallarta's most popular gay nightclubs, along with links to other hotspots of the Paco Empire. Three more sites are *http://www.gaypuertovallarta.info*, *http://www.gayguidevallarta.com*, and *http://www.gaypuertovallarta.news*.

For links to the scenes in Acapulco, Cancun, Guadalajara, Huatulco (beach life in Oaxaca State), Manzanillo, Mexico City, Tijuana, (Tijuana?), and Veracruz you can type in *http://gaymexico.net*. This site also provides access to Mexico's largest gay chat room. Another site *http://www.geocities.com/mexicanguide* has message boards for some areas.

Finally, as much as I hate to bring y'all down, there's a report called *Mexico: Treatment of Homosexuals* written by Andrew Reding in November 1997 and subtitled *Prepared for the Resource Information Center of the Immigration and Naturalization Service, U.S. Department of Justice.* Both genders will be interested in Reding's conclusions.

Partyin', Brewskis, Fiestas, and Fandangos

One of my personal joys of living in Mexico is being able to observe and participate in the celebrations that take place here. Go to *http:// www.mexconnect.com* and look in the Festivals and Holidays section for a calendar of many of the country's celebrations and observances. You can find a month-by-month listing of all the major holidays at *http://www.mexonline.com/ holiday.htm.* Each area and each village has particular festivities that are traditional and meaningful to them, and there are also plenty of regional and national events that take place throughout the year.

Many expatriates miss out on the spice of life that comes with living in Mexico by avoiding these events. One Mexican Independence Day, in one of the more

popular *gringo* enclaves, seven of us walked to the church for the ceremony leading up to the reading of the *"Grito de Dolores"*, the Cry of Dolores, the call to revolution by Father Hidalgo in 1810. This re-enactment is carried out in most of Mexico's cities and towns and is one of the major celebrations. Our group had a wonderful time, and even though we stayed late, we saw few other *gringos* out enjoying the entertainment and street dancing. All evening long we saw only six other foreigners and four of them were clearing out

EL JARABE,
WILLIAM GENTES, 1985

of the area as quickly as they could. The next year we saw eight or ten non-Nationals there, so that shows a bit of progress. My advice is to throw yourself into the activities around you. You'll enjoy yourself so much more if you make the attempt to integrate into the community. One night my daughter Abby, son-in-law Brian, four-year-old grandson Asa and I were the only foreigners sitting at another celebration under a huge open-sided tent at midnight listening to some very polished and entertaining musicians. We felt no threat or discomfort at all.

Indio, Sol, Modelo, Pacifico, Corona, Dos Equis...

Incidentally, you can buy *cerveza* in nearly every grocery store here. Brewing companies have their own retail establishments that sell their entire range of alcoholic beverages along with a limited selection of snacks, soft drinks and sometimes, a few grocery items. They usually carry their promotional products with the company logo stamped on coolers, shirts, towels, hats, dominoes, coasters, t-shirts, trays, sports balls, beverage glasses, neon signs, and posters.

Liquor stores are pretty much liquor stores all around the world. They're here and you'll be able to recognize them by the words *Vinos y Licores* painted on the outside. If you're not sure, ask any drunk you happen to stumble over. If you don't see *Vinos y Licores* just look for a sign reading *licorería* and you'll be in paydirt city.

Here's an interesting little item. Minors are prohibited by law from buying tobacco products, but it's a common sight to see small children totin' big bottles of *cerveza* or *tequila* down the street. Evidently it's okay to send 'em on down to the corner *tienda* for a booze run if you're not in strollin' shape towards the end of the evening.

Chapter 19

You're Not in Kansas Anymore

The Bellerin' Blue-Haired *Gringa*

I'd stopped by to get some money from the ATM but I saw the guy was working on it, so I walked across the street to sit on the plaza and wait. I'd just settled in on a bench when I heard the screeching. Human female screeching. Off to my right, just on the other side of where the cabbies were parked. The cab stand is on one side of the street and the cop shop is on the other and she was parked in the street between them. As were the eight or ten cars behind her. She chose to park there, but the others had no choice. The cabbies were all out of business because the traffic backed up on the street had them blocked in. Got the picture? Gringa from Texas, big white Dodge sedan, prematurely blue hair.

Evidently I'd missed a good part of the show up to this point but I quickly saw that the cabbies were trying to get her to move the Dodge so they could get out and earn a living. She, on the other hand, had been wronged at another location and was hell-bent to report her woes. "I'm here for the police", she shrieked, standing beside the open door of the car and waving her arms in the direction of the police headquarters across the way, "the police".

Again, several of the cabbies asked her to move. Again she refused. Now it was a challenge, taken up with good humor by most of the affected group. A few suggestions in both Spanish and broken English as to where and how the car could be placed, all met with stout resistance from the screeching gringa, and with a jerk at the steering wheel to emphasize her claim that the car could not be turned. The drivers of the cars behind her sat patiently, some grinning and enjoying the show. And she was puttin' on a performance. Every time a cabbie approached she shooed him away. Each time a policeman stuck his head out the door she shrieked and waved. Somewhere a horn tooted and she turned her attention to the traffic she had backed up.

Now you have to understand that there's a certain group of folks, not just here, but everywhere, who believe that the world revolves around their own little piddlin'-ass problems, and nothing else matters. This particular member of that group was upset because after she'd parked beside the road somewhere she'd flung her car door open into the path of a passing vehicle and gotten it reconfigured. She was now upset because the other driver didn't stop. Let me explain. She was at fault, but she felt as though she had the right to inconvenience half the town just because she felt like it.

After a few minutes reinforcements came rollin' up in The War Wagon. About six or seven flak-jacketed, M-16 totin' city cops came pilin' out of that Chevy short bed. The driver walked to the screecher to take the report. The others took the safe route and walked on over to the cop shop and disappeared inside. As soon as her attention was diverted by the officer, one of the braver cabbies jumped into the Dodge and to the laughter and cheers of his compadres, and the shouts, applause and honking of the other drivers, he pulled it out of the way. Almost everybody was happy now. Miss Congeniality was still raving. Perhaps even more so.

Day One

Here's a little scenario you'll probably encounter at one time or another. You've pulled up in front of the place you've rented, unlocked the door and started unloading the Volvo. One or two things are likely to happen. All of them quaint. All of them cute and picaresque. Each a potential threat to your finances and sanity.

Neighbors of all ages might come out to see exactly what's going on and who you are and what you're totin'. Smile and nod. Speak if you know an appropriate pleasantry.

Someone may come over and offer to help you tote. Let him. Or her. Or them. They're just curious and need to gather plenty of information to report to the shy ones. Offer a Coke in appreciation of their help.

Someone may petition for employment as your maid, or gardener, or major domo, or just about any damn thing. Don't hire anyone right now. *Don't* hire *anyone* right now.

Or, the street could be silent and the neighborhood seemingly deserted without one person seemingly aware of your arrival. Custer probably thought the same.

A local festival could be in full swing and the crowds walking to and from the *plaza* are hindering your efforts at unloading by trying to get you to join in the festivities. You're not up for that right now.

Women and children may shyly promenade up and then back down the street to observe your activities. This technique is employed by the C.I.A. in hotspots around the globe. Smile. Stay calm. Make no sudden moves.

This is a good time to stay sane and steady. Do not attempt to ingratiate yourself with anyone.

The cute little boy standing by the drive may already be plotting the best way to set fire to your dog. See the match box in his hand? I'm always amazed that no matter where I go in Mexico I can always count on one constant. Little boys with matches. Odds are better than even that he also has a stash of explosives somewhere in his clothing. Firecrackers.

Once again, do not hire a maid or gardener today. You don't know the local labor market. They do. You could end up with the most expensive hired help in town. Any town, including Palm Beach or Palm Springs.

Be careful of the overly friendly lady who's trying her best to converse with you in English that's even more pitiful than your Spanish. Amway is big in Mexico as are Avon and Mary Kay. The Mormons, Hare Krishnas, and Jehovah's Witnesses are here too.

The biggest decision you should make right now is where you'll have dinner tonight. And whether to have *seven* or *eight margaritas*, and whether you want to be coherent and mobile tomorrow. My advice is to forget about tomorrow, and relax tonight.

Your mission at this point is to get yourself and your goods into the house sans soap, salvation, or the satisfied smiles of newly-prosperous household employees or salesladies.

Unless you're willing and able to employ half the neighborhood, you need to establish that you're not just another wealthy *gringo*. Observe. Watch. Gather information. Then act, because you'll have begun to understand the ebb and flow and routine of your newly chosen part of the world.

Do the neighbor ladies come out early each morning and sweep the walks and pick up trash in front of their houses? Do they scrub the sidewalk with an old broom? You should too.

Do they use a hose or toss pails of water in wide sweeping arcs to wet the street in front of their houses to hold down the dust? You should too.

Do they leave the house carrying an empty brightly colored woven plastic shopping bag and come back later with a day's worth of groceries? You should too.

Do they wander to the *plaza* in the afternoon or evening to sit and visit, or simply watch life as it unfolds? You should too.

Get a Leg Up

Before and after you take the plunge into life SoB, get a leg up on Mexico's people and their cultural ways with help from these from these folks:

http://www.peoplesguide.com Carl Franz is, in my opinion, THE single best source of general information on Mexico. He and Lorena Havens have extensive experience here. Even if you already have 372 books about Mexico, your library is lacking an absolute essential if you don't have *Carl Franz's The People's Guide to Mexico*. Order it from Carl or from any bookstore if it isn't on the shelf. I've purchased many copies as new editions come out and passed the older ones along to deserving friends and visitors—one of whom evidently stole the latest.

The best web resource to learn about life in Mexico is *http://www.mexconnect.com*. You'll find information about specific towns and geographical areas, Mexican cooking, history and shopping, and a multitude of other useful topics. There are several non-commercial interactive forums where you can ask questions and offer your own opinions and experiences. Don't believe everything you see posted on these forums. Log on every few days and read what's being said. You'll quickly develop a sense of who knows and who doesn't.

By the way, do not, and I repeat *do not,* log onto one of those forums and ask a question like "Will some-

PLAYA DE BRASIL,
WILLIAM GENTES, 1989

one tell me all about living in Queretaro?" Would you take time to answer someone who asked the same about your hometown of West Podunk? Probably not.
Be specific and ask questions that can be answered in a few words or a series
of short sentences. Otherwise you're likely to be ignored.

For an excellent look into Mexican culture and the misunderstandings that can
arise between *gringos* and Mexicans, read chapter four of *A Place Where the
Sea Remembers* by Sandra Benitez. Read the entire book for an exceptional
look at some of the people of the Pacific Coast of Mexico. You'll gain some
valuable insight into the Mexican thought process and learn that not everything that you might interpret as a slight is intended to be. This lady has a
respect for the people and the culture that shines through in her loving novel.

Maintain Your Perspective

Is everything perfect in Mexico? How boring! You're going to encounter problems, challenges, and aggravations. You'll either learn to live with em, or head
on back to "Paradise".

There could be roosters. Roosters. The ones that they train to fight to the
death, or close to it, probably understand the need to get a good night's sleep.
The others crow all night long. And all day long. Round the clock crowers,
these Mexican roosters. And the ones with featherless necks are flat-out ugly
on top of being annoying. The ones who live outside my bathroom window, on
the neighbor's roof cough all night long. Never make a sound after sunrise or
before sunset. Nocturnal hackers.

The good news is that usually they won't wake you. The barking dogs have
already done that. Or the mosquitoes buzzing and dive-bombing your ears all
night long.

Mosquitoes. Barking dogs. Dead animals in the road. Trash in the streets. Wild
critters roaming the night. Creepy crawlies. Dust. Narrow roads. Fireworks at
all hours of the day and night. Heat. Torrential downpours. Bad roads. People
who don't have the decency to learn to speak English. Electrical failures. Poor
public services. Bureaucracies. Workers who agree to, but then never show up
to do a job. Undrinkable water. Non-operating public telephones. Septic tanks.
Loud music half the night long. Stray dogs poopin' in the streets. Horses poopin'
in the streets. Donkeys poopin' in the streets. Chickens poopin' in the streets.
Live animals on the highways. Dead animals on the highways. High gas prices.

Now some folks look upon these little distractions as Major Problems. My guess
is that roosters and dogs and mosquitoes generate more complaints in traveler's
tales than the next ten whines combined.

Here's a hint. Think of these things as Problems To Be Solved. If you're sensitive
to noise, you probably already own a set of really good earplugs. Or a white

noise machine. Or a cassette player and the Astral Sounds tape. Or whale songs.

And the mosquitoes? You can buy Raidolitos mosquito coils to burn to chase the little critters away, or turn on your floor fan and direct the airflow over your body. Or sleep under a mosquito net. Have one made of cotton netting because some of the cheaper nylon ready-mades have a real tendency to restrict airflow. But, don't let a dog or cat near it, nylon or not.

Regardless of what the C of C boys may say, mosquitoes are definitely a health threat in coastal areas at certain times of the year. You'll see signs posted offering inoculations for dengue prevention. Even if you get bitten by the right kind (or wrong kind) of skeeter you're probably not going to die unless you were pretty well ragged out to begin with.

Even though Mexico has some incredibly cosmopolitan cities, most of the country is rural and agricultural. Roaming these wide open spaces you'll see farm animals. Horses, donkeys, mules, cattle, sheep, goats, hogs. Chickens, ducks, geese, turkeys. And lots of dogs and cats. Most of em runnin' free. Occasionally you'll see a horse or cow or pig on a rope. You'll also see cars, trucks, tractors, buses and motorcycles.

These two groups are not compatible.

What you see lying beside the road, often covered with quicklime, is the result of old meeting new. The clash of the modern with the traditional. Real life. And death. I guess if you've lived in a city all your life it might be a shocking to see, but for those of us who grew up in small towns and rural areas it's a familiar sight.

My son's friend was killed recently in North Texas when he topped a small hill on a country road and ran into a cow. It's something that happens frequently on rural roads. As an insurance adjuster I worked many of these claims.

In the Eye of the Beholder
One day we were cruising around Jocotepec when we saw two *gringas* out walking their dogs. I pulled over and asked if they knew of any houses for rent.

"Oh God" the older one said, "I hope you're not thinking of moving here. There are nine churches in town and the bells ring constantly. And each one has its own saint and festivals. Firecrackers go off all year round. Music plays all night long. It's a living hell."

She'd just described some of the reasons I moved to Mexico. Festivals, music, noise. That also means all sorts of parades and entertainment, food, drink, fun. And multiple opportunities to learn about the customs and the cultures of the area—and to meet the people. It sounded like a living heaven.

I've lived within two blocks of four different churches here. The bells are comforting and reassuring. They mark the passage of time. They tell me that there's a constant in this world. They speak to me of history, tradition, sacrifice, and of victory. I'm not religious, but I *am* affected by them.

Are they such a problem, these events of life? Everywhere you go you must cope with distractions and inconveniences. Mexico owes you nothing. Accept her, or reject her, but don't complain about her.

They buried our friend's mother today. In Seattle. But she was with us for a while in San Juan Evangelista where we'd driven over to find some artisans we'd heard about.

Guillermo crafted beautiful and intricate Virgens and angels from clay. His brother Tranquilo made tiles, lamps, hollow balls. We bought a few items but we were

La iglesia vieja, William Gentes, 1995

here to see the old maestro, Señor Sixto. We had been directed to his home, but we stopped first to explore the church and cemetery across from his house.

It was one of those places that not only draws you to itself, but holds you once you're there. We stood on the stones of the courtyard and she suggested that perhaps we should say a prayer for our friend and his father, and for the soul and spirit of his mother. For some reason I said no. Not yet. We walked the few steps to the bare black dirt of the cemetery and stood, looking, searching.

They were there. All. From the poorest to the grandest; all equal now. We sat on the heavy wooden plank suspended on the two pillars of rough concrete. At our feet were two mounds of black dirt. Under them, the remains of two of those of this village. Atop them, nothing.

To the left, far to the side, a smaller mound. A child? No marker, but a brilliant red bougainvillea planted precisely in the center of the mound of black dirt. No marker? No; marked well, and appropriately for this beloved.

And here, steps away, the crypt of one of the mothers of la familia *Rojas. Land-owners. People of substance and wealth.*

And here. "Look", she urged. At first I saw only a large slab, covered over completely with the ugly factory-made tiles with the raindrop pattern painted on before glazing. "I hate those", I said.

No argument. She didn't look up. She answered, almost in a whisper, "They just wanted something nice." I was silent. Shamed.

Here the marker was a stone of the field. Uncut. Unlettered. A stone of the field.

And everywhere, partially planted in the black dirt of the mounds, one gallon cans, most still bearing the faded blue and white labels reading San Marcos Rajas Verdes de Chiles Jalapeños. *Vases. Once, and sure to be again, flower filled.*

And here, side by side, two leafless poinsettias with but a few flags of identifying red on each. One at the head of Mama's grave, and one at the head of Papa's grave? No other markers.

No markers in many places.

But love everywhere. And respect. For family. For self. For tradition. For God. For the ancient and endless struggle to exist; to be.

There was no need for someone to tell the stories we saw that day. No need for someone to say that this person was, or that the family of this person has, or that the people here…

The story of the place, the story of the people; their character, their beliefs, their struggles, their joys, their courage, their lives and their spirits, down to the very core of their souls and the basest and the most glorious essence of their beings was told by the dry black dirt carefully mounded about these loved ones.

And by the stones. The stones of the field. Lovingly chosen, and carried here, and placed… confidently. Yes, that's right, they would have said. It looks good.

And they would have stood close together, holding each to the other, looking, seeing much more than was there.

And by the plants. Each entrusted with the task of reassuring each of those who came to this place that life in some form does indeed continue on forever.

Much was told to us. By many.

Now.

Now was the time to talk to God.

We talked quietly as we walked over the stones to the low, wide doorway of the church. Of faith. Of belief. Of majesty. Of awe. Of the peaceful beauty of the certainty of the true believer; relieved of the need to think or to question.

What must the natives have thought five hundred years ago when confronted by those who turned their world upside down, shook it clean of all they knew and worshipped, and offered them back an alien god who had endowed their conquerors with powers unknown to them, to be greatly feared. And obeyed.

And what architectural marvels they produced, these true natives. This church stands today, strong, solid, alive. Needed and wanted by this village, by these people. As it was by those who lie beside it under the black dirt.

This church stands today as a refuge, a symbol. This church stands today as the soul of this village. The true natives took unto themselves the spirit around them, infused it into the stone, and caused it to grow. Not nurtured by an alien god, nor the priests. Nurtured by the true natives. By the ones who rest here today beneath the mounds of black dirt. The true natives.

With one long step over the low stone threshold we entered into a new world. Quiet. Still. Cool. Calm. It's here. The spirit. There's no other explanation, it has to be the spirit. The spirit of the true natives, mixed with the spirit of the true believers. The spirit. God? No. The spirit. He's here; He has to be here, but they're much stronger. He's here because they willed Him here. We're here because they willed us here.

I've sat quietly in the Sacre Cour and listened to the pure sweet voices of the French nuns singing ancient songs of praise and thanksgiving and ritual in celebration and recognition of the wondrous powers of their magnificent God. In the hot still night of a war zone I've squatted on my heels on the slowly cooling deck of my boat, listening to the chants and prayers of the Buddhist monks offering thanks and reverence to their God. I've sat through hundreds of replays of fundamentalist tirades and offered myself up for salvation in their church. I've prayed strongly and fiercely to my God for the life of my injured beautiful boy. Today, maybe for the first time, I knew He was there. And the true natives. And the true believers. And we felt her too.

Thirty benches. Wooden. Plain. And we sat side by side near the back, not touching, not talking. We two and the spirit. Of the true believers. And of the true natives. And of God.

And finally we spoke. Quietly. Of how difficult it was not to believe. Impossible. And we offered our prayers. And there were tears.

And the simple majesty, the strength of this small church outshone any that had gone before. Perhaps tomorrow it will once again be just another of the hundreds of small stone churches constructed by Indians laboring as mere slaves, but today it was the source of comfort and wonder and the symbol of miracles past and miracles yet to come.

Perhaps tomorrow the cemetery will be just another small wind-blown patch of black dirt in just another small village near just another small lake in Mexico, but today it delivered the story of the grand history of a people. And provided a place for her to touch us as she passed.

Today it brought the true message. Everything is as it should be.

And you won't change it, nor will I. Things will happen as they happen and we're free to accept or decline.

Politics—Don't Go There!

On the pages of one of his books, *The Jeweler's Eye*, William F. Buckley relates the story of his father's expulsion from Mexico after backing the wrong side during the Revolution. Unless you're just aching to see what a Mexican military escort looks like, I suggest that, unlike Mr. Buckley, you refrain from getting involved in Mexican politics. They will not be impressed by the fact that Bubba Clinton's boys rented out the Lincoln Bedroom to you and that little brunette from the shipping department or that you were elected Trash Monitor back in Fumble Falls for twelve consecutive terms. **Stay completely out of Mexican politics.**

If you feel compelled to pursue and indulge some of your own leftover or latent political fantasies you'll probably be able to do so within your own circle of friends and enemies. It won't escape your notice that the larger *gringo* societies usually provide an arena for internecine power struggles where citizens of sometimes dubious intent can flaunt their self-deluded superiority and unload huge amounts of bile and bilge water. Feel free to join right in if you wish. Me and the boys'll be sittin' over here in the shade drinkin' and offering up our full thanks and appreciation for your efforts to entertain us.

In some areas, and God strike me dead as a dinosaur if I'm lyin', the office of President of the Dog Pound is considered by some *gringos* to be a post worthy of fighting over and causing great rifts within the community. Diff'rent strokes, I guess. I learned my lesson about indulging in politics years ago and I'm stayin' clear of all of it.

Absentee Voting

If you want to keep up with your U.S. voting chores you can contact the party of your choice at either *http://www.democratsabroad.com* or *http://www.republicansabroad.com*. You can find contact information for Senators, Congresspeople, and State Governors at the Federal Voting Assistance Website at *http://www.fvap.gov*. Canadians can access voting information at *http://www.elections.ca*. Click on the "English" button and when that page opens, look up on the header bar and click "International" to get details about absentee voting in Canadian elections.

You can also drop by the nearest U.S. or Canadian Consulate to pick up the federal forms required to register to vote in your country of citizenship. If you're successfully integrating into the true Mexican lifestyle, you'll soon discover that you don't care much who's runnin' for what, anywhere in the world.

Crime and Punishment

It's reasonable to be concerned about crime and your personal safety in Mexico. Just like in your city or town there are areas of serenity and areas of chaos. Looks can be deceiving. While you're seeking your new home you'll find that even though a section of town might appear to be a bit shabby and rundown, it's usually very safe. Many of the neighborhoods where you'll choose to live are not going to look like NoB suburbia. People here seem to be constantly working on their houses which means you'll see a lot of construction materials and debris everywhere.

The *gringos* most likely to become the victims of burglary or robbery are the ones who live in the tonier *gringo*-heavy neighborhoods who conspicuously flaunt their material possessions. From what I read it seems that in some areas of the U.S. the thugs in the poorer neighborhoods prefer to work their mischief close to home, choosing their victims from among their neighbors. You'll find the exact opposite situation here. Unless you consciously choose to live in a dangerous crime-ridden neighborhood, you should never have to worry about your safety. Believe me, your Mexican neighbors are aware of every move you make, every person who gets close to you or your house, as well as what you eat at each meal. They're better security than a Rotweiller with an attitude. It's not at all uncommon, after one of my wall-bending sneezes, to hear someone outside my garden express a polite *¡Salud!*, the courteous Mexican "to your health", or gesundheit.

Currently, my front porch seems to be the neighborhood gathering place. The older neighbors come over in the early evening to sit and watch the stream of life as it flows down *calle Porfírio Diaz*. Soon after dark, the teens come together to sit and hold hands and gaze fondly at one other with that strained look of lust and frustration that some of you may remember from your own teen years. Your neighbors will recognize the people who don't belong in your neighborhood and can size them up faster than you can.

Still, use common sense. The fundamentals of safety apply pretty much everywhere. In most of the places I've lived, I've usually left everything unlocked even when I wasn't home for the day. I certainly don't suggest this to you, but I feel safer SoB than I did in neighborhoods NoB. Of course, I'm behind high walls that surround the garden. Are they burglar proof? No. I've had to borrow a ladder and send a neighborhood kid over my wall more than once to open my gate after I locked myself out. And my neighbors would have no trouble dropping down into my *jardín* from their flat roofs if they wished. But they don't and they won't.

Crimes that do occur in very upscale urban areas are murders, rapes and attempted rapes, car-jackings, car thefts, armed robberies, burglaries—the whole gamut of petty and serious crimes. Usually these are sensationalized because a certain segment of the population tends to Chicken Little every episode. Once you look closely, there's usually an underlying reason for the more serious crimes against individuals. Personal grudges, *gringo* on *gringo* crimes, drug involvement, or folks purposely placing themselves in dangerous situations are pretty good explanations for most of the stories you hear.

This is not to say that there are no dangers here but don't fixate on the sensational and inflammatory bias rampant in NoB newspapers. Keep your perspective intact. Many Mexicans with families NoB grieve for at least one son, daughter, nephew or cousin who has been the victim of violent crime in Los Angeles, Chicago, or Toronto. Again, common sense will be your best guide. Don't flash large amounts of cash in public or wear tons of expensive jewelry. Don't park on the darkest, most deserted street you can find or start up and keep rolling a virulent feud with someone. Don't open your door to strange men or go walking alone on the beach at 2 a.m., as was the case with a young female tourist I knew who was attacked but thankfully not raped. Common sense…don't leave home without it. If you do take leave of your senses, or if someone happens to relieve you of some of your worldly possessions, or if you or your auto gets damaged, you can lessen the financial impact of your loss with insurance.

Life on the Street

Since we've just discussed insurance and crime, here's another *regalo* for you. You're going to be amazed how quickly you relax and how quickly your worries and concerns about those two things lessen. Living in small-town Mexico is similar to small town America or Canada, of the late '40s and '50s. There is a tremendous amount of street activity in the evenings. Folks get out and visit with each other. They go to the *plazas* and to the *cenadurias* for their evening meal. There's a sense of community, of belonging, of shared experiences, hopes, dreams and needs.

LAS GAVIOTAS, WILLIAM GENTES, 1995

The Mexican people are warm, expansive, generous and accepting. There have been many times that I've sat down for my evening meal and was immediately taken into conversation by one of the strangers sitting nearby. Most of the time I had no in-depth understanding of our conversation because of my limitations with the language but I always knew I was accepted and welcome. At first that may seem strange to you because the idea of sitting down with strangers is no longer common NoB. In many of the small *cenadurias*, or dinner places, there will be few tables. You just look for a vacant chair, walk over and motion to it and ask, "*¿Con permiso?*", with your permission, the elegant Mexican "May I?". Hell they do it in the French Quarter in Nawlins all the time, and the tourists there think it's quaint and friendly.

You'll see families out together with the children playing and the young parents visiting each other. Folks will set up tables or booths to sell food and drinks. You'll see the teens out, posturing for one another, flirting, and dancing if some-one has music, but you won't feel threatened because those youngsters are not about to risk having someone report to their parents that they were misbe-having in public.

In the towns where you'd want to live, the streets are perfectly safe. Remember that your neighbors are usually out walking and greeting each other, not riding around in their cars. They want safe streets too.

And Fandangos

As far as integrating into the community goes, my big breakthrough came in San Antonio Tlayacapán late one afternoon as Pirata the One-Eyed Wonder Dog and I returned home from a long walk. The street was abuzz with activity. As I passed the *herrería* I asked Ricardo what was going on.

"The Virgen *is coming."*

"Which one?"

"Zapopan."

"She was here just two months ago."

"She's coming again."

"Why?"

Shrug. "She's coming."

When it comes to Mexican Virgens, *there are no whos, whats, wheres, whens, whys, or hows, they simply ARE.*

I put Pirata in the yard, got my rake and machete *and fell in with the rest of the folks. Everyone in the 'hood was out sprucing things up. I learned that the* Virgen *had never before come down* La Paz, *our street, so this was an extra special event.*

We chopped and pulled weeds and threw them behind the rock wall of the vacant lot next to my house.

We gathered loose rocks and threw them behind the rock wall of the vacant lot beside my house.

We trimmed trees and bushes and threw the limbs behind the rock wall of the vacant lot beside my house.

We scooped up the pile of sand left over from an old construction project and threw it behind the rock wall of the vacant lot beside my house.

The vacant lot was no longer a mere vacant lot. Even before Her arrival, the Virgen had caused a milagro in the neighborhood. She had effected a miraculous change in status from vacant lot to neighborhood dumpsite.

Beside my house.

We worked cutting, cleaning, raking, and burning the dried grass on the roadside until dark was well settled around us. There were to be no obstacles in Her path, no errant overhanging limb to snag or snare, no unsightliness to offend Her eye.

I went to bed satisfied that we had prepared well for Her visit.

I woke up to discover that we'd only just begun. My maid Maria, Ricardo's mother, showed up with a huge bundle of palm fronds. These were to be attached to every vertical surface along the street. Walls, gates, doorways, utility poles. Everywhere.

Maria instructed Ricardo and his younger brother Jose to string the streamers she'd bought the night before along the street. High above the street. Luckily we'd been building a mirador on the roof of my patio so I'd already borrowed a ladder we could use.

The entire town was in on the preparations now. Each neighborhood seemed to be trying to out-do one another with their decorations along the route taken by the Virgen. Each street was decorated differently, each displaying the style and will of the senior señora. La Doña. Balloons here. Palm arches there. Rose and bougainvillea petals everywhere. Ornately cut paper streamers above. Christmas lights along here. Hand painted banners there. Love, devotion, hope, thanks, joy, respect, adoration, expectation throughout.

The Virgen is coming.

We all worked until the middle of the afternoon, and as the last knot was tied to secure the last streamer high above the street, I prepared to shower and change before She came. As I turned to go to my house, I saw them. A long, single-file line of Aztec dancers rounded the corner two blocks away. I stood with the rest of my neighbors, my friends, as the line twisted and wove its way toward us.

Silent, except for the rhythmic rattle of the nut husks tied in rows around their ankles and their labored breathing, the dancers led the procession. Maybe twenty had been chosen for this honor. And behind them, priests and altar boys. And behind them the Virgen, serene and secure in Her plexiglass case, firmly fastened to the carrier bolted to the floor of the covered pick-up in which

She was riding. And behind Her walked many of the faithful and devout of the village.

And we stood and watched. Tired and dirty, but proud that we were ready, that we had showed our respect. The Sign of the Cross was offered many times. Even by some of us infidels. Mexican Virgens wield a power that defies logical understanding. Especially to us infidels.

In less than thirty seconds, the entire procession had passed the place where we waited. I turned to where Ricardo stood, just a few feet away. His eyes were as misty as mine as he smiled and softly said, "That's all".

Not quite. It was the beginning of my acceptance into the community. The devout little ladies who passed by, heads covered with their widow's shawls now smiled and spoke first. The very reserved *tienda* keeper began to warm to me. The neighbors all displayed a different attitude.

On *Dia de los Muertos*, The Day of the Dead, I set up my altar in front of the house. Not strictly to traditional form, but with many of the elements and colors. The only one on my block.

When the priest posted the notice of his intent to judge the altars erected on December 12th to honor *La Senora de Guadalupe y Juan Diego,* I prepared a shrine for judging. Again, non-traditional, but I was participating. One of only three participants on my street.

And then I was elevated. My efforts were rewarded.

They came early and were not to be denied. They beat on the door ferociously until I got up, found something to put on, stopped by the bathroom to pee, and stumbled my way to the door, wondering just who in their right mind would be rousting me out at the ungodly hour of 9 a.m.

My neighbor Rosa. And a young girl of ten or eleven.

I understood and returned Rosa's greeting, but not much that followed. The child served as our translator. Mas ó menos. The gist of the conversation was that Rosa was asking to use my truck that evening for our neighborhood posada.

I agreed. Just let me go lie down somewhere until this wave of early rising nausea sweeps on past. Oh, ¿a que hora? Tres. Fine.

After at trip to the plaza where Joaquin, the street washer, managed to scrape my truck fairly clean, I drove home to figure out where to park. Right here in the intersection of La Paz and San Jose? In the middle of the street? Several of the neighborhood ladies immediately sprang into action. That pitiful earthbound platform was quickly converted to a portion of Heaven. A blue tarp was suspended from a rope strung across the road from the rooftops and allowed to drop down behind the cab and to the bed of the truck. Next, chairs were placed on either side of the bed to serve as a base for the large sheets of paper painted and wadded to look like rocks. Now you know; there are rocks in Heaven.

Then the tailgate, which had been lowered, was covered with a white rug. The ladies placed huge wads of chicken wire around the truck bed and covered them with sheets and cotton batting to simulate clouds. Large palm fronds, attached to the far corners of the bed, finished the set.

Pirata and I had shopping to do so we ambled off for a couple of hours. On our way home, the translator rushed up the road to tell me to report to Rosa. I walked next door and knocked. Rosa and Maria ushered me in. This was a different Maria, not my maid. Maria, Guadalupe. Lupe. Lupita. The *Virgen de Guadalupe has inspired many Mexican mothers when it came to baby naming.*

I'd walked into a frantic costume constructing session. Rosa pointed to a chair at the dining table and I sat. That's when it dawned on me that I hadn't been invited for coffee and chit chat. She slapped a homemade beard down in front of me closely followed by what appeared to be a gold cardboard lumberjack's saw blade. In a split second she produced a roll of tape and grabbed up the saw blade to wrap around my head. A crown! I was being fitted for a crown.

Maria was standing by with the next item. As soon as I was properly sized, I was jerked to my feet for the next fitting. This little item appeared to be one of Maria's old nightgowns. Lavender. Silky. Maria is a healthy little gal but no way is she gonna match me for sheer bulk. Needless to say, the garment was much too short in the arms and much too short in length. Just a perfect fit for a Mexican festival. After all the tryings-on were finished, I was instructed to report back at 5:30, so I vacated the premises before they thought of something else to do to me.

At 5:30, Rosa sent her son, Firestarter, the neighborhood pyromaniac, to fetch me. There were to be no excuses for not showing up.

A few minutes later I found myself standing in the bed of my gaudily decorated truck, on a cobble-stoned street in a small Mexican village, dressed in a clingy lavender gown with a red sash draped over my shoulder, wearing an itchy homemade beard of fake hair glued to a piece of cardboard, and a shiny gold cardboard crown, screwed down so far on my head that I was half blind and totally deaf. It was a very sophisticated look. In addition to looking like a goober, I was totally clueless about what my role would be.

But here came the translator, dressed as an angel. Evidently, my entire theatrical debut was to consist of standing stock still with my arms spread, hands palms up, presenting my son Jesus Christ to the world. JC was played by

Rosa's son. The one who will set fire to your dog if he gets a chance. Definitely not typecasting. Only a group of Mexican Catholics would buy me as the Old Testament God Yahweh and pyro boy as Jesus.

It turned out to be a pretty cool gig though. Just to my left and facing up calle San José sat Santa. He had a blue tarp hanging behind him too. "On the tarp" was a painting of the Virgen de Guadalupe with a priest painted off to the side. Santa and I were the first two tableaus in the presentation. The procession formed about a block away, up by the sewage treatment plant. They spent quite a bit of time singing and re-singing that traditional Mexican hymn of thanks and joy, Jingle Bells. Jingle Bells. The Havah Nigilah would have been equally appropriate.

The Jingle Belling finally ceased and the procession began. I froze into position as Joseph and Mary approached. My ass began to itch. The beard began to tickle. Something flew up my nose. I'm sure a scorpion was climbing my leg. I was miserable, God or not. It suddenly dawned on me why I had been chosen. All the other men in the neighborhood had been there, done that, and weren't about to be caught again.

One of the things that I dearly love about Mexican parades and processions is that anybody is free to join in at any time. Or opt out. Stumble and stagger along the cobblestones 'til you need a break and then just get up on the sidewalk and watch for awhile. Rejoin once you're rested. That's how Pirata and I get into all of 'em. Show up, fall in. Nobody cares. Nobody's in charge except the priest and he's got his plate full off somewhere else.

So here they came on foot, Mary and Joseph following my interpreter angel with the spectators crammed together so tightly in the street that M and J and the angel were struggling to stay upright.

They approached and drew nigh unto Heaven—the young children up front, the ladies of the village choir to my right, the priest beside them with his street evangelist's portable bullhorn, and beside him, the guitarist and the banjo picker.

The priest spoke, the choir sang, the crowd responded with syncopated group clapping, the whole "no room at the inn" ditty was run through about seventy-eight times, and then they headed off to the next stop. Deaf and blind through most of it because of my ill-fitting crown, I was distracted by thoughts of what that scorpion might be up to. After the last stop, I was able, though not entirely willing, to take off the costume. True, I was a bit tired of the beard and crown. But now I got to join the parade. Whatever was in my nose had evidently burrowed down into the soft tissue and smothered, the scorpion had gone to greener pastures, and I finally got to scratch my behind.

*Jingle Bells. God. Jesus. A banjo picker. Candles. Nightgowns. A bullhorn-totin'
priest. Santa. A bigdamn Texas truck. Hot as hell in December. Big blue tarps
everywhere.*

*Eventually I fell out and headed home to the bathroom. Experience tells me I
really missed some goodies. Neighborhood* posada *tableaus can consist of
anything from a dinosaur hatching to an alien invasion. It all makes sense to
me though. If the only musicians in the neighborhood are a guitarist and a
banjo picker, then there's your band. You could hire a band, but they aren't part
of the neighborhood. If the only way to man the tableau assigned to your
street is to trick the* gringo, *trick away. If the only costumes you have lend
themselves to a scene depicting a Scottish log tossing festival, chop down a
tree and press the kilt. All is as it should be.*

Spontaneous "Fiestas"

*As we walked down
the block, we could
hear the music.* Ran-
chero music. *We
crossed the street, en-
tered the square and
saw a nice-looking
older gentleman play-
ing a keyboard and
singing to the accom-
paniment of a really
good karaoke set-up.*
Señor Musico. *He
alone would have been
enough to satisfy all
but the most discrimi-
nating and demanding
of music fans but there
was more. Much more.
We were about to be
treated to a perfor-
mance by the*

EL MUSICO,
WILLIAM GENTES, 1995

Chapala Square Dancing Society.

It wasn't the petticoat and silk neckerchief bunch, but real square dancers. Absolute show stoppers. A black three-legged dog tried to horn in on the act but the dancers successfully fought off all challengers to emerge as the evening's most appreciated. Running a close second to them though, were two over-tequila-ed, good-time Carlitos who held the audience enthralled with their performances.

The taller, younger, better groomed of the two danced in a waltzy bliss. Eyes closed, and with a slight smile on his lips, he silently sang along with Señor Musico. His cohort, on the other hand, was a frenzied, crazed, jumpin' jack with a bobbin', weavin', crouchin' left foot over right and right foot over left jivin' style. Totally oblivious to tempo and rhythm, he danced himself free of his sandals more than once. Black curly hair, expertly styled to present the appearance that he'd slept on it and forgot to brush, along with a manic wildness in his wide open eyes and a perpetual open-mouthed grin, his looks perfectly suited his square-wide ramblin' style.

Wilfredo the Waltzer stayed pretty well within an eight foot square right in front of Señor Musico but Santos the Stepper cut a wide and rowdy path through most of the plaza, gainin' on several occasions, the snarlin', snappin' attention of the black three-legged dog. Actually he had four legs, he just couldn't get one of the back ones to stay down.

It was similar to the problem Jumpin' Jack Santos was havin'. He couldn't get either of his to stay down for more than a nano-second until he planted both of 'em to devote a full sixteen beats to what I believe was the Gene Kelly patented, Funky-Monkey-Pickin'-Up-Peanuts routine. Those particular moves also seemed to involve shootin' the moon at Señor Musico. We're still grateful our seats put us dead ahead of him when that particular maneuver took place.

We had serious concerns that the show might come to a premature close when we saw one of Chapala's finest stride purposefully onto the square from behind the bandstand, but she kept moving right along with only a quick glance at the floor show. We were also concerned that Cujo might lose control and take a hunk outta Santos' ass, but he finally seemed to be more interested in the tortilla scraps that he was bein' fed by the old señora sittin' on a bench across from us. Not that Santos didn't go out of his way to aggravate him anyway.

All in all it was a great show and still in full swing when we waved an *adios* to *Señor Musico* and drifted on down to the *malecón*.

I know what you're thinkin', and I agree that it's a cryin' shame that Broadway doesn't do enough of those shows anymore.

And speaking of shows, Mexico is the only place in the world where I can hang out with a movie and stage actress. I tried it in a couple of other places and all I have to show for my efforts are a few restraining orders. And as a bonus, the mayor of Melaque lets me hang out with him, too. Lara Gallardo and Alejandro Lazareno Craviato are currently working together to form a group of volunteers to help with their efforts to save the eggs of the turtles that nest on the Coco Beach area of Nayarit State. If you want more information or want to help, and I hope you do, you can contact them at either *tortugazul2001@hotmail.com* or at Lara's B&B address, *casadelsolmex@hotmail.com*. Or e-mail me and I'll get the information to them.

Folks, that's it for now. There are four information-packed appendices that follow that you'll want to explore. If you can't find answers to questions you have, feel free to contact me at *don@headformexico.com*

Or check out my website at *http://www.headformexico.com*. I also have a monthly column on Mexconnect that you can access at *http://www.mexconnect.com*.

Appendix I

Of Course I Know What I'm Talking About, But You Need To Hear From These Folks Too

Personally I wouldn't make an expensive life-altering decision based on what one person told me, and I hope you won't either. Here's a list of other resources you can check and I strongly suggest that you do.

General Information About Mexico

This is **Very Important Information**: The websites below will take you to a list of Mexican Consulates in the U.S. and Canada. Some of the individual consulates will have websites of their own, which will be organized differently from the others. Some seem to load the English link rather slowly so be patient. A few are only in Spanish.

The site for the Mexican Embassy is: *http://www.embassyofmexico.org*

http://www.nafinsa.com/consulatedir.htm

http://www.enespanol.com/atlanta/mexconsulate/list.htm

http://www.embamexcan.com/english/indexenglish/html

http://www.mexonline.com/consulate.htm

http://www.canada.org.mx

http://www.move-to-mexico.com

http://www.state.gov/p/wha/ci/mx

http://www.embpage.org

Equally important are the U.S. and Canadian websites that follow. These provide specific, official government regulations and requirements for international travel.

http://www.customs.ustreas.gov/travel/travel.htm is the U.S. Customs Service site for international travelers.

http://aphis.usda.gov/index.shtml is the U.S. Department of Agriculture website where you will find information about moving plants and animals across international borders.

Canada Customs can be found at *http://www.ccra-adrc.gc.ca/customs/individuals/faqs-e.html.*

http://www.canada.org.mx is the site for the Canadian Consular Services and provides information on the various agencies and regulations regarding moving plants and animals in and out of Canada.

http://www.inspection.gc.ca is the Canadian Food Inspection Agency Site.

http://www.nafta-customs.org/english/hoursmx.htm provides a chart showing the operating hours of ports of entry along the U.S.-Mexico border.

http://www.caa.ca is the site for the Canadian Automobile Association.

http://www.aaa.com is the website for the American Automobile Association.

The best—no doubts, no arguments, no dissent accepted—news site featuring news of the world from the Latin perspective is found at *http://www.hispanicvista.com*. This site is in English and is amazingly comprehensive, offering a variety of viewpoints and articles on issues of interest and concern to Latinos and gringos. You can spend hours on this one, reading old as well as current and updated news and opinions.

At *http://www.go2mexico.com* you'll find links to a number of free worldwide news sources.

There's no website here, but you can subscribe to an excellent travel and retirement newsletter at <u>Adventures in Mexico</u>

> Apdo 31-70

> 45050 Guadalajara, Jalisco, Mexico

Our Canadian short wave radio fans can access information about Radio Canada International broadcasts at the RCI website *http://www.rcinet.ca* or e-mail them at rci@montreal.radio-canada.ca. If all else fails, call (514) 597-7555.

TIME Latin American Edition

http://aola.com/canales/voces

NEWSWEEK

http://www.newsweek.msnbc.com

SLATE

http://slate.MSN.com

MACLEANS-Canada

http://www.macleans.com

FIFTY PLUS-Canada

http://www.50plus.com

TV GUIDE

http://www.tvguide.com

SKEPTICAL INQUIRER MAGAZINE (just because...)

http://www.csicop.org

CBC ONLINE NEWS

http://www.cbc.ca

On Mexconnect you'll find a Living in Mexico Survey with questions responded to by people who are actually living here. It gives specific information in a number of areas: housing costs, entertainment, activities, etc., as well as general attitudes. Follow the instructions to links at: *http://www.mexconnect.com/survey*

You might want to let them know what you found useful.

This should be a very valuable tool in your planning kit. Type in *http://groups.yahoo.com*. Now look for "Join A Group" and scroll down to "Regional". When the new screen opens, click on "Countries" and scroll down the alphabetical list of countries and click on "Mexico", then on "Mexico Groups". This explanation is a lot more complicated than the actual process. Anyway, you'll find chat groups and sources that can address your concerns, or answer questions that crop up. Scroll through the index of sites and pick out the ones that catch your interest.

Other Internet resources are:

http://www.mexico-travel.org is the website of the Ministry of Tourism and is a great place to start your research. This site provides links to each Mexican state as well as travel info. There is an English version available.

http://www.mexicoautotravel.com is a site you need to visit if you intend to drive in Mexico. I'm not recommending their services but their information is invaluable. Note that contrary to their statement, auto insurance is currently mandatory in Jalisco State.

The Travel Mexico online newsletter is written by the editors of the Traveler's Guide to Mexico and is offered free of charge. Send an e-mail to editor@mail.travelguidemexico.com and on the subject line type in "Request for Subscription." The website is at http://www.travelguidemexico.com

Don Humphrey's Kicking Back in Baja site at *http://www.angelfire.com/falcon/sundog/kicking.html* offers a list of the majority of the Mexico message boards and forums. Don offers country-wide real estate listings for sales and rentals as well as other good stuff.

If you have a specific question about an area go to *http://www.virtualmex.com/resource.html*. Here, on the Mexico Information Volunteers and Tips page you'll find folks who can help you. A number of volunteers, myself included, post notices for areas we know well. Browse through the postings until you find the person you believe will be best suited to answer your questions. E-mail them directly. This is a valuable free service.

http://www.go2mexico.com is a site that offers free on-line elementary Spanish tutorials. Click on Spanish Helper.

http://www.itunisie.com/nihed/spanish.html offers "Basic Spanish for the Virtual Student". Free.

http://www.mexiconetwork.info is a relatively new site that's a collaboration of three of Mexico's major Internet information providers. This one is very worthwhile.

http://www.mexconnect.com is the best internet resource dedicated to Mexico. You can literally spend days on this site gathering an impressive amount of useful and practical information. There are also a number of regular contributors who share their Mexico experiences and expertise. Check out my monthly column at their new subscription site http://www.mexconnected.com.

http://www.mexicofile.com is another favorite site. Although its not as extensive as Mexconnect, it's very attractive.

http://www.mexicanwave.com is billed as "Europe's Gateway to Mexico". There are a few items that will interest you. Very colorful but somewhat limited in content, its still definitely worth a visit. I sense that they'll be expanding in the very near future. Check out the shopping section for a look at Mexican crafts and furniture. Sign up for their free monthly newsletter.

http://www.lloyd.com.mx advertises Mexican financial services and instruments, and insurance available in areas with large gringo populations.

http://www.planeta.com is a great ecology-oriented site.

http://www.mexonline.com is a site with literally hundreds of bits of useful information from descriptions of individual cities to holidays to embassy and consulate listings to driving information, as well as customs requirements, medical tips, history, culture, shopping, and real estate. You can also sign up for the @migo! Newsletter, an online monthly compilation of special interest articles about Mexico. It's free and potentially of great value to you.

http://www.elantiquario.com is the website of a gorgeous art, antiques, and folk art magazine that is published in Guadalajara. They have a few online articles that you can access to get an idea of the interests served by their writers. This is not a stuffy arts publication; it resonates more like a cultural history book. E-mail them at *elantiquario@infosel.net.mx* or call them in Guadalajara at 011-52-33-3827-1990 or 3827-0378 and fax to 011-52-33-3640-1292.

http://www.thelist.com/countrycode.html shows you Internet providers in Mexico.

http://www.go2mexico.com is a commercial site with excellent information about purchasing real estate in Mexico, as well as a link to all the Mexican Consulates NoB. I strongly suggest you look at this one.

http://butterflywebsite.com/michmon/index.htm is a site devoted to the Monarch butterflies.

http://members.tripod.com/~Post_119_Gulfport_MS/legionet.html will lead you to a list of webpages for American Legion Posts in Mexico.

Canadians will want to check out this company geared specifically to them. It offers a free subscription to the CRA magazine.

Canadians Resident Abroad, Inc.

305 Lakeshore Rd. E.

Ontario, CANADA L6J 1J3

Phone: 905-842-0080 or FAX 905-842-9814

e-mail: *cra@canadiansresidentabroad.com*

http://www.canadiansresidentabroad.com

Canadians might also want to check out an excellent and extremely useful selection of articles at *http://www.voyage.gc.ca*. These are free Consular Affairs Publications that can be downloaded from your computer. Some of the titles are:

Bon Voyage, But...Information for the Canadian Traveller

Her Own Way: Advice for the Woman Traveller

Mexico: ¿Qué pasa? A Guide for Canadian Visitors

Retirement Abroad: Seeing the Sunsets

Working Abroad: Unraveling the Maze

You can also go to *http://www.dfait-maeci.gc.ca* to find these articles online, or call 1-800-267-8376 or 613-944-4000 to have them delivered by mail. If you go online, you need to click on the "Travel" logo on the left side of the screen. This is a very informative site and should be visited by Canadians as well as by folks in the U.S.

http://www.teach-english-mexico.com is a great site for potential teachers. You can e-mail Shirley at *info@employnow.com*. They offer a really splendid newsletter aimed at job seekers that provides a great deal of information about various cities. There's a lot of information you can apply to your personal situation.

http://www.teachandtravel.com offers information about resident and online classes that allow you to earn an ESL teaching certificate, as well as a other specialty teaching certificates. Ms. T and I think their cost of living estimate for Mexico is about a third what it actually should be. Be careful.

http://www.teflfarm.com is a great place to read articles written by working teachers. You'll find ideas that will make your teaching more interesting and effective.

Look on http://www.transabroad.com the website of a very interesting magazine, Transitions Abroad. This book is not directed solely at those who are interested in Mexico, even though it lists good job openings and addresses for teacher training programs.

You can also go to *http://www.SolutionsAbroad.com* and click on the "Business" heading, and then "Finding a Job" to see some other options for work.

Another source of information is *http://www.overseasjobs.com*. After you check out these sites you'll begin to understand just how grim the Mexican job market is for freelance job seekers outside the teaching or highly specialized technical or professional fields.

Travelers Guide To Mexico is a huge (460+ pages) magazine written and printed by a bilingual staff in Mexico City. The book presents an in-depth look at 19 Mexican cities, offers maps of each area, and relays an amazing amount of information about the country and the people. For more information go to *http://www.travelguidemexico.com*.

Books

Carl Franz's The People's Guide to Mexico edited by Lorena Havens. This is the classic guide to the people, land, and culture of Mexico. Carl and Lorena have lived and traveled in Mexico for over thirty years, and the stories of their Bohemian adventures are both instructive and entertaining. This is not glitzy Mexico, but rather an affectionate, and clear-eyed look at the lives of the common people. 'Nuff said? Every good bookstore either has it or can get it.

http://www.peoplesguide.com is a "must visit" site that contains an amazing variety of useful and entertaining information. Any book with Carl's name on it will be of great value to you.

I recently discovered Backcountry Mexico- A Traveler's Guide and Phrase Book by Bob Burleson and David H. Riskind. I've never met these guys, or even heard of them before, but I can tell you that they're the real deal. Anyone who's spent any time in Mexico will be able to see that these guys have "been there, done that." In addition to short descriptions of rural Mexican life and culture, they provide a course on how to behave down here and how to deal with locals of all kinds. This is a full course phrase book as well as a glossary of common terms. If you need to tell someone "The flies around here are terrible", these old boys show you how. Buy this book, even if you never actually get to the backcountry. Ask for it at your local bookstore. I found mine at Sandi's in Guadalajara.

Western Mexico—A Traveller's Treasury by Tony Burton

Tony Burton is a geographer and naturalist who makes you wonder how he unearthed all the facts and details he includes in this (much more than a) travel book. I recommend this book very highly.

Box 4

Ladysmith, BC

V9G 1A1 Canada or

e-mail Tony at *tonyburton@pacificcoast.net*

Costalegre: The Little Known Beaches Of Jalisco by David Ramsey is a colorful and informative magazine-sized, 33-page introduction to the beaches and villages of the Pacific Coast between Puerto Vallarta and Manzanillo. I lived in one of these villages, La Manzanilla, and I'm familiar with most of the places Mr. Ramsey talks about. His information is as accurate as the print media allow us to be, considering the rapid changes in all parts of the world. The pictures are gorgeous. If you're considering the beach life, this book may be of great value to you. To order, contact the author by e-mail at *hernansma@prodigy.net.mx* or by postal mail at Apdo #515, 37700 San Miguel de Allende, Guanajuato, Mexico.

Aztec by Gary Jennings

This is a well-researched and very cleverly written novel of the "history" of the Aztecs, from their days as wandering scavengers, through their defeat at the hands of Cortes and a few hostile tribes. Every good bookstore has it or can get it for you.

Aztec Autumn by Gary Jennings

The story begun in Aztec continues in this book. One of my Mexican friends says this is the better of the two, but I liked them both equally.

Broken Spears – The Aztec Account of the Conquest of Mexico edited and with an introduction by Miguel Leon-Portilla

History, they say, is written by the victors. Not here. Ask for this one at your bookstore. As a history major I highly recommend this easy to read, footnoted, one hundred and eighty-two pager. It appears that Jennings borrowed heavily from this book.

Stones for Ibarra by Harriet Doerr

This book is set in the Mexico of the '60s. Excellent characterizations, great story, excellent side stories. I only wish that I felt the author had more accep- tance and appreciation of Mexican customs, culture, and individuals than she displays. Aside from that, this book will give you a sense of what living among the Nationals might be like for you. A friend independently offered the same opinion of the tone of the book that I did—that it reads as though it were written by an accountant. This book won the American Book Award, the Bay Area Book Reviewers Award, the American Academy and Institute of Arts and Letters Harold D. Vursell Award, and the Godal Medal of the Commonwealth Club of Califor- nia. So much for my piddlin' ass little review.

A Place Where the Sea Remembers by Sandra Benitez

It took me a couple of chapters to really get caught up in the magic of this novel and it was well worth the effort. It turned out to be an outstanding and gentle explanation of the Coastal Mexican culture, told in an entertaining and satisfy- ing way. This book rings true, and is very high on my list of all-time favorites. This work earned the 1994 Minnesota Book Award, and if I had any influence I would load it to the gunwales with other awards. I'm probably in love with Mrs. Benetiz and her wise and loving soul. Order this book through your local bookstore.

Speaking of living among, and understanding the locals, GeraldW . Petersen wrote a splendid little supplemental textbook called Life In A Mexican Town pub- lished by the National Textbook Company of Lincolnwood, Illinois. Mr. Petersen has created the imaginary town of Altagracia set in the southern part of the central plateau of Mexico that encompasses many of the towns I've written about. The book describes everyday life in the town and covers just about every facet of its social structure. Have your bookstore order it. Some of the terms he uses are a bit different from those in this book (INSS *vs.* IMSS) but they in no way detract from the truthfulness and value of his descriptions. You'll learn everything from table manners to how towns are laid out. This is one of the better resources for those who have not had the pleasure of visiting the interior of Mexico.

The Irish Soldiers of Mexico by Michael Hogan

This book tells the story of a group of Irish-Catholic U.S. Army deserters, as well as other Americans and Europeans, who fought for Mexico during the 1846-48 Mexican-American War. This book has a few faults but it also tells a story that our government has tried to suppress for over a hundred and fifty years, so for that we owe thanks and appreciation to Mr. Hogan. In Many Mexicos, Simpson alludes to the story of these soldiers, but he had a much more "company" line than Mr. Hogan presents. I strongly urge you to buy this book because you'll learn something new and interesting.

Try a local bookstore or

Fondo Editorial Universitario

Madero 687

44100 Guadalajara, Mexico

FAX 52-33-827-1026

e-mail: *74052.3431@compuserve.com*

The Cross in Mexico by VirginiaB. deBarrios

A guide to all things religious in Mexico, this book offers up good history, and explanations of the various *Virgens* and *Santos*. Churches, pilgrimages, celebrations, and art and symbolism are all carefully explained. Excellent reference, easy to read.

Try a local bookstore or

Editorial MINUTIAE MEXICANA, S.A. de C.V.

Insurgentes Centro 114-210

06030 Mexico, D.F.

FAX: 55-5232-0662

This publisher prints a series of small inexpensive guides about many aspects of Mexican life, history, ecology and culture. Ask for a list.

Midlife Mavericks: Women Reinventing Their Lives in Mexico by Karen Blue is a wonderful affirmation of both how easy and how difficult it is to make a major lifestyle change and actually move to Mexico. Real women tell you how and why. This is good reading for both genders. Blue is partnered with Judy King in producing an online newsletter I'll tell you about shortly.

http://www.mexicoblue.homestead.com

e-mail: *mexicoblue@prodigy.net.mx*

800-636-8329

I can assure you that if you subscribe to their newsletter, Judy and Blue will get you up to speed regarding Mexico's many holidays (look under the Guadalajara/ Lake Chapala heading). But for a complete overview of all the Hispanic holidays go to your local bookstore and ask them to order The Latino Holiday Book, From Cinco de Mayo to Dia de los Muertos-the Celebrations and Traditions of Hispanic Americans. Valerie Menard is the author, and the publisher is Marlowe & Company. You'll learn the reasons, customs, activities, and foods associated with various holidays, not just in Mexico but throughout the Hispanic world.

History

In case you want to know more about Mexican history and culture, here are two good books that are relatively easy to read:

Many Mexicos by Lesley Bird Simpson was written in 1941. Even though it's dated, it has been revised and still serves as a good general overview of Mexico. You'll enjoy its entertaining and humorous tone.

Many Mexicos may be out of print. Check with your local bookseller or search for used copies on *http://www.amazon.com* or with used or rare book dealers.

Distant Neighbors: A Portrait of the Mexicans by Alan Riding is one of those books that everyone recommends and few seem to have read. A chapter on the nature of the culture, a couple of chapters of history, and then Riding launches into an outstanding explanation of modern Mexican business, politics, and foreign relations, particularly those with the U.S. Good book, even if it is a slower read because you want to stop occasionally to think and remember the events of recent history as you go along.

A wonderful website that offers free access to worldwide historical archives and articles is Don Mabry´s Historical Text Archives. For those of us like me, who are history buffs, this is a gold mine. The site is well-designed and easy to use. And did I mention free? Type in *http://historicaltextarchive.com* to learn about the French Connection to Mexico. Find out why Empress Carlota went mad, and how the belltower of the Templo de Guadalajara in Puerto Vallarta, just off the *malecon* near the Plaza de Armas, came to be modeled after her crown. Dazzle the less informed with the full rundown on Maximillian, Carlota, Napoleon the Third, the Pope, and the French attempt to establish a foothold in North America while the U.S. was distracted by the War of Northern Aggression.

The A&E Television Network and The History Channel offer Mexico: A Story of Courage and Conquest, a set of four color videos, each 50 minutes long, that provides a very good overview of the story of Mexico from before the arrival of Cortes through the war with the U.S. I bought my set at a book fair in Guadalajara but you can get Barnes&Noble to order it for you.

Mortgage Lenders, Maybe

Much of the information in this book is aimed primarily at renters. If you want to know about Mexican-U.S., dollar-based, home mortgages you can contact these folks about mortgages that they may (or may not be) offering. The Mexican home mortgage market is extremely limited and lenders come and go with some high degree of regularity, so there's a good chance the info in this section won't hold up for long. Check 'em out anyway, if you're interested.

You can get information about "Credi Dolar" programs from the General Hipotecaria group at *http://www.generalhipotecaria.com.mx*

e-mail: *viviendamedia@generalhipotecaria.com.mx*

You can also contact Rofigra Global Resources by e-mail at *jhrfii@yahoo.com* or 626-444-0409 or 866-763-4472 and Paula McGowan at 719-633-2211 or e-mail her at *pamcgowan@aol.com*. One thing this group requires and provides is a complete title search. They're watching out for you. Check out some of the real estate sites I've listed below to see how important this is.

Bank United is at 800-545-4870 ext. 8005 and you can contact their Mexico representative Sharon Tognietti at *pennytog@aol.com*. Look at http://osmx.com/financing.htm.

Irwin Mortgage Company is doing business in Manzanillo and Guadalajara, represented by Alejandro Leiva Uribe. Phone or fax 3-121-5179 or call toll free in Mexico to 800-545-4870 X 8203.

Golden Shores Financial is at *http://www.gfsonline.com*.

Collateral Mortgage is at *http://www.mcorazon@compuserve.com* or 210-804-1400 or 800-370-1130.

Canadians might want to contact the nearest Scotiabank Inverlat branch. They advertise that they offer mortgages to both *gringos* and Mexican Nationals. *http://www.scotiabankinverlat.com*.

I'm not affiliated with any of these folks in any way. This information is provided to give you a place to begin your research if you wish to explore this option. If you're really serious about buying land or a home in Mexico you should check out the Move2Mexico website. They have a very good article on what is required and what you can expect during the entire transaction. Go to *http://www.move2mexico.com*. When the homepage appears, scroll down and see that the last item on the sidebar to the left is titled "Buying Property in Mexico".

Click on the title and start gathering info. Then spend some time looking at the other features. You can also find the same info, written by Dennis Peyton at *http://www.mexonline.com/realesta.htm.*

The best site devoted to real estate information I've found is *http://www.mexicorealty.com.* Much of the info you'll find here is by an Arizona attorney, Lisa Larkin, Esq. E-mail her at *mexicorealty@aol.com.* Click to all the sections of her website and you'll have an extremely full picture of what's involved in buying property SoB. I'm not a big fan of lawyers but I'm making an exception in Ms. Larkin's case.

Here's a fun little book that will carry you through many of the complexities of the Mexican real estate market with its accompanying headaches and heartbreaks.

The Gringo´s Investment Guide—Every legal thing you need to know about buying real estate in Mexico by Ginger Combs-Ramirez with legal consultants Rene Ramirez-Ortiz, A.L. and C. Bruce Combs, C.P.A., J.D. Try B&N or write to Monmex Publishing, Box 1158, Ennis, Montana, 59729.

Online News
For keeping up to date on happenings back in the USA and Canada, you might want to try these free newspaper sites:

http://www.latimes.com

http://www.refdesk.com (general interest)

http://www.jewishworldreview.com (national)

http://www.worldnetdaily.com (non-mainstream)

http://www.nytimes.com

http://www.washingtonpost.com

http://www.houstonchronicle.com

http://www.houstonchronicle.com (national)

Canadian readers can also look at these sites for a start:

http://www.globeandmail.com (national)

http://www.thestar.com (Toronto)

http://www.vancouversun.com

http://www.calgaryherald.com

http://www.montrealgazette.com

http://www.thetelegram.com (St. John's)

http://www.ammsa.com/sage (Saskatchewan)

You may wonder why I included the "Aboriginal" or Native American paper at the end of this list, so I'll explain. Most people don't know how closely linked are the histories of Canada and the United States. Most people are unaware of the enormous contributions by the early Canadians who helped in the development of both countries. Our common concerns about the status and actions of the indigenous population were dealt with quite differently, and I believe better, by the RCMP. The Great Plains by Walter Prescott Webb is a classic text on our shared history and should be required reading in the foreign community.

http://www.bbc.com is one of my favorite news sites. The European perspective is much broader and less self-serving than what we're used to on this side of the pond.

And just for fun, and a different set of views, look at *http://www.rtumble.com*. It's the Rough and Tumble website, "A Daily Snapshot of California Policy and Politics" and it's much more interesting and entertaining than the cut line would indicate.

Rolly sent this one to me and I love it. Cartoons from all over the world are found at *http://cagle.slate.msn.com*. Check it out if you have a sense of humor, or if you want to see how we're perceived by editorial cartoonists in other countries.

One last thing. Your hometown newspaper may have an online edition. Use the Google search engine to find out. *http://www.google.com* will get you there and all you need to do is type in your search request. For instance, Dallas Times Herald.

Here are some places you might want to consider for your retirement home.

Places to Live

Colima, Colima

This is a beautiful city (and State) in a very diverse part of the country. It may well be one of the overlooked retirement possibilities of Mexico. It's definitely worth checking out. It's hot in the summer and you'll need some Spanish language skills. I've included some volcano websites here because there's a smoking volcano quite near Colima city. There's not a lot of information out there about this area because, to the best of my knowledge, fewer than 300 *gringos* live in Colima city. The downtown area is clean and attractive with a wonderful selection of department stores, shops, restaurants, hotels, and tourist services. The University of Colima is there as well, and a dance troupe from the school performs traditional dances throughout the country.

Colima is the capitol city of Colima State, the third smallest state of Mexico. It is also the third oldest city in Mexico, after Veracruz and Mexico City. The geographic features of the state include the beaches of the Pacific coastline; volcanoes (including the Archipelago of Revillagigedo which is composed of four volcanic islands); fresh water lagoons occupied by many species of birds, reptiles, and animals; waterfalls; coconut, banana, and mango plantations; as well as many farms growing an amazing variety of fruits and vegetables. There are several significant archaeological sites and the famous salt making town of Cuyutlán within its borders. There is a National airport in Colima city and an International airport near Manzanillo, about two and a half hours away on an excellent toll road system, as well as a few private airstrips.

After a few rough days of fact-finding and sightseeing through the area, a friend and I recently treated ourselves to a night at one of the four star hotels in the downtown area. For around $90 US we got the executive suite (after a bit of hagglin'), and for an additional $60 US, a room service dinner and a bottle of wine. The room was huge, with a separate dressing area, two vanities, an extremely large closet, a first-rate and very comfortable king-sized bed, elegant furnishings, a balcony that wrapped around both sides of our corner room that provided an excellent view of the volcano, and an immense bathroom with a two person, side-by-side whirlpool bathtub. In the US, we couldn't have afforded even a comparable meal, and I can assure you that most hotels offering the same amenities NoB wouldn't let me in the lobby. Colima remains reasonable in contrast to some of the more popular and well-known desitinations.

http://www.davestravelcorner.com offers seven very informative webpages about Colima. Just go to *http://www.davestravelcorner.com/articles/colima/intro.htm* and click on the arrow on each page to move to the next page.

http://www.visitacolima.com.mx

http://www.volcano.si.edu/gvp/volcano/region14/mexico/colima/var.htm is the website of the Global Volcanism Program of the National Museum of Natural History of the Smithsonian Institution.

http://volcano.und.nodak.edu/vwdocs/volc_tour/mex/9Colima.html

http://www.wunderground.com/global/stations/76658.html is *the site where you'll* find weather reports for Colima.

http://www.mexweb.com/colima.htm has a one-page description of the area.

http://www.tourbymexico.com/colima/colima.htm is a site that offers descriptions of the five Colima State towns, as well as the Nevado de Colima National Park.

http://www.gomanzanillo.com/old_articles/elsalto/index.htm takes you to an article about the El Salto waterfall and recreational area.

http://www.latinamericavacationguide.com/travel/colima)_Overview.html gives you a short description of the area, plus links to other sites.

http://www.guiacolima.com opens in Spanish but has an English link.

Costalegre Area of Colima, Jalisco, and Nayarit

For those of you who dream of retiring to a small village at the beach, this is an area to consider. The entire stretch of coast between Puerto Vallarta, Jalisco and Manzanillo, Colima is easily accessible via Mexico Highway 200, although the road is pretty twisty and narrow. This is a strip of road that scares even me at night. You'll find reasonably-priced housing in many of the towns although inflation, coupled with wealthy *gringos*, have driven prices up in others.

http://www.tomzap.com has links to La Manzanilla and other parts of the Costalegre.

http://www.costalegre.ca is billed as the site "Designed With The Canadian Travelers In Mind", and there's a ton of info those of you 'twixt and 'tween Canada and Mexico can use.

http://www.lamanzanillamexico.info

http://www.lamanzanilla.com

http://members5.boardhost.com/casalibertad

And again, there's David Ramsey's book Costalegre: The Little Known Beaches Of Jalisco. Not intended to be an atlas of the entire coastline, this book will show you what much of the area looks like and what various locales offer. As I said earlier, Mr. Ramsey has done his homework well.

Guadalajara/Lake Chapala Area, Jalisco

The Guadalajara Colony Reporter is an English language weekly newspaper published in Guadalajara.

http://www.guadalajarareporter.com

e-mail: *reporter@informador.com.mx* or *editor@guadalajarareporter.com.mx*

http://www.mexicopost7.com is the American Legion Post 7 website in Chapala.

http://www.go.to/americanlegion.com is American Legion Post 9 in Guadalajara.

Mexico's Lake Chapala and Ajijic The Insider's Guide to the Northshore for International Travelers by Teresa A. Kendrick and six very knowledgeable contributors is the best and most useful local guide I've ever seen anywhere. If you're considering this area, you need this book. Many locals refer to it regularly, and have dubbed it "The Bible". Sure she's my editor. Who wants someone who's not intimately acquainted with the subject helping them with a project this big?

http://www.chapalaguide.com

e-mail: *ajijic@chapalaguide.com*

The Complete Lake Chapala Review is a monthly publication that normally prints several good pieces about the lakeside community as well as other parts of the country. Lots of advertisements. These are to your benefit, as you'll be able to answer a lot of your questions when you see services advertised. Paid sub- scriptions available to the U.S. and Canada.

http://www.lakechapalareview.com

e-mail: *review@laguna.com.mx*

El Ojo Del Lago—the above description fits this publication also.

http://www.chapala.com

e-mail: *ojodellago@laguna.com.mx*

The Lake Chapala Society is a group of volunteers organized to assist the local expatriate community. These folks publish a phone book and coordinate a wide range of services. They also provide a library and a video library for their mem- bers.

e-mail: *lsc@laguna.com.mx*

Canadian Club of Lake Chapala is an invaluable resource for Canadians.

http://www.mexconnect.com/amex/canclub or *http://www.canadianclubmx.com.*

e-mail: *canclub@mexconnect.com*

A well-researched and continually updated comprehensive orientation to both Mexico and the Lake Chapala area is Mexico Insights Seminars. These presen- tations are conducted each week by Judy King and Karen Blue, two well-known writers, observers of the local scene, and long-time residents of the area, with a brief introduction and slide presentation by Teresa Kendrick. Their program in- cludes information about the cost of living, climate, health care options, activi- ties and culture of the Lakeside communities. The seminars include discount coupons from local merchants. Participants are entitled to e-mail support if ques- tions arise later. Contact them at *seminar@mexico-insights.com* or at their website *http://www.mexico-insights.com.* I suggest you subscribe to their on-line monthly magazine about the Lake Chapala area that details current trends as well as cultural and historical events. For subscription information e-mail *mexicoblue@prodigy.net.mx* or *judyking@laguna.com.mx.* These ladies are friends who I respect and hold in great affection so of course I'm prejudiced, but their offerings are worth every penny. They'll speed your learning curve about the area by leaps and bounds. That's why I asked them to contribute a thought or two to this book.

Another group, R&R in Mexico Seminars is headquartered in Guadalajara. You can access them at *http://www.rr-mexico.com* or by e-mail at *order@rr-*

mexico.hypermart.net. They offer a quarterly newsletter and several books about Mexico living and retirement.

http://www.mexconnect.com has a series of forums where you can post questions and read comments posted by area residents and visitors. When the home page opens, scroll down to read the index on the left side of the page. Click on "Forums" and then choose the area in which you have an interest, then after you've read all those, go back to the index and begin exploring the rest of Mexico.

http://www.mexconnect.com/mx_/colmrta.html has a cost of living chart

http://www.chapala.com

http://guad.8m.net is a gay friendly information site.

http://www.allaboutguadalajara.com

http://www.mexweb.com

http://vive.guadalajara.gob.mx is the "Official Program of the Guadalajara City Hall" and is designed to promote tourism. You'll find a lot of good information here. The site loads in Spanish, but if you scroll down on the right side of the page you'll find the "English" button.

http://www.mexicanwave.com/travel/Guadalajara

http://www.americansociety.org is the website of The American Society of Jalisco, A.C. The e-mail address is *info@amsoc.hypermart.net.* This is a very active gringo service group in the Chapalita section of Guadalajara. They publish an interesting and chatty monthly newsletter entitled "The Voice". They also operate a thrift shop for those who need to pick up an odd or interesting item from time to time. These folks are active and very helpful.

http://www.virtualmex.com/guadala.htm

http://www.epinions.com/content_47115832964 has a link to visitors' reviews of Guadalajara. They cover quite a few subjects and provide a collection of opinions about what the city and the surrounding areas have to offer.

http://www.davestravelcorner.com/articles/guadalajara/intro.htm will lead you to an excellent review of the city and its many attractions.

Manzanillo, Colima

Manzanillo and the State of Colima, Facts, Tips, and Day Trips by Susan Dearing is a 150-page guide to the area. It contains a wealth of information about how to move gracefully through the day to day events of life, as well as valuable travel tips. This is much more than a simple city guide in that it offers you a look at the customs and the culture. The lady has been here for about ten years and knows what's what. A dollar from the sale of each book goes to one of the local charities which helps homeless or underprivileged children. I highly recommend this book. It may seem a bit pricey but it's worth every cent. I refer to it frequently.

http://www.gomanzanillo.com/guidebook/index.htm

e-mail the author at *susan@gomanzanillo.com*

Phone: 011-52-314-333-0642

FAX 011-52-314-333-3678

Mail orders can be sent to:

> Susan Dearing
>
> Apdo. Post. #295
>
> 28861 Santiago, Colima
>
> Mexico

along with a check or money order for $29.95 US.

http://www.gomanzanillo.com is an excellent site for a wide variety of local information.

http://www.manzanillomexico.com

http://www.manzanillo.com

http://www.mexonline.com/manzanillo.htm

http://www.tomzap.com is an interesting and useful site that provides a message board and where you'll find a bit of information about a few of the lesser known coastal towns and villages.

http://www.davestravelcorner.com/articles/colima/intro.htm and follow the instructions in the Colima section to explore these 14 pages.

Help! The Manzanillo Foreign Community Association, A.C. Membership in this group includes a subscription to their newsletter <u>As The Palapa Turns.</u>

http://www.manzanillohelp.com

E-mail: HELP!@bay.net.mx

Phone: 011-52-314-334-0977

FAX: 011-52-314-334-0977 or 334-2477

If you need to look up a business in the Manzanillo TELMEX Directory you'll be pleasantly surprised to find that, unlike some other tourist and retirement destinations, it provides an index in English. In many cases it's not going to help much if you call and don't speak Spanish, but it will tell you where to go for help or service. Used in conjunction with one of the many excellent city maps provided by the local Manzanillo Tourism Bureau Office you'll be able to find your way around like a native. You can contact the Tourism Bureau at *manzanillo@bay.net.mx* or *sectur@bay.net.mx*. From the U.S. and Canada you can call 011-52-314-333-1380 or 333-3838. Brochures and maps are available in most hotels and many restaurants.

Mazatlan, Sinaloa

http://www.pacificpearl.com is the website of the local newspaper. There is a bit of free online content, and inexpensive online subscriptions are available.

http://www.themelville.com is a commercial site for an assisted living facility that also offers a great deal of information

http://www.maztravel.com is a commercial site that can also be useful

http://www.mexonline.com/mazatlan.htm

http://www.mexconnect.com/mex_travel/tmcdonald/tmmazatlan.html is a tremendously helpful and well-done site.

http://www.maztravel.com/maz/retire.html#assist will take you directly to a site that offers a cost of living chart and a medicine cost chart.

http://mazatlan.com.mx is difficult to navigate, but is another source of good information.

http://www.radiofree.mazatlan.com has a great community forum and many links

http://www.mazcity.com.mx

Morelia and Patzcuaro, Michoacan

You'll probably need to speak some Spanish if you intend to be comfortable in these two cities. Patzcuaro is a beautiful colonial city; Morelia has more cosmopolitan shopping. Even though their personalities are different, I paired them because they're close to each other.

http://www.mexconnect.com/foromichoacan is a message board where you can post questions and read the postings of others to gather information.

http://www.flyingcolorsart.com/source/scrap/patzcuaro.html has great pictures

http://www.groups.yahoo.com/group/MoreliaConnect

http://www.mexicanwave.com/travel/Morelia

http://www.mexicanwave.com/travel/patzcuaro

http://www.mexonline.com/morelia.htm

http://www.mexonline.com/patzcuaro.htm

http://www.mexonline.com/fm-mich.htm offers info about the State of Michoacán.

http://www.tourbymexico.com/michoa/michoa.htm has nice photos

Puerto Vallarta, Jalisco

Here's a *regalo*. If you decide to move to PV, or if you just want to check it out, cross the *Rio Cuale* into Old Town via the bridge nearest the Bay of Banderas. The street at the foot of the bridge is *Aquiles Serdan*. Turn left, unless you're driving, then you'll have to go to the next street. Go two blocks and turn right. There will be a big grocery store on your right at the end of the block you just turned on to. Go inside and turn to your right, look right, and you'll find the greatest bulletin board in Mexico for rentals.

http://www.todopv.com is an excellent site to begin exploring PV.

http://www.allaboutpuertovallarta.com

http://www.mexonline.com/puertovallarta.htm

http://pvmex.8m.com is a gay friendly site with several good links.

http://www.vallartatoday.com

http://www.puertovallarta.net has good links to photos, ads, and other PV websites.

http://www.vallarta-info.com is an outstanding site. The webmaster has provided prices in U.S. dollars for many goods and services. Don't be frightened by some of the prices in the real estate sales and rental section.

http://ww.inside-vallarta.com is an interesting site.

Vallarta Lifestyles is a quarterly magazine available for $29.95 US. Send it to 705 Martens Court, #78-299, Laredo, TX 78041-6010. (This is the drop address for a private mail service operated throughout much of Mexico, so if you rent a box from them your address will look similar.) Anyway, Vallarta Lifestyles is affiliated with A.M.P.I., the Mexican Real Estate Association so you'll be bombarded with real estate promotions. There's also good information about PV attractions. Their website is *http://www.virtualvallarta.com*.

http://www.pvmirror.com is the site for an excellent on-line newspaper with a wide variety of information about the PV area.

The Times is a weekly newsletter for English speakers in the PV area.

e-mail: *do-it!in-vta@pvnet.com.mx*

Bahia de Banderas News bills itself as "The Area's HOTTEST Newspaper". It has an online version. And though it's geared to the "party hearty" crowd, it runs a few serious articles and its classified ad section could prove useful.

http://www.BanderasNews.com

e-mail: *Editor@BanderasNews.com*

San Luis Potosí, San Luis Potosí

http://www.angelfire.com/ok/Sanluis/index.html

http://www.mpsnet.com.mx/mexico/slp.html

San Miguel de Allende, Guanajuato

http://www.infosma.com is the best, most informative, and easily navigated city site I've ever seen.

http://www.sanmiguel-de-allende.com

http://www.portalsanmiguel.com

http://www.mexonline.com/sma.htm

http://www.mexicanwave.com/travel/san_miguel

http://www.mexweb.com/colonial.htm#San

http://www.virtualmex.com/miguel.htm

http://www.internetsanmiguel.com/index.html

The newspaper is Atención San Miguel

http://www.infosma.com/services/communic.htm#Newspapers

Phone/FAX: 011-52-415-152-3770

e-mail: *atencion@unisovo.net.mx*

This paper has the best rental listings I've ever seen anywhere in Mexico. Go to their site to find out first-hand what the rental range is. They'll be at:

http://www.infosma.com/atencion/rentals.htm

When you get to SMA stop by the *Biblioteca Publica*, or Public Library to get an idea of what's going on in the city. SMA is a colonial city whose character is maintained due to strict zoning and building codes. However, most modern conveniences are available. You can buy a copy of *Juarde*, the directory of SMA residents and many local businesses.

Tepic, Nayarit

This is one of my favorite cities. Modern, clean, safe. Not a lot of *gringos,* but lots of *gringo*-style services.

http://members4boardhost.com/Nayarit. This is a beautiful site. Scroll down on the message board to "The List" to see why Alice and Cliff decided to move here.

http://www.tourbymexico.com/nayarit.htm

http://www.turnay.gob.mx has an English language link.

http://www.members5.board.com/casalibertad

VERY IMPORTANT FM-3 INFORMATION

Here's something that they may or may not tell you when you receive your FM-3 in the U.S. or Canada. **You must register your FM-3 with *Migración* in Mexico within 30 days of issuance.** This information is on page 2 of the FM-3 booklet. In Spanish.

You can register it at any Port of Entry or at any *Migración* office in the country. You might want to do it when you cross the border, or if you're headed for a *gringo* enclave there will be an OMH or two who can direct you to someone who can help you get the job done.

This must be done. No excuses, no exceptions. Fines are levied for those who fail to follow the law. Deportation is an outside possibility.

In every area where *gringos* have settled you'll find a business set up by an English speaker who you can hire to facilitate your paperwork and solve bureaucratic problems. Check around, the locals can direct you to them. Purists scoff, but after all the frustrations I encountered when I decided to renew my FM-3 without assistance I now utilize their services for almost anything involving paperwork.

In March of 2002 the National Immigration Institute (INM) of the Mexican government was supposed to begin issuing electronic ID cards to the 900,000 or so foreigners permanently living in Mexico. The card will contain the holder's name, age, gender, occupation, address, and fingerprints and was scheduled to cost 50 pesos. By using the card, the government would be able to track our movements into and out of the country. Some might consider this another version of Jorge Orwello´s *Hermano Grande,* but after 9/11 it makes sense to have a way to monitor the people who cross your borders. As of publication the cards have not been issued.

APPENDIX 2

SOME TRAFFIC LAWS AND REGULATIONS

You may laugh at some of these statements, but you *will* see the bulleted regulations on your driver's license test. Here are a few versions of what you'll need and what to expect when you apply for your Mexican DL.

First, do you really need a Mexican DL? No, the one you have now is just fine and is accepted as long as it doesn't expire. If you can't keep it current, then the answer is yes.

How do you go about getting a Mexican DL?

Here are the items you'll need to present to the authorities. First, a copy of your current driver's license if you have one, even if it's expired. This will eliminate the need to take a road test. Then you'll be required to present a laboratory report of your blood type. Argue with me that your blood type is on your current license and that should be proof enough, but don't count on it *being* enough. Remember the *Constancia de Domicilio*? Bring a copy of that along with a copy of your FM-3. There's someone out there who will tell you that a Tourist Visa will suffice. But normally you'll need the FM-3.

Now you have a choice of ways to proceed. In some places you can employ one of the area "expediters" to help out. Your "expediter" will tell you to show up where and when they tell you, sign a completed test form, have your photo taken, get fingerprinted, turn over all your previously gathered paperwork, and become the almost immediate possessor of a Mexican DL good for four years.

Sometimes you might have to wait a few days if the local cop shop doesn't have the modern processing equipment.

Other "expediters" might have a different arrangement. Their scenario could be similar to the foregoing, with the exception that you will be required to take the written test. In this scenario, a local police officer who is somewhat fluent in English will read each question along with four possible answers and "hint" at the correct answer.

The real deal, and most to be dreaded, is the straight-up official application. In this potential nightmare, you'll be expected to actually take the test, in Spanish, and sometimes pass an eye examination. All is not lost if you're confronted with this situation. The authorities will usually allow an interpreter to read the test to you, along with each set of answers, and you'll be required to provide the correct choice of A,B,C,or D. Some jurisdictions will want to know about this arrangement beforehand. If you need the help of an interpreter you must hire one yourself.

Most of the following information will be familiar to you and some won't. Some of it will be pure common sense and some will be downright bizarre. This information was translated from official documents by my *amiga* Guadalupe Raygosa of San Antonio Tlayacapan.

Laws and Regulations

•   There are two categories that govern traffic in Mexico: laws and regulations.

•   Speeding must be avoided, but if you do it is an infraction of the law.

•   You are not permitted to use red lights on a private vehicle. These are reserved for use by social service vehicles such as fire trucks, ambulances, and police cars.

•   A traffic officer (Highway Patrol) cannot stop you unless you have committed an infraction of the law or regulations.

•   If you own a Mexican-plated car and your license plate, circulation card, and the window sticker are stolen or lost, you must report the loss as soon as possible and cancel them. You must notify the proper authority, *Ministerio Publico, Procuraduria,* and S.V.T. (DMV). This must be done so that you don't get blamed if a vehicle with the stolen items is involved in a crime or an accident.

•   The speed limit in school zones, and near churches, markets, theaters, and other public areas is 10 KPH (Kilometers Per Hour).

•   It is an infraction if your car does not have a windshield.

•   At intersections, streets without traffic signs have preference.

• On one-way streets you must always park to the left side. You must park no more than 50 cm from the curb. That's about 20 inches. On two-way streets you park to the right. That means both sides, doesn't it?

• Drunk driving is a felony.

• Do not drive with pets, children, or large objects in the front seat.

• When the highway is not marked, you must drive on the right side of the road.

• The traffic authorities, in descending order are the Governor, the municipal Mayor, and the Secretary of Traffic and Transport (S.T.V.).

• The objectives of the laws and regulations are: to keep order in the traffic, to make transportation easier, and to enforce the obligations and rights of drivers, passengers, and pedestrians.

• It is an infraction to cover your auto license plate.

• It is an infraction to drive backwards (in reverse) for more than 10 meters (about 33 feet).

• It is an infraction to park on the sidewalk. You should think about the handicapped such as wheelchair users and the blind.

• The Social Service agency emergency vehicles, in ascending order are fire trucks, ambulances, police cars, and highway patrol cars. To obtain preference they must have on the flashing lights and the French horn.

• At the intersection of streets of equal importance if there are no signals, you must stop totally and yield the right of way to the vehicle to the right. Never trust the other driver because s/he may not know this rule.

• It is an infraction to drive at night without lights. It doesn't matter if you forgot to turn them on, or if they don't work. That's why it's important to check your headlights and directional signals.

• The regulations say that you must stop on all right turns. It doesn't matter if the traffic light is on or the traffic officer is on duty, you must stop to let pedestrians and other cars pass. After all this, you may turn right.

• For safety, and also because it's a regulation, you must park a minimum of 6 meters (about 21 feet) from any intersection on the narrow streets. (Think of the big trucks trying to turn.)

• It is against the regulations to drive a car with the license plate placed in the wrong place.

• It is illegal to drive a car with a crushed or broken windshield.

• It is an infraction to drive while you are wearing earphones.

•   You must not follow a Social Service vehicle (police, fire, ambulance or other emergency vehicle) if it goes on an emergency call. You cannot stop within 25 meters (about 68 feet) of where the police, ambulance personnel, or firefighters are working.

•   When you enter a traffic circle you must stop to let the cars in it proceed.

•   When making a left turn onto a highway across traffic from a side road, you must be sure there are no cars coming from either direction before turning left onto the highway. You must then drive on the right side of the highway.

•   The classifications of traffic circulation from least to greatest are: streets, avenues, and highways.

•   Your vehicle can be impounded for the following reasons:

←   Driving without license plates

←   Being parked in a prohibited place

←   Driving without car papers and driver's license

•   If you are issued a traffic ticket you have a fiscal debt. If you pay the ticket from the first to the fifth day you get a 50% discount. From the sixth to the fourteenth day you may discount 25%. After that you pay full price.

•   It is illegal to pass where streets and roads cross.

•   Your car's papers are not transferable so when you sell a car you must go to the D.M.V. to report the sale.

•   At a railroad crossing you must stop completely and look both ways. If no train is coming, you may proceed.

•   If you are involved in an automobile accident you must report it to the authorities. It is allowable for the parties involved to work out an agreement among or between themselves, except when somebody gets badly hurt or dies, or if National property is damaged.

•   The driver's license is valid for four years and must be renewed 30 days before it expires (Chapala area).

•   You can not pass on the right side. This will not only result in a ticket, it is dangerous to your life and the lives of others.

•   You may not stop your vehicle in a pedestrian crosswalk.

•   You may not park in a prohibited zone, but you may stop to discharge or pick up passengers.

•   You can be ticketed if you drive too slowly and impede the flow of traffic.

- If you think you were unjustly ticketed you may report to
  - ← Oficina de Inconformidad
  - ← Delegacion Regional
- If a speed limit is not posted, the maximum speed allowed is 50 KPH, but only if the traffic and circumstances allow.
- You may never stop on a curve.

Mechanical Considerations

- You must tune your car every 10,000 KMs or every six months, but you should change the air filter every 5,000 KMs.
- When diesel motors are cold, sometimes you need to use aerosol ether to help them start.
- If your car catches on fire, try to disconnect the battery immediately and try to put out the fire with a rag or dirt. Sometimes a car catches fire because of a short circuit or a gas leak. It is important to have black tape.
- In the cooling system of the car, the water pump makes the water circulate.
- When a car is not getting power it is because the alternator is failing.
- A diesel engine explosion begins from the compression and elevation of the temperature. These engines do not use spark plugs.
- A gas engine explosion begins from the spark of a spark plug.
- All re-cap or renewed tires must be on the front.
- Before driving, it is a good habit to check oil, water, fluids, and tires. You should look to make sure nothing is under the car.
- When the wheel of your car shakes a lot, it is because it needs to be balanced.
- If your brakes fail, you must stay calm and brake with the motor, and use the emergency brake. Ask someone if they have had this experience.
- The emergency brake works by an air belt. (Trucks only.)
- The minimum air pressure for a compressor must be 80 to 100 pounds, but this applies only to heavy trucks.

Defensive Driving

- You must try to avoid having an accident by not drinking, not speeding, not being distracted, and respecting the traffic laws.

•   The requirements for a good driving experience are knowledge, ability, road conditions, and time to reach your destination.

•   Defensive driving is the ability to drive from one place to another without having an accident, even if the other driver is impolite and commits errors, and the driver encounters adverse conditions.

•   Before taking a curve you must slow down as you enter it and accelerate smoothly out of it. If driving at night, be prepared to dim your lights.

•   Reaction time is understood to be the time it takes to remove your foot from the gas and move it to the brake pedal.

•   The rule of two seconds helps us to keep the proper distance between cars.

•   Distraction is another problem that causes accidents. To avoid this, don't smoke, don't look at yourself too much in the rearview mirror, don't look at the radio dial, and don't turn your head to watch pedestrians or the girls.

•   When you pass another car you must go back to the right lane as soon as you see it completely in the rearview mirror. If a car is passing you, take your foot off the gas and give the other car time to pass.

•   If your car slides to the right, don't accelerate, don't apply the brakes, and steer to the right.

•   If you get a flat while driving, hold tight to the steering wheel, take your foot from the gas pedal and let it lose speed alone, and begin to steer toward the right side of the road.

•   If your hood flies open while you're driving, the first thing to do is slow down. Keep calm, look out, and then get to the right side of the road. This is why it's a good idea to check it after you check under the hood.

•   When you park on a one-way downhill street you must turn your wheels to the left. If the street is two-way, you must turn the wheels to the right.

•   When a car follows too closely behind you it is very dangerous.

•   Remember, your mood influences your driving.

•   When you must stop on a steep hill because of car trouble you must first turn on the emergency lights, then set the emergency brake, and put out emergency signs.

•   Defensive driving allows you to have time to react.

But There's More
If you bought a *Guia Roji* map, you found a complete set of road signs. These signs are divided into three categories: Regulatory, which are predominately

red and white, with black print; Warning, which are black and yellow; and Informative, which are blue and white. Study them because a significant number of questions (enough to cause you to fail) will be on sign identification. Concentrate your efforts on the first two categories.

See ya on the road!

APPENDIX 3

HERE'S SOME ADVICE AND A FEW RESOURCES FOR U.S. AND CANADIAN VETERANS

Mexico can be a great option for those of you who are retired from active duty, on disability pensions or other types of benefits, surviving spouse payments, and burned out on the day-to-day existence you're hackin' through now. If you need a part-time job at a fast food palace or the local grocery store to supplement your meager pension, then a new life SoB might do you a world of good. I feel better physically and much more at peace psychologically and emotionally since I made my permanent move. You're not going to live The Life of Riley on an income less than what's required by the Mexican immigration law, but if you can meet their minimum requirement and learn to adapt to the ebb and flow of local life you'll be a lot better off than in many places in the U.S. and Canada.

For those of you who have specific concerns about health and mobility, I'll provide information about some of the more commonly asked questions. However, just as I stressed in the medical advice chapter, and everywhere else, *check things out for yourself* before you come down for good.

First, personal mobility. There are only a few cities that are relatively wheelchair friendly. Some municipalities have installed wheelchair ramps at street intersections, and there are good sidewalks and paved streets that can be navigated. I know several guys here who are wheelchair bound and who are able to access the *plaza* and a few essential places. There will be a great many stores, restaurants and government offices that will be impossible to enter without help, though. The up side is that domestic care is relatively inexpensive, and if you choose to hire live-in help, the living space you provide for them is considered to be half their salary. If you need to have grab rails or ramps installed, the cost will be a fraction of what you'd pay up NoB. They probably won't be shiny chrome, but they'll help you haul your ass wherever you intend for it to land.

I'm not specifically recommending or endorsing this facility, but if I were a wheelchair user, or if I required medical monitoring I think I'd check out The Melville in Mazatlan to see what they offer. Try *http://www.themelville.com*. The prices I've seen advertised seem to be reasonable, and Mazatlan is a beautiful small city. You'll also be able to avail yourself of the free entertainment supplied by the timeshare salespeople who work the streets as diligently as the hookers on Sunset Strip.

Here's a website you might enjoy. The British have a much healthier attitude in regard to many things, including disabilities. Go to *http://www.bbc.co.uk/ouch/ thelab* to get the BBC-sponsored take on the problems some of us encounter. Some bits are funny, some provoke anger, but they all make you think. Not much PC here.

Next, free medications and medical supplies sent out by government clinics, hospitals, or other care facilities won't be sent to an address in Mexico. Number one, it's not legal under current Mexican law and two, it's too undependable, even if it were legal. I personally know people who have medications forwarded to them by friends in the U.S., using the regular postal service, UPS, and FedEx and the like. I wouldn't depend on this kind of arrangement for myself. I just buy what I need from a local pharmacy. Or visit the witch.

In Chapter 16 I wrote about what you might expect in the way of special medical equipment. If you need specific information about an area and what services you can expect to find there, I suggest you contact the American Legion post in the area and direct your questions to the Post Service Officer. Ask for a referral to the Department Service Officer if the local SO can't answer your questions. As you're well aware, the people holding these positions change, so keep asking until you get the answers you need.

Another option is to contact the Service Officer of the Military Order of the Purple Heart in Mexico. You don't need to have been awarded the medal to receive assistance from this organization. David Lord is certified to provide service and to submit claims to the Veterans Administration. Contact him at *Mexicodirect@infosel.net.mx* or *info@mophmx.com* or call 011-52-33-3164-1106. David arranged a program that allows vets to use the services of the

Mexican Army Hospital in Guadalajara at a greatly reduced cost. Contact him directly for more information about that. At present David, along with several others, is working to form a Mexico branch of the MOPH. He operates a Mobile Service Unit that travels to a number of towns and cities to assist vets. He also helps Mexican Nationals who served in the U.S. Armed Forces, as well as the widows of these men who may not realize that they could be eligible to claim benefits. David does not charge for this assistance and does not accept donations. He was recently elected to serve as Service Officer of the American Legion Department of Mexico.

Here's a list of websites you can explore. Let me strongly encourage you to investigate your options and your obligations *prior* to making a move. There are landmines within the bureaucracies of all countries as well as other hostile territory. Be careful.

Veterans Affairs Canada is at *http://www.vac-acc.gc.ca*.

Army, Navy, and Air Force Veterans in Canada can be contacted at *http://www.anavets.ca/org.html*. E-mail them at *anavets@storm.ca*

The Royal Canadian Legion-Dominion Command is at *http://www.legion.ca* and the e-mail address is *info@legion.ca*. Mail them at:

> 359 Kent St.
>
> Ottawa, Ontario
>
> Canada, K2P OR7
>
> Phone: 1-613-235-4391
>
> Fax: 1-613-563-1670

Old Age Security and Canada Pension Plan information can be located at *http://www.hrdc-drhc.gc.ca/isp/common/home.shtml*.

A list of American Legion Posts in Mexico can be found at *http://members.tripod.com/~Post_119_Gulfport_MS/legionet.html*

Keep in mind that you do not need to be a member of the Legion in order to apply for assistance from them. It's a good idea though, in my opinion, to join and to support a local post if you're able and eligible. Some posts also allow Associate Memberships, so look for ways to join. I belong to a post in Guadalajara and in 1976, served as Sergeant-at-Arms of the American Legion Department of Texas.

Disabled U.S. vets should utilize the website of the Foreign Medical Program at *http://www/va.gov/hac/fmp/fmp.html*. E-mail them at *hac.fmp@med.va.gov*. You can call 303-331-7590 or fax 303-331-7803. You can apply for reimbursement for medical care of any service-related disabilities and conditions for which you receive compensation. Check this site to see what eligibility requirements affect your specific case.

Some of you retirees are going to have Tricare questions. You can go to *http://www.tricare.osd.mil/tfl* or to *http://tricare15.army.mil.*

The U.S. Veterans Affairs website is at *http://www.va.gov.*

Go to *http://www.cem.va.gov* for death and burial information.

The website for the Veterans of Foreign Wars is *http://www/vfw.org* although there are currently no active VFW posts in Mexico that I'm aware of.

http://www.vets.com is an interesting and extensive site with hundreds of links to useful and entertaining information and articles.

You may need to contact the National Personnel Records Center (NPRC) at *http://www.nara.gov/regional/mpr.html.* If you need to download form SF 180 to request records you can go to *http://www.nara.gov/regional/mprsf180.html.*

Federal Benefits for Veterans and Dependents is a booklet you can order by calling 1-800-827-1000, which is the VA toll-free hotline. Or try *http://www.va.gov/pubaff/fedben/00fedben.pdf.*

You might also want to look at *http://www.Military.com.*

The Social Security Administration website is *http://www.ssa.gov.*

If you fully utilize these sources along with the rest of the information in the book you should find answers to most of your questions. Let me suggest that you contact one of the many qualified Service Officers of any one of the national veterans organizations before you finalize your move. These folks are trained to answer your questions and they can direct you in your planning. They can also alert you to possible problems you might face if you decide to move SoB.

In the past few years a class of what some of us would consider less than desirables has sprung up to "help" vets who are in dire financial straits due to illnesses or other disabilities. These folks offer to purchase the future benefits they're scheduled to receive. They offer to buy rights to life insurance policies, lottery winnings, future lawsuit or insurance disability payments, and…veterans benefits. If you're approached by one of these agents, be damn sure you understand what the ramifications will be. The VA has improved in the past few years, and I'd sure feel more confident about dealing with them, than a pack of "compassionate and helpful" businessfolks who were trying to do me a "favor" or offering me a "service" that permanently negated my agreement with my government.

Here's what one of our fellow vets has to say about his move to Mexico and his impressions of life SoB.

A Single Vet's Perspective

As the former Vice-Commander of the American Legion, Department of Mexico, I can tell you that there are twenty American Legion Posts between the Rio Grande and the Panama Canal. The Department of Mexico encompasses all of these posts. The largest of them, with over 300 members, is Lake Chapala Post Seven located at Calle Morelos #114 in Chapala. Their telephone number is 52-376-765-2259 and their website is http://www.mexicopost7.com. This was one of my first stops when I arrived and I suggest that you do the same if you plan to come to a town where a Post is located. At the end of this article I'll give you a list, current as of July 2002, of all the Posts in Mexico, and contact information for each one. If you qualify for membership please consider joining your local Post. Some Posts offer Associate memberships for the benefit of those who are not eligible, so that our Canadian and Mexican friends are welcome to take advantage of many of the services offered by individual Posts. If you're not fluent in Spanish, the local Post can help you with your entry into the area.

Once you're here you'll find that you might need to have your VA records transferred. We're all under the jurisdiction of the

BILL O'BRIEN, FORMER VICE-COMMANDER, AMERICAN LEGION, DEPARTMENT OF MEXICO CHAPALA, JALISCO, MEXICO

Houston Regional Office. Contact them by mail at:

Department of Veterans Affairs

Houston Regional Office

6900 Almeda Road

Houston, Texas

Fax 713-794-3818.

E-mail for general information: *houstonfsi@vba.va.gov*.

Having lived on Lake Chapala's "Northshore" for about two years now, I've gained some insight into living in this part of Mexico that I'm happy to pass along to my fellow veterans.

Since housing is going to be one of your major concerns, here's a single man's viewpoint. First, don't buy a house for at least six months—longer would probably be better. Give yourself some time to get oriented before you make such a big investment. Find a neighborhood you like and then search for a low-cost rental, something in the two-hundred to two-fifty range. In most towns you won't have much trouble finding something in this price range. Then hire a maid to sanitize the place—it should run you about twenty dollars or so plus the cost of cleaning supplies.

You may need to exterminate, paint a bit, and add a few things like curtains and a throw rug or two, but you'll end up with a place that's comfortable and fixed up to suit you. The advantage here is that by putting out a bit more money and effort during the first month or two, you'll save hundreds of dollars in rent in the long run. Your personal appearance and comfort can be taken care of by a part-time maid hired to clean your place and do your laundry. Depending on where you live, this cost can be as little as a dollar or so an hour.

If you end up settling on Lake Chapala, you'll find that you'll have money to burn as there's not a lot of nightlife or single unattached *gringas* in our age range. Of course, there are many beautiful local ladies but you should spend some time with someone who has dated or married a Mexican woman. Some have good stories and some are scary, but all of them will help you decide what to do if that's something you're interested in pursuing.

I'm exploring other parts of Mexico to see if I want to move with the seasons or if there are more exciting places to spend part of my year. A big advantage of being here is having the freedom and the money to do this. In New York a garage would cost me $500 a month, but in Mexico for the same money I can find a good selection of furnished houses.

Even if you decide the Northshore is not for you, it's still a good place to use as a base while you search for your dream location. Most of the things you're used to having are available and you'll be able to keep in touch with friends and family, and keep up with world events while you compile information about other places to live. You're already ahead of the game by purchasing this well-researched book to help you plan your move.

Look me up when you get here but if you don't come to Chapala, please stop by one of the Posts below.

Frank M. Valentine Post Nine

Carretera a San Nicolas #61

Chapala, Jalisco

(El Mirador Bar & Restaurant)

Phone: 376-765-5032

E-mail: *xeno214@aol.com*

Lake Chapala Post Seven

Calle Morelos #114

Chapala, Jalisco

Phone: 376-765-2259

E-mail: *hsbmjb@hotmail.com*

Cuernavaca Post Ten

Apartado Postal # 4-464

Cuernavaca, Morelos

Phone: 777-315-6276

Guadalajara Post 12

Phone: (cellular) 33-3-899-8369
Commander- David Lord

E-mail:
mexicodirect@infosel.net.mx

Garcia-Jiminez Post 11

Apdo Post #154-B, Central
Camionera, 82010

Mazatlán, Sinaloa

Phone: 669-985-2047 (Commander-Sam Pelzman

E-mail:

pelzman@mzt.megared.net.mx

Billy Payne Post 18

San Bernabe #519

Colonia San Jeronimo Lidice

D.F. (México City)

Phone: 55-5-595-0735

New Post-No Officers Elected Until October 2002.

Rocky Point, Sonora

E-mail: *hansill@prodigy.net.mx* or *nuestroffuturolnv@aol.com*

Thomas E. Proulx Post 8

Faroles 10-A,

San Miguel de Allende, Guanajuato

Phone: 415-152-1389

E-mail: *iaun@unisono.net.mx*

There's one more item that might help you save money on an exploratory trip to México. If you look at the Armed Forces Vacation Club website at *http://www.afvclub.com* you'll find information about reduced cost ($249 a week) vacation lodgings in desirable travel destinations. Active duty and retired service personnel, 100% disabled veterans, DoD civilian employees and teachers, and other categories are eligible to sign up for this program. It's worth looking at.

BILL O'BRIEN

APPENDIX 4

BOATS, GUNS AND HUNTIN', FISHIN' POLES

You outdoorsy types might wonder how your lifestyle will change if you move to Mexico. There are some important things to know about boating, hunting, and fishing SoB.

Boats

Let's look at boating first. For actual "been there, done that" professional instruction and guidance I recommend that you get a copy of *Mexico Boating Guide — Baja, Sea of Cortez, Pacific Mainland, Gulf Coast, and Yucatan* by Captains Pat and John Rains. It costs about $42 US and it's loaded with information. The Captains have extensive experience along Mexico's coasts and they provide detailed information about marinas, safe harbors, hurricane holes, and the services and supplies that will be available in each location they write about, as well as local color and a million other things. I bought the book and even though I don't own a boat, I enjoyed reading about the places and things they write about. They're at *http://www.mexicoboating.com, http://home.san.rr.com/caprains*, or Post Office Box 60190 San Diego, CA 92166, and toll free 888-302-2628. This is a must-have, and it leads you to a lot of other valuable information and services.

If you're going to tow a smaller boat across the border you can get plenty of information at *http://www.mexonline.com/boatmex.htm*. One of the biggest issues around towing your boat to Mexico is to make sure your policy covers your trailer. Some companies *require* that you notify them that you will be towing a trailer and will want you to provide detailed information about the trailer and the boat. Some policies are worded to deny coverage completely if you have a wreck while towing an undeclared trailer of any kind. That means they may not pay for damage to the tow vehicle that you thought was covered. Check this out with your company before you cross the border. The same applies to jet-skis, motorcycles, ATVs, or anything else you hitch up and haul in, including a camper trailer.

At *http://www.tijuana.com/info.html* you can find a bit more about bringing your boat into Mexico, as well as some general border crossing information. Scroll down and click on "Getting There by Boat".

On the website of the Mexican Consulate in Austin, Texas you'll find an on-line manual designed to provide official information about bringing your vessel into Mexican waters. Type in *http://www.onr.com/consulmx/English/boat_eng.html* to read the 5-page report.

A longer and more detailed 18 page explanation provided by <u>Latitude 38</u> boating magazine can be found at *http://www.mexconnect.com/mex_/ sailingregs.html*. <u>Latitude 38's First Timer's Guide to Mexico</u> gives you a great deal of information about all aspects of SoB boating.

There are companies that can truck your boat down for you or you can arrange for a floating delivery, just like anywhere else in the world. Captain Rains is just one of many experienced mariners who can provide that service. The websites listed above will also tell you how long you can keep your boat and trailer in Mexico, as well as how to handle things if you have to leave the country temporarily without them.

Guns and Huntin'

Here's the one that will really be disastrous if you don't handle it correctly. Earlier you read what the U.S. Department of State says about bringing guns into Mexico. Don't. If you absolutely have to, here's the way to go about it.

First, take a look at the website of the Consulate General of Mexico in Denver, Colorado. *http://www.consulmex-denver.com/eng/services/hunting.html* will get you there. The primary thrust of this page is to tell hunters coming down on an FM-T what to expect, as well as what weapons are allowed and which are forbidden. For a hunter's perspective type in *http://residents.bowhunting.net/ awesomehunting/mexicogunpermits.html* to find the article General Information on the Procedures for Getting Hunting Firearms into Mexico. This is not official information but it gives you the writer's experience.

For the official word from the U.S. Department of State look at the press release of December 6, 2000 titled U.S. Customs Provides Helpful Hints on Required Documentation for Hunting Trips in Mexico. This release states that certain firearms may be imported into Mexico, subject to certain provisions and approval by several Mexican government agencies. They say that around 2,000 permits are issued each year, however they don't tell you who to contact or how to get legal approval. That information is in another press release titled Firearms Arrests in Mexico that you'll find at *http://travel.state.gov/gunsrel.html*. Here they tell you:

"The only way to legally import firearms and ammunition into Mexico is to se-cure a permit in advance from the Mexican Embassy in Washington, D.C. or from a Mexican Consulate in the United States. Mariners who have obtained a Mexican firearm permit should contact Mexican port officials before attempt-ing to enter Mexican waters, to learn about specific procedures to report and secure weapons and ammunition."

If you plan to try this allow yourself *plenty* of leeway. If you read the entire press release you can see why it's important to follow every law to the nth degree. The NRA won't be able to help if you screw up down here.

Canadian citizens will need to contact the Mexican Embassy in Ottawa or one of the other Mexican Consulates. If you're driving to Mexico from Canada you'll travel through a number of individual states in the U.S. Each state has different requirements for transporting weapons and you'll more than likely be expected to know and abide by them. However, if you follow the guidelines of the federal gun control law, (the Brady Bill) you should be in compliance with all local or state laws.

Begin what is probably going to be a long and aggravating process by check-ing out the website of the Canadian Firearms Centre at *http://www.cfc-ccaf.gc.ca*. Ramble around for awhile until you find links to other informative sites. One of them will be the U.S. Bureau of Alcohol, Tobacco and Firearms at *http://www.atf.treas.gov*. You probably remember them from the botched job they did in Waco, Texas a few years ago.

If you do manage to get your armory into the country you may be able to enjoy some good hunting, but only in certain areas under specific conditions. For a good overview of the Northern states and what's available there go to *http://www.mexonline.com/huntmex.htm*. This site has an older chart showing the seasons and limits for various birds as well as White-Tail Deer. Wild pigs are not listed on the chart but they're down here too. There's also a link to SEMARNAP, the agency that manages natural resources in Mexico.

Fishin' Poles

Things get a lot simpler when your sporting equipment consists of a rod and reel. If you want to fish in Mexican waters you'll need a license. Some say you only need it for coastal waters while others claim you need it for inland waters, too. Buy the license anyway. It's inexpensive and worth the peace of mind you'll get by being prepared for any strange interpretation of the regulations by law enforcement representatives.

What are the specifics of Mexican fishing regulations? Let Gene Kira at *http://www.bajadestinations.com/afish/afish2001/afish000022/afish000022.htm* tell you. I'd bet a good spinnin' reel that you'll never get this site to open but on the off-chance you do, it's very interesting. The main idea is that there are some strange and surprising sportfishing regulations in Mexico and that even as an experienced fisherman, he was unaware of many of them. His enlightenment came courtesy of a small inexpensive booklet written by an international consultant. You can get your own copy of *Mexico Sportfishing Regulations, English, Spanish*. It's 24 pages long, 14 of them in English. If you're interested in stayin' on the right side of the Mexican game wardens you can order the booklet from Bernard R. Thompson, MIRA Associates, P.O. Box 33782, San Diego, CA 92163-3782. Telephone him at 619-260-1637 or Fax to 619-543-0454. The e-dress is *mexinfo@ix.netcom.com*. It's just $10.00 US.

Mr. Kira has an engaging writing style and even if you can't open the site above you can still use the short address and find his weekly columns as well as links to information about the books he's written. *http://www.bajadestinations.com* will get you in the door and adding */books/kom/kom.htm* will get you to the books page.

Another way to secure a Mexican fishing license is spelled out in *How to Obtain a Mexican Fishing License* at *http://bajaward.com/license.html*. It's fairly area-specific, it's humorous and it provides a realistic look at how things usually work (or not) SoB. The author also gives you a quick introduction to the infamous Forma 5 with which you'll become well acquainted after you attempt a few transactions with government entities that require you to pay money. You'll normally need 3 copies, all originals. No photocopies, no carbon paper, nothing but originals. You'll understand after you've done it once. Read the article.

Of course offshore fishin' is a whole other game, and the boat captains usually take care of everything, but check things for yourself. There are approximately 62 kajillion charter boats available in Mexico and if you'll use the links on the websites I've provided, or put your search engine to work you won't have a bit of trouble finding plenty of folks who can get you on the water and headed toward a trophy. Many areas and captains are enforcing catch and release programs so whatever your philosophy is in that area you need to make sure it matches with the boat policy.

THE AUTHOR,
THE CONTRIBUTORS, AND THE CREDITS

About the Author

Don Adams has traveled in Mexico since the early '60's and lived on and off there for years before retiring to live there full time five years ago. After service in DaNang, RVN in 1966-67, he graduated from Midwestern State University in Wichita Falls, Texas. A man of many interests, he has worked as a long-haul truck driver, catastrophic loss insurance adjuster, manager of an auto-body repair shop, teacher and coach, and owned a landscape company. He has two grown children and two grandchildren. He has published articles in specialty magazines, won awards for his fiction, and currently writes a monthly column for the world's largest Mexico-related website. Don continues to travel extensively in Mexico, indulging his passion for the country's people, culture, history and natural beauty. This is his first full-length book. He is currently researching a book on the history and craft of the Zapotec weavers of Teotitlán del Valle, Oaxaca, Mexico. Contact him at *don@headformexico.com*

The Contributors

Teresa A. Kendrick

Teresa A. Kendrick is a professional journalist, writer, researcher, editor, and publicist who has lived and worked full-time in Mexico since 1994. She is the author of the book, "Mexico's Lake Chapala and Ajijic: The Insiders Guide to the Northshore for International Travelers", numerous articles on travel, fine art, folk art, health and culture, and is a former newspaper columnist, and radio and television reporter. She has loaned her skills to create and expand many cultural organizations throughout the years. She lives in Ajijic, Jalisco and can be reached at *http://www.chapalaguide.com* and at *ajijic@chapalaguide.com*.

Karen Blue

Karen Blue, known by friends as "Blue," chucked corporate life in 1996 at age 52 to live and write in Ajijic, Mexico. She has published several articles in English language newspapers and authors a monthly column on Mexico's largest

Internet site, titled "Living in Mexico—From a Woman's Perspective" at *http://mexconnect.com/mex_/travel/blue/askblue.html*. In the late eighties, she co-founded both the Silicon Valley and San Francisco chapters of the National Association of Women Business Owners. Blue holds a BA in Business Management. She held several corporate management and consulting jobs in Silicon Valley in both business-to-business marketing and international customer service organizations. She has two grown children and two young dogs. Her days are spent enjoying the beautiful weather of the Lake Chapala region, making soft-sculptured dolls, writing a novel—Leap Into Life— traveling, and marketing Midlife Mavericks. She and her friend Judy King publish a monthly newsletter, Living at Lake Chapala...Mexico Makes Sense, and present weekly newcomers seminars in Ajijic. She also plays bridge, Scrabble, Mah Jongg, Pinochle, and Cranium when she can hogtie people into joining her. Blue welcomes comments and questions. She can be reached by e-mail at: *mexicoblue@prodigy.net.mx*. Visit her website at: *http://www.mexicoblue.homestead.com* or at her newsletter website at *http://www.mexico-insights.com*, e-mail *seminar@mexico-insights.com*.

Mark Farley

Mark Farley made his first trip to Puerto Vallarta, Mexico in 1984, fell in love with the country, and since then has lived in Morelia, Guadalajara, Mexico City, Cuernavaca, Guanajuato, Merida, Xalapa, and San Luis Potosí. As a teacher of English as a Second Language, Mark discovered how motivated students can earn higher salaries as bilingual employees and feels that he is making a valuable contribution to the country that has received him so well. Mark is currently the Program Director for InternetWorks, a Guaranteed Placement Program, and provides important job, housing, and travel information for The Teach English in Mexico Newsletter. He is also the author of *The Teach English in Mexico Employment Guide*. In 1993, Mark won 1st place for "Best TV Commercial" in a large market at WSNS-TV in Chicago for a Spanish language commercial he wrote, produced, and edited. Mark attended both the University of New Mexico in Albuquerque and the University of Illinois in Chicago. He graduated in 1984 with a Bachelor's Degree. Mark is a current member of both CATESOL and TESOL organizations and his company InternetWorks is a member of the Better Business Bureau of the Southland. You can contact Mark at *http://www.teach-english-mexico.com* or e-mail him at *info@employnow.com*.

Bill Haslbauer

Bill Haslbauer and his wife Neva retired to Mexico in late 2000. Bill graduated from North Texas State University in Denton, Texas with a BBA in Management, a BS in Industrial Arts and enjoyed a career in Purchasing and Material

Management with several companies, predominately Texas Instruments. He has served as a school board member and as a representative to the Texas Association of School Boards, on the county selective service board and the economic development council, on the regional Junior Achievement board, and at one time, the Greater Dallas Homeowners Association board, and as president of his neighborhood homeowners association. The Haslbauers have three grown children who were very supportive of their move to Mexico. Bill enjoys meeting new people and seeing new things.

Judy King

Judy King has carved her own niche at Lake Chapala to showcase the knowledge gained from a dozen years of living in Mexico learning the "how-to's" for expatriates and understanding some of the cultural differences that make Mexican life a daily adventure. Her professional life focus has been designing and writing projects and promotion for adult education, chambers of commerce, newspapers, real estate sales and management to comfortably ease participants into new roles.

In January 2002, she joined forces with Karen Blue to develop and present newcomer's seminars and a fact and insight-filled monthly magazine, "Living at Lake Chapala." Through these venues and from articles on *http://www.mexconnect.com*, "The Lake Chapala Review" and speaking assignments for U.S. and Canadian tour companies, she serves as a local resource for writers. Judy provided information to the staff of Forbes for their 2000 and 2001 "Retirement" issues and International Living Magazine's Mexican buyer's guide and real estate market updates. She is currently researching and writing books on Lake Chapala construction tips and techniques and about the virgins, saints and crosses. E-mail Judy King in Ajijic, Jalisco, at *judy@mexico-insights.com* or *http://www.mexico-insights.com* for information about the "Living at Lake Chapala" magazine and seminars.

Bill O'Brien

Bill O'Brien served with the 2nd Battalion, 7th Marine Regiment, 1st Marine Division where he spent 13 months as a machine gunner. He participated in 17 combat missions and was twice wounded in close quarter combat. He holds numerous medals and decorations for his service. After his discharge he was self-employed in the construction business for many years.

He is a service-connected disabled veteran as a result of his wartime injuries and currently lives in the Lake Chapala region of Mexico. Bill rates the good weather, the laid-back lifestyle, and the lower cost of living as the three major reasons for his satisfaction with his life in Mexico.

Bill is a former Second Vice-Commander of the American Legion Department of Mexico and currently serves as Alternate Department Executive Committeeman. As a member of Chapala Post #7 he served as chairman of many committees and as Post Service Officer. He is also a Life Member of the Disabled American Veterans, and a member of both the Military Order of the Purple Heart and the Veterans of Foreign Wars.

Georgina Russell

Georgina was born in Guelph, Ontario, Canada and graduated from Guelph Collegiate Vocational Institute and the University of Waterloo with a Bachelor of Arts Degree.

She served as Assistant Media Librarian for the Audio-Visual Centre, Graduate Secretary Combinatorics and Optimization and later Administrative Manager Math Faculty Computing Facility at the University of Waterloo. Georgina is also a founding partner of Focus on Mexico.

She has two children, Melissa, a diving vacation resort manager in Roatan, Honduras, and Jason, an engineer in Toronto, Canada. In Ajijic, she is involved in the Lakeside Education Fund and sings in the Lakeside choir, Cantantes Del Lago.

Ron and Georgina met while working for the Audio-Visual Centre, University of Waterloo and were married in 1991. They enjoy spending late spring at their cottage on the Bruce Peninsula in Ontario and the rest of the year in Ajijic.

Ron Russell

Ron was born in Brampton, Ontario, Canada and is a graduate of Ryerson Polytechnic University with a Degree in Radio and Television Arts and Sciences. He was selected in 1989 to serve as the Commonwealth Relations Trust Bursar representing Canada as an educational media specialist for study/ambassadorial visit to the United Kingdom.

Ron served as Production Supervisor for the Audio-Visual Centre for the University of Waterloo and has received many accolades for his writing and production services. As Director, Ron was instrumental in introducing new technologies to campus including dial-up and satellite videoconferencing, digital video facilities and high technology classroom learning facilities.

Over the years he served on national and local committees, co-chaired national media competitions and performed public service volunteer work in his community. He is a founding partner of Focus on Mexico. He continues to write for periodicals, produce multimedia presentations and stay abreast of developing technologies.

The Illustrations

Chapter 1

Nostalgia William Gentes, 1992, Print on paper, courtesy Isabel Fuente & Lara Gallardo Collection La Sirena B&B, Melaque, Jalisco, Mexico

Chapter 3

Los Danzones William Gentes, no date, Print on paper, courtesy Isabel Fuente & Lara Gallardo Collection La Sirena B&B, Melaque, Jalisco, Mexico

Cerca de isla alarcrán William Gentes, 1980, Original print on paper, courtesy Isabel Fuente & Lara Gallardo Collection La Sirena B&B, Melaque, Jalisco, Mexico

Chapter 4

Merienda William Gentes, 1996, Print on paper, courtesy Isabel Fuente & Lara Gallardo Collection La Sirena B&B, Melaque, Jalisco, Mexico

Chapter 5

¡¡¿Leña?!! William Gentes, 1980, Print on paper, courtesy Isabel Fuente Palma Collection Isabel Fuente Tours, Ajijic, Jalisco, Mexico*La Hamaca* William Gentes, 1993, Print on paper Bob and Smokee Wilson La Sala de Smokee, Ajijic, Jalisco, Mexico

Chapter 8

Medio Dia en Sonora William Gentes, 1992, Print on paper, courtesy Isabel Fuente & Lara Gallardo Collection La Sirena B&B, Melaque, Jalisco, México

Bandido William Gentes, no date, Print on paper, courtesy Isabel Fuente & Lara Gallardo Collection La Sirena B&B, Melaque, Jalisco, México

Piedras por Pancho William Gentes, 1990, Original print on paper, courtesy The Studio Art Gallery , Luisa Julián, Ajijic, Jalisco, Mexico

Chapter 10

En la playa en Melaque William Gentes, 1993, Print on paper, courtesy Isabel Fuente & Lara Gallardo Collection La Sirena B&B, Melaque, Jalisco, Mexico

Con tarugos a bañarse, que hasta el jabon se pierde William Gentes, 1982, Print on paper, courtesy Isabel Fuente & Lara Gallardo Collection La Sirena B&B, Melaque, Jalisco, Mexico

Chapter 11

Acarajas, Brasil William Gentes, 1989, Print on paper, courtesy The Studio Art Gallery, Luisa Julián, Ajijic, Jalisco, Mexico

Tiendita Ajijic William Gentes, 1988, Print on paper, courtesy Isabel Fuente & Lara Gallardo Collection La Sirena B&B, Melaque, Jalisco, Mexico

Chapter 12

La familia de Gabriel William Gentes, 1982, Print on paper, courtesy David Merryman, Re/Max Fénix Realty San Antonio Tlayacapán, Jalisco, Mexico

Vestigios William Gentes, 1978, Print on paper, courtesy The Studio Art Gallery Luisa Julián, Ajijic, Jalisco, Mexico

Cariño maternal William Gentes, 1978, Print on paper, courtesy Isabel Fuente & Lara Gallardo Collection La Sirena B&B, Melaque, Jalisco, México

Chapter 14

Rosca de Reyes William Gentes, 1995, Print on paper, courtesy Isabel Fuente & Lara Gallardo Collection La Sirena B&B, Melaque, Jalisco, Mexico

Chapter 16

Danza de los viejitos William Gentes, 1982, Print on paper, courtesy Marguerite and Carl Marxsen Collection La Floresta, Jalisco, Mexico

Chapter 18

Caballos, pistolas y mujeres infieles William Gentes, 1983, Print on paper, courtesy Isabel Fuente & Lara Gallardo Collection La Sirena B&B, Melaque, Jalisco, México

El Jarabe William Gentes, 1985, Print on paper, courtesy Isabel Fuente & Lara Gallardo Collection La Sirena B&B, Melaque, Jalisco, México

Chapter 19

Playa de Brasil William Gentes, 1989, Print on paper, courtesy Isabel Fuente & Lara Gallardo Collection La Sirena B&B, Melaque, Jalisco, Mexico

La iglesia vieja William Gentes, 1995, Print on paper, courtesy Linda Samuels, Ajijic, Jalisco, Mexico

Las Gaviotas William Gentes, 1995, Print on paper, courtesy The Studio Art Gallery, Luisa Julián, Ajijic, Jalisco, Mexico

El Musico William Gentes, 1995, Print on paper, courtesy Isabel Fuente & Lara Gallardo Collection La Sirena B&B, Melaque, Jalisco, MexicoAbout the Designer

About The Artist

WILLIAM GENTES,
MELAQUE, JALISCO, MEXICO
1917-2000

Born June 21, 1917 in Brooklyn, New York, William Gentes studied art at both Hobart College and the New York Art Students League. He began his long career as a sign painter, an activity he always claimed to enjoy as it allowed him to work outdoors in the open air. He matured into a sensitive and accomplished printmaker who found in Mexico and its working people the perfect subjects through which to express his exceptionally warm and affectionate outlook.

His long love affair with Mexico began in 1971 when he moved to Guadalajara with his wife Adele, and their children, Bill and Gaye. Several years later, the northshore of Lake Chapala, an hour's drive south, became home after the children completed their education.

On our many field trips and holiday excursions, Bill always had his sketch pad at hand. It was captivating to see Mexico through Bill's eyes and then to see those sketches transformed into colorful linographs. Bill lived life to the full. His parties, which always carried a Mexican theme, were enthusiastically shared and enjoyed by his large coterie of artistic friends. For them, he gave generously of his time and energy, conducting workshops and making his presses available to aspiring artists. His puckish sense of humor never ceased to amuse us.

Bill's eternal optimism made him an engaging friend. His compassion and understanding for his fellow man leaves no doubt in my mind that it was an honour and privilege to have known him, a vanishing breed of man. Bill died July 26, 2000.

James Avery, Paris, France, August, 2002

About the Designers

Mary Rickman-Taylor designed the book with an eye to making it a useful guide for readers who are not only arm-chair adventurers but also folks seriously interested in making the transition to a retirement South of the Border. She has produced and designed more than twenty books over the last 19 years, and has worked with publishing houses ranging from Bantam Books to

New American Library. One of her specialties has been assisting authors make the transition from manuscript to self-published books as the publishing business moves into the true era of publishing on demand. She also is the Research and Analysis Coordinator for AIBT-International Institute of the Americas, a group of career colleges located in the Southwest with campuses in Phoenix, Mesa and Tucson, Arizona and Albuquerque, New Mexico. She can be reached at *publisher@coalinga.net*.

Marianne Carlson

Marianne Carlson has been living in Ajijic, Jalisco, Mexico for the last five years. In addition to running Galérias Avant Gourd y Papagayo and her internet business, MexicoEtc, on which she sells Mexican dollhouse miniatures, she supports herself by doing all types of computer work. Marianne can be reached at mariannecarlson@prodigy.net.mx or when she is in the gallery at 16 de Septiembre #13, Ajijic.

Joseph Philipson

Joseph Philipson has been involved in creative problem solving for corporate and small businesses since 1977. He is the principal of The Philipson Agency, Marketing Communications & Graphic Design, in Boston, Mass. and Ajijic, Jalisco, Mexico. He can be reached at jxxp@prodigy.net.mx.

INDEX

ISBN 1553695623-3